D1069255

ANATOMY OF THE McMARTIN CHILD MOLESTATION CASE

Edgar W. Butler
Hiroshi Fukurai
Jo-Ellan Dimitrius
Richard Krooth

University Press of America,® Inc.
Lanham · New York · Oxford

Copyright © 2001 by
University Press of America,® Inc.
4720 Boston Way
Lanham, Maryland 20706

12 Hid's Copse Rd.
Cumnor Hill, Oxford OX2 9JJ

Library of Congress Cataloging-in-Publication Data

Anatomy of the McMartin child molestation case /
Edgar W. Butler ... [et al.].
p.   cm
Includes index.
1. Buckey, Ray—Trials, litigation, etc. 2. Buckey, Peggy McMartin—
Trials, litigation, etc. 3. Trials (Child sexual abuse)—California—
Los Angeles. I. Butler, Edgar W.
KF224.M215 A53   2001   345.73'025554—dc21   2001027030 CIP

ISBN 0-7618-1983-5 (cloth : alk. paper)

⊖™ The paper used in this publication meets the minimum
requirements of American National Standard for Information
Sciences—Permanence of Paper for Printed Library Materials,
ANSI Z39.48—1984

Dedicated to Virginia McMartin and those who, believing that they were being unjustly accused and prosecuted, fought to preserve their personal integrity and their civil, legal, and human rights

Contents

Preface

In the step of history, children and women have often been the most vulnerable to physical abuse and sexual violence, hunger and distress, and legal exploitation and manipulation. And in modern times, the likes of the European and Salem witch hunt trials, focusing on vulnerable women and young children, have been periodically revisited, each people and nation experiencing nuanced versions of their own frightful and nightmarish episodes.

The *cause celebre* in the United States in the 1980s and 1990s was the McMartin sexual molestation case, beset by the psychological uncertainties and ambiguous legal status of young children who were cleverly pressured to undergo therapeutic evaluations and medical and anatomical examinations for the sign of sexual abuse and were unwillingly forced to stand witness against those being criminally charged. Those accused of sexual abuse were also jailed, condemned by the public, prosecuted and convicted by the press, and their assets and means of survival were jeopardized and lost despite the fact that there was no adult witness or any conclusive forensic or material evidence to substantiate the sexual abuse or molestation.

This book details the painful, torturous, and often unbelievable turn of events in the McMartin episode and offers a critical window on Salem by the Sea, revealing how civil society and the criminal justice system have mindlessly and brutally dealt with young children, their parents, defendants, and their families under the guise of pursuing justice and equity.

The detailed account of the McMartin case raises many important and serious questions about our criminal justice system, criminal court proceedings, conducts of the mass media, the legitimacy of legal participation by therapeutic and rehabilitative industries, and the effectiveness of their services. Specific questions include the pervasive and outrageous display of prosecutorial misconduct politically orchestrated by the district attorney's office, prosecutors' crafted utilizations of therapeutic and rehabilitative agencies to perform quasi-prosecutorial and inquisitorial functions, a back-scratching alliance of prosecutors and reporters of the local media, and prosecutors' unfettered discretion and abilities to selectively disclose and release pre- and post-indictment information on defendants and their alleged crimes.

There are other serious questions that call for greater scrutiny as well. How should the community act and react under circumstances of suspected sexual abuse of young children? How should the police, other governmental agencies, and the press handle such sensitive matters involving children? What role should private therapeutic agencies play in soliciting and constructing evidence of molestation from alleged child victims? When do parents, other interested parties, and the public at large have the right to know about suspected sexual acts against vulnerable children? How shall the civil, personal, and economic rights of accused parties be protected or secured? What recourse should they have if their rights are violated?

Our original and direct involvement in the McMartin case began in 1985 as trial and jury consultants in the case. While we assisted the defense counsel in preparing trial strategies, selecting the final jury, and submitting defense motions, we also tried to make critical and objective assessments of the entire McMartin episode. Such outside perspectives and third-party evaluations were certainly needed because we were also local residents in Southern California where the McMartin case had the maximum impact on our daily activities and operations of local schools, church, church-run preschools and clubs, and other private volunteer organizations due to rumors of suspected child molestation and satanic ritual practices.

Our involvement in the trials also gave us ample opportunity to critically assess and evaluate the media, prosecutors, the judge, legal experts, defense attorneys, and other key players in and out of the courtroom. Our overall analysis of the case suggests that, despite the adversarial and strained relations that existed between McMartin defendants and the parents of allege child victims throughout the episode, the whole McMartin incident has also equally infected, poisoned, and victimized children, their parents, the McMartin Seven, and the defendants' families.

With us, we ask you to make the critical evaluation and assessment of the McMartin saga and judge the circumstances, charges, and defense of this nightmarish story.

Acknowledgments

This book took almost ten years to complete, captivating our attention and energy from the very beginning of our involvement.

Though we have been interested in academic research on criminal matters for many years and have observed many criminal trials as social scientists and participating jury consultants, no case to our knowledge has ever matched the McMartin episode in terms of significant twists, fascinating facts, and disturbing information. Indeed, some details of the McMartin affair are still being uncovered and evolving, leaving our inquiry an account yet to be closed, hopefully prompting interest in its future social and judicial implications.

That future matters, too. For though the two McMartin trials resulted in not guilty verdicts for the McMartin defendants, we cannot leave the matter to rest. Indeed, a certain uneasiness has accompanied our own involvement in the McMartin episode as jury consultants, leaving us with a healthy skepticism towards so-called criminal justice and those able to mold its contours using their political leverage and social influence— reinvigorating our still unfulfilled determination to uncover their motives and to question the legitimacy of their claims to power and authority.

Though we have worked hard to bring this study to a successful conclusion, we have also relied on the help and support of others. So here we wish to express our indebtedness to those who contributed to the research effort.

At various stages of completion, discussions about the manuscripts were held with Professors John I. Kitsuse, John Brown Childs, and Dane Archer in the Department of Sociology at the University of California, Santa Cruz. We also appreciated the support, encouragement, and assistance of Professors Bill Domhoff, Dana Takagi, Pam Roby, and Dana Hagler, Susan Curtis, Lin Weyers, Christina Cicoletti, and other office staff members in the Department of Sociology, as well as Bill Hyder, Ken

Garges, George Sisson, and Jane Nyberg of the Computing and Facilities of the Social Sciences Division at the University of California, Santa Cruz.

At the University of California, Riverside, we are particularly indebted to Cathy Carlson, Robin Whittington, and other office staff who were extremely helpful and facilitated completion of the manuscript; we also would like to thank the late Larry Sautter and his staff of the Academic Computing Office at the University of California, Riverside. The University of California, Berkeley, too, made research facilities available, as did the Department of Public Services and its chairman Larry Brewster at Golden Gate University, San Francisco.

Several persons contributed their expert knowledge in the period before this particular manuscript took formation. Notable here are Dean Gits and Danny Davis, defense attorneys in the McMartin child molestation trials in Los Angeles; Abby Mann and Myra Mann who wrote the script for the award-winning HBO movie, *Indictment: The McMartin Trial.* In addition, Mr. Ray Arce, formerly of the Jury Commissioner's Office, Los Angeles County, over the years, was very helpful to us. A number of staff members in the Los Angeles Criminal Court Building facilitated our efforts while we were going through the McMartin transcripts and we offer them thanks for their courtesy and assistance.

As a theoretical backdrop, we were guided in part by the work of two of our colleagues, Dr. Homero Yearwood of the Criminal Justice Department at Sonoma State University and Professor William J. Chambliss of George Washington University.

Funding for this study came from a number of sources. We thank, in particular, the following: the Intramural Research Program at the University of California, Riverside; the Social Sciences Division and the Committee on Research Grants in the Faculty Senate at the University of California, Santa Cruz; and especially the Superior Courts in Los Angeles County.

We also appreciate the assistance of Dr. Robert West, Editor and Diana Lavery, Assistant Editor of University Press of America. Our appreciation is also extended to the assistance provided by Angela von der Lippe, former Senior Editor for the Behavioral Sciences, Harvard University Press and Kim Nelson, her assistant, in thoroughly going through the earlier version of the manuscript. Anonymous reviewers with their helpful comments also assisted in making useful revisions and strengthening the manuscript.

Finally, the book could not have been completed if it had not been for the outstanding efforts, dedication, and continued support and encouragement from our collaborators, Professor Emeritus Millie Almy in the Education Department at the University of California, Berkeley; oral historian and essayist Ann Baxandall Krooth in Berkeley; human rights attorney Karl W. Krooth also in Berkeley; Robin Chanin in Santa Cruz, and Zoë Sodja and Cheryl VanDeVeer of the Document Publishing and Editing Center at the University of California, Santa Cruz, who provided an admirable job of editing and proofreading the manuscript.

Needless to say, we accept full responsibility for the contents and the views presented in this book. They are based upon our participation and observations at the trials, reading of trial transcripts, newspaper and television reports and accounts, and personal interviews. Finally, once again, this project could not have been completed without the genuine encouragement and support of Diana Lavery, Helen Hudson, and the office staff at University Press of America.

Edgar W. Butler
Hiroshi Fukurai
Jo-Ellan Huebner-Dimitrius
Richard Krooth

Chapter 1

An Overview

The longest and costliest trial in U.S. history, the McMartin child sexual molestation case, finally came to a close in 1990, seven years after the first charges were filed. Two juries in two separate trials could not render guilty verdicts in the case, but it is still premature to assume that the case is actually over. The acquittals have brought countersuits by the former defendants against those who made the original charges.

The McMartin case will be remembered as one charged with high emotion and complicated by a media that acted as both accuser and judge. In a rush to judgment, the accused were portrayed as pariahs. Reputations were ruined by an unchecked media; mere allegations were reported as fact; children's stories were prodded and coaxed from them and then treated like gospel; and the presumption of innocence was nowhere to be found.

In retrospect, it now appears that the case was the incendiary capstone of a period of social devolution in Los Angeles, where there already existed deep feelings of helplessness and resentment. The McMartin legal drama was acted out against a backdrop of the escalating social ills of drug addiction, the emergence of AIDS, racial uprisings, gang wars, drive-by shootings and police violence. There had already been an explosion of sexually-overlaid advertising, juvenile prostitution and personal-victim crime, including brutal assaults, forcible rape, and child abuse. This aggressive and violent social atmosphere drew much attention to the Los Angeles area, where the younger generation often displayed their contempt for social convention and flaunted their disregard for the law.

In this milieu in the summer of 1983, an alcohol-addicted mother reported that her 2 1/2-year-old son had been sodomized by a school aide,

Raymond Buckey, during day care hours at the McMartin Preschool in Manhattan Beach. Despite a lack of opportunity for such an offense to occur—the child had only attended the preschool for a little more than ten occasions over several months and had only been in Raymond Buckey's care a couple of times—Buckey was arrested. He was, however, released for lack of evidence.

The complaining mother continued to make bizarre charges, including that her son and family dog had been sodomized by her husband, an AWOL marine. In a letter to the district attorney, she alleged that Peggy McMartin Buckey, Raymond's mother and owner of the preschool, was involved in ritualistic practices featuring a "goatman" and a church. She said, "Ray flew through the air," and "Peggy drilled a child under the arms."

With these new charges, the police sent letters to 200 parents naming Raymond Buckey as a child-molesting suspect, but which also boldly pronounced that there was no evidence to connect the preschool and other employees with these acts. Their investigation continued for the next six months. Nearly 400 children who had attended the school were interviewed at the Children's Institute International, a private agency which offered therapy and counseling for abused children. A complaint filed by the Los Angeles District Attorney's office listed 41 children as potential victims.

The media spread the word as quickly as it could. They accused the soon-to-be defendants of drugging, raping and sodomizing children; killing horses and rabbits, mutilating corpses, drinking blood, and sacrificing a baby in a church. The state and federal authorities armed with search warrants spread out over neighboring southern California counties and out-of-state sites, but found no photographs, videotapes, or any other hard evidence.

In the wake of the massive publicity and mass hysteria following the original McMartin charges and building on the pathological implications of the case, the ring of suspicion grew to enclose other preschools in the area. Although no formal charges were ever brought, some were investigated as suspects of child molestation, after their names had been released to the media by the prosecution. Seven other South Bay preschools closed amid the same accusations. Yet only a single person at one of these schools was ever charged with a criminal violation of sexual molestation, and that trial ended with a hung jury.

Nonetheless, despite a dearth of evidence, a grand jury indicted Raymond Buckey, his mother Peggy McMartin Buckey, her mother Virginia McMartin, and four other preschool teachers on charges of child abuse perpetrated over a ten-year period. They each entered a plea of not guilty; however, Raymond Buckey and Peggy McMartin Buckey were held without possibility of bail.

The preliminary hearing on the case was an extended ordeal lasting 18 months. Each of the seven defense attorneys cross-examined 13 child witnesses. The testimony covered so-called "naked games," satanic rituals, secret tunnels, cemetery visits, animal sacrifices, sexual abuse after being taken on a boat, car, and airplane, and molestation in caves, carwashes, and elsewhere. At this point, though, the children's testimony was uncorroborated by any hard evidence—there were no known secret tunnels or rooms that the children could remember, no evidence of satanic practices, no airplane tickets, no adult witnesses, no photographs, and no defendants willing to plea bargain and testify against the other defendants for immunity or leniency. Yet, by the close of the preliminary hearing, the judge decided that all seven should stand trial on 135 counts of child sexual molestation.

Then came a momentous turn around: Citing insufficient and incredibly weak evidence, the newly elected District Attorney Ira Reiner decided that the charges should be dropped against five of the original seven defendants. Reiner disclosed that these five defendants had had irregular contact with the school when the alleged acts took place and that it was "not likely" that there had been "massive molestation" at the McMartin school. For the two remaining defendants, the trial finally began in the Los Angeles Central Superior Court.

Meanwhile, the personal toll reached its highest point for some of the key players of the case. The mother who had originated the first charge died before she could be called to testify. A defense investigator committed suicide the night before his testimony. A young man whose girlfriend's house had been searched for evidence also killed himself. The McMartin Preschool was set on fire numerous times, as was Peggy McMartin Buckey's hair by her jailhouse inmates. The defendants were becoming impoverished. And a defense attorney was attacked by a TV crew for defending the "devil."

Fearing a possible loss of state and federal funding, a prominent medical expert was also forced to withdraw from testifying for the defense after the DA's office and state attorney general contacted his university department chair concerning his potential testimony. Realizing no American medical expert was willing to testify for the defendants, the defense had to rely on testimony from a foreign medical doctor.

The prosecution team was beset by an entirely different set of problems. Aside from the news of a love affair between a key child therapist for the prosecution and the TV reporter who broke the McMartin story, more serious were the allegations of a romance between a prosecutor, an editor of a local newspaper, and a superior court judge. The personal lives of some essential players spilled haphazardly into the legal arena, which raised the obvious questions of professional ethics and the objectivity and viability of the prosecutorial charges.

Lasting nearly three years, the trial cost over $15 million and reputedly became the longest criminal trial proceeding in U.S. history. It resulted in a not guilty verdict for one defendant, a not guilty verdict on most counts and a hung jury on other counts for the second defendant. A subsequent trial for the remaining defendant, Raymond Buckey, resulted in a hung jury.

The Goal and Purpose of the Book

The McMartin case may prove to be one of the most important legal cases in U.S. history. It engrossed and fascinated many experts and professionals in a wide variety of fields—some testified in court, while others worked with alleged victims, parents, and the prosecution. Other professionals worked with the defense counsel and supporters of the defendants. The case affected the way the criminal justice system and criminal court proceedings handle child sexual molestation accusations and resulted in legislative action that further protects sexually abused children in and out of the courtroom.

The present authors variously participated in the McMartin trial as community surveyors, jury consultants, assistants to defense counsel in selecting the McMartin jury, and observers of testimony by children and expert witnesses during the course of trial. Thus, this book is based on our collective experience in the McMartin case. For the defense, we performed analyses of potential jurors by examining data obtained from a community survey in the Los Angeles Central Superior Court Judicial District, pre-*voir dire* jury questionnaires filled out by potential jurors assigned to the McMartin case, and in-court assessments of jurors' verbal responses and non-verbal behavior during questioning by attorneys and the judge. We also assisted defense counsel in developing trial strategies including jury challenges and other motions to obtain extended *voir dire* conditions in an effort to select "unbiased" peers to try the unpopular defendants. Given the constant media scrutiny and the court's ultimate decision denying a change of venue to a new trial site, it was of paramount concern for the defense to obtain individualized *voir dire* screening sessions to carefully assess and evaluate jurors' biases and prejudice against the defendants and their alleged crimes. We developed, utilized, and statistically analyzed *voir dire* protocols to assist in the selection of jurors and alternates.

We also assisted defense counsel in the second McMartin trial, performing similar analyses and selecting the jury that tried the lone remaining defendant, Raymond Buckey. We attended many court sessions to observe the jury trial as the case proceeded.

In our opinion, the McMartin case illustrates the worst aspects of what could happen to the accused, undermining the legitimacy of the criminal justice system and criminal court proceedings, when guilt is assumed without adequate investigation of the possibilities of innocence; when irresponsible and biased media reports overwhelm the public; and when prosecutors purposefully use the media to distort the facts. The prosecution also suppressed crucial evidence during the preliminary hearing and trial, including the original accuser's letter indicating her inability to separate fantasy from reality and the fact that her son was unable to identify Raymond Buckey in a photo lineup, in fact pointing out someone else. Prosecutors also relied on perjured testimony by discredited jailhouse informants who curried special favors from the prosecution and were on the DA's payroll for more than ten years; and the district attorney deliberately attempted to heighten name recognition for political gain, neglecting the constitutional rights of the accused.

The McMartin incident also raised a number of social, legal, and judicial issues that will undoubtedly involve the courts in legal clarification for years to come. During the trial a number of constitutional issues were also raised, though they were not discussed as such. Constitutional issues would have been raised in appeals had any of the defendants been found guilty of even one charge.

Other potential arenas of controversy involved prosecutorial misconduct; retroactive versus prospective application of laws; judicial decisions made, and then reversed for no obvious legal reasons, but rather from media attention and due to political pressure.

One of the original district attorneys, Glenn Stevens, left the prosecution team and joined the defense in the trial. He argued that the original charges filed against the McMartin defendants were based on very weak, if not false evidence. Thus, the possibility of invidious prosecution was raised by the defense, and the claim of misuse of legal processes was subsequently made in court, but was quickly thrown out. Alleged perpetrators who were never found guilty of a single charge thus appeared to have no avenue of redress of their grievances against the government, despite an apparent violation of their constitutional rights.

Outside the courtroom, the media played an early, prominent role in the case, generating widespread publicity through reporting that was decidedly biased against the accused. Their unrestrained sleuthing and demands won them access to information from the prosecution that was then used to publicize the case. The invasive and pervasive nature of their reporting forced the defense to call for a change of venue in search of jurors who were able to review the facts with minimal outside influence. Furthermore, the media neglected to report any evidence or testimony that was even remotely favorable to the defense.

Of particular concern, too, was the media's power to ignite mass hysteria regarding child sexual abuse, both in the Los Angeles area and elsewhere. Only smaller local newspapers and some isolated national media coverage presented a more even-handed approach. So, clearly there were ethical considerations with respect to media coverage that need to be critically examined in future child molestation cases.

The investigative techniques employed by the prosecution also warranted closer scrutiny. Their techniques led to confusion, inadmissible evidence, and evidence that was so tainted that two different juries refuted its merits. Of particular importance was the role of therapist interviews used to elicit evidence from the children that would stand up in court. For instance, the key therapist, who treated the alleged child victims and generated the evidence upon which the prosecution later relied to bring charges against the defendants, held no professional license to conduct such interviews. This raised serious questions about the impact a lack of "professional" knowledge could have on the children who were interviewed, and ultimately on the credibility of the evidence itself.[1]

In the context of protecting children, for instance, the California Penal code addressing "lewd and lascivious acts" with children under age 14 states specifically that the court shall consider the needs of the child victim and whatever is necessary and constitutionally permissible to prevent psychological harm to the child.[2] Many questions could be raised about the failure to apply this aspect of the Penal Code during the pretrial therapist interviews and the trial.

Still another controversy emerged in the McMartin case about the reliability and validity of medical evidence. As demonstrated during the trial, different interpretations of medical evidence may or may not indicate the presence of sexual abuse. The criteria for making such judgments has clearly not been universally agreed upon and accepted. Even when there is a consensus of opinion indicating sexual abuse has occurred, without further evidence it offers no clues as to who may be the abuser or where and/or precisely when the abuse took place.

Without solid forensic evidence, other problems arise as well. In the McMartin case there were conflicting interpretations of the medical evidence, and there was no corroborative material evidence. Thus, the trial turned on an evaluation of the testimony of young children compared to that of the alleged perpetrators. Some assert that children do not lie, especially about sexual molestation; while others are just as certain that young children (as well as adults) can be manipulated into saying whatever is wanted by either molesters and/or criminal investigators, therapists, parents, or other authority figures. The McMartin trial paid little attention to children's memory retention limitations and post-event activities, and how these may have had an impact on the testimony of both prosecution and defense witnesses.[3] While new studies and research are emerging in the field of child sexual abuse, clearly more research is needed to cover these important matters.[4]

Not explored during any phase of the McMartin episode were the obvious implications of the charges being brought by a socially isolated and mentally ill mother and the consequences of the mass hysteria it generated. Nor were there any questions asked in regard to the full cooperation of an uncritical Manhattan Beach police department, which acted in concert with the mass media.

Moving to an even higher level, both the original text of the U.S. Constitution and the Fifth Amendment state that, "In all criminal prosecutions, the accused shall enjoy the right to a speedy and public trial, by an impartial jury ... and to be informed of the nature and cause of the accusations; to be confronted with the witnesses against him; to have compulsory process for obtaining witnesses in his favor." The defense and prosecution wrestled over these points during the trial. The right to a speedy trial certainly was abrogated; and with the defense questioning the nature and justification of accusations, the degree of publicity became a point of contention throughout the trial.

The case also raised additional concerns in the following areas: economic impoverishment of those accused in molestation cases, as well as for taxpayers who are unjustly burdened; continued government funding for therapists and diagnostic centers that treat alleged child victims and parents who are drawn into unfairly influencing their children to aid the prosecution; so-called child sexual abuse therapeutic and rehabilitative industries intimately linked to the prosecution, which have been accused of manufacturing both perpetrators and their victims through faulty diagnosis and treatment.

These concerns have led us to document this account using a variety of citations. We cite the trial transcripts, after spending substantial time going through the thousands of pages. We do this because some of the material included in this volume may strain believability, and much of what is cited was never reported by the media. We also cite some academic and scholastic literature when it seems appropriate. The importance of the media in this case led us to frequently cite television programs, newspapers, and magazines. The McMartin case in our opinion would have been a "non-event" except for the media and the prominence of some of the crucial players in the case, including the DA and some of the parents of the McMartin children.

Organization of the Study

This book thus traces the beginnings of the McMartin episode through its various phases up until the moment that the final pages were written in mid-2000. As trial participants, critical observers of the McMartin incident from its start, as well as residents of Southern California communities where the McMartin case had maximum impact for many years, we carefully address, discuss, and critically analyze constitutional, legal, and social issues and problems associated with the McMartin case and other similar child sexual abuse incidents. Not only do those issues and problems of child abuse trials need to be examined, but also they will likely remain important both for alleged victims and assumed perpetrators.

To begin chapter 1, we simply set the stage for the remainder of the book by sketching some historical background and by describing the evolution of the McMartin child molestation case. In chapter 2 we present an analysis of some of the social processes involved in publicity surrounding the McMartin charges of child sexual abuse, enumerate the first charges against the McMartin school personnel, discuss the initial arrests and lack of evidence, show how the investigation was expanded by searches and raids, analyze why more defendants were added as the case progressed, evaluate information presented at the preliminary hearings, and list the final charges against the defendants.

Chapter 3 illuminates the McMartin episode as a media blitz and evaluates the influential role that television, newspapers, and other electronic media had in bringing the McMartin defendants to trial. The extent of bias confounded by prosecutorial and media collusion is explored, revealing the implications and impact of pre-trial publicity on the defendants and their possibility of receiving a fair trial.

The focus of chapter 4 is on guilt or innocence from the public's point of view as demonstrated by letters to the editor, radio talk shows, and television presentations. In addition, we present information from several surveys judging and evaluating the public's perception of guilt, innocence, and their views of the criminal justice system, especially in relationship to allegations in sexual crime cases.

The following chapters cover the nuances of the McMartin proceedings. Chapter 5 examines the preliminary hearings, including prosecution and affirmative defense testimony, presents the evidence, explores prosecution misconduct, and covers the declining number of charges against the accused and dropping of five defendants.

Chapter 6 describes various pre-trial events that took place prior to the selection of the McMartin jury. It includes a section on prosecutors' doubts about the validity of the charges, death of the first complaining mother, denial of bail for Raymond Buckey, motions for a change of venue and jury challenges, and other pre-trial matters such as various defense charges of misconduct by the prosecution, and implications of misconduct for future trials.

Chapter 7 focuses on procedures that were used in impaneling the McMartin jury, with an emphasis on the prosecution and defense's views of desirable jurors, the use of peremptory challenges, and the final selection of the jury and its alternates. The defense strategy of utilizing experts from *Scientific Legal Services* in selecting the final jurors and alternates is discussed in some detail, including analyses of pre-trial defense motions requesting a change of venue, extended *voir dire* conditions, and jury challenges; a description of how community surveys, behavioral observations, and psychological evaluation techniques were utilized to carefully select those seen as the most unbiased persons in the jury pool against the defendants and their alleged crimes.

Chapter 8 delineates testimony and evaluates evidence as presented by children, parents, therapists, expert witnesses, investigators, and others. It describes comparisons of child testimony between the preliminary hearing and trial. This chapter also examines the believability of medical experts and credibility of videotape testimony by children that played an important role in jury decision-making.

Chapter 9 presents further information related to the jury making decisions regarding to the guilt or innocence of the defendants. It also describes how to the jurors interpreted evidence and what influence various kinds of evidence had upon the verdict. This chapter presents the verdicts as well. How the judge influenced the verdicts by his instructions and in directing jurors how to evaluate the evidence is explored. An analysis of the jury's deliberations and the process of developing consensus in the jury room are also presented.

The first trial's aftermath is the focus of chapter 10. The media's response, its soul searching, public demonstrations and outcry, and an evaluation of evidence as reported by jurors are emphasized. The chapter also examines personal losses suffered by the original McMartin Seven, children, and their parents, and discusses societal costs of the McMartin episode, including the burden on the criminal justice system and the jury system, as well as the economic successes of child sexual abuse rehabilitative and therapeutic industries.

Chapter 11 focuses on the second McMartin trial—the trial of the lone defendant, Raymond Buckey. The discussion includes the prosecution's decision to retry Raymond Buckey, jury selection, the judge's instructions to the jury, the verdict, and aftermath of the second trial. The chapter also presents in-depth analyses of experiences of child witnesses in the criminal court system.

Chapter 12 is concerned with the broader implications of the McMartin trials. It alternatively focuses on constitutional rights of the alleged victims of child abuse and on the constitutional rights of alleged perpetrators of sexual abuse of children. How the experiences of children may make them not only victims of molesters, but also of the criminal justice system itself is explicated. Implications of trial by the media, reputations destroyed, and jail time without guilt being ascertained are several of the constitutional areas explored in respect to alleged perpetrators. The chapter also examines the abuse of power by the prosecution, civil rights violations of alleged perpetrators and child victims, use of videotaped testimony by alleged child victims in court, and admissibility of hearsay evidence in child sexual abuse cases. Recent California and U.S. Supreme Court decisions on the use of videotaped testimony and the admissibility of hearsay evidence are discussed and examined. The chapter also presents possible court-initiated strategies to control the extent of media publicity and pervasive scrutiny, influencing jurors' decisions for the final outcome of the trial.

Chapter 13 explores several issues that were raised during the trial such as (1) possible remedies to protect alleged victims and assumed perpetrators; (2) countersuits filed by the McMartin Seven and the courts' decisions on those cases; and (3) a possible "recipe" for reforms in child sexual abuse cases and other highly publicized trials.

Finally the last chapter brings the McMartin phenomenon up-to-date, including the death of Virginia McMartin, one of the original McMartin Seven, a grandmother of two defendants, and a co-owner of the McMartin Preschool, who passed away in December 1995 at age 88. The TV journalist whose report started the McMartin episode also died, in 1992. The chapter also discusses a recent ruling of the civil trial which awarded monetary compensation to a couple who was initially accused by the prosecution along with the McMartin Seven. The chapter also discusses other California sexual molestation cases and compares the structural aspects of criminal prosecution of those incidents with those of the McMartin case. Finally, we update continuing controversies surrounding prosecutorial misconduct and mismanagement of the Los Angeles DA's office, especially after their failure in bringing conviction of O. J. Simpson, in which some of us participated in the selection of the Simpson jury and trial preparations assisting the defense counsel.

Conclusions

At the beginning of jury selection in the first McMartin trial for her daughter and grandson, Virginia McMartin then in her late 70s was waiting outside the courtroom, knitting, and pondering somewhat on the bench, while defense attorneys and we were debating about defense and trial strategies. Virginia was more stoic and determined. A devoted Christian Science follower, she was the principal defense witness warrior who vehemently refuted molestation charges in the courtroom and relentlessly fought for the freedom of her daughter and her grandson. Her outburst soften angered the judge and prosecuting attorneys. But for all of us involved in the trial, the whole McMartin embroglio reaffirmed her faith, though there was sadness knowing that she would never be fully exonerated in the court of law.

We hope that this book is about that faith—that justice will be done, however arduous the judicial path and however long the legal road. For this book attempts to lay the framework of the social and political pressures on the McMartin case by providing insightful analyses and illuminating the extraordinary aspects of the McMartin incidents that have never been covered by the media, the made-for-TV movie, or scholars.

Due to the numerous sociological and legal issues that the McMartin case raises, we hope this study will also draw the interest of lawyers, social scientists, social workers, civil rights and child advocates, students of politics and philosophy, of law enforcement people working in the child sex abuse arena, and, of course, residents of Los Angeles where the case had its maximum impact over so many years. Further, we hope that this book helps provide a methodological and practical framework within which to critically examine individual child sexual abuse cases, to eliminate sources of prosecutorial misconduct, and to contribute to the intense debate concerning the present search by legal and academic researchers for more equitable criminal justice proceedings to protect both child witnesses and alleged perpetrators of sexual abuse against children.

Chapter 2

The Evolution of Charges

In 1983, the McMartin Preschool in Manhattan Beach, California, was placed under police surveillance after Judy Johnson, a 39-year-old, part-time salesperson with a history of alcohol abuse and mental illness, said that her 2 1/2-year-old son was molested by school aide Raymond Buckey at the reputable Virginia McMartin Preschool. Less than a month later the police sent a letter warning 200 parents and naming Raymond Buckey as a child-molesting suspect:

> September 8, 1983
> Dear Parent:
> This Department is conducting a criminal investigation involving child molestation (288 P.C.) Ray[mond] Buckey, an employee of Virginia McMartin's Pre-School, was arrested September 7, 1983 by this Department.
>
> The following procedure is obviously an unpleasant one, but to protect the rights of your children as well as the rights of the accused, this inquiry is necessary for a complete investigation.
>
> Records indicate that your child has been or is currently a student at the pre-school. We are asking your assistance in this continuing investigation. Please question your child to see if he or she has been a witness to any crime or if he or she has been a victim. Our investigation indicates that possible criminal acts include: oral sex, fondling of genitals, buttock or chest area, and sodomy, possibly committed under the pretense of "taking the child's temperature." Also, photos may have been taken of children without their clothing. Any information from your child regarding having ever

observed Ray Buckey to leave a classroom alone with a child during any nap period, or if they had ever observed Ray Buckey tie up
a child, is important.

Please complete the enclosed information form and return it to
this Department in the enclosed stamped return envelope as soon as
possible. We will contact you if circumstances dictate [the] same.

We ask you to please keep this investigation strictly confidential
because of the nature of the charges and the highly emotional effect it
could have on our community. Please do not discuss this investigation
with anyone outside your immediate family. Do not contact or discuss
this investigation with Raymond Buckey, any member of the accused
defendant's family, or employees connected with the McMartin Pre-
School.

THERE IS NO EVIDENCE TO INDICATE THAT THE MAN-
AGEMENT OF VIRGINIA MCMARTIN'S PRE-SCHOOL HAD
ANY KNOWLEDGE OF THIS SITUATION AND NO DETRI-
MENTAL INFORMATION CONCERNING THE OPERATION
OF THE SCHOOL HAS BEEN DISCOVERED DURING THIS
INVESTIGATION. ALSO NO OTHER EMPLOYEE IN THE
SCHOOL IS UNDER INVESTIGATION FOR ANY CRIMINAL
ACT.

Your prompt attention to this matter and reply no later than
September 16, 1983 will be appreciated.

HARRY L. KUHLMEYER, JR.
Chief of Police
(Signature of John Wehner)
JOHN WEHNER, Captain
Investigation Division

As indicated, Raymond Buckey had been arrested, but then released
for lack of evidence. In a letter to the district attorney, the complaining
mother also alleged that Peggy Buckey was involved in satanic ritual
practices: Her son was taken to a church where he witnessed a baby being
beheaded, and he was forced to drink the blood. It was later determined
that Johnson's son had attended the McMartin Preschool only 14 times
over a three-month period and had been in Buckey's class no more than
two afternoons.

The McMartin Preschool had been a Manhattan Beach institution
for over 30 years when child molestation charges were first made in 1983.
Until then the school and its operators had unblemished reputations, and
it was considered the best in town. Many sons and daughters of Manhattan Beach's elite attended the school. The school also accepted problem

children. For many years the preschool had a long waiting list of those who wanted their children to attend, and at the time of the alleged molestations had a six-month waiting list.

One of the preschool children's fathers later said that the McMartins and their employees must have been "masters of deception," able to play roles of upstanding citizens while being child predators.[1]

What types of people were the accused, then? In 1977, the local chamber of commerce had presented Virginia McMartin, the school's founder, with the "Rose and Scroll," Manhattan Beach's highest honor, and commended her as the "Citizen of the Year." The school's teachers were devoted Christian Science Church members, whose friends and relatives said refused to drink, smoke, or curse. Babette Spitler, one of those charged, had previously worked in a center for abused children. Bette Raidor had turned in her own son for growing marijuana, and Mary Ann Jackson usually donated three days a week to the church.

They seemed an unlikely vehicle of misconduct. Yet, as the investigation enlarged and more daycare workers at the school became molestation suspects, the embroglio split the Manhattan Beach community into McMartin supporters on one side and on the other many parents and allies who believed that children had been molested at the school. "Everybody is concerned about ... [child molestation] here," one local resident was quoted as saying. "Nobody can relax, as long as the case is active, until it's over."[2] Little did the neighbor know that the case would take years before there would be even a preliminary resolution and that the case would still be underway some seven years later.

First Charges

In the six months following the initial accusation, nearly 400 children who had attended the school were interviewed by Kathleen MacFarlane at the Children's Institute International (CII), with 41 diagnosed and listed as "victims" in a complaint filed by the state. Apparently in a hurry to file the complaints, the district attorney made a cursory investigation, and charges were filed after only one-third of the children were interviewed. Claiming that the McMartin Preschool was linked to a child pornography ring, authorities armed with search warrants spread out over three counties and visited 11 locations.

On February 2, 1984, Wayne Satz, on Los Angeles television station KABC-TV (Channel 7) reported the allegations. More than 60 children, he fulminated, "have now each told authorities that he or she had been keeping a grotesque secret of being sexually abused and made to appear in pornographic films while in the pre-school's care—and having been forced to witness the mutilation and killing of animals to scare the kids into staying silent."

T.V. news anchors introduced Satz's reports with pronouncements of the teachers' guilt; and the accounts were heralded by a Channel 7-sponsored, full-page newspaper advertisement with an emotive prop—a battered teddy bear, with one eye missing and its stuffing spilling out.

Blitzing Los Angeles and Southern California, the media soon brought on a witch hunt. On May 24, 1984, a federal grand jury was impaneled to investigate "various aspects" of the case, possibly with a focus on pornography.[3] Grand Jury hearings began seven weeks later on July 12. But in an intriguing turn of events implying a DA set-up, Deputy District Attorney Glenn Stevens suggested that no photographs existed and that the federal authorities would not find any photographs because there were none to be had.[4] The grand jury's indictment meanwhile charged seven persons with 115 instances of molestation and listed 18 children as victims.

Turning to the mass media, Deputy District Attorney Glenn Stevens alleged that drugs had been used to make the children submit to sexual molestation. He was quoted in the newspapers as saying that the children were given shots, pills, and liquid drugs to make them woozy, drowsy and less likely to offer resistance to sexual assault.[5] Several parents affirmed that their children had an inordinate fear of needles, which they attributed to their youngsters having been administered drugs at the McMartin school. Though these allegations freely circulated in the media, no charges involving drugs were *ever* filed in official complaints.

Initial Arrests and Lack of Evidence

On March 22, 1984, a grand jury indicted Raymond Buckey, his mother Peggy McMartin Buckey, his grandmother Virginia McMartin, and three McMartin teachers for abusing children over the previous ten years. Mary Ann Jackson was arrested at her home after returning from a trip. She said that she was "asked to turn and face the wall—they handcuffed me and I was taken away."[6]

Bette Raidor was arrested at her daughter's home. Raymond and his mother, Peggy McMartin Buckey, were arrested at their homes in Manhattan Beach. Babette Spitler was arrested near the headquarters of the city's school system where her two children were enrolled. In nearby Orange County, Peggy Ann Buckey, Raymond's sister, was arrested in front of her students in a La Palma High School classroom where she taught deaf children.

Based on prior arrangements, television cameras were freely allowed to accompany the police while they arrested the defendants in their homes. Only the physically disabled grandmother, Virginia McMartin, was allowed to surrender voluntarily. As the principal accused, Raymond Buckey and Peggy McMartin Buckey were viewed as dangerous and were held without bail.

On April 2, the *Los Angeles Times* reported on the use of therapeutic puppets to coax from the children stories about molestation—rape, sodomy, oral copulation, and fondling. They said that they had witnessed the slaughter of animals to scare them into silence and as threats against them and their parents, and that they had been forced into pornography and prostitution.[7]

Some children described playing a "doctor" game involving physical exams and taking rectal temperatures. Prosecutors said that they were able to identify 389 children who "admitted" that they had been molested at the school.

Los Angeles Times reporter Cathleen Decker said that her reports were based strictly on the children's accounts to their parents and social workers, though she embellished her account with emotion-laden words ("young victims," "tormented secrecy," "the assailant") and an absence of qualifying adjectives such as "charged" or "alleged." Using similar terminology, most of the press in the Los Angeles area sensationalized the case.

Evolution of Criminal Charges

In March of 1984, the district attorney officially charged the defendants with child molestation. Virginia McMartin was charged with a single count of fondling a child; her granddaughter, Peggy Ann Buckey, was charged with one act of molestation. Her daughter Peggy McMartin was charged with 15 counts, allegedly involving oral copulation, fondling, and penetration with a foreign object. Mary Ann Jackson was charged with four counts involving lewd conduct and fondling and one of oral copulation. Babette Spitler was charged with six counts of fondling, while Bette Raidor faced 12 counts of fondling, oral copulation, and rape with a foreign object. Raymond Buckey faced 75 charges of molestation, oral copulation, fondling and penetration with a foreign object.

In May, nearly 100 additional charges of child molestation were lodged against the seven defendants.[8] Though the original grand jury indictment had listed 115 instances of molestation involving 18 children at the McMartin Preschool, the new complaint covered 208 instances of molestation and named 42 children as victims. Two children in the original complaint were dropped. But, for the first time, a count of conspiracy was added to the complaint, bolstering the argument that all defendants were in league and should be tried at the same time, using the same evidence implicating one another.

The complaint charged Virginia McMartin with 12 counts of molestation, which called for a prison sentence of 96 years. Raymond Buckey faced 97 counts with a possible prison sentence of 776 years. McMartin's daughter, Peggy Buckey, was charged with 49 counts of molestation; McMartin's granddaughter was charged with 14 counts; Babette Spitler was indicted on 22 counts; Betty Raidor was named in 32 counts; and Mary Ann Jackson was charged with 15 molestations. In addition, there were specific charges of using "force or fear" to carry out the conspiracy which allowed the defendants, if convicted, to be sentenced consecutively on each individual count rather than concurrently. Further, some defendants were accused of having acted in concert while molesting individual children.[9]

The district attorney's office did not rest. Prosecuting attorney Lael R. Rubin announced on August 8, 1984 that the seven teachers had committed 397 sex-related crimes involving children in addition to the 115 for which they had already been charged.

The preliminary hearing was scheduled for mid-August, 1984. The defense sought a closed hearing, arguing that the media were only interested in "selling sin" and that the publicity would make it difficult if not impossible to impanel impartial jurors. The district attorney's office took no position one way or the other. But Jeffrey S. Klein, a lawyer for the *Los Angeles Times,* several other newspapers and television stations, argued that the case had aroused wide public concern that compelled media attention under the First Amendment.[10] Preliminary Hearing Judge Aviva K. Bobb ruled that the hearings would be open to the public, but reserved the right to close the hearing whenever she thought it necessary to protect the defendants' rights. Yet she refused requests to photograph and broadcast the hearing.[11]

Expanding the Investigation

In July, 1984, it was disclosed in court that 30 additional individuals were being placed under investigation.[12] Prosecutors refused to name these persons or to indicate what charges might be filed against them. Charles Henry Buckey, father of Raymond Buckey, learned from Deputy District Attorney Glenn Stevens that he was considered a suspect, though

Stevens refused to comment whether the senior Buckey's arrest was imminent. No charges were ever filed against the elder Buckey. Even though these "additional suspects" were never charged with a crime, the prosecution continued to hint at allegations of child pornography and photographs to the media.

A climate of fear, meanwhile, hung over the Greater Los Angeles childcare community. Suddenly, on March 11th, a number of sites were raided and searched, but no reports of recovered evidence were made public.[13] Four months later, in July of 1984, nine new locations in the South Bay were raided. Additionally, two local markets and several other residences, including the homes of friends of the defendants were raided. Dragnets covered sites identified by the children as being places where they had been taken, molested, and photographed. Acting on the children's assertions that they had been photographed, the FBI entered the case, looking for the sale of photos of unclad children from the McMartin Preschool.

To discover evidence connected with the alleged child molesters, Municipal Judge Michael Tynan freely signed search warrants. Kent Well, a weight-lifting friend of Raymond Buckey, was thus fingered for a search and his home was raided. The young man's parents, Philip and Kay Well, recounted a fishing expedition on the morning of March 11, 1984, for evidence in their home and the family car. The Manhattan Beach police left with some family photo albums.[14] And for others, as the "witch hunt" went on, the media provided ample publicity, but no evidence—naming names in the case—though no additional persons were legally charged.

The district attorney's desperate hunt for hard evidence was then extended. Since the schoolchildren had insisted that they had been molested and photographed in a professional studio, the police secured a search warrant and raided the studio of school photographer Hanson Williams. Without any charges being filed, the police appeared at his Palos Verdes home, broke into his studio where 30 years of negatives, photographs, and childhood scenes were stored. The police put Hanson, his wife, daughter, son's wife, 3-year-old granddaughter, and 3-month-old grandson in the living room and proceeded to comb the house and take what they pleased. But no nude photos of children were found, and no charges were ever filed against the photographer or any member of his family.

Civilian groups took up where the F.B.I. and police had failed. In November, Hermosa Beach councilman John Cloffi, spokesman for Parents Against Child Abuse, posted a $10,000 reward for purported pornographic photographs of the McMartin Preschool children, supposedly nude and engaging in sex acts with the defendants. He stated that :

> We know the photographs are out there and we know for a fact that these children were abused. We would like to make sure that these defendants are convicted. And getting a photograph will help.[15]

No pornography was found despite offers of monetary rewards, however. And as of 1999, no such photographs have ever been found, and no one has come forward to claim the reward money.

Another alleged perpetrator was Ray Fadel, owner of Harry's Market in Manhattan Beach. Several McMartin children had identified his back room as the place where they were taken and molested. Raymond Buckey was said to have worked there once as a box-boy. Though Fadel was never charged nor officially named as a suspect, once the district attorney's office publicized these unsubstantiated charges, his store became subject to a boycott and was emptied of customers. *The Beach Reporter,* a local newspaper, wrote in an editorial that if merchants frequented by the McMartins are suspect, "then over a 30-year span you might as well suspect 90% of this community."

As the official investigation proceeded, parents of McMartin children saw suspects lurking everywhere. Frustrated by what they viewed as slow and inept police investigative procedures, some parents transformed themselves into amateur detectives. Many were seen diligently rummaging through neighbors' garbage, trying to identify suspects in supermarkets and restaurants, taking down license plate numbers, following cars, and driving their children through various neighborhoods—expeditiously in search of evidence of what they believed was a wide-reaching conspiracy of pedophiles, pornographers, and satanic cultists.

They harassed anyone remotely connected with the case. They gathered information on people who had not even been charged. They spent their time driving by each of 40 locations from a list provided to them by the district attorney to see if any of these sites rang a bell with their children. They quizzed their youngsters and gave the children rewards for each new name they were able to elicit as a suspect.

Parents sifted garbage seeking various homeowners' identities and used clues in discarded mail to determine what kind of work the owner did and where. In one instance, parents were more discerning than the district attorney's office, forcing a sheepish Manhattan Beach police detective to admit that a person identified by them at a posh residence under investigation did not exist.

Many parents lost their sensibility, monitoring their children's emotive reactions as if each was a source of unquestionable validity. A single impression could set the witch-hunt in motion. When one of the children was eating brunch in a restaurant with her family, she pointed out a woman and identified her as "the one who hurt me." The father quickly sent his wife and children outside, obtained the woman's name from the restaurant owner, looked up the address, and in hot pursuit drove by with the child, who pointed out the house as the place where she had been photographed and abused. The father promptly notified the authorities, but he had merely traveled another blind alley.[16]

In this crucible of paranoia, children became prosecutors, taking command of their parents' emotions. The entire community seemed hostage to the accusations; people in leadership positions shrank from their responsibility to quell the rumors and wild charges. As the stigma of purported child abuse spread its ugliness, no one whose child attended the school wanted to discuss it publicly. Manhattan Beach Mayor Russell F. Lesser reported that one concerned mother even called the school district asking for a list of names of children who attended the McMartin school so that she could ensure that her kids would not have any contact with them.[17]

The search reached new heights in March of 1984, when the *Los Angeles Times* reported that specialists from the sheriff's crime lab were investigating a vacant lot where children from the McMartin school said they saw animals killed and buried, supposedly to frighten the children into silence.[18] The sheriffs took over the task from parents who had decided to do their own digging when the authorities did not respond quickly enough to their request.[19] And during the course of the excavation, fragments of a tortoise shell and what appeared to be several small animal bones were recovered. Though no underground passageways, as reported by the children, were found in the field, one of the parents, Arvin Collins, insisted—"but that doesn't mean that they don't exist." Another parent, Joe Cipolla, said that his son had witnessed "animal sacrifices and devil worship here, and right over there"—under an avocado tree in the vacant lot—and that "is where he said the devil lived."[20]

Devils also took carnal and carnival form, the children thought. One 7-year-old male child told the prosecution that he was taken on excursions to a "farm" where he saw Raymond Buckey beat and kill a horse with his bare hands and to a "circus house" where people were dressed in elephant costumes. Another 10-year-old boy described how he and other children were taken to a church several times for candlelit ceremonies, where hooded, black-robed people stood in a circle and moaned. Raymond

Buckey also purportedly cut up a rabbit, warning, "if you tell anyone of the secrets that happened at the school or here or anywhere, then this will happen to you."

In response to this and other stories about butchered rabbits, a raid was conducted on the home of a girlfriend of an uncharged suspect— Robert Winkler. Some of the McMartin children had identified Winkler as one of those persons who had molested them. Winkler was already in the country jail pending a preliminary hearing on earlier charges that he had molested children he had contacted through a baby-sitting service at a Torrance motel.

Surprisingly, the raid on this home produced a pair of rabbit ears, a black cape, and black candles. Adult sexual material was also found, but no child pornography. Deputy D.A. Rubin contended "there may well be a link between this Robert Winkler and Raymond Buckey."[21] Yet no charges against Winkler, his girlfriend, or anyone else resulted from the raid. And for unknown reasons, Winkler later committed suicide.

In March of 1985, goaded by McMartin preschool parents, specialists from the sheriff's crime laboratory began digging up the area surrounding the McMartin school. While there were numerous excavations made, continuing up until 1991 when the school was torn down, no evidence linked to the child molestation case was ever found.

Manhattan Beach was consuming itself alive. Any "witch" the McMartin school children pointed to was immediately a suspect to the police, the district attorney, and the California Department of Social Services. When McMartin children identified the Manhattan Ranch Preschool and Kindergarten as among the places they were molested, the ring of suspicion widened.

In May 1984, a parent complained to police that her 6-year-old daughter had been molested at the Manhattan Beach Preschool and Kindergarten. The school, about a mile from the much publicized and now closed McMartin Preschool, had been in operation 14 years, enrolling 130 students. The parents of six other children made similar allegations, including a charge of nudity by a Torrance resident whose 4 1/2-year-old son had attended the school for more than two years. She said that she was particularly disturbed because when she picked up her son one day she found his underpants were missing. The teachers told her that it had been a hot day and they had taken them off so the children could run through the sprinklers. "I told them, if you want to take my son's clothes off, you should call me." She did not withdraw her son from the school, though she refused to sign school permission slips so that her son could be taken on field trips.[22]

One parent also thought that it was "peculiar" that she was required to tell the school in advance when she would pick up her child, not realizing that the teaching staff needed to have this information to maintain work schedules and to retain accountability for the location of the children.[23] Other testimony about the Ranch school seemed to transform the most ordinary situations into the extraordinary. One parent said that her son sometimes experienced painful bowel movements and developed rashes around his genitals. A physician attributed these physical difficulties to straining when attempting bowel movements. Her son sometimes also became angry and depressed and showed his feelings by biting a bedpost— a sequence that certainly could be caused by many forms of stress and frustration.

Even though an investigation was begun, evidence against the Ranch school was weak and unsubstantiated. Though the inquiry failed to establish a link between the Ranch school and the McMartin Preschool, the State Department of Social Services went into action, ordering the Ranch school temporarily closed. Pandemonium ensued. "It was an emotional scene," reported the maintenance man who observed parents coming to pick up their children from the school for the last time. "The kids were upset and parents were crying. The kids hugged their teachers good-by, and mothers were crying with tears on their faces."[24] After the state lockout, police and social service officials remained tight-lipped about school activities and purported charges.

The news media was the first to inform some parents about the closure. One parent, Jan Steinwald, said that his daughter attended the school three days a week, and he could not believe the accusations because he had been "extremely happy" with the school since enrolling his daughter. He said that his daughter "loved it very much. Frankly, I don't see how anything . . . could have happened here." The school was "wide open. Parents could come and go anytime. We looked all over [for a school] between Santa Monica and Manhattan Beach and liked this one best."[25]

The state filed temporary closure papers, alleging that unnamed investigators had found a "substantial threat to the health and safety of the children." The state alleged that:

Since 1979, children who were clients of the another school [McMartin Pre-School] were taken to the Manhattan Ranch facility. These children while at the Manhattan Ranch facility, were physically and sexually abused.

On one or more occasions, during the aforementioned period of time, children from the Manhattan Ranch facility were taken during school hours to the other preschool [McMartin], where the children were physically and sexually abused.[26]

Liz Brady, a spokeswoman for the state, said that "we don't know the extent of it yet, how many children are involved, but we're afraid of what it might develop into."[27] Subsequently, the only person arrested was a 17-year-old playground aide at Manhattan Ranch on suspicion of child molestation involving children at *that* school—the only employee ever charged. The police spent more than a month investigating the 17-year-old aide, arrested him on suspicion of molesting seven children, held him in a juvenile detention facility, and charged him with 97 counts of molestation. Even these charges may have lacked foundation, for what would usually appear as normal child care and school playground activity had suddenly became suspect.

Assisted by investigators from the Los Angeles County District Attorney's office and the Sheriff's Department, the Manhattan Beach police implicated other Ranch preschool teachers as well. Together they searched the school and its grounds, seized records and raided homes of nine school teachers. Yet Manhattan Beach Sgt. Jim Noble announced that they found "nothing substantial," adding that none of the teachers were considered as suspects.[28]

Clearly, rumor, allegations, false charges of conspiracy, and an over-anxious police department overwhelmed the Manhattan Beach Ranch Preschool and Kindergarten. No evidence was ever produced that could support claims it had swapped children with the McMartin Preschool so that students could be sexually and physically abused. Yet these charges led the State Department of Social Services to order the school closed, but by then the owners had already done so because of hecklers who had driven by and shouted ugly remarks and over concern for the children's safety.[29]

Though all of the original charges against the Manhattan Beach Ranch school sounded powerful and conclusive, no supporting evidence was ever produced, either then or since. Running a preschool had become a dangerous business in both Hermosa and Manhattan Beach.

Jail and Bail

Conflicting juridical decisions about jail and bail also ran their course in the McMartin case, with little coordination taking place among several courts. Then Superior Court Judge Ronald M. George ruled that all defendants be held without bail after determining that their release would pose a danger to public safety.[30] A lower level municipal court judge then fixed bail for four defendants on some counts, while not changing a higher level Superior Court judge's order that they be held without bail on other counts. The Los Angeles Sheriff's Department indicated that no one would be released until the confusion over which court had jurisdiction was resolved.[31]

Those charged were held in custody because of their supposed danger to the community. There was no court review of the facts that would merit such a conclusion. Deputy District Attorney Lael Rubin had argued that releasing the defendants from custody would pose a danger to the children and parents involved in the case.[32] A witness for the prosecution, Colleen Mooney, testified that she believed that some of the children were "terrified" and feared that they might be harmed and maybe even "killed" if the defendants were released.[33] But not all the overlapping courts were convinced by the argument.

To add to the jurisdictional conflicts, a California appellate court, which is on a higher level than municipal or superior courts, conditionally ordered that Babette Spitler, on original bail of $400,000, be released on her own recognizance on all counts because she did not receive a speedy preliminary hearing on the child molestation indictment.[34] She was not to leave the state, to waive extradition if she did leave the state, and to appear in court whenever required. However, her bail of $400,000 was reinstated by the California Supreme Court, which has jurisdiction over all other courts. Her attorney, Eliseo Guana, then requested that her bail be reduced to $125,000.

To add further to the jurisdictional problems, after being released from jail, Babette Spitler learned she was wanted under a bench warrant from the superior court for failing to appear at a hearing, even though she had been free upon her own recognizance under orders from the higher level appellate court; the warrant was to have her appear to post bail.[35]

As in many other aspects of the case, moreover, the difference of opinion among various courts forced Spitler to pay the monetary and personal costs. When intercourt disputes were more or less settled, Spitler was released from jail after posting $400,000 bail, insisting that she would be "vindicated" of all charges against her.[36]

Bette Raidor, whose bail was set at $750,000, also sought similar relief, which she received under an appellate court order.[37] Despite the state Court of Appeal order for her release, however, Raidor was not released. When her attorney, Walter R. Urban, asked Superior Court Judge Ronald George for her release, the judge denied the request, stating that the appellate court had not specified whether the municipal or superior court should act on the order.

Virginia McMartin and Mary Ann Jackson were actually freed on bail. But Peggy McMartin Buckey's bail was set at $1 million, while Peggy Ann Buckey's bail was set at $250,000. Raymond Buckey was being held without possibility of bail.[38]

Conclusions

Delayed by investigations by different criminal justice departments and confusion over jurisdictional powers—including local, state, and federal agencies—the actual trial was a long way off. Non-judicial and extra-legal factors also influenced the way in which the public viewed the case. Pre-trial publicity of the investigations, the reactions of parents of alleged child victims, and other influences shaped the ways in which the general public, the prosecution, and potential jurors evaluated the McMartin episode.

Consuming months of testimony by witnesses for the prosecution and by the defense, the preliminary hearing brought forth parents of the alleged victims, therapists, child witnesses, medical experts, and many others. In itself, it seemed like a trial.

But in fact the trial was yet to begin. There were a series of critical steps that took place prior to the actual trial, including the development of procedures for selecting and impaneling a jury that would sit in judgment during the first trial. There also were other cumbersome legal procedures that used up a substantial amount of time and resources.

Even before then, pre-trial publicity about the defendants and their alleged crimes joined the prosecution's disclosure of pre-indictment materials to the media, empowering the purveyors of words, sounds and pictures to shape and construct the way in which news stories of child molestation were reported to the public. This power of unlimited persuasion is the focus of the next chapter.

Chapter 3

Pre-Trial Publicity: A Media Event

There may be no way to adequately protect the rights of suspects in cases where the charges are so gross and involve so many alleged victims that the public's demand to know the details seems to outweigh other considerations.

The McMartin case—with the enormity of its charges and the large number of children claiming to be victims—may fall into that category. Certainly no responsible news organization could ignore the case. It's heartbreaking to contemplate children being victimized, and it's a natural thing to presume the defendants' guilt.

Yet what if the McMartin Seven aren't guilty? Or what if not all are proved guilty? Because of the intense coverage, the lives of the innocent would be ruined.

> Howard Rosenberg, "McMartin case as media spectacle," *Los Angeles Times,* June 20, 1984

From the beginning, the McMartin case developed as a media event with sensationalistic mass publicity. Each television commentator and newspaper reporter seemed determined to outdo the others in developing the more sensational, sexual aspects of the case. The presumption of guilt by most of the mass media generated public hysteria. One Oscar and Emmy Award winner saw the case fitting the theme of a "witch hunt."[1] And a television program, in which children from the McMartin Preschool appeared, focused on the "sexual house of horrors"—children, incidentally, who were not witnesses but who had supported the district attorney's charges against the defendants.

Members of the media waged a frantic, competitive struggle in the preliminary stages of the McMartin case, moreover, each seeking access to all documents, videotaped interviews, and other materials from both defense and prosecuting attorneys. As the preliminary hearing for the trial was opened to the media, then closed, and then opened again, the media's search for anything that could be construed as breaking news seemed at times almost desperate.

In an attempt to control publicity-hungry networks, the prosecution and defense agreed to keep the details of the case sealed—the prosecution seeking to protect any evidence they might have that would ensure conviction, and the defense wanting to keep inadmissible evidence out of the hands of the media.[2] Publicity about the case was even being read in Tokyo newspapers in Japan. To find a jury that has not been tainted by the mass media, attorney Eliseo D. W. Guana, representing accused Babette Spitler, stated that "we may end up holding the trial in Borneo," his offering only partly in jest.[3]

The legal shield against the media was continuously pounded and penetrated. During testimony in the preliminary hearing, Judge Aviva K. Bobb had initially prohibited television, still cameras, and sound equipment from the courtroom, yet did not restrict the public's right to attend.[4] Quickly moving on the offensive, the Radio and Television News Association and the *Los Angeles Times,* joined by ABC, NBC, CBS, and Cable News Network (CNN), waged a court battle to have the hearings open to them, advocating that public interest demanded the proceedings be broadcast by TV.[5]

Newspaper, television, and radio commentators were meanwhile, on the *qui vive,* in constant attendance from the very beginning of the case. A *New York Times* reporter described the scene: "Each time the cortege [of defendants and attorneys] approaches or leaves a courtroom on the seventh floor, brilliant lights flash on. Television crews, lying in wait like hunters, lunge forward and aim their cameras at the group."[6]

Such waves of publicity, though, engendered further injustices as well. A few lawyers argued that in such an atmosphere innocent adults might be prosecuted and their lives forever ruined by mistakes or fantasies concocted by children and overzealous prosecutors.[7] These possibilities seemed to escape much of the media scrutiny. Objective and investigative news reporting seemed almost lost, as the maddened coterie of scribes and camera hounds conducted their trial by flashing images, accented adjectives and conviction by postulation, titillating readers' emotive lives in efforts to gain circulation and the broadest viewing audience.

Television and the McMartin Case

The media blitz, initiated by the prosecution, created the illusion that the charges were believable. Though the case began September 15, 1983 with the arrest, then release, of Raymond Buckey, the police continued their investigation until late March 1984, when seven teachers and administrators were arrested and indicted by a grand jury.

The press had temporarily held off; several journalists who were ready to report elements of the story for more than a month awaited further police action. Then on police cue, the blitz began; props and sensationalized charges against the McMartin seven grabbed public attention, with the added bonus of widening news circulation, and eliciting an ever-wider police response that traumatized child witnesses, their parents, defendants, and the community.

Certainly no print or electronic media organization could ignore the case. Yet, there were few shields or barriers protecting the rights of the suspects in the face of these massive charges. For the media gave little consideration that the defendants had families, reputations, jobs, personal resources, and integrity to protect. There was almost no recognition that the defendants had the right to vindicate themselves personally and in a court of law. To most of the media, the defendants were guilty beyond any reasonable doubt though the trial was not to begin for several years. Media distortion thus mined the case's tortuous pathways, seducing advertisers and the public, increasing revenue, and keeping itself alive and well.

KABC-TV (Channel 7)
Breaking the McMartin case on KABC-TV on February 2, 1984, reporter Wayne Satz sensationalized and editorialized, offering little recognition that the charges of molestation were allegations and not facts. Perhaps the most extreme example of biased sensationalism was KABC's full-page newspaper ad featuring a child's teddy bear, mauled, one eye missing, its stuffing spilling out.[8] None of these props were ever part of the case or of the material presented to the court.

Yet, teddy bears, rabbit ears, chicken bones, and *Playboy* magazines were to become hallmarks of the press in its reporting of the McMartin case. The KABC ad reported that the station had beaten everyone with the news and that the news could prove to be a catalyst in crime prevention. The May 1985 full-page newspaper ad for KABC noted that:

> We beat everybody with the news, but we feel lousy because the story is so awful.... This is a sick, sick story.

Satz, both a lawyer and reporter who had specialized in stories of police malpractice and brutality, won a Peabody Award for his report of police shootings of civilians and two Golden Mike awards for his

McMartin stories.[9] Yet, Satz's reporting and the newspaper ad raised a serious problem—"the balance between reporting and pandering [to public emotions], the conflict of telling a story and protecting the innocent."[10] Not coincidentally so did KABC's ad, which appeared the day before competitive ratings were being made, an obvious ploy to focus the attention of the television viewing audience, in a deliberate attempt to exploit the case to increase its rave reviews.[11]

Similarly, it was later revealed that a social worker who had interviewed the children had transmitted testimony and documentary evidence, which were subject to protective orders in the criminal proceedings, to the KABC station and its news reporter, Satz.[12] And thereafter, KABC in Los Angeles (Channel 7) became an important dispenser linking fact and fiction during the early phase of the preliminary hearing.

A "20/20" Segment on McMartin

One of the major TV pieces on the McMartin case was a "20/20" segment which was primarily the work of a free-lance reporter—Ken Wooden. In the process of designing the program, Wooden was accused of pressuring the prosecution to allow court-restricted airing of his interview with a counselor of the Children's Institute International (CII), by threatening to broadcast copies of the institute's videotaped interviews with the children. A compromise agreement was made, with some parents and children to appear on "20/20"—ostensibly to warn other parents whose children might be in danger of being molested. To protect them, the children and their parents were photographed from the back or in silhouette and their images blurred. Their voices were also electronically changed and distorted so that they could not be identified.

The program displayed what was claimed to be a police report identifying Raymond Buckey as an accused pedophile; pictured deputy prosecutor Lael Rubin talking about the children's "frightening" stories; showed how CII therapists used puppets to draw information about school events from reticent children; and displayed bizarre sexual drawings that some of the children had made of the McMartin teaching staff, drawings that ABC correspondent Tom Jarriel advised viewers—"tells us much about their teachers."

The children's impressionable interpretation of the world was to be believed, Jarriel implied, regardless of where they had obtained it. Events and their images were conveyed second-hand from the children's stories as told to their parents, who then recounted them for "20/20" viewers. The awful things, that they said their children had told them, happened while in, what Jarriel alleged to be, a "sexual house of horrors." Thus flowed adult accounts about children having been taken from the school and used as prostitutes and participants in pornographic movies. There was no other conclusion to draw but that those charged were guilty, despite the use of the journalistic qualifier "allegedly" (used six times in the 25-minute segment) and the disclaimer that "the defendants in this case are innocent until proved guilty."

Both Jarriel and "20/20" host Hugh Downs went the last mile for the prosecution, too, relaying a third-hand account of the alleged events— from the children to the parents, who told Jarriel, who then retold the story to the "20/20" national TV audience (each of whom in turn might have retold the story many times):

> Downs: How deeply marked are these children, Tom, and will they recover from it?
> Jarriel: Psychologically, perhaps never, Hugh. One little boy, for example, asked his mother, "Mommy when I die, will the bad memories go away?"
> Downs: My God!

"20/20" purposefully presented the case as an object lesson to advise parents how to protect their children against sexual abuse at child care facilities. But the lesson could not help the parents of the McMartin school children, Jarriel said, for the "information comes too late." Assumption of the defendants' guilt was then extended by Jarriel's comment on what the parents said—"By sharing what they have learned, they can now hope to prevent this type of tragedy from happening to other kids."

Yet, some viewers missed this message. Even though it was KABC-TV's Wayne Satz's report on the McMartin Preschool allegations that originally sensationalized the case, KABC-TV in Los Angeles refused to broadcast the McMartin "20/20" segment because it contained interviews with the alleged child victims.[13] A controversy over whether or not the program had had access to the videotaped interviews carried out at the CII accounted for a variety of countercharges, with Judge Michael A. Tynan issuing orders restricting access to the tapes and barring anyone from making them public.[14]

The local ABC television outlet, Channel 7, reversed its own internal policies by deciding not to televise interviews with alleged child molestation victims, though the station's real reason may have been fear of law suits.[15]

In a *Los Angeles Times* review of the "20/20" segment, however, Home News editor Rosenberg concluded that it was probably impossible for the McMartin Preschool case to be treated fairly in the media. He argued that the term "allegedly," no matter how many times used in the "20/20" TV program, did not lessen the program's ultimate message— *guilty!* Rosenberg argued that as the defendants were fully identified, with "allegedly" thrown in, was "like calling Hiroshima an alleged bombing."

In further reviewing the context of the "20/20" version, Rosenberg also noted that "most TV news is [an] instant theater, a sort of foil-wrapped video TV dinner that reaches a quick boil and then evaporates. The purpose is to stimulate emotions, not minds. The emphasis is on what viewers see, not what they learn or absorb."[16] He criticized the "20/20" presentation as pro-prosecution, with virtually no defense arguments being presented. On the program, he said, three children, none of whom were to testify at the trial, detailed "alleged widespread molestations and physical and mental torture" at the McMartin Preschool.

While their faces were not seen and their voices were distorted, the parents and children appearing on the "20/20" segment were easily recognizable in Manhattan Beach, exposing the children to harassment. Shocked by their own vulnerability, some families moved to ensure that their children would not be further exploited by TV or the courts.

Modern media has a ready alibi for its infringements: The public's right to know the danger it faces. The media, moreover, overlooked its own blind spot, that programs might impair a defendants' right to a fair trial by making it virtually impossible to find an unbiased jury. A serious question of ethics was also raised by Rubin's appearance on the television show, talking about the children's frightening stories. The program, designed to transform viewers into a jury of peers, presented as "evidence" bizarre drawings that the children made of the McMartin staff, and showed how therapists used puppets to elicit tales of sexual abuse from the children. As Rosenberg's review noted: "Minutes earlier, Jarriel had emphasized that 'the defendants in this case are innocent until proved guilty.' He was wrong, of course. They had just been convicted on national TV."[17]

Why would so many children who were being abused remain silent about the abuse, the "20/20" program asked. The program's answer was that the children were "brainwashed into silence" by their teachers. An army brainwashing expert wearing combat fatigues—the ultimate prop—claimed that the brainwashing was similar to incidents in Vietnam. Solely basing his conclusions on the "20/20" interviews with the children conducted by Tom Jarriel, the army expert announced that without a doubt, the children had been brainwashed by their teachers.[18] For presumed balance, defendant Bette Raidor and her attorney, Walter Urban, were briefly interviewed on the program—they, of course, denied the brainwashing charges.

To detect child abuse, the program also offered five easy steps, which even parents of the allegedly molested children thought were too simplistic; they questioned the credibility of the program and how it might reflect upon their own credibility.

Another View: The "60 Minutes" Segment

Perhaps the first national attempt at unbiased reporting of the McMartin case was the "60 Minutes" segment. The program was aired after the preliminary hearing and the dropping of five defendants from the case. Centering on the views of former Los Angeles District Attorney Robert Philibosian, who had initially filed the charges against the McMartin defendants, interviewer Mike Wallace elicited the lawman's opinion of no sympathy for the released five defendants, but sorrow for the child victims. Philibosian criticized what he perceived as the new District Attorney Ira Reiner's error in dropping charges against the five, arguing that both a grand jury and a preliminary judge had indicated that the five should be tried for child molestation. The former DA also noted that the grand jury and preliminary judge had heard ample evidence, day-in-day-out, and determined that all seven should stand trial. He commended CII for the great job they did in eliciting information from the children on sexual abuse at the school.

Wallace also interviewed CII Director Evans. Asked if any hard evidence had ever been found, such as photographs, animal bones, tunnels, or evidence of satanic rituals, she replied "[N]one," but added that medical evidence had proven that abuse had taken place. She also said that CII was not attempting to develop evidence, but that their procedures were for diagnosis and treatment, not law enforcement. Nevertheless, the therapeutic procedures were videotaped, and subsequently, we will see, the videotapes became part of the important evidence presented during the trial.

In her interview for Wallace, Lael Rubin, the chief prosecutor, was adamant in her belief that all seven of the alleged perpetrators were guilty of child abuse at the McMartin Preschool. She said,"[C]hildren were molested there," adding that she had ample evidence of abuse which would be presented in the courtroom at the appropriate time. She recounted the problems that some of the children had suffered such as sexual irritations, infections, etc., but discounted any possibility that these could have arisen from sources other than sexual abuse at the school.

Similar allegations were made by a parent, Tim Wheeler, who also insisted that the testifying children were pioneers. Wheeler, an attorney in Los Angeles, said that his two children were seven and eight years old when they had been molested at the preschool. His older son implicated two teachers, and his younger son said that he had been forced to play games like "Cowboy and Indians," in which he had to take off his clothes and let people touch him.

Though Wheeler discounted testimony by the children on specific questions, he expressed his belief that the overall picture was one that demonstrated that the children had been molested at the school. Agreeing with him, according to Wheeler, were other parents who also believed that charges against the five should not have been dropped.

In an interview, the new District Attorney Ira Reiner defended his decision to drop the charges against five of the former defendants. He said that on the basis of weak evidence, he was obligated to drop the charges against them. He told interviewer Wallace that the whole case had developed "massively out of proportion" to what actually had taken place at the McMartin Preschool.

For her part, accused Virginia McMartin told Wallace that no evidence of tunnels, photographs, satanic rituals, etc., would ever be found because none ever existed. In a moment of levity, she offered to take Wallace to the avocado tree where children claimed the devil lived, if he wanted a corroborating interview with him.

Sounding eminently composed, Raymond Buckey offered that he was allowing the interview on "60 Minutes" at that time, despite previously refusing others, because he believed that the public was finally stepping back from the hysteria that initially surrounded the case. "I am not a monster," he insisted, denying to Wallace that he had ever had a single instance of a sexual encounter with any of the children. He told Wallace that he believed that the children had been told what to say and that this was then reinforced by the therapists, parents, and prosecution attorneys. He said that five of the other defendants had been released on the basis of evidence similar to that which was still being held against him. Apparently, he concluded, the authorities needed a "scapegoat" and it was he. "They have ruined me and my family" all over petty politics, he recounted. Peggy McMartin Buckey finally put the case in a broader frame: It was a witch hunt.

The Print Media and the McMartin Case

Following television's lead, the print media, led by the *Los Angeles Times,* the largest and most widely-read newspaper in southern California, seemed to lose its journalistic balance, helping to create a climate of public furor over the McMartin case. Waiting a couple of months after the KABC-TV broadcast by Wayne Satz, a *Los Angeles Times* article on April 2, 1984, further polemicized the case. The *Times* launched its army of reporters, sensationalizing the case; they reaped the benefits of a wider audience, increased circulation, but perhaps lost objectivity by neglecting in-depth exploration of known facts. The *Times* tried and convicted the defendants without a trial and without presenting any defense evidence. Running more than 25 stories on the case in a mere six weeks, plus many others on child molestation, the *Times* outdid all rivals big and small.

Other soul-wrenching press and television reports picked up the rear, each attempting to keep alive allegations that sometimes disappeared or died in the courts. Pinpointing the Buckeys, arguing guilt by association, the media linked the McMartin center with other day schools and residents throughout the area, accusing all as part of a ring of child-molesters.

The real conspirators may have conclaved elsewhere. Charges of collusion between Chief Prosecutor Lael Rubin and *Los Angeles Times* reporter Lois Timnick surfaced when it appeared that Rubin was giving out-of-court "evidence" to the reporter for her "news" stories. Rubin and Timnick had long shared a strong stand against child abuse.

Rubin might well have stepped over the bounds of ethics when she provided information to Timnick that Raymond Buckey had been coun-seled for "sexual problems" involving young children, by a Dr. Frank Richelieu, pastor of the Church of Religious Science in Redondo Beach, a community near the McMartin Preschool. Both in and out of court, Dr. Richelieu hotly denied that such counseling ever took place, stating, "I never counseled Raymond Buckey for child abuse nor molestation. I coun-seled him for matters dealing with himself. He was drinking. We never discussed sexual molestation at all. I read the *L.A. Times* article and it was ridiculous. I don't know what they were basing it on."[19] Dr. Richelieu also noted that if the counseling had been about child abuse, he would have been compelled to report it to law enforcement officials under the child abuse reporting law. Prosecutor Rubin was never able to produce substantiating evidence of her charges floated in Timnick's articles.

A word about Timnick, who had been working as a reporter for 18 years, seven of them at the *Times:* As a single mother, Timnick felt strongly about child abuse, and as another *Times* reporter, David Shaw, wrote, "she has spoken publicly on the subject [of child sexual molestation] and was interested in it before McMartin hit the headlines; she wrote nine byline stories on child abuse the year before McMartin—the major rea-son she was assigned to the story in the first place. She knew—and cared— about the subject."[20]

During most of the case, David Rosenzweig was the metropolitan edi-tor of the *Los Angeles Times.* He had continued to print prosecution-ori-ented stories, setting the tone of the newspaper's negative coverage towards the defendants. This also fit into the logic of a romance between the prosecutor Rubin and Rosenzweig that started at least a few months before the defense began to present its case in trial; critics argued that this helped explain the *Times* bias and its refusal to cover the defense's evidence. Although there is no compelling proof for this assertion, Rosenzweig felt the heat, subsequently removing himself from any role in trial coverage.

As McMartin parents began to see news coverage momentarily turn against them, many dropped pursuit of legal action. The sensational headlines were gone for the time being and major national media like *Newsweek* and *Time* began to question if there had ever been any substance to the original charges. A few smaller circulation publications did in-depth investigations of the defendants' pasts, revealing that they were not monsters, but ran their preschool on the basic premise of a shared love of children. However, with perhaps the exceptions of a few "pro-defense" coverage papers like the *Daily Breeze* in Torrance—another nearby beach community—the dailies covering the case consistently aided and abetted angry parents and supporters of the prosecution.

In addition to the media impact upon the alleged perpetrators, the blitz affected the community, bringing on more accusations, child-care facility closings, and the unconscionable misuse of police powers. The McMartin school, meanwhile, became a site of curiosity seekers; it was broken into several times, and set afire. Messages such as "ONLY THE BEGINNING" and "RAY MUST DIE" were spray-painted at the preschool. Some were calling Manhattan Beach "Salem-by-the Sea"—a place of intense private sleuthing and snooping, capped by accusations and abuse of those stigmatized without evidence of wrongdoing, and found guilty without a trial. Thus, the community succumbed to fear, as police surveillance and public hysteria increased.

Political Publicity

The cult of personality that addicts Hollywood, stars, and Los Angeles aficionados was not foreign to the Los Angeles District Attorney's Office. Most DAs sought name recognition as a stepping stone to the State Attorney General's Office, then to the governor's seat or a senator's office.

From the beginning of the McMartin case, there had been charges that the district attorney was using the case for political purposes. Such allegations were publicly raised and made part of the court's record when formal charges were made by Forrest Latiner, one of the defense attorneys, that the prosecution was manipulating a willing media by feeding them pre-indictment and confidential information about the defendants. Latiner went further, implying that District Attorney Philibosian had repeatedly exploited the sensational aspects of the case by publicly speaking to the media, angling for conviction of the defendants. Latiner anticipated that complaints against the defendants would be made just prior to the election, following Philibosian's repeated attempts to exploit the sensational aspects of the case for his own publicity. There was even a charge that Superior Court Judge Ronald George was aiding the district attorney in his election bid and thus should not be allowed to sit in judgment of the defendants.[21]

Defense attorney Daniel Davis also made written motion in municipal court, arguing that Philibosian had unconscionably exploited the McMartin case to heighten his name recognition during his election campaign, that he violated ethical standards by making statements about the case outside of the courtroom and facilitated investigative and other prosecutorial procedures which, in themselves, had been psychologically and socially harmful to the children involved. Davis also accused Judge George of biases in favor of the district attorney's office in order to further his own judicial career and to help Philibosian's election prospects. Attacking the very foundation for bringing the case itself, Davis argued that Philibosian and his legal entourage—Deputy District Attorneys Reuben A. Otega, Lael R. Rubin, Jean Matusinka, and Eleanor E. Barrett— should be compelled to testify in court about the way they handled and shaped the McMartin case.

Jean Matusinka, a deputy district attorney and head of the child abuse unit in the Los Angeles District Attorney's Office, for instance, had handled the early phase of the McMartin investigation and had contacted Kathleen MacFarlane at CII to interview nearly 400 children.

In the motion to disqualify the district attorney filed by the defense attorney, Daniel Davis specifically stated:

> ... after the arrest of Raymond Charles Buckey in September 1983, interim District Attorney Robert H. Philibosian retained the services of political advisors to direct him in his campaign for his presently appointed position. In response, Philibosian's political advisors undertook research and surveys, determining Philibosian was in need of better public name recognition, and that he should publicly identify himself with criminal prosecution involving child molestation or abuse charges.
>
> Accordingly, Philibosian seized upon the McMartin Preschool case and began intensely zealous efforts to exploit the case for political publicity value. In so doing, Philibosian directly and indirectly promoted extensive media disclosure of incremental rumors, suspicions and information, developed though his office's investi-

gation of the case. Throughout, Philibosian presented himself to the
public in close association with the prosecution of the case, often
choosing to seat himself at the counsel table, during the most highly
publicized aspect of the case. On each such occasion, he made no
statement or action within the courtroom, but merely sat in front of
the attending public and television cameras. Thereafter, he would
conduct an informal press conference outside the courtroom, expressing a variety of opinions, purported facts and accusations regarding the case, the defendants and evidence.

Conflict between politics and prosecution had been actual and
apparent in literally all of the aspects subject to the discretion of the
District Attorney, including release of criminal records, surveillance
of defendants, arrest of defendants, bail recommendations, discovery of evidence, intimidation of defendants and their defense staff
and prolonged failure in filing a complaint.

Early in the investigation, Raymond Buckey's prior arrest record
was released to the public. Shortly after original charges were dismissed against him, he and his entire family were subject to unnec-
essarily intense and harassing surveillance. Although several defendants made explicit requests for voluntary surrender, the District Attorney instead caused surprise physical arrest substantially
covered by news media, for no other purpose but to obtain political
notoriety and advantage.[22]

The defense argued that the district attorney must remain free from
personal involvement that appeared to bias his judgment by factors extra-
neous to his objective and impartial handling of the case.

Preliminary Hearing Judge Bobb declared that she could not make
the decision about whether or not the district attorney's office could manage the case until the State Attorney General's office disqualified the office
of the Los Angeles District Attorney. If the Los Angeles District Attorney's
office was precluded from prosecuting the case, the State of California's
Attorney General's office would eventually become the prosecutors. But
the Attorney General's office was opposed to becoming the prosecution
in the McMartin case. Since the state disagreed with defense attorney
Davis, there was no reply to the court and thus the local district attorney's
office continued to remain in charge of the prosecution. The court also
ruled that Judge George did not need to be disqualified.[23]

In a written statement filed with the court, Philibosian also denied all
of the defense charges, though Philibosian later lost the bitterly contested
election to Ira Reiner, who became the new Los Angeles District Attorney in December, 1984. And later, Judge Ronald George was nominated
to become a Supreme Court Justice in the State of California.[24]

Impact of Media Coverage

The McMartin Preschool case generated an enormous outpouring of media attention, a focus crucial to how the case was perceived by the public and in the community. In child molestation cases, past studies show that a number of predictable factors are generally correlated with media coverage. Almost all multiple victim cases have received extensive media attention, as have the cases in which the sexual abuse was of long duration. Eighty-eight percent of cases prosecuted attracted media attention, as did 100% of the cases in which there was a conviction or a guilty plea.[25] The cases that have escaped media attention tended to be ones with lone female perpetrators, lone juvenile perpetrators, and no white victims. When only racial and ethnic minority children were victimized, the cases have not been considered as newsworthy and they normally have not drawn much public scrutiny or media attention.[26]

At its zenith, the McMartin Preschool was considered the best day-care school in the City of Manhattan Beach, where 90.2% of residents were white, the highest concentration of white residents in Los Angeles County which was demographically proportioned: 45.6% whites, 10.2% blacks, 33.3% Hispanics, and 10.3% Asians and Pacific Islanders.[27] While the majority of county residents were thus racial and ethnic minorities, Manhattan Beach has been regarded as a white enclave in the county with residents from the middle and upper class (e.g., 0.6% black, 4.8% Hispanic, and 4.1% Asian and Pacific islanders).

The McMartin defendants were white and worked and lived in a scenic oceanfront community located on the south side of Santa Monica Bay in Los Angeles County. The defendants' backgrounds were identified with residents of sandy beaches and picturesque settings, popular for affluent Angelenos. Similarly, the McMartin Preschool enrolled the children of many of the county's political elite and prominent professionals. Almost all of the alleged victims were white and belonged to the upper and middle class, and their racial and social class backgrounds might explain the mass hysteria and the community's reactions to the allegation of child molestation at the preschool. Parents and local police were able to mobilize both state and federal criminal justice enforcement agencies into the investigation of the case, attracting public attention and high publicity by the media.

Extensive media coverage also brought a number of other significant and crucial actors into play. Politicians and policymakers sensitive to publicity revealed a deep concern for growing public anxiety. Prosecutors, yielding to the pressure to take action in fighting crimes, went into combat on the media-exposé of multiple sexual abuse and ritualistic satanic practices. Similarly extensive media coverage identified alleged victims and their families, besieging them with reporters, prosecutors, investigators, licensed officials specializing in child molestation cases, and allies. The alleged victims and their parents also found themselves playing unaccustomed roles as highly visible public figures, appearing on TV shows both locally and nationally.

Conclusions

Clearly the McMartin case focused on child-care facilities and potential childhood sexual abuse in California and elsewhere.[28] The door was opened for a concerted effort to educate young people about child sexual molestation.

Massive publicity by print and electronic media also opened another door: hysteria, influencing and encouraging the young to see child abuse everywhere, even in the most innocent places and acts.[29] As there were possible mitigating factors on both sides of the proceedings, the media should have tread more lightly, exercising self-restraint in its reporting until sufficient facts were gathered, sifted, and evaluated in a court of law. But the media failed to give notice and honor to the principle that a person accused is assumed innocent until proven guilty by measured legal steps—violating the rights of both alleged victims and perpetrators.

The courts did protect the rights of the accused to confront the witnesses against them, and the media's right to free access to information, but embroiled attorneys and judges in a tangle of legal opinions. The public's demand to know details remained important, but what was just as important was that lives should not be ruined; the alleged acts might not have happened and the supposed perpetrators might be innocent.

The line of demarcation between the public's right to know and protection of the alleged victims and perpetrators was never located in the McMartin case.[30] An unresolved, broad and burning social issue was thus revealed by the media's treatment of the McMartin episode: In child molestation cases, how should the injured or accused be protected rather than terrorized by press and electronic handling of such a highly emotive issue? The next chapter focuses on a community survey conducted by the present authors concerning the McMartin incidents and presents critical comparisons with empirical findings of a national survey conducted by the *Los Angeles Times* on the same subject.

Chapter 4

Pre-Trial Publicity: The Public's View

The media gave life to the McMartin preschool case, forcing it into the consciousness of greater Los Angeles, and sending shock waves of apprehension across the nation. Pre-trial publicity had an impact on the public's perception of the guilt or innocence of those gravely charged with child molestation. Public revelations, with the cooperation of and manipulation by an eager media using preindictment investigative materials, aided the prosecutors' attempts to shape both evidence and the trial outcome.

In covering the revelations of the McMartin case in 1985, the *Los Angeles Times* led the field, conducting a national opinion survey on child sexual abuse issues. Appearing in two weighty articles, the survey findings focused readers' attention on child molestation. The defense team meanwhile angrily reacted, attempting to sharply restrict media exposure of the defendants and the prosecution's evidence, measures necessary to secure a fair trial. Raising its shield, the defense asked social scientists to conduct a content analysis of both print and electronic media reportings on the McMartin defendants, in order to assess media influence on public opinion regarding the possible outcome of the trial. This analysis included a community opinion survey to determine the linkage of media publicity, public perception of the defendants, and alternative trial outcomes judged by potential McMartin jurors who resided in Los Angeles County. The results suggested that a fair trial would be in jeopardy, compelling the defense to seek a change of venue from Los Angeles to an alternative location where residents might have had minimum exposure to the McMartin allegations.

Recounting these steps, this chapter focuses on pre-trial publicity and its influence on the public's view of the McMartin defendants and the alleged crimes. In outline, the following account delineates: (1) the analysis of the *Los Angeles Times* opinion survey; (2) the two types of empirical analyses made by defense-recruited social scientists to assess the possibility for the defendants to receive a fair trial, emphasizing the need to select impartial jurors; and (3) the opinion survey of potential jurors who resided in the Los Angeles Superior Court judicial district— the trial site for the McMartin defendants. By placing emphasis on the analysis of opinion survey results, biases against the McMartin defendants by potential jurors residing in the Los Angeles Central Superior Court jurisdiction were revealed.

The *Los Angeles Times* Opinion Survey

The media has changed its mien in modern times. Since the early 1980s, the mass media has transformed its news reporting style from traditional, narrative news stories to more investigative, objective, and seemingly scientific methods, offering more credibility to its news stories. The media began to turn to a number of scientific methods, including telephone surveys and structured, objective interview techniques, in hopes of providing strong legitimacy to their news stories and their investigative reports.

The *Los Angeles Times* was no exception. In the midst of reporting the latest developments about the McMartin case, the *Los Angeles Times* had managed to carry out a national public opinion survey and collect information on the issues of child abuse, sexual molestation, and the causes and consequences of childhood experiences. Conducted during eight days ending July 25, 1985, the *Los Angeles Times* survey was national in scope, including the states of Alaska and Hawaii.[1] Two substantial articles in the *Times,* on August 25 and 26, reported and analyzed the results, compared reported sexual abuse victims with nonvictims, and divided victims of child abuse into those who were "penetrated" and those who were "not penetrated."

The original intent of the survey was to provide in-depth analyses of child molestation and shed critical insights into the causes and consequences of childhood sexual experience. Relevant to the McMartin defendants, however, the survey and reported articles failed to ask the deeper questions of the defendants' innocence as victims of overzealous prosecutors, a maddened media, and angry parents. Rather, the articles added to the fear and possible dangers of child sexual abuse in the community, stressed the destructive consequences of childhood sexual experiences, and set the frame for public outrage against would-be-molesters and free-thinkers alike.

The survey was also a set-up to solicit answers that reaffirmed the point of view the *Times* sought. For instance, in considering the difference between "innocent people being tried for crimes of child sexual abuse they did not commit," as opposed to guilty people never being brought to trial, the article emphasized that about two-thirds of respondents were more concerned about the guilty not being brought to trial than the innocent being tried for alleged child molestation. The analysis also found no differences between abuse victims and non-victims in their willingness to talk about the danger of child sexual abuse and the adequacy of laws dealing with the problems.

Similar results were obtained when respondents were asked about respecting the rights of alleged perpetrators versus protecting alleged children victims from psychological damage. The definition of abuse was broad as well. Virtually all respondents also said that child sexual abuse takes place when a sexual act has been "attempted," even though it may not have been completed. Further, over two-thirds of both victims and non-victims believed that when "an adult made sexual remarks or indecent suggestions to a child," that would be an example of child sexual abuse. Even a larger percentage believed that showing a child photographs of naked persons constituted sexual abuse, though somewhat fewer persons considered adult exposure to be an example of child molestation.

In all of these responses, the percentages varied relatively little and typically within the sampling error (+ or - 3%). In all instances, alleged victims were slightly more likely than non-victims to report a greater percentage of assumed child sexual abuse.

Those who reported that they were sexual abuse victims said that most of their abuse was related to exhibitionism, while many also reported experiences involving oral copulation or sodomy. About a third of the sexual abuse reported took place within the home, and about half of the experiences took place with a person in a position of authority. Most sexual abuse took place before the victim was 14, and over two-thirds of the abuse was a one-time experience. Many victims never reported the abuse, and when it was reported about 70% said that nothing was done about it. The person most often told was a parent, next a sibling, then a friend.

The questionnaire also compared the extent of "suffering" by a child when the family moves and/or parents get a divorce with a child's exposure to pornographic magazines, playing sex games with another child, and with sexual abuse by an adult. The most traumatic experience, according to these respondents, was sexual abuse by an adult (78-81%), followed by divorce (33-34%), then exposure to childhood sex and pornographic magazines (13-16%), and finally a family move (3%). For these questions, the variation in response between abuse victims and non-victims was virtually non-existent.

A similar finding was observed for the expected influence that a child sexual abuse experience would have on a person in his/her adult life. There was substantial agreement that most damage would be mental, rather than physical or social. There also was agreement that children are most often molested by someone who is known to the child, again with virtually no difference of opinion between victims and non-victims. However, victims were more likely than non-victims to agree that sexual assault within families is very common.

Victims were also more likely than non-victims to believe that sexual assault and child molestation are serious problems, but the vast majority of respondents reported that sex crimes are not serious in their community. About two-thirds of the respondents believed that those who sexually abuse children are mentally ill and that children who submit to sexual abuse do so because they are afraid.

Prevention of child sexual abuse, according to these respondents, was possible through more public education and more severe punishment of offenders, with some emphasis on therapy. The model of appropriate punishment would be jail for 20 years or more. The majority viewed the possibility of rehabilitation of the offender as being somewhat likely, with little variation between victims and non-victims. Victims reported the major reasons for not reporting sexual abuse as fear and a feeling of guilt.

Finally, reported victims of child sexual abuse were more likely to have talked and/or read about child sexual abuse than non-victims. Victims were also somewhat less likely to be satisfied with how "authorities" handled the McMartin investigation. Those persons who reported that they were child sexual abuse victims were more likely than non-victims to believe that the children involved in the McMartin case were sexually abused.

Unfortunately, little information was gleaned in this general survey about the actual social or psychological consequences of childhood sexual abuse and whether or not these early childhood experiences made any difference in the future, adult lives of the victims.

While the national survey of child abuse and child sexual molestation raised public awareness of the problem and its nuances, the media also examined and scrutinized the McMartin defendants and the charges against them. Such publicity, prior to the trial, focused the issues and exerted significant influence over public perception of the guilt or innocence of those charged.

Defense Analyses of Pre-Trial Publicity and Public Opinion

While massive pre-trial publicity raged against the accused, potentially influencing the outcome of the trial, and the media proved that the public was overwhelmingly biased against those charged, the defense attorneys were not idle. They sought testimony from two Duke University professors to substantiate these biases.

Robert M. Entman's analysis of several thousand pages of press coverage between 1985 and 1987 concluded: (1) "the early coverage of the McMartin Pre-School case was extraordinary in amount, scope, sensationalism and negativism toward the defendants"; and (2) while "later coverage was more balanced," as a result of this publicity, assembling an impartial jury was highly unlikely.[2]

John B. McConahay also conducted a telephone survey of 453 people in the Los Angeles area. The defense considered his analysis important and necessary because the 1986 community survey revealed that pre-trial publicity had exerted significant influence on public perceptions of the outcome of the trial. The survey of prospective jurors also illustrated that well over 90% of respondents believed that both Raymond Buckey (97.4%) and Peggy Buckey (92.7%) were guilty as charged.

The question asked was: *"Do you think that Ray Buckey is ... definitely guilty, probably guilty, probably not guilty, or definitely not guilty?"* A similar question was asked about Peggy McMartin Buckey, with only a slightly lower percentage believing that she was guilty as charged.

In addition, 81.9% thought that Raymond Buckey was part of a child pornography ring, 95% thought Peggy McMartin helped cover up the sex crimes, and 74.7% thought that the five defendants against whom charges had been dropped were still guilty. The survey also found that of those aware of the case who had an opinion, only 42.4% thought the investigating police and social workers might have planted ideas in the children's minds; only 22.0% thought that the stories of satanic rituals and mutilations were so absurd as to cast doubt on the children's credibility; only 27.2% thought that the career concerns of the police, social workers, and prosecutors had kept the case going; yet 71.7% thought that if the defense lawyers had not intimidated the children, more of the charges against the defendants would still be pending.

Similarly, there was a general and widespread concern in Los Angeles about child sexual molestation. It ranked second to cocaine trafficking among crimes that the respondents perceived as serious problems; and some of those concerned with child sexual molestation advocated harsh and unusual punishments such as castration or beheading for those convicted of the crime. Further, only 15.2% of the sample agreed that a person accused of child molestation was probably not guilty, and 71.5% of the respondents agreed to take the word of a child over that of an accused adult in child molestation cases.

Survey of Potential Jurors in the Los Angeles Central Superior Court District

The present authors conducted another survey in 1986 to examine potential jurors who resided in the Los Angeles Central Superior Court Judicial District, the district from which the McMartin jurors were to be chosen. The list of eligible jurors was obtained from the Jury Services Division, Los Angeles County. While all of these eligible jurors were already placed on the Master File to be called into jury service, the actual respondents who were contacted and sent questionnaires were not allowed to appear at the courthouse and serve in the McMartin trial, a condition agreed upon by both the prosecution and defense attorneys before the survey questionnaires were sent. The survey proved to be of great importance because the sample of eligible jurors was comprised of residents of the Central Superior Court Judicial District—the actual trial site for the McMartin defendants.

Our survey was different from the earlier survey by Dr. McConahay in a number of ways. For example, it covered the targeted population of residents who were already classified as eligible to serve on the jury, while McConahay's survey did not screen for jury qualification, only for those who were over 18 years of age. Secondly, our sample of those jurors came from the general population of eligible jurors living in the area of the actual trial site, while the previous survey was based on information drawn from general residents of Los Angeles County.

Thirdly, the previous survey was conducted by telephone interviews, while our survey questionnaire was sent and returned by mail. The self-administered mail survey provided more valuable information on response rates, and how jurors respond to jury summonses when the jury commissioner's office attempts to contact individual potential jurors by mail. The use of the mailed, self-administered questionnaire helped define three different types of sample respondents: (1) those who actually filled out and returned the questionnaire, (2) those who failed to receive the questionnaire (i.e., undeliverables), and (3) those who received the questionnaire but were unwilling to return (i.e., recalcitrants).[3]

The survey was a shadow of the jury summons process. Given the filtering logic of the procedural steps in jury selection, rarely do all eligible jurors appear at the courthouse. This is because jury summonses sent to prospective jurors may never reach them. For instance, it is possible that some eligible jurors may have moved and left no forwarding address. Such jurors may be classified as "undeliverables" and are automatically eliminated from jury duty because they obviously failed to receive the summons. By the same token, persons who refuse to return the summons are considered "recalcitrant" or unwilling to respond and are eliminated from jury service. According to the 1983 report released by the Jury Commissioner's Office in Los Angeles, approximately 44% of all potential jurors were classified as nonrespondents: 25% undeliverables and 19% recalcitrants.[4]

Similarly, varying degrees of geographical mobility affect the undeliverable populations. According to the 1990 U.S. Census, for example, 17% of whites move annually, while 18% and 23% of blacks and Hispanics move. Thus, a larger proportion of minority populations do not receive jury questionnaires or jury summonses. Also, racial minorities and the poor may often feel skeptical about judicial participation because they view the court system as subjugating and discriminating against them as traditionally oppressed and indigent populations. They have a strong sense of distrust of police, courts, and other criminal justice and judicial systems. As a result, they are reluctant to respond to jury qualification questionnaires or summonses, and constitute a large proportion of nonrespondents, thereby making themselves unavailable to serve on juries.[5]

By concentrating on these realities, our survey was important because it already screened the groups into nonrespondents, less likely to serve on actual juries, and those who returned the questionnaire and thus were more likely to serve. The attitude and opinions of the latter group were more important than the nonrespondent, because their views were more likely to represent those who were to serve on the actual McMartin jury.

Lastly, our survey relied on the same address listing of potential jurors sought by the jury commissioner's office. Thus, the random sampling of survey respondents allowed the present authors to generalize the findings and to evaluate the attitudes and willingness to serve for the general population in the jurisdiction.

Sample Size and the Response Rate
While the 1980 U.S. Census provided the basic information on prospective jurors in the Central Superior Court district just prior to the trial, census data failed to offer more up-to-date and accurate breakdowns of eligible jurors in 1987. Plus, the U.S. Census did not collect information on attitudinal and ideological profiles of the population. The defense team thus proceeded to obtain a list of the prospective jurors from the Jury Commissioner's Office in Los Angeles County in order to examine socioeconomic and attitudinal characteristics of qualified jurors in the judicial district. Those jurors had already been placed on the 1987 Master File for jury service. After the pool of randomly selected prospective jurors was created, survey questionnaires were sent to 1,000 jurors in the Los Angeles Central Superior Court Judicial District. A total of 407 prospective jurors responded to the questionnaire (41% response rate). These responses were then computerized and carefully studied. The response rate in our survey (41%) was similar to the initial response rates in other self-administered questionnaire surveys.[6] But it was lower than the response rate of Los Angeles jury qualification questionnaires survey (56%) in which the jury commissioner's office reported that only 44% of prospective jurors failed to respond to qualification questionnaires.[7] The response rate in our survey could have been higher if we sent the follow-up questionnaire to prospective jurors who failed to respond. Since the jury commissioner's office did not track down the nonrespondents, we decided not to follow up the undeliverables and recalcitrants. However, for the purpose of examining relations between the mass media and general perceptions on the defendants and child molestation, the community survey provided important information on the jury profile and analytic defense strategies for scientific jury selection.

Community Survey Findings
Survey findings indicated that prospective jurors in the jurisdiction had been fully aware of pre-trial publicity surrounding the McMartin case. For the period between 1984 and 1986, 98.5% of respondents said that they had heard or read about the subject of child sexual abuse. Similarly, 96.7% of jurors said that they had specifically heard or read about the McMartin Preschool case over the same period.

The survey findings coincided with those of the 1986 telephone surveys conducted by the Duke researchers. The 1987 community survey also revealed that almost all respondents believed that the children involved in the McMartin Preschool case had been sexually abused (97.9%). For the question, *"[D]o you think that most of the children involved in the McMartin preschool case were sexually abused, or some of them were, or a few of them were, or do you think that none of them were sexually abused?"* only 2.1% of jurors in the LA Central jurisdiction felt that none of children were molested at the preschool, while 33.3% of jurors believed that most of them were molested, 51.8% believed that some were, and 12.8% that a few were. This finding was of great significance since the trial was not to start till the following year, and preparations for careful jury selection could be made.

The results further suggested the extent to which massive publicity had already exerted significant influence on the general perception of prospective jurors. Similarly, while charges against five of the original seven defendants had been dropped, the majority of eligible jurors still believed that they were guilty of molesting children (58.2%). While the figure in the Central Superior Court District is somewhat lower than similar findings in Los Angeles County (74.7%), the majority of prospective jurors in the jurisdiction still believed that the five pre-school teachers were guilty of the child molestation charges. Similarly, though a large number of eligible jurors was not sure whether Peggy McMartin Buckey was guilty of the crime, 86% of those who already decided the outcome of the trial said that she was guilty of child molestation.

Another significant finding was that more than two-thirds of the respondents (70.4%) were not satisfied with current California law dealing with sexual abuse like that charged against the McMartins. The majority of the respondents further questioned the credibility of testimony by children. The survey results showed that 63.6% of prospective jurors in the jurisdiction thought that children could be trained to testify about things, such as sexual abuse, that had not really occurred.

While the telephone survey had found that 71.5% of L.A. residents would take the word of a child over that of an accused adult in child molestation cases, the majority of potential jurors in the L.A. Central jurisdiction felt that the same child could be taught or coerced to make false statements regarding sexual abuse. Though critical analyses of the community survey revealed that significant influence had been exerted by the publicity surrounding the McMartin case, survey findings also revealed that potential jurors in the jurisdiction were more likely to be cautious about the credibility and viability of testimony by children on sexual molestation. This finding was of great significance because it provided valuable information for possible defense strategies in the trial. Further, if testimony were presented in a way to accentuate the possible coaching and coercive methods utilized by interviewers and therapists who first questioned the alleged victims, survey findings revealed that it might be possible to generate serious doubts about the legitimacy and credibility of the charges brought against the defendants.

Criticism of Mail Survey by the Print and Electronic Media

While the present authors' survey was being conducted, an interesting turn of events took place. The opinion survey was sharply criticized by Lois Timnick, staff writer for the *Los Angeles Times,* in the November 11th issue,[8] even though she had published several articles about the earlier *Times* survey of childhood sexual abuse.[9] Similarly, KABC (Channel 7) evening news questioned the survey's intent, criticizing the defense's potential use of survey results.[10]

The media criticized our community survey for attempting to discover public attitudes and perceptions of potential jurors on these critical issues of prejudicial bias. They did so despite their own responsibility in shaping public attitudes and perceptions.

While Timnick's November article was highly critical of the survey, at least one survey respondent who had not intended to respond did so after Timnick's news articles blasted its logic:

> The entire questionnaire raised my suspicions until I saw today's *Times*. Now I know it's OK to respond. Having been very involved in the last 4 years as juror and as a supporter of [a] falsely accused teacher, I couldn't help feeling paranoid.[11]

The survey questionnaire also had open-ended questions, allowing respondents to add their comments and express their opinions on the McMartin episode.[12] Comments were highly informative and varied, illustrating a wide range of opinions about almost every aspect of childhood sexual experiences. While the majority of eligible jurors in the Los Angeles Central jurisdiction felt that the defendants were guilty, they also expressed their doubts and skepticism with respect to the credibility and viability of criminal charges against the accused. To demonstrate how the public felt about childhood sexual experiences, the McMartin defendants, and other aspects of the criminal justice system, a few comments are presented here to illuminate the issues for the reader to judge.[13]

Several respondents stated that they refused to answer the questions because they thought that the survey questionnaire was biased either toward the defendants or the prosecution, with each respondent's interpretation dependent on his or her perspective and opinion on the issue of child sexual abuse. As an example of an assumed pro-prosecution bias in the questionnaire, one person responded:

I would think that in a survey as this, one should not be able to decipher the conclusions that are expected. Your questions appear to assume the guilt of *all* people charged with sexual abuse.

Another person wrote that:

I think ... that your questions elicit an apparent bias against defendants that would not exist if your questions were clearer.

An assumed pro-defense comment took the following form:

It is obvious that the questions have been framed to bias the response to a predetermined conclusion.... I think that child abuse is a terrible thing. I also think that this survey is not going to do a thing towards stopping child abuse. It's too slanted.

Another respondent said that:

I did not answer the questionnaire because I felt it was a requested questionnaire conducted by you for the McMartin defense, and frankly those Bastards can burn.

The responses brought out a variety of other reactions, confirming that almost everyone who did respond had fixed opinions about the McMartin defendants and their alleged crime.

The Media and Pre-trial Publicity

The survey results illustrated the power of the mass media to determine guilt or innocence in the public's mind. Unfortunately for the defendants, survey results showed that potential jurors who lived in the jurisdiction had already made up their minds on the adjudication of guilt. Survey results thus reaffirmed the defense's contention that massive pre-trial publicity had influenced prospective jurors in the jurisdiction and that the general tone of the mass media was primarily against the defendants. And yet, an anomaly surfaced: Almost all of respondents' comments on the media were negative, one person noting that:

The news media is always looking for a big story. Despite claims, the news is biased, inaccurate and superficial. The public does not get a true picture of any criminal trial.

Another respondent said:

> Due to the media coverage, the reputation of those persons accused
> has been completely distorted, whether they are guilty or innocent.

And another person fulminated that:

> It might be wise to minimize media coverage to assure that preju-
> dice of the general public does not result.

The media was also condemned for not focusing on facts:

> I really feel that the public never really knows the facts due to the
> news media.

Or too many facts:

> I feel that the news media should not bring out so much information
> about a case before it even goes to trial.

One respondent commented on the "20/20" segment on the McMartin case:

> I am of the opinion that many incidents are blown out of proportion
> by interpreters. I listened to the interviews that took place last week
> on the 20/20 program on channel 7 [KABC]. Those being inter-
> viewed were the 5 whose charges against them were dropped. They
> convinced me that they were not guilty. I did not feel the same way
> about the Buckeys, especially the son. I also feel that children of the
> ages involved in the McMartin case are mimics and can easily be
> persuaded. This cannot be applied to all children, but, there are many.

Finally it was pointed out how the media undercut knowledge:

> In the McMartin case, I think it has been so sensationalized that we
> will never know the "truth."

And that is what opened the door to the possibility of a fair review by
potential jurors seeking a truth that had yet to emerge.

Testimony by Children in Sexual Abuse Cases
Was it possible for the survey to anticipate the conclusions expected to
be reached by jurors in the McMartin trial? The majority of eligible
jurors had clearly questioned the credibility of testimony by children in
sexual abuse cases. In addition, there was considerable belief (70.4%)

really occurred. Thus, despite respondents' general belief that the defendants were guilty of sexual molestation, these prospective jurors also demonstrated skepticism regarding the credibility of children's testimony in such cases. The skepticism revealed by the survey was later shown in the McMartin trial to be a crucial factor in determining the guilt or innocence of the accused.

There were those who uncritically accepted the reliability and validity of a child's testimony. Among those believing that children can accurately report such abuse was one who wrote the following comments in the questionnaire.

> Young children usually exaggerate and sometimes lie, but in the case of sexual abuse, I don't think that a child could conjure up such a scenario. I'm very sure some may do it for attention or to jump on the bandwagon, but I strongly feel that 99% [of the] claims of abuse made by a child are true, and convictions cannot be made because a child's claim will usually change because of pressure, fear and the fact that he/she wants to block it out of her/his mind. As far as the McMartin case is involved, we'll never know exactly what happened and to whom it happened and all the other sick details, but we all know that it did happen. I don't think children are capable of plotting such a devious plan by making up the whole thing. And if they did, then children are a lot more evil and sick than I thought they were.

Another person had comments about the law and children's ability to remember past events:

> I believe the current laws are inadequate with dealing with the problems of child testimony. Therefore, the child's rights are *not* as protected as the child abuser. I think children should be allowed to testify on closed circuit TV and that cross-examination should be limited. Frankly, I find the suggestion that a social worker or psychologist could implant a sexual incident in a child's memory that really didn't happen as ludicrous. The jury should hear the child's testimony, the medical evidence and the social worker testimony plus the defense and render a verdict.

On the other hand, some respondents questioned the ability of children to accurately answer questions posed in the courtroom. For example, one person who had recently served on jury duty said:

> Children have short attention spans and are unaware of what is expected from them in their testimony.

Another respondent said that:

> Even at 8 children can fantasize and can be led on by adult (paren-
> tal) questioning. Children always pickup on what parents say and
> follow parental lead—it's part of the child wanting to please the
> parents. Often parents and children are not aware of it even happen-
> ing.

Similarly,

> Courts are strict about inadmissibility of testimony flowing from
> "leading questions." They must be even stricter when the testimony
> is a child's, otherwise the lawyers' tendency to suggest and supply
> answers to their own questions is out of control. When children are
> to testify, questions should be literal, not abstract, and opinion or
> speculation need to be avoided. Children's testimony should be al-
> lowed on videotape, with news coverage limited or ruled out, at
> least until the trial is resolved. The right of all parties to a fair trial
> comes before any *immediate* right to know.

Guilt and Innocence

Only a few respondents discussed the guilt or innocence of the defendants in detail. Among their comments was one which not only implied
innocence but demonstrated the impact of the McMartin case upon other
teachers.

> My daughter is a school teacher. One of her teacher friends told her
> that she had taught with [one of the defendants] and said of her that
> there was no one more loving or caring than her. During this trial I
> saw the teachers withdrawing from touching children in any affec-
> tionate way. Many children K[indergarten] to 3rd grade ask for hugs
> or kisses from teachers—who often are their mothers away from
> home. It was a scary time.

Another person, perhaps divining the ultimate outcome of the trial, noted that:

> People are innocent until proven guilty. The McMartins have not
> been proven guilty. That does not mean that they are innocent. My
> understanding is that some charges were dropped because parents
> refused to allow them [their children] to go through the meat grinder
> of our legal system, *not* due to lack of evidence. The law must be
> amended to make criminal trials less difficult for victims or for people
> who believe that they are victims.

Notwithstanding the above comments, most respondents, similar to the general public, assumed that the defendants were guilty. One respondent made the following comment:

> I think the law deals much too lightly with most criminals. It seems that the victims are made to look more at fault than the criminal. Child abuse is one of the most horrible crimes. Whatever happens to these people [the McMartin defendants] it won't be bad enough.

Another person also apparently thought that the defendants were guilty, noting that:

> Anyone who would hurt a child (especially sexually) doesn't deserve to breath the same air as that hurt child. Even the severest punishment would not console the child ever. He/she when a grown adult probably will be severely distrusting/disoriented and possibly mentally disturbed. If I could have my way I'd wipe [the defendants] off of the face of this earth and straight into hell.

A little less drastic comment was made by another respondent:

> There is no question in my mind that the defendants are guilty of violating the boundaries (of affection and physical demonstration of affection) required and in fact needed by primary school children. I do not find it difficult to believe the testimony of the children involved in this case. I do not believe that the accounts need be necessarily documented or in chronological order or overly precise as might be required in a trial for and involving only adults. There is I believe a *sense* of the occurrence.

The Judicial System and Investigations
of Child Abuse by the Prosecution

Several respondents had made critical comments about the criminal justice system. Among them was the following comment that undoubtedly would be agreed with by the McMartin parents.

> Children, victims of sexual abuse, in my opinion, are put through further trauma and abuse in our current judicial system.

A touchy subject also was discerned by a perceptive respondent who noted that:

> I guess my concern is in exposing young children to the embarrassment of publicly discussing such sensitive and personal subject matter, and *then* choosing to deem that testimony of no limited value.

Another person advocated severe punishment of defendants when proven guilty, but not keeping anyone in jail receiving free education and health coverage until they were convicted.

Severe criticism of the prosecution's investigation of McMartin was also made by respondents. The following comment was made by a person who had recently served as a juror.

> To focus on the McMartin case it seemed to be mishandled in the investigation and the grilling of the children was handled poorly.

Child Sexual Abuse Over Time

It did not seem credible to some respondents that child abuse at the McMartin Preschool could have taken place over a long period of time without ever being noticed prior to 1983. As an example:

> How could all these people commit such terrible things to children for such a long time without someone knowing about it? There are no [adult] witnesses. I'm sure if someone knew of these things were taking place they would of been found or came out and said they knew these things happened. What evidence [exists]?

And the following:

> Whatever happened to a speedy trial? How can anyone expect a child to accurately remember what happened to them two years ago? Could an *adult* recap with *accuracy* an incident two years ago? Should the children be expected to? Having a 5 year old daughter myself, I would be hesitant to put her through the processes of [sic] trying to revive an accurate account of something so traumatic. Such a shame, because this time the system failed miserably, regardless of the outcome, *whenever* that may be [underscores by the original respondent].

Political Implications

A number of respondents questioned the political motivations of District Attorney Robert Philibosian and his prosecutors. They were critical of possible mishandling of the case by the prosecution's office even from the very start of the McMartin episode in 1983. One respondent gave the following critical assessment of the prosecution's handling of the case.

> I'm quite convinced that the entire case is one of political harassment without regards to the rights of the defendants. To totally impoverish persons by such lengthy harassment without mandatory

money remuneration to them because of the prosecution and court action is in itself a crime. Those in the McMartin case should be paid *all* the money they've lost, *all* defense fees, and for loss of property and business. A large sum should be assessed to the prosecution branch and courts to the extent that even the individuals and sitting judges should be held accountable. The abominable actions of these prosecuting attorneys and the judges should not be tolerated by society and punitive action should be taken against them. To hide behind the cloak of "justice" and the following immunity granted them "by law" is an affront to the purpose of justice. *Innocent* until proved guilty, and protection under the Constitution of human rights [underscores by the original respondent].

Another person who had served as a juror was quite critical of the DA's office, noting that:

In my own experience as a juror I have seen the DA's office bring two, extremely weak cases to trial. These incidents cause me to wonder about the competency of the DA's office, as well as the motivation behind some prosecutions—e.g., the McMartin Pre-School case. I suspect that there is more to the case than child sexual abuse; for example politics.

Perhaps the most severe condemnation of the political aspects of the case were made by several respondents, one writing:

Cases such as the McMartin case are just a stage for the DA and etc. attorneys to make a name for themselves regardless of who gets hurt. This 'showboating' includes the judges.

Another one said:

Guilt or innocence doesn't seem to be the objective of a trial, but which attorney puts on the better dog and pony show. The only winners in a trial are the legal fees [paid the attorneys].

One person who had jury experience and lived in Manhattan Beach had the following view of the whole process.

The McMartin pre-school teachers were tried in the media, and whether guilty or not, are ruined. I have served on several juries, and know better than to judge a person on any evidence other than presented under oath in court before I'd set an absolute judgment or

even preponderant judgment of these people. The pillar of the law
is that one is innocent until proved guilty beyond a reasonable doubt.
I cannot have a firm opinion on Peggy McMartin Buckey's guilt or
innocence unless I hear the facts in evidence. I have seen the hysteria and vigilante attitudes firsthand at my church in Manhattan Beach;
I see bumper stickers reading 'I believe the children.' I have heard
the doctor's testimony affirming that many of the children were sexually abused, as evidenced by scar tissue. It seems that something
went on at the McMartin Pre-School, but proof as to who did what
is needed before someone is found guilty. I have a youngster who
was in pre-school at the time (not at McMartin). I cannot accept the
outrage of parents who expect their children's testimony to be taken
literally when the kids are stuck in a charged environment and are
experts at fantasy (in the 2 - 5 bracket). If it happened to mine, I'm
pretty sure I'd know soon thereafter.

Conclusions

In child sexual abuse trials, insofar as is possible, it is important to find
unbiased and impartial jurors to evaluate evidence. Unless impartial jurors are available, it is the mass media who sits in judgment. In the
McMartin case, the vast majority of the functionaries making up the mass
media had already tried and convicted the defendants; it only remained
for jurors to follow the print and electronic mass media to do the same.
The analysis of the community survey in the Los Angeles Central Superior Court judicial district revealed that the media had exerted a powerful
influence upon the general public's perception of guilt and innocence of
the McMartin defendants. Yet, it was clear that only relatively impartial
jurors could conduct a fair reading of the evidence.

Going forward, the next chapter presents critical analyses of the preliminary hearing, including affirmative defense strategies, testimony by alleged child victims, their parents, therapists at the Children's Institute International, presumed medical experts of child sexual abuse, the declining
numbers of charges against the accused, prosecutorial misuse of its discretionary powers such as cult practice fabrications, illegal delays in reporting
alleged sexual abuse and supporting evidence, and conflicts among prosecuting attorneys. As we will see, the preliminary hearing demonstrated the
difficulties of establishing credible evidence against the McMartin defendants while protecting the rights of both the child victims and the accused.

Chapter 5

Preliminary Hearings

The McMartin legal embroglio began with an in-court preliminary hearing. Aside from police investigations and grand jury indictment, California law requires that a preliminary hearing be held in criminal cases to determine if there is sufficient evidence to hold a trial. By denying the allegations of child sexual abuse, the defendants effectively demanded a preliminary hearing to determine the nature and extent of any evidence.

The nightmare of the community was logically extended to the courtroom, where the preliminary hearing for the seven defendants was being heard. It was a hectic scene. All of the defendants, defense attorneys, and prosecutors were crammed into a small seventh-floor hearing room, more like a compartment, in the Traffic Court Building in downtown Los Angeles. Jockeying for position at the long counsel table were seven defendants, seven defense attorneys, and three prosecutors. Ranging behind them at the courtroom rail sat a scattering of earnest legal assistants, assorted news reporters, and intractable supporters of the defendants wearing large buttons emblazoned with the simple acronym FRIPAC, standing for "Friends and Relatives of Innocent People Accused of Crimes."

The lengthy preliminary hearing caused an extended delay before the actual trial. Much of the hearing focused upon legal motions involving admissibility of evidence, modes of testimony, availability of records, the prosecutors' charges made outside of the courtroom to the mass media, and a preliminary hearing decision by the defense to take the unusual tactic of presenting an "affirmative defense"—setting the stage for a quasi-trial before the actual trial. Experts testified to the children's existing emotional conditions, prior to the actual presentation of evidence by the children or their parents, creating the impression that a factual basis existed for their postulations. Often there was no apparent logical, legal connection between the children's testimony of alleged sexual abuse and the findings and testimony of prosecution experts—despite court procedures that generally require a proper evidentiary foundation be established before a witness can be asked to testify as an expert.

To understand the logic—and illogic—of the proceedings, this chapter explores the McMartin preliminary hearing. It also presents an analysis of the prosecutors' misconduct and possible misuse of power. Needless to say, the awesome power that prosecutors exercise is susceptible to abuse. Such abuses most frequently occur in bringing charges and controlling the information used to indict and convict.

The focus of this courtroom tour, then, is on process: the presentation of evidence by the prosecution and defense; the prosecutors' rationale for dropping charges against five defendants; the role played by the judge; an evaluation of some of the evidence presented; the prosecution's misconduct and withholding of evidence; the move of one prosecutor to the side of the defense; defense tactics; bail for the defendants; and the process of moving towards an actual trial. Those various issues are explored in relation to their impact on both the alleged victims and the defendants.

The Affirmative Defense

Ordinarily, preliminary hearings in California are used by the prosecution to demonstrate that a case should be brought to trial. In the McMartin case, however, the defense decided to wage an initial attack—presenting what is called an "affirmative defense." An affirmative defense requires that the defense produce its own evidence at the preliminary hearing, instead of waiting to present it at the actual trial, in order to show a lack of sufficient evidence to bring the case to trial.

The preliminary hearing was fraught with factual quirks and legal nuances from the beginning. The defense requested the names of prosecution witnesses in advance so that careful plans could be made for their cross-examination. Preliminary Hearing Judge Aviva Bobb agreed and ordered that the defense be told 48 hours in advance who the prosecution's upcoming witnesses would be, but Deputy District Attorney Lael Rubin refused to abide and justified her refusal by stating that she was "outraged at the abuse of the order by the defense in intimidating witnesses."[1] Subsequently, Judge Bobb found Rubin in contempt of court and fined her $200, causing some consternation about her standing with the state bar association, but ultimately stayed the payment to give her time to appeal the fine.

Virginia McMartin requested that she be allowed to serve as her own attorney because she was out of money and facing penury. She complained, "because of the lies they've taught those children, they've taken my livelihood, my home, my reputation."[2] Prosecutor Lael Rubin opposed such a substitution. The judge also denied the request, ruling that "it would disrupt this preliminary hearing and deprive Mrs. McMartin of Mr. Brunon's representation, which I believe she truly desires." Virginia McMartin then threatened not to show up to court unless the "sheriffs come and drag me there."[3] This was a threat the judge would not abide, and during the next few days Virginia McMartin was persuaded by her daughter Peggy McMartin Buckey and grandson Raymond Buckey to be quiet in the courtroom so that proceedings could continue. And ultimately, attorney Brunon was funded by Los Angeles County as her defense counsel.

Outside the courtroom, besides dealing with the evidence, the defense team also faced a fury of emotions. One technician on a television crew had a run-in with a defense lawyer in which a punch or two were thrown in an elevator. The lawyer was accused by the technician of "defending the devil."[4] In the courtroom, too, testimonials elicited by the prosecution did not go unchallenged.

The Judge and Other Court Players

Having already been mentioned in previous sections, the names and backgrounds of the main players in the preliminary hearing need only be summarily presented. Daniel Davis, representing Raymond Buckey, graduated from the University of Texas law school, was a former captain in the military police, and by the preliminary hearing, had tried fifteen molestation cases and had won them all. Dean Gits, a Beverly Hills defense attorney for Peggy McMartin Buckey, was a cum laude graduate of William Mitchel College of Law in St. Paul. He was a deputy public defender for nearly nine years before going into private practice. With more than ten years of criminal trial experience, he was appointed by the court to the McMartin case. Each of the other five defense attorneys was both experienced counsel and prominent in his own right, including: Walter Urban (for Betty Evans Raidor), Eliseo D. W. Guana (for Babette Jane Spitler), William Powell, Jr. (for Mary Ann Jackson), Forrest Latiner (for Peggy Ann Buckey), and Bradley Brunon (for Virginia McMartin).

The prosecution team included Lael Rubin, the chief prosecutor, whose past experience was in prosecuting organized crime cases. Graduating from the University of West Los Angeles School of Law in 1978, she began to distinguish herself after joining the district attorney's office. Like Rubin, another prosecutor, Glenn Stevens, had never prosecuted a child abuse case prior to the McMartin case. He had been assigned to the prosecution of L.A. gangs. The only member of the three-person prosecution team who had previous experiences in child abuse case was Christine Johnson.

Municipal Court Judge Aviva K. Bobb was appointed to become the presiding judge for the preliminary hearing. Judge Bobb had not been involved in a child molestation case prior to the McMartin. She was originally a traffic court judge, one of the last appointments of former Governor Jerry Brown. She knew little about child sexual abuse and sexual molestation, having mainly handled misdemeanor trials on drunk driving, petty theft, and drug possession.

The preliminary hearing was generally chaotic. The contest starred three prosecutors, seven defendants, each with their own attorney, sparring technological armies from the media, McMartin supporters and detractors, the curious, and the always-present, insatiable publicity seekers. Amidst the pandemonium, Judge Bobb was criticized by the attorneys and the media for not maintaining sufficient control over the hearings, making contradictory rulings—allowing, then disallowing, child testimony by closed-circuit television—and by closing parts of the testimony to the public and the media. Her inexperience kept her from quelling or guiding the attorneys who hotly argued over each and every issue in the case.

Many questions asked by both defense and prosecuting attorneys seemed irrelevant, yet the judge allowed them to delay the hearing by legal maneuverings that were best left for the trial itself. For instance, time was spent considering whether the public and press should be excluded from the courtroom; whether or not defendants should be the subject of joint or separate hearings; and if the children should be allowed to testify by closed-circuit television or be required to testify in person in the courtroom.[5]

As an evidentiary base, the videotaped interviews conducted by Kathleen [Kee] MacFarlane at the CII with the alleged child victims were considered by the prosecutors to be the core of their case against the defendants. And as expected, the defense argued that they needed to have copies of the tapes to answer charges against their clients in court.

The defense argued that the prosecution's case rested upon these videotapes and that they were much like other recorded statements which traditionally have been provided to the defense in other cases in California for over 25 years. The defense thus demanded that they should have unlimited access, but the prosecution insisted that the tapes were private and the children's and parents' right to privacy would be violated if they were released to the defense. Superior Court Judge Ronald M. George refused to allow the defense to have and keep their own copies of the tapes, but permitted the tapes to be viewed by defense lawyers and their staffs, indicating that anyone who violated the confidentiality conditions that he set down would be held in contempt of court.[6]

But the courts could not agree. Later, in August, 1984, Judge Bobb ordered that the defense be given copies of the videotaped interviews of the children. But Superior Court Judge Ronald M. George issued a stay which effectively delayed their distribution. His ruling was based on the prosecution's argument that multiple copies of the tapes might increase the probability that they would become available to the media, and that showing them publicly could cause lifelong scars for the children and their families.[7]

A legal contest then emerged over whether or not the alleged victims would have to testify in open court, or whether, in order to avoid having to face the seven defendants, they could testify from a room adjacent to the courtroom via closed-circuit television.

Lacking material evidence and adult witnesses, the prosecution insisted that the use of videotaped testimony be allowed. The defense argued that the public should be excluded from the courtroom and that the children should testify in person, rather than by videotape, and be subject to cross-examination. Deputy District Attorney Glenn Stevens countered that the use of the videotaped interviews would be sufficient to build a strong case, possibly add counts to the indictment, and spare children the trauma of having to testify at several hearings and trials.

The mother of one of the children later told a U.S. Senate panel that her daughter "would be too terrified to speak" if she had to face the suspects in court.[8] Kathleen MacFarlane of the CII also told the court that many children were terrified of the defendants and believed that they had magical powers. But Judge Bobb ruled that no statutory authority existed for using closed-circuit television testimony and that the prosecution had failed to show that open court testimony would cause psychological harm to the children.

Still another issue was raised over medical testimony on child sexual abuse. The defense found that many prominent medical experts in the U.S. were reluctant to testify for them because of the high visibility, publicity, and emotional nature of the case. And on December 26, 1985, Judge Bobb unilaterally decided to rest the defense case when the defense indicated that its medical experts would not be available until early January,

1986. Defense medical testimony was deemed especially important because the prosecution had presented hearsay evidence by one medical doctor who testified that several other doctors had found physical evidence consistent with sexual molestation.[9] Where that molestation had occurred and by whom was never shown, however, and the preliminary hearing did no more than to show that sufficient evidence existed to merit a trial of the matter.

An Open or Closed Hearing?

Conflict also emerged over whether or not the public and the news media should be excluded from the courtroom. The California Penal Code, amended in 1982, permits closed preliminary proceedings if the judge believes that it is necessary to protect a defendant's right to a fair trial; thus, the media and public right to know was deemed to be secondary to the right of a defendant to a fair trial.[10] As the McMartin defense argued that extensive media publicity had already made it quite difficult to find a fair-minded jury for the subsequent criminal trial, the decision on an open or closed hearing became important.

The defense sought to close the preliminary hearing, insisting that the news media were only interested in sensationalizing the case by distorting the factual information and that publicity would make it difficult to find impartial jurors for the actual trial. Mary Ann Jackson's attorney William Powell Jr. added that the media attention would mean that even if outrageous charges were later dropped against his client, the publicity would make her "indelibly identified as one of the seven." Attorney Powell thus argued that:

> It's not the extent of the media coverage alone, but it's the negative public reaction that would certainly follow from that media coverage of these types of areas that concerns us as far as the ability to have a fair trial.[11]

A simple request to close the hearing was within the scope of the law prior to 1983, when the alleged crimes took place, and attorney Powell argued that the law should apply to this case. But for this law to apply, however, it required the consent of both the judge and prosecution.

And that was not a simple matter. The defense then recalculated: if the hearings were to be open to the media, the defense would waive the clients' right to a preliminary hearing and proceed directly to trial. However, Deputy District Attorney Glenn Stevens flatly refused, insisting that the preliminary hearing was necessary for videotaping purposes should any witnesses become unavailable at the trial, as well as to spare children the trauma of having to testify at both the hearing and the trial.

Attorneys for the *Los Angeles Times* and several other newspapers and television stations jumped into the legal tangle with their own vision. They heatedly argued that the case had aroused wide public concern, and that therefore the proceedings should be conducted openly in the interest of accurate and objective reporting. Any attempt "to put a finger in the dam" by closing the hearing would only result in the spread of "hearsay, rumor, and innuendo," *Times* attorney Jeffrey S. Klein stated, adding that, "the public wants to know what is going on behind these locked doors. And reporters, doing their job, will try to find out. They'll talk to the people who are sitting in this room. And then whoever decides to talk to the press will control what the public knows."[12]

Judge Bobb now ruled that the preliminary hearing would continue to be open; however, she ordered a closed hearing during testimony of numerous expert witnesses, because, she said in a confusing word choice, that "it appears to me that there is a possibility, there is a reasonable likelihood that there may be substantial prejudice from the testimony I may receive which would impinge on the defendants' right to a fair trial."[13] These expert witnesses were testifying in support of a prosecution motion to allow child witnesses to testify by closed-circuit television. The prosecution argued that the young witnesses would suffer psychological damage if they were forced to testify in an open court and had to confront the accused.

The defense argued against such a procedure as it denied the accused the constitutional right to confront their accusers and that it would be better to remove the public and the press from the courtroom rather than remove the testifying children. The defense argued that a closed courtroom virtually halted the public disparagement of the accused, as well as blocked the media from further slanting the public's perception—making it possible to pick an impartial jury.

There were several other conundrums that had to be confronted and resolved. Prosecutors had argued that closed-circuit testimony would minimize the trauma to child witnesses. Yet the media seemed not particularly concerned with the welfare of the children and sought to have them testify in open court in front of defendants, arguing that the public had a right to know what was going on in the courtroom.

Judge Bobb finally ordered that the children had to testify in open court in front of defendants. However, media access to the courtroom was restricted to the extent that they were prohibited from publishing any materials which might publicly identify the witnesses—Judge Bobb issuing her ruling:

> Because of evidence of discrimination against children who attended Virginia McMartin Preschool by members of the Manhattan Beach community, I believe that I am mandated by Penal Code Section 288 (c) to protect the anonymity of the present witness child and other alleged child victims from whom testimony will be elicited.... The ruling with regard to the anonymity of the alleged child victims is subject to proof that the right to privacy has not been waived by the filing of a civil suit which states the name of the alleged victims or by agreement to have the name published by the media. I would at this time ask the media, in addition, not to publish biographical material from which witnesses could be identified.[14]

As mentioned earlier, despite the concern of Judge Bobb, Los Angeles Superior Court Judge Ronald M. George said that she "had abused her discretion and exceeded her jurisdiction" in closing the courtroom during testimony by two psychiatrists and a clinical social worker called as expert witnesses by the prosecution. Judge Bobb nonetheless rejected defense concerns on an open hearing:

> The defendants have moved that the public be excluded from the courtroom for the preliminary hearing.... I ruled that this preliminary hearing would be open to the public subject to further court order at such time as this court determines that exclusion of the public is necessary to protect the defendants' right to a fair and impartial trial.... I do not find that the exclusion of the public from the preliminary hearing, including this cross-examination, is necessary at this time to protect the defendants' right to a fair and impartial trial. Therefore, the defendants' motion is denied.[15]

Of course, media representatives were overjoyed with this ruling awarding access, though the judge herself was not absolutely clear that such arguments applied to preliminary hearings. Thus, she said, the issue would eventually have to be taken to a higher court, the California Supreme Court.

Parental Testimony

Parents had their say in both the media and courtroom. Some of the most vocal parents, however, did not testify and the mother who brought the first charges had no chance to do so. Though she had charged her husband with molesting their own child, he refused to testify and neither the prosecution nor the defense called him to take the witness stand.

Some parents spoke only to the news media, not in court, and many reporters did not make clear distinctions between the parents' hearsay statements to the media and parents' sworn testimony in the courtroom. The media's failure to make clear distinctions regarding parents' accounts of molestation was considered to be another example of its bias in favor of the prosecution.

Substantial parts of parental testimony were hearsay and circumstantial at best. Both parents and the district attorney's office looked for a way to explain how it was possible that the alleged abuse of the McMartin school children could have gone on for years without disclosure. Lacking any forensic or material evidence to back their claims, they came to the conclusion that the children must have been drugged before they were abused. Yet neither the parents nor the DA logically deduced that, if the children were in fact drugged, they would remember little if anything about supposed abuse, and would likely fantasize about what happened, if anything.

Playing to the press, prosecutor Glenn Stevens announced on August 8, 1984, that some McMartin children had been given shots, pills, and liquid drugs to make them drowsy and less likely to offer resistance to sexual assault. As proof, at Raymond Buckey's preliminary hearing, Stevens relayed this hearsay by stating that "[O]ne child ... described the drugs' effect as 'making me feel like I was asleep even though I was awake.'"

One mother also testified that her 3-year-old son appeared to have been drugged when she picked him up one day at the school. "I couldn't wake him up," she said. "He acted like he was real sleepy, like maybe he was drugged." She said that he slept through her carrying him to the car and the drive home.[16]

Such weak evidence, presented without considering other factors that might have had an impact on the child's sleep, was bolstered by a checklist of circumstantial events that might have had many simple explanations, though each was used to implicate Raymond Buckey in unspecified acts of child molestation. Thus, this mother said that she unexpectedly arrived at the school one day and was asked to wait in the yard for her son; then she noticed a sheet had been hung over the window of Buckey's classroom; that at other times her son complained that "his fanny hurt"; that the child was diagnosed as having herpes of the mouth while attending the McMartin school; that her child and other molestation victims continued to see those they called "the other bad people" driving around the neighborhood; that she and other McMartin parents were reluctant to leave their children with baby-sitters, fearing attempted kidnaps of kids who were going to testify.

Another parent who testified in open court, the wife of a Manhattan Beach police officer, said that she did not suspect molestation until the alleged activities at the school became public. With four of the defendants charged with molesting her son on 13 different occasions, she stated that her son sometimes behaved oddly and had occasional physical problems while attending the school in 1979 and 1980.[17]

There was, then, fear, unbounded suspicion, almost pathological numbness in the emerging situation—and a lack of appreciation that weak, circumstantial evidence was hardly evidence at all. Little consideration was given to the circumstances that the mother, for example, may have been asked to wait because classroom activities were in process; the window may have been covered because movies were being shown or the children were taking a nap. The child's fanny may have hurt because it was chapped and uncared for by the parent. The herpes could have come from a variety of sources in the school, at home, or elsewhere. Maybe the parents themselves pointed out "the other bad people" in their neighborhoods. Was there any real threat of a kidnap? All of these possibilities made as much sense as the other suspicions posited by the parents, not to mention a myriad of other possibilities.

What became clear, as the parents testified, was that their stories were becoming further removed from any material evidence. For instance, two other mothers testified that their children were afraid of needles and shots. One said that her 4-year-old son "would become panic stricken when I took him in [to the pediatrician] for shots." Another testified that her son developed a similar fear during the three years he had attended McMartin, from ages two to five. "To this day, he still cannot have a shot," she said, adding that he had talked to his parents "about why he is so afraid of shots and needles"—but, because it would be hearsay, she was not asked to recount her son's explanation. The child's own testimony would be that he had been drugged at the school, Deputy District Attorney Lael Rubin promised.

Though a dozen children said that they had been given pink pills or pink liquid they thought were drugs, drugs were not a significant part of what had transpired at the school, according to one unidentified investigator. Rather, he said, the children were fearful of physicians because of the physical examination and rectal temperatures that had been taken during the "doctor game" at the school. "That's why they're so afraid of doctors," said this unnamed source close to the investigation, "they were hurt so much."[18]

In presenting the defense, the attorneys called upon more than 20 witnesses, including some of the children's fathers, in an effort to demonstrate that the children had fabricated their descriptions of sexual abuse.[19] For example, defense attorney Daniel Davis sought to find out how the father of a 5-year-old girl had obtained the information from her that she had been sexually molested. "Now this may put you in an admittedly awkward situation, sir, but did you tell your daughter that Ray [Raymond Buckey] had done bad things to other children?" Davis asked. The father, whose identity and occupation were not disclosed in court, sat in the witness box for approximately 20 to 30 seconds before answering: "Well, we probably mentioned that to find out if our children had been molested. We had received a letter from the Manhattan Beach Police Department asking us to talk to our kids."

Another parent who testified was the father of a boy born in 1975 who had attended the McMartin Preschool on every Monday, Wednesday, and Friday from January 1979 to June 1979. During the testimony, it was revealed that the father was a police sergeant as well as a colleague of the chief investigating officer in the Manhattan Beach Police Department—the chief accuser in the case. His testimony also revealed that his department had been facing the civil suit that had been filed by the McMartin defendants, so no love was lost between the police and the accused. Attorney Dean Gits, representing Peggy McMartin Buckey, disclosed:

> [The witness] is a Sergeant of Police, is a co-worker ... [of] the Chief Investigating Officer—chief accuser in this case—Jane Hoag. He has access to information that the ordinary citizen would not have, and for any number of reasons going to motive, [holds] bias, intent, knowledge, demeanor while testifying—all of the matters that the fact finder is entitled to consider—his employment and associations in this case is [sic] clearly subject to cross-examination.[20]

Attorney William Powell, Jr., representing Mary Ann Jackson, blew the whistle:

> Additionally, ... if he is an employee of the City of Manhattan Beach and the defendants have sued the City of Manhattan Beach for a sizable sum of money such as $4,500,000, his testimony could be biased in favor of—or against the defendants in this case because it directly impacts upon his remuneration.[21]

Parental testimony had failed to produce any credible materials to support the allegations. Their testimony lacked forensic verification, such as pictures, and was ultimately of little consequence in substantiating that child molestation actually took place.

The defense contended that these sexual abuse charges were based upon fantasy rather than fact. The fantasies were derived from responses to suggestive questions first posed by apprehensive parents, police officers, and then CII therapists who had been asked by prosecutors to interview the children to determine if they had been molested.

Therapists' Testimony

Who, then, could testify to the charges of molestation? The McMartin case was without question a difficult, emotional one, especially for the alleged child victims. While the investigation and questioning by police and therapists undoubtedly was traumatic, further trauma could be expected inasmuch as each alleged victim was to testify in person. One psychiatrist who testified several hours for the prosecution told a reporter that "those kids are dead. It's seven to one in there, and even I was flustered."[22]

The prosecution had as its goal trying to establish that there was no adult guidance of the children's accounts, while the defense contended otherwise. The defense charged that unrelenting coaching took place during the professional therapy sessions at CII, where the prosecutors had referred the distraught parents.

Kathleen MacFarlane of CII said that she believed the children were frightened and thought that they or their parents might die if they testified against the defendants. MacFarlane also stated that she was experienced with techniques for counseling children suffering from a denial syndrome after being molested. She said that she hoped to bring out the truth by making each child feel she/he was not the first to divulge sexual abuse— which she called "yucky secrets," a phrase the children easily understood and responded to by telling her what, if anything, they knew about sexual abuse. MacFarlane thought that this induced response relieved the children, taking the onus off each one to be the first to tell. And under substantial prodding, about 360 of the 400 children interviewed told astounding stories of being molested by teachers, being photographed nude and in sexual situations, seeing animals sacrificed, and knowing of hidden passageways beneath the school.

The most damning child testimony was the description of a game supposedly played at the preschool called "Naked Movie Star," which the children explained on videotape during therapy sessions. One typical 8-year-old witness was presented on videotape answering questions about this game. In the tape, MacFarlane is holding and speaking to and through an alligator puppet, trying to elicit and sometimes pressure the child's response about seeing the game; however, the child insists he only heard about the game and was never present to see it. The videotaped interview recorded the following interactions between MacFarlane and the boy:

> BOY: Well, I really didn't hear it a whole lot. I just heard someone yell it from out in the—someone yelled it.
> MACFARLANE: Maybe, Mr. Alligator, you peeked in the window one day and saw them playing it, and maybe you could remember and help us.
> BOY: Well, no, I haven't seen anyone playing "Naked Movie Star." I've only heard that song.
> MACFARLANE: What good are you? You must be dumb.
> BOY: Well, I don't really, ummm, remember seeing anyone play that 'cause I wasn't there, when I ... when people are playing it.
> MACFARLANE: You weren't? You weren't. That's why we're hoping maybe you saw it. See, a lot of these puppets weren't there, but they got to see what happened.
> BOY: Well, I saw a lot of fighting.

Interviewers at CII used other puppets called "detective dog," "alligator," "Mr. Snake," and "Mr. Sparky."[23] The pressure on the children seemed overdone and overwhelming, and at least one child was interviewed twice by two different CII interviewers because in the first interview, the child insisted that she had not been molested.[24]

The CII also tried to cover up both the explicit and subtle pressures they exerted on the children. During expert testimony, Dr. Astrid Heger, the medical examiner for the prosecution, testified that she had not interviewed any of the children, though subsequent testimony demonstrated that she had. A pediatrician associated with the Los Angeles County University of Southern California Medical Center and a CII consultant, Dr. Heger said to one young child who kept insisting that she had not been molested, "[I]t's time to get down to business, no more joking, no more kidding around."[25]

Rather than thoughtful and therapeutic prodding to elicit information from a possibly traumatized child, the professional suggestions, coercions, pressures, and affronts to a child's sense of self and ego may have been more calculated than merely to release the child from harboring secrets. The danger is that the method might also have encouraged fabrication and, in legal terms, "lead" the witness beyond the border of truth—though this particular child was able to resist at least in this session.

In more formal terms, this is an area of investigation and concern, known to all social scientists as "interview acquiescence." Most competent researchers are well aware of the potential impact an interviewer can have upon a patient-subject, and they, therefore, attempt to guard against it.[26] In this instance just the opposite was observed.

With the children's stories obviously disjointed and inconsistent from one version to another, prosecutors objected to the defense asking child witnesses to reconcile the statements they made during the videotaped interviews at CII with those made in court. Spencer Eth, a Los Angeles child psychiatrist, said in his testimony that, for children, reconciling contradictory statements may be difficult or impossible. He added that some questions represented a clear threat to the children's psychological well-being and resulted in a humiliating sense of defeat as the children struggled to reply.[27] Outside of court, the defense stated that Eth's testimony was a "red herring" and had been presented because prosecutors were concerned about their witnesses' credibility.

The checkered role that the CII played in the case was clearly central to the defense. Parents testified that they were sent by police, prosecutors, or others to the CII to have their children interviewed. There, therapists had spent many hours with the children using dolls and puppets to elicit "yucky secrets." The defense contended that the therapists were not qualified for such endeavors and that they had manipulated the children into giving answers the therapists wanted to hear.

The key interviewer, Kathleen MacFarlane, testified as an expert witness as a director of Diagnostic Center at Children's Institute International, a 90-year-old private therapy center. The prosecution tried mightily to make her an expert witness: "observing the emotional and physical effects on children while testifying and relating such observations to the emotional well-being of those children and those effects induced in those children after they leave the courtroom."[28]

But MacFarlane admitted under cross-examination that she was not licensed as a social worker in the state of California. Nor was she licensed as any type of therapist, psychotherapist, or other medical professional in any state in the U.S. She had received a B.A. in Fine Arts from Denison University in Ohio in 1969 and post-graduate education with a master's degree in social work from the University of Maryland in 1974.[29] She had worked at the National Center on Child Abuse and Neglect in the Department of Health and Human Services, Washington D.C. prior to her employment at CII, and had been in private practice as a psychoanalyst between 1974 and 1982.

She received a number of prestigious awards for her service in child sexual molestation investigation, including the California Sexual Assault Investigators Association Annual Award in recognition of distinguished service in 1983, and the Governor's Award for recognition of outstanding contributions to improving the quality of services to victims in 1984. She also published a number of scholarly papers explaining CII's interview techniques and defending against possible challenges in a courtroom setting to the legitimacy of their techniques. She stated in one of her articles:

> In the best of all possible worlds, it would be advisable not to ask children leading questions, in order to avoid the concern that children are responding to suggestions that certain things occurred or that they are being compliant and acquiescent to an adult authority figure. But, in the best of all possible worlds, children are not sexually assaulted in secrecy, and then bribed, threatened, or intimidated not to talk about it. In the real world, where such things do happen, leading questions may sometimes be necessary.... As a consequence, those who take on the task of evaluating alleged child victims must also be prepared to become the objects of attack when cases enter the legal system and their conclusions and techniques are challenged.... However, for those who can withstand the process in the interest of insuring that the voices of sexually abused children are heard, the risks and the battles are part of the job.[30]

She argued that leading questions, as well as using anatomically explicit dolls, constituted important elements of interview techniques that elicit children's accounts of sexual molestation. She had followed Dr. Roland Summit's theory of the child sexual abuse accommodation syndrome, that children never lie about molestation, the accepted belief among many psychologists, social workers, and child abuse experts.

In her testimony, MacFarlane also revealed that she had not shown the parents the entirety of the children's videotaped interviews, but that the parents had only been exposed to small segments of videotapes showing children describing sexual abuse. The defense requested that the parents view the entire videotapes to see how their children had been exploited by the therapists. "What we hope will happen is that the parents will get so angry when they see the tapes that they will withdraw their children as witnesses," one defense attorney argued.[31]

The question of professional credentials also surfaced during the testimony of another interviewer, Jane McCord, a therapist at the Richstone

Family Center. Having interviewed one of the alleged child victims, McCord testified that the child should not testify in the presence of the defendants. Judge Bobb indicated that McCord was not a licensed psychologist and therefore could not qualify as an expert witness, and as a non-licensed practitioner, McCord could not invoke the doctor-patient privilege of confidentiality, and that her testimony should be given less weight than normal. The testimony established the fact that two of the key therapists in the case were professionally unqualified—and unlicensed. And the children they may have influenced were the only witnesses for the prosecution.

Children's Testimony

The children's general renditions dovetailed nearly perfectly—almost too perfectly, as if rehearsed many times over. In almost every instance, however, details of what allegedly transpired were either missing from the children's accounts or they were unbelievably bizarre. "I don't remember" was a seemingly well-learned refrain when both the prosecution and defense were on the trail of what might have really happened. Thus, though the patterned, general stories told by the children often linked tightly together and corroborated one another, the details were still vague.

The children were paraded up to, and grilled on, the witness stand. The district attorney's office meanwhile was videotaping the children's testimony for use at the trial should any of them later be unavailable due to psychological or other reasons. As they launched their affirmative defense, the defense attorneys each wanted his own turn to question the children, knowing that it might be the only opportunity to actually do so. A contest of opinions ensued among the attorneys, as well as with Judge Bobb, who repeatedly cut off some lines of examination as being irrelevant and too time-consuming for whatever evidence they would yield, thus consistently upholding the prosecution's objections to defense questions.

Throughout the preliminary hearing the prosecutors also argued that the defense was harassing the child witnesses, and that Judge Bobb was empowered under the Evidence Code to exercise reasonable control over the mode of interrogation of a witness—in order to make it as rapid, distinct, and effective as possible to ascertain the truth, and to protect each witness from undue harassment or embarrassment.[32]

Defense attorneys sometimes did not agree with each other, either, each realizing that they had a legal commitment to protect their own client; they, thus, resented any court curtailment of their legal right to cross-examine witnesses. Dean Gits, representing Peggy McMartin Buckey, had wanted a separate preliminary hearing for his client so that he could place each witness under a legal microscope. But the judge refused, insisting on a combined hearing for all seven defendants, Gits retorting "I cannot help it if I was joined in." What he demanded was an opportunity to examine each and every witness; and when prosecutors objected that many of his questions had already been asked, he protested—"not by me."

So, one after another, as each child witness took the stand and was asked questions by prosecution and defense attorneys, they grew tired, their studied stories blurred, and the weakness of their accounts became obvious. Each told different stories at different times; they contradicted themselves; they could not explain inconsistencies in different versions they told and retold on examination and then cross-examination. The children clearly proved to be unreliable witnesses—perhaps caught mediating between their sense of the truth, their fantasies, and the post-event influences and pressures of their parents, the police, therapists, and media. It would be no picnic on the witness stand for them.

The first child to testify was Willie, a 7-year-old boy in the first grade. He described several games played at the school when he was 4 to 5 years old, each emphasizing "touching" and "nakedness." One game was called "Cowboys and Indians," he said. The teachers "were the Indians ... they would put us in jail ... with our clothes off ... and touch us."

In the "Alligator Game," he continued, "we'd take off our clothes, crawl around and when we were on the floor, they would touch us." In "Naked Movie Star," he explained, they had the naked children doing "tricks" and turning somersaults, while being photographed as they sang a song that went "What you see is what you are, you're a Naked Movie Star." In "tickle," he said, "the kids take off their clothes, and the teachers tickle them in the butt and on the penis."

Pointing to Raymond Buckey, he insisted that Buckey had touched him with his hand and his penis "in the mouth and in the butt and on my penis." "Did that hurt?" Deputy District Attorney Glenn Stevens asked of the alleged sodomy. The boy's answer was "yes." The boy added that his genitals had been touched by three other teachers while Virginia McMartin watched and photographed him; during the games the teachers watched, participated, or photographed them. But when Stevens pressed him for details, "don't remember" was the frequent reply. During his fourth day of testimony he even replied, "don't remember," when asked whether Virginia McMartin had photographed him during the naked games.[33]

During two hours of cross-examination by Peggy McMartin Buckey's attorney, two inconsistencies in the boy's testimony emerged. In his initial statements, the boy said that the game of "Cowboys and Indians" was played naked in the classroom. Under cross-examination he said that the same (or a similar) game was played fully dressed on the playground. Asked if he had ever played the game inside, his reply was "no." Again, the boy was asked, "[T]hey didn't play Cowboys and Indians inside?" "No" the young witness replied. "So the teachers never chased you and put you in [a pretend] jail inside?" "No," the boy replied.[34]

His inconsistency was a key factor in evaluating the remembrances. He testified that he was driven by the teachers to a farm, a circus house, and unfamiliar "strangers' houses" where some of the children "got touched," while others waited in the car. However, his testimony was not detailed as to who was among the "we got touched there" and who waited in the car, not able to see what actually happened.

The child's testimony suggested that he had not actually seen the things to which he testified. Virginia McMartin's attorney, Bradley Brunon, seized the possibility that this boy had been influenced by someone who had predesigned his stories. Brunon implied in statements, inflected to sound like questions, that the child had invented the bizarre stories to please his parents, a therapist, and prosecutor Stevens:

> Brunon: They told you they wanted you to say that Ray [Buckey] touched the kids on the penis and butt?
> Boy: Yes.
> Brunon: Did you say that Virginia McMartin watched the molestations so that he [Deputy District Attorney Glenn Stevens] wouldn't be sad?
> Boy: Yes.

Brunon then asked him a series of questions in which the boy described being helped by his teacher "Miss Peggy" to dry off and dress after playing in the school's wading pool. "She had to touch you on your bottom and your penis, didn't she?" "Yes," the boy replied.

Though the youngster stuck to his earlier stories of playing naked games, in response to other questions, the child testified that he had never seen any adults naked except his parents and that he did not remember anybody watching naked games at the school—both apparent contradictions of his testimony in direct examination. When asked if "[T]his is just telling the story these people want you to tell? You're not nervous, but just telling the story that Shawn [Connerly, a CII therapist], Mr. Stevens [the prosecutor], and your mom—that everybody—wants you to tell?" "Yes," the boy replied.

The child later appeared exhausted and ill, taking deep breaths, which Judge Bobb attributed to "the exhaustive cumulative effect of three days" of testifying. But defense attorneys dismissed the discomforts as "the effects of being caught in prevarications."

On the fourth day of testimony the following exchange took place, with the attorney asking the boy if a psychologist had said—

> Latiner: She [a CII therapist] thought Ray was a mean guy?
> Boy: Yeah.
> Latiner: She said she thought Ray had touched you on the penis?
> Boy: Yeah.
> Latiner: She kind of made you say that?
> Boy: Yeah.

Outside of the courtroom, Forrest Latiner, the defense attorney for Peggy Ann Buckey, stated that an adult could get this boy "to say anything you wanted him to say."[35] To prove this, the defense prepared to show a videotaped interview with the boy conducted by CII, that defense attorney Brunon said "shows brainwashing." The defense also felt that the testimony of the first witness had been successfully impeached.

The second child on the stand was a 10-year-old boy who testified, in street language, about body parts and alleged sexual acts that had taken place when he was four. He testified to being sodomized and sexually molested by all seven defendants. He also asserted that the children had been made to pose for pornographic pictures.

The boy charged that after the teachers had helped them undress, during naked games played to records, the children were told to walk or dance in a circle until the music stopped, then stand still or lie "posed" spread-eagle on the floor while Raymond Buckey or his sister Peggy Ann Buckey photographed them. He also said that Raymond Buckey showed him nude photographs of himself and of other naked children he did not know. He told the boy, "[H]ere's you and you're going to be a star."

The boy also testified that he and other children were sometimes taken to such locations as the storeroom of a market and an unfamiliar house, where "they [the teachers and the strangers] would touch us.... We would play the 'Naked Movie Star' game over by the fireplace, by the brick hearth." He said that he had been forced to orally copulate Raymond Buckey; that Buckey had masturbated him and inserted his fingers and objects into his anus; and he and other children bled from the anus after being touched by Buckey.

Among other allegations, the boy said that Buckey had sexual intercourse with his sister in the children's presence, showing the children what they were supposed to do to the female teachers, including touching the woman's breasts and genitals with their hands and mouths, and allowing the women to touch them on their genitals and in their anuses. He further said that Virginia McMartin had "touched" him on the chest and penis while he was naked.

The boy also testified that he had watched the bloody mutilation and killing of a pony, rabbits, chickens, and birds at a church and at a farm; the teachers warned him and the other children not to tell "any of the secrets" or their parents would be treated the same way. "Were you scared when you saw the pony bleed?" the prosecutor asked. "Yes," he replied. "I didn't cry out loud, but tears came down my eyes. I didn't say anything or scream. I didn't tell anyone because I thought that my parents would be hurt if I told those secrets."

Defense attorneys believed that the child's memory of events six years earlier was hazy at best. "His story [of alleged sexual abuse at the school] is a broadbrush picture that's missing too many details. We're going to try to see how much he really remembers," said Betty Raidor's attorney Walter Urban. Walter Powell, Jr., defense attorney for Mary Ann Jackson, focused on such details as the size of the room where the children were allegedly taken from their classes to be abused. The boy had testified that it was an empty, unused classroom; after saying he could not remember the entrance to "the secret room," he later described it as being entered through a doorless doorway from another classroom. So attorney Powell wanted the witness to show the location of its entrance, whether it was carpeted, and what kind of light fixture it had. He also directed the child to draw a diagram of the room's relation to the rest of the school. Outside of the courtroom Powell told reporters that he doubted that such a room ever existed.

The child's testimony also changed about the "Naked Movie Star" game—one day testifying that it was played weekly, the next day stating that he was forced to play it only four or five times. "What you've got is a combination of fantasy, an effort to please, and fact," attorney Powell said of the boy's testimony.[36]

The boy's testimony, meanwhile, became increasingly bizarre. He described children being taken to Harry's Market and being told to remove their clothes and then being "touched" in a back room inside the store. Though there was no storeroom, the owner Rasheed (Ray) Fadel told reporters there was an outside compressor room with open doors and an indoor wine cellar. The boy could not make up his mind if Fadel had watched from the outside or inside. The boy testified that Fadel had come to the door to talk with one of the teachers, but couldn't remember whether the man was actually inside the storeroom. "Was there ever any person not a teacher in there?" questioned defense attorney Bradley Brunon. "The store owner, Ray," the boy replied. "He was watching the games." "Did it happen on more than one occasion," the boy was asked. The reply was, "[Y]es." "You now remember that he came in on [at least] two occasions and watched the games?" "Yes," the boy answered.

In later testimony, the boy had Fadel in the room and said that he participated in the game activity. "Two of the men who touched you were Ray Buckey and Ray [Fadel], the owner of the market?" attorney Daniel Davis baited the hook of contradiction. "Yes," the boy replied.

Outside of the courtroom, Fadel denied the allegations. "That's not true at all. I don't know where he's getting his stories. He is making up stories."[37] He denied that his store had ever been used or that he had been a spectator at the so-called naked games. Yet Fadel also told two different versions about the defendants. He said that Peggy McMartin Buckey was a customer and that Raymond Buckey worked for him as a box-boy for several months in 1976; on the other hand, he said that he did not know the defendants at all.[38]

Perhaps the most amazing story told by this witness was that of animal sacrifices at the well-attended St. Cross Episcopal Church in nearby Hermosa Beach. The boy testified that live animals were chopped to bits at candle-lit ceremonies involving black-robed people who sometimes wore masks. The defense asked about door locks and other details that might undercut the prosecution's claim that the defendants conspired to silence the children by frightening them.

Under cross-examination, the boy repeated how he and other children were taken to a church. While there, adults wearing masks and black robes danced and moaned, and Raymond Buckey went to the altar and killed pet rabbits, turtles, and birds, threatening to kill the children's parents the same way if they told of their sexual abuse.[39]

The child witness, when questioned about the alleged sacrifice of a rabbit, recounted how, "Ray went outside and came back with the rabbit. He put it on the altar and cut it to pieces." The child said that he was molested by people in robes. He also insisted that the rabbit bled when it was cut up, and the blood went all over the altar. Asked about drinking cat's blood at the church ritual, the boy responded, "[N]o," but then picked up the idea several days later, when asked during cross-examination if he was forced to drink the blood of an animal, he calmly replied "[Y]es." He elaborated the rabbit blood incident, saying that he had seen the rabbit but didn't know what color it was. When he was asked what he drank the blood out of, Judge Bobb cut off the defense attorney after prosecutors argued that it was irrelevant, and that the evidence that might result was not worth the time needed to get it. Defense attorney Latiner disagreed, arguing, unsuccessfully, that such details were needed to prove that the child was fabricating the incident.[40]

Attorney Latiner asked Judge Bobb if she could imagine such an occurrence at the St. Cross church. "If you can, your honor, then we should stop cross-examination at this point and let all the children say what they will and go to trial." Outside of the courtroom, defense attorneys noted to reporters that no caretaker at the church had ever found the remains of any animals and that police investigators had not found traces of blood on the altar.[41]

The defense proposed that the child could be swayed into believing that he was remembering what he was only imagining. As confirmation of this thesis, the young witness recounted that, when confronted with questions or suggestions about what allegedly happened at the school, "I'd make a picture of what that looked like in my mind and think, 'does this picture look familiar?'"

Sometimes, he said, he then remembered again, and sometimes differently, from the first imaged impressions he made. As his memories of age three to four were being triggered at age ten, he tried to sort them through, to figure out what actually happened. But he also became confused and told different stories. One particular important change was that in his story to the therapists at the CII, he said that the cowboys abused and photographed the Indians, while in his testimony he said that Indians had abused and photographed the cowboys.

The third child witness was an 8-year-old girl. She testified that when she was three, she had been raped, photographed, tied up, placed in a dark closet, and forced to watch her teachers slash a turtle. On cross-examination, the witness said she could not remember things she had previously testified to or gave answers inconsistent with earlier testimony. Though in previous testimony she repeatedly had identified "Ray, Miss Betty, and Miss Peggy" as teachers who had sexually abused her, when asked by defense counsel who touched her, she replied "I can't remember."

The witness also said that she could not remember how she was touched or who threatened her. While she had previously testified that she had been forced to touch Raymond Buckey's penis, she replied that she had never done so. She also replied "[N]o" to a defense question of whether "anything" had ever been placed in her vagina or anus. On redirect questioning by the prosecution, however, she said that she thought "anything" meant like a stick or an object and was not thinking of a hand or penis.

Defense counsel Dean Gits requested that since she was bombarded with suggestive materials and was exposed to professional coaching, the 90-minute videotape of the child's exposure to diagnostic and therapeutic treatment be shown. He wanted the judge to "see what went on." Played in court, the tape showed social worker-therapist Shawn Connerly leading a 7-year-old girl through a series of play activities on the floor—drawing, looking at pictures, and using puppets and naked dolls, acting out suggested scenarios of what had happened. On the tape, Connerly told the child that 183 other children had already told her "yucky secrets," that the McMartin teachers were all "sick in the head" and deserve to be beaten up, and that her help was needed in figuring out what happened at the school—or what might have happened—when the children were "touched."

"Think Mr. Ray might have done some of that touching?" Connerly asks the child. When the child shakes her "Rags Raccoon" puppet in a gesture of "no," the therapist then asks, "[W]here do you think he would have touched her, Rags? Can you use your pointer and show where he would have touched her?" The child is then encouraged to keep pointing to different parts of the body, until the child has included the doll's private parts. "What part of Mr. Ray would have touched her?" the therapist asks and keeps going until the child points to the doll's genitals.

The defense argued that this was a form of setting untruths and fixing fantasy in the child's mind—of "brainwashing" by the therapist Connerly and the Institute. "Here you see the germination of fabrication," Gits told reporters outside the courtroom. "It may have been a play event—with suggestions hidden underneath."

Prosecutor Rubin agreed that the questions asked on the tape were "leading" the child, but they were for therapeutic purposes not intended for court use and not part of the district attorney's case.[42] Nevertheless, the appearance of professional coaching and fabrication was now being examined by the defense; this apparent coaching and the lack of objective, scientific assessments of the children's statements, along with other parts of the child's testimony, clearly made the children's accounts seem less credible and unreliable.

The next child to testify was extremely nervous at first, but became more comfortable as testimony proceeded. His testimony, riddled with contradictions, involved a number of important discrepancies, and he admitted to giving false statements. The gist of his testimony, is as follows:

- In 1984 he had testified that on one occasion two women were in the house, and another time four women were there, when the children were allegedly undressed, put in a closet and then taken out one by one and photographed; but in 1985 he testified that no female teachers were ever at the house.
- He identified Raymond Buckey as the photographer in 1984, but now said the camera was operated by a stranger.
- In 1984 he said he had seen teacher Betty Raidor partly naked; but in 1985 testimony he added Peggy McMartin Buckey.
- At his earlier appearance in the preliminary hearing he said Buckey had molested him at the house; but at the following week's appearance he said Buckey had not molested him at the picture-taking session at the house.

This witness also embellished his earlier accounts with new allegations, that the children played a naked game called "horsie"—a "lookout" game in which he said he sat atop a jungle gym watching for the unexpected arrival of parents, while his classmates were being molested inside the school.[43]

The defense argued that in the earlier statements none of the young witnesses indicated that they had been molested, but that therapists had then planted the notions in their minds; thus, they maintained, the prosecution and therapists had coached the children's stories before preliminary hearing testimony began. This particular youngster, however, insisted that he had told his mother that he had been sexually touched by a teacher and forced to play naked games *before* being interviewed by a CII therapist, insisting "I told her before [being taken to the CII, seeing news accounts or being given information by adults] ... some of the things I said in court—like that Ray touched me in my private parts and that we played some naked games." He further said that Betty Raidor and Raymond Buckey had stripped and "showed me their private parts." The term private parts, though, made his testimony suspect, as such designations are not usual components of a child's vocabulary.

In other testimony, in a breathless tumble of early witness-stand fear, he added, "[T]his man would put us in a closet. They'd take one kid out and take pictures of their private parts out in the big room.... I would go over to the chair and one man would tie us with our backs turned facing the wall and put a blindfold over our face. The men would take pictures of my bottom." This, he testified, was done with a large camera in a studio-like setting with two big umbrellas and bright lights. This child witness apparently thought that he saw his own bottom being photographed while he was blindfolded sitting on a chair.

On cross-examination, the defense attorneys were stung by the child's new accusation that he was fondled, sodomized, and forced to orally copulate Raymond Buckey in the bathroom of the school. The child drew a picture of the bathroom, containing several stalls, though the bathrooms at the school contained only single toilets. The boy said that he did not mention these incidents earlier because he was confused by the district attorney's questions. The district attorney, outside of the courtroom, said it was probably because the boy was too embarrassed to mention them.[44]

The fifth child to testify was a 9-year-old who testified to events that were said to have taken place five years earlier. The substance of his account had several different elements:

- Raymond Buckey and a man the witness did not know had sexually abused him and other children while a van they were riding in had its curtains down in a car wash.
- Raymond Buckey sodomized him and forced him to perform oral copulation at the school; Buckey also pointed a gun at him and other children, killed a school hamster, and threatened them with death if they told anyone secrets about the sexual abuse.
- At a strange house, a movie, showing several McMartin pupils playing a game while naked, had been shown by Raymond Buckey to a man and two women the witness did not recognize, as well as to several McMartin children.
- Driven to the house in a green van, the child said that he had seen Raymond Buckey receive money for the movie.
- "They showed pictures of us [the children]," the boy testified. "Ray's friend worked the movie camera. It showed us walking and dancing and playing 'Naked Movie Star.' Ray gave him the film and the guy would give Ray the money."

Deputy District Attorney Christine Johnson contended that the alleged movie was sold as pornographic material: "Ray turned over the film and received money."[45]

The sixth child witness to testify insisted that she had been raped and sodomized with pencils during a game called "horsie." Over a period of five and a half days, during 11 hours of testimony, she said that she had played naked games with Raymond Buckey and other children at the school while photos were being taken.[46] She testified that she had been taken on an airplane ride with two women named Leslie and Sandy, as well as taken to a "costume" house where Buckey and a stranger dressed in a costume had given them bubble baths.[47] Also, she had met a man called Fireman John dressed in a fireman's hat and outfit, who then changed into a ghost costume. Nothing "bad" happened during these times, according to the girl.

Her testimony was guided by outside pressures. At one point, she indicated that her therapist, parents, and the prosecution told her what to say on the stand. Inconsistencies also noted by the defense were that the girl testified that she had never touched Raymond Buckey with her mouth, but that he had forced her to orally copulate him.

Another young 8-year-old girl testified that she had been raped during a nap at the school. During her six days of testimony, she said that she had been forced to play a game called "doctor" in which Raymond Buckey had raped her and threatened to kill her parents if she told them about it.

Her testimony to the grand jury and in open court resulted in discrepancies. One contradiction involved photographs. Defense attorney Dean Gits said to the young girl, "you told the grand jury that Ray didn't take any pictures during the game of 'Naked Movie Star.' Were you telling the truth?" The answer was, "[Y]es." The attorney then asked, "[W]ere you telling the truth when you told us in court that he did take pictures during 'Naked Movie Star'?" "Yes," she answered again. The judge indicated that she, too, had questions about the credibility of this particular witness.[48]

The eighth child witness called was an 8-year-old boy who testified that Raymond Buckey had molested him and that Buckey had "sticked his fingers in my butt" during a game called "tickle." The boy also testified that pictures were taken during the "Naked Movie Star" game and that there were threats of death if he said anything about the incidents.

To obtain credible testimony from any of the children was difficult. The cross-examination revealed that this particular child's response was influenced not only by CII's Kathleen MacFarlane, but also by his parents. The following testimony shows the extent to the parental influence:[49]

> Davis: Did you ever see two other children playing the Naked Movie Star game when you were at that school?

Boy: No.

Davis: Did you ever see one other child playing the Naked Movie Star when you were at that school?

Boy: No.

Davis: Then, [boy's name], how do you know that two children a day played the Naked Movie Star game at that school?

Boy: I'm guessing.

Davis: And why did you guess, [boy's name]?

Boy: I don't know.

Davis: When you told the grand jury that all of the children had their pictures taken during the Naked Movie Star game, were you guessing then?

Boy: What do you mean? At a time?

Davis: The question you were asked, [boy's name], was, "when he [Ray] took pictures in the Naked Movie Star game, who did he take pictures of?" and you said, "the whole school." You never saw anybody else playing the Naked Movie Star game, so were you guessing when you told the grand jury the whole school had their pictures taken in the Naked Movie Star game?

Boy: Lots of people got molested so they probably most of them played it....

——

Davis: [boy's name], yesterday, you told Mr. Gits that someone told you that all of the children were molested. Do you remember that?

Boy: No.

Davis: Well, did anyone tell you that?

Boy: Well, they told me a few people were molested so I think they were all.

Davis: Is that part of the reason, [boy's name], that you think that you were molested?

Boy: I know I was molested.

Davis: All right. When you say, "they told me a few children were molested," who do you mean "they"?

Boy: My mom.

——

Davis: And you said that your mother told you that a few children were molested. You mean more than two children when you say a few, didn't you?

Boy: Yes.

Davis: All right. You mean three or more children, didn't you?

Boy: Yes.

Davis: So when your mother told you that, [boy's name], you believed her, didn't you?

Boy: Yes.

Davis: And it's because of what she told you that you believe all of the children were molested, correct?

Boy: Yes.

Davis: Now, when you refer to a few children that your mother said were molested, what did she tell you about those children?

Boy: That they were molested.

Davis: And the word she used was "molested," wasn't it?

Boy: Yes.

——

Davis: ... when you talked to Kee [Kathleen MacFarlane] and she asked you if you ever got to places where animals and stuff like that—ever got to go to those places, and you told her no, I asked you why did you tell her no and you said, "because I didn't think I was molested then."

Now, when you were talking to Kee with the puppets, you didn't think you were molested then, did you?

Boy: No.

Davis: You began to think you were molested after you talked to Kee with the puppets, correct?

Boy: Yes.

Davis: Now when you talked to the grand jury—remember the grand jury, [boy's name]?

Boy: Yes.

Davis: Did you think then that you had been molested?

Boy: I don't know.

Davis: You weren't sure then, were you?

Boy: No.

While other child witnesses provided similar versions of sexual abuse experiences, it was the thirteenth witness who gave accounts of molestation different from other child witnesses. A 9-year-old girl testified that she had been raped and sodomized by Raymond Buckey, molested by Buckey's mother and by Betty Raidor at a Manhattan Beach car wash, inside a "green house," and at a farm. She also said that she was photographed by Raymond Buckey and several strangers and served as a "lookout" to warn Buckey when other people were approaching. She said, "I was outside swinging on the swing. Inside was Ray and some children. They had their clothes off. Ray was molesting and abusing the children. I'd run in and tell Ray the child's mother was coming. He'd put the children in the bathroom and [tell the mother], 'Go in the little yard, and they'll be there.' He got the child dressed, peeked out the door and said he had found the child in the classroom." Also she said that "for little girls he [Buckey] was sticking his penis in their vaginas and his fingers in their behind, and for little boys, he [put] his penis in their butt." According to her, Peggy McMartin Buckey and Betty Raidor penetrated her with fingers and rubbed themselves against her.

Anything this child could be goaded to say, the judge allowed. And Judge Bobb would not allow defense attorney Daniel Davis to object to *any* questions when this child was testifying, saying that she *assumed* that the attorney was objecting to all of the questions being asked by prosecutors—not exactly a discerning way to make rulings from the bench.

Whom the children would accuse was almost anyone's guess. A 10-year-old boy identified photographs of Los Angeles City Attorney-elect James Kenneth Hahn, movie actor Chuck Norris, a priest, and four nuns as being among the "strangers" who allegedly killed animals, molested children, and participated in weird rituals at a church altar. Defense attorneys said that the testimony was preposterous. Hahn noted that great care must be taken in utilizing photographs because when children incorrectly label individuals as molesters, "their lives could be ruined."[50]

Forrest Latiner, one of seven defense attorneys, noted outside of the courtroom that "these children are simply picking out pictures because they were put in front of them with the suggestion that there's somebody in there they ought to recognize." "The two [child] witnesses we've had so far don't remember who they picked out a year ago."[51]

A 10-year-old boy's testimony included that he and other children had been tied up and bullwhipped until they could hardly stand, and had used knives and hypodermic needles to kill animals at the preschool almost every day. He also said that he was molested in a van after he had gone through a car wash, went to a farm where he was naked and bullwhipped, and was taken to a cemetery where they were forced to dig up bodies and watch teachers hack them with knives. According to the testimony, the children would get down into the grave and as they dug would place the dirt in their shirts and haul it out of the grave. They used pickaxes, shovels, and pulleys to pull the caskets out of the graves. After the casket was opened, the defendants cut a few pieces from the body. According to the testimony, sometimes the body would bleed. The boy testified that he had been forced to go to church and pray to "three or four gods" while nuns and priests chanted—and if they refused to pray, they were hit on the back by the priest. Defense attorney Forrest Latiner was quoted after the testimony as saying "[P]icture seven little dwarfs with pickaxes marching to a grave in broad daylight.... It's totally unbelievable."[52]

"We stand by the testimony of our witness," prosecuting attorney Glenn Stevens replied. "He was terrorized and taken to a cemetery ... and awful things happened." Stevens said that he did not know the name of the cemetery. During cross-examination, the child's statements led to further confusion, when Dean Gits applied logic to the witness's answers, attorney Latiner being moved by the ridiculous to an unprofessional, emotional response:

Gits: Who would decide which body was going to be dug up, [boy's name]?
Boy: The teachers.
Gits: And would the teachers give the kids shovels so that they could help dig up the body?
Boy: Yes.
Gits: So they'd have to bring the shovels along with them when they went to the cemetery, right?
Boy: Yes
Gits: Did they bring any wheelbarrows along with them when they went to the cemetery, [boy's name]?
Boy; No.
Gits: Anything else, any other utensils besides shovels that they brought with them to the cemetery?
Boy: A few pickaxes.
Gits: Okay. About how many pickaxes?
Boy: Three—two or three.
Gits: And could each kid have a shovel?
Boy: Yes.
Gits: Well, then when—
Stevens (prosecutor): I'm sorry.
Court: Mr. Stevens.
Stevens: I'm sorry to interrupt counsel. Mr. Latiner appears to be laughing.
Latiner (attorney for defendant, Peggy Buckey): Your honor, I'm covering my face.
Court: Mr. Latiner as well as another attorney appeared to be snickering ... apparently in response to answers the child was giving. A few minutes ago, I looked at Mr. Latiner and tried to indicate to him by a gesture that he should stop laughing or snickering at the witness.... There is no reason for any of those gestures.... I know this feeds into your defense but you cannot emote this way in front of the witness. It's unfair and unnecessary.[53]

The same witness said that three of the defendants had taken off their clothes and fondled "my butt and penis" during naked games at the school. He testified that the defendants had threatened to shoot and "slice up" his parents and burn down his house if he told about the games. Photographs were also taken during the naked games according to this witness.

Still another child victim testified that children had often been drugged while being molested. One young girl testified that the teachers had fondled her and given her medicine that made her sleepy. She had been forced to undress and pose naked for the "Naked Movie Star" game, she said. She added that Raymond Buckey and his mother sometimes were undressed during the naked games while Virginia McMartin watched. They killed a cat to frighten her into silence.[54] Yet, she gave different responses to the same question in the videotaped interview and in court.[55]

Gits: And after you were shown the pictures [of the teachers], the puppet lady said to you, "we know that you know all about this stuff, but maybe you could remember ... like, um, do you know if there was somebody in any of these pictures that maybe scared the kids and told them not to tell some of the yucky secrets?" and you said, "No."

She said, "No?" and you said, "I don't remember anything there," and she said, "Oh. Do you think you could help us remember?" and you shook your puppet's head, "no."

And then the puppet lady said, "Do you think, do you think?" and you said, "no."

Now when you told the puppet lady that nobody scared the kids at the school, were you telling the truth?

Girl: No.

Despite the nagging question of the puppeteer's failure to elicit the truth, the puppet lady undoubtedly left an impression on the child.

In December, 1985, a 7-year-old boy testified via closed-circuit television that he played naked games and a game called "Cowboys and Indians" in which, "[T]hey'd put us in jail; they'd touch us in jail."[56] The touches took place on the penis, according to the boy. The young boy also testified that Raymond Buckey had cut the ears off rabbits and injured other pets in front of the children and threatened to harm their parents if they told anyone about the sex games. The child's statements were often unclear and confusing, in response to defense attorney Dean Gits' questions:

Gits: Why did you tell the grand jury you went to the house [for a nude photography session] in a red convertible [rather than in a green-and-white van you described in 1981]?

Boy: I don't know.

Gits: Were you lying?

Boy: Well, I'm not sure. I think I might have. I think I was.

Gits: Why did you lie?

Boy: I don't know.

One of the more perplexing aspects of the testimony by the alleged victims were the numerous references to the "Alligator Game" and "Naked Movie Star" games. The children found it very difficult to give specifics, and their standard response was "I don't remember."[57] However, there were some clues, far from conclusive though, that these games might have been related to the therapy at CII. Kathleen MacFarlane had used an alligator puppet as a way of drawing information and shaping the accounts of the children. She appeared to have a fixation on nakedness, which undoubtedly affected the children's accounts, though they might not remember details of things that they did not experience or that did not really happen.

It began to be apparent that some parents had discovered that their children were being manipulated to testify to things that may have compromised their children's sense of security and truthfulness. One child scheduled to testify had actually been withdrawn by the parents, even though the parents were unaware that the child was still scheduled to testify. The mother said that there was "no way" that she would permit the child to testify if her therapy records were to be made public. Similarly, the father of another child scheduled to testify changed his mind after his older child had testified for eight days under what he considered "intolerable" conditions. He said that even closed-circuit television would not help. He also said that two therapists recommended that his younger child not testify.[58]

There is, then, some evidence that the children's accounts were influenced by adults who had learned the intimate language of the alleged vitimizations from the CII therapists. The therapists served as the all-important link between the fantasies of Judy Johnson and the young children.

Even though Johnson's original charges regarding her son were never followed up, her stories of satanic ritual abuse might have helped condition and pre-program the CII and, through its personnel, the children's stories that were presented in court. Since information on Judy Johnson was never revealed during the preliminary hearing, the defense did not have any opportunity to assess any information that could have cast doubt on her credibility. Rather, this information was purposefully and illegally suppressed by chief prosecutor Lael Rubin. What is significant is that the complete documentation of her long history of mental illness, alcohol abuse, and her bizarre charges was not released to the defense or to the court until the end of 1986, long after the preliminary hearing. California law now makes such withholding of evidence punishable by fine and/or report to the state bar association for possible disbarment proceedings.

It was quite serious that CII interviewers were not properly trained or licensed to practice as psychotherapists in conducting the interviews, that their methods were one-dimensional and leading, and that they knew of Johnson's claims. An alternative interview method such as criterion-based content analyses might have been more effective in extracting valid and credible information from the alleged victims; such scientific methods were not used in the CII interviews. Here it is only possible to speculate that the systematic use of more scientific assessment methods in the McMartin case might have ended the nightmare for the children, parents, and defendants long before the case ever reached the courtroom.

Medical Evidence and Medical Experts

The only expert forensic evidence presented by the prosecution was the testimony of doctors that some McMartin Preschool children showed medical signs of abuse—which the defense challenged, arguing that there was absolutely no evidence that any child was sexually abused or that any sexual molestation had taken place at the McMartin Preschool.

Much of the prosecution's medical expert testimony was offered without laying a proper foundation, with the key medical expert stating what the alleged victims told her—clearly hearsay evidence—in conjunction with detailed medical examinations.

Judge Bobb allowed Dr. Astrid Heger, a pediatrician at the Los Angeles County-University of Southern California Medical Center, to testify as to what the allegedly abused children had told her when she took a medical history from them and their parents. As she also worked as a consultant to the CII, a close observer of the preliminary hearing hinted that her testimony may well have been a foregone conclusion before the McMartin case itself ever emerged. Legally, her testimony probably should have been limited to the technical and medical domain, rather than stories the children allegedly told her.

Dr. Heger testified that she had examined 150 former McMartin students, including 30 of the 42 children involved in the case, and found physical evidence of sexual abuse and assault in six of them.

In order to investigate the traces of possible child abuse, Dr. Heger used a colposcope, a magnifying device equipped with a camera that takes three dimensional photographs, to examine the vaginas and anuses of alleged victims of child molestation. A colposcope is a binocular device which permits 30-power magnification, thereby allowing microscopic examination of various physical areas. A camera is attached to the colposcope and takes stereoscopic slides to preserve the results of the exami-

nation. The medical device is relatively new and in order to make testimony legally admissible for the examination of sexual abuse victims, the
use of a colposcope has had to meet the stringent requirements of the so
called Kelly-Frye rule. The Kelly-Frye rule requires that a new scientific
technique must meet a two-pronged test in order to be admissible: First,
the reliability of the method must be established by expert testimony.
Second, the witness giving the testimony must be properly qualified to
give a competent opinion on the subject.[59]

In California, *People v. Mendibles* (245 Cal.Rptr 553, 1988) first established that a colposcopic examination met the requirements of the Kelly-
Frye rule. Dr. Heger was involved in the Mendibles case as the medical
expert who had examined alleged victims of child molestation with a
colposcope.

The credibility of testimony based on colposcope examinations was
also reiterated in *People v. Luna* (250 Cal.Rptr. 878, 1988) in which the
court stated that the Kelly-Frye rule applies to the colposcope because of
the Mendibles decision and that it had been in use since 1977 to study
cervical pathology and as a tool for clarifying the diagnosis of sexual
abuse. The colposcope had previously been used in Brazil, for example,
to determine if brides were still virgins.

A colleague suggested that Dr. Heger try it out on the McMartin children. Heger had limited experience with the equipment, which at times
malfunctioned. She showed 42 slides and testified that they evidenced
sexual abuse.

The method itself does not provide certain proof of abuse. There had
been some earlier debates about the reliability and credibility of testimony based on the examination of child victims by colposcope.

Dr. Heger testified to what she believed were genital and rectal injuries which she said were most likely caused by forced penetration by an
object "the size and consistency" of a male sexual organ or, in other cases,
a blunt object. She said that the shapes and patterns of scarring and the
precise size and locations of the injuries were such that they could not
have been caused by bowel problems, masturbation, the insertion of pencils, or falling on sharp objects. She explained that scarring patterns, particularly in young children who are not yet sexually active, can provide
evidence of years-old abuse, even in cases where there was outside force,
but no penetration.

Dr. Heger recounted that in some of the children she found evidence
of "painful, forceful penetration," all of which are indications of sexual
assault and abuse. These injuries were not only visible to the naked eye,
but also by the colposcope's magnified, three-dimensional photographs

of external genital areas. Dr. Heger said that her findings were consistent with the children having been repeatedly sodomized and raped.

Judge Bobb allowed Dr. Heger to testify freely, thereby violating the standards of presenting evidence in the following ways: First, the personalized feelings of pain on the part of the alleged victims could not be recognized by an expert; second, such pain was alleged to be the consequence of forced penetration, which clearly had yet to be proven; and third, the unproven latter instance was assumed to be caused by sexual assault and abuse—extrapolating a legal conclusion about the commission of a crime from unproven facts. Clearly, the judge showed poor judgment and should have required that expert testimony be limited to the medical issue of the children's existing physical condition, should have excluded such conjecture about the causes, and should not have rejected defense motions to strike parts of the testimony.

Finally, Dr. Heger did not note that the abuse she assumed, as a result of her examinations, could have taken place anywhere—while with relatives, with parents at home, with playmates outside the school milieu.

Several medical experts called by the defense said that they could not make definitive conclusions about sexual molestation from photographs; they would have to examine the child, take a history, or at least have information provided by the examining physicians.[60] Dr. Robert ten Bensel, a nationally recognized child-abuse expert from the University of Minnesota, conducted blind studies of Heger's slides. He asked medical experts to evaluate them and found that there was no correlation among the experts' independent evaluations. Experts called to the witness stand to support Heger's conclusions could not do so. One expert circled areas on a slide of a normal anus, saying that there was evidence of abuse.

Although not admitted at the trial, a research finding by Dr. John McCann, a child-abuse expert at the University of California, San Francisco, challenged Heger's medical evidence. McCann used the colposcope on 114 normal, unabused girls and a smaller number of boys. The small bands that had been thought to be vaginal scars were found in more than 39% of the girls examined by colposcope and in 15% of the girls when the exam was done by the naked eye. But when he realized they were appearing in 26% of the children he examined, he consulted an anatomist, who found that the phenomenon had been identified as a congenital condition in 1936. The dilation commonly associated with sexual abuse was found in 49% of the children.[61]

The ultimate conclusion was that the medical testimony was at least suspect and at most probably completely misleading, insofar as it indicated sexual abuse; and, if there had been sexual abuse, there was no medical or any other forensic evidence that it had occurred at the McMartin Preschool.

Potential Bias of CII Personnel

The defense attorneys felt that CII personnel were not employing objective and systematic validity check methods in evaluating the children's statements and might have their own individual biases against alleged child molesters which influenced the way the children had been interviewed. One of the defense tactics, then, was to examine potential biases of CII personnel and the prosecution's medical expert. The defense attempted to find out whether these adults had ever been victims of child molestation and whether such childhood experiences might have colored their views and influenced their examinations and interviews.

As the primary medical examiner of the children, Dr. Astrid Heger was asked by the defense whether or not she had been molested when she was a child. She refused to answer the question. The court ruled that if she did not answer, it would infer that she had been molested and it might affect her credibility.[62] The court also presumed that Kathleen MacFarlane had been a molestation victim. Sandra Krebs, another CII therapist who had been trained by Kathleen MacFarlane in the case, admitted in a videotaped interview that she was a sexual abuse victim.[63] Krebs told children on tape, "I was a molestation victim, and it's all right for you to tell me."[64]

Dr. Heger denied in court that she was biased in any way as a result of being allegedly sexually molested in her childhood. While she initially stated that she had not had any personal contact with the alleged victims, she later revealed that she in fact had interviewed some of the children in person and obtained information on their alleged molestation at the preschool.

Would such personal encounters potentially bias Dr. Heger as an expert witness? Although interviewers are instructed to remain objective and to avoid communicating personal views, past research suggests that interviewers often give cues that may influence respondents' answers.[65] Even when verbal cues are avoided, nonverbal communication can often escape the interviewer's control. Sometimes even the interviewer's race, gender, age, and personal biases can influence respondents who, in an attempt to please the interviewer, may give socially admirable but potentially misleading answers.[66]

The defense thus tried to establish that the CII interviewers and the prosecution's chief medical expert were personally biased against the defendants in the McMartin case because of their own childhood moles-

Lender:

DO N

‖‖‖‖‖‖‖‖‖‖‖‖‖‖‖‖‖‖‖‖‖‖‖‖‖‖‖‖‖

Responder Req. No.: 8370316

MINITEX: MII01

Printed Date: 23-DEC-2008
Need By: 18-JUN-2009

Rep

Title: Anatomy of the McMartin child molestation case
Author/Article Author: Butler, Edgar W.

Volume/Issue: **Article Date:**

Article Title:
Publisher Info: University Press of America; Lanham, Md.; c2001.

ISBN/ISSN: 0761819835   OC 4582/156
                                IWIDIR(G2
                                2WILSG2m
Edition:
Description: 346 p. ; 23 cm.
Copyright Compliance:
Call Number: N/A
Database/#: MnPALS/U-SYS01 LCN: 2001027030
Request Notes:

Pickup Location

Ba

tation experiences, and that their personal prejudices influenced the way they had interviewed and evaluated the alleged child victims.

Prosecutorial Misconduct

Cult Practice Fabrications

The defense also contended that the prosecution had distorted the accusations against the defendants, engaging in egregious legal misconduct on a number of tactical fronts. Medical evidence supplied by experts, as well as testimony by parents, therapists, and the alleged child victims, suggested that the district attorney's office might have indiscriminately identified suspects and manufactured evidence by using unrelated cases and creating artificial links with the McMartin Preschool—building upon a prefixed image of a conspiracy with occult and satanic connections. These images were then exploited by the media to focus public attention on the case and release a wave of hatred and condemnation of those accused.

The happenstance of a similar case allowed the prosecution to "corroborate" the McMartin charges without any linking of evidence that McMartin satanic rituals and sacrifices actually took place. Robert H. Winkler, a bearded, long-haired 35-year-old unemployed man, had been charged in nearby Torrance with molesting children he had met through a baby-sitting service. Unable to produce bail, Winkler had been held in jail. Although there was no known link between Winkler and the McMartin defendants, the children were shown pictures of bearded men, and some picked out Winkler as one of "the strangers" involved in the alleged molestations.

Recounting so-called "cult" evidence found at Winkler's home, Deputy District Attorney Lael Rubin attempted to link Winkler with the McMartins:

> I think that it is highly significant that, after having testimony from two children about the manner in which [defendant Raymond] Buckey cut off rabbit ears, rabbit ears were found in the same place [Winkler's home] with what is obviously cult material. I think it is tremendously corroborative of what these kids are saying. There may well be a link between this Robert Winkler and Raymond Buckey.[67]

Winkler volunteered to take a lie-detector test, adding that he had never met Buckey.[68] Later, Rubin said that she did not know whether any charges would be brought against Winkler.

If such corroborative "evidence" against an alleged conspirator did not bring charges, there must have been something phony about the evidence itself. Indeed, there apparently was no legal basis to charge Winkler, and ultimately Rubin did not. However, Winkler was publicly named as a suspect, though the district attorney did not include him on the list of suspects provided to the defense attorneys as required by law.

The district attorney's loose-cannon approach to the naming of suspects, nonetheless, continued unabated. Defense attorney Forrest Latiner said after perusing the list, "we have the names of over 75 people, including some of prominence, who have been so identified. They'd be very disturbed to know that their pictures were picked out in the first place, or to have their names revealed to the media in the second place."[69]

The prosecution "floated" charges against many people who were never officially charged with a crime. Defense attorneys, meanwhile, wrangled over whether or not a court "gag order" would be desirable, but ultimately decided that the media and public needed to hear their contention of prosecutorial malfeasance—and that precluded their attempts to secure a gag order.

Illegal Delays in Reporting Sexual Abuse

The defense charged the CII with illegal behavior when it did not report hundreds of alleged cases of sexual abuse within the 36 hours required by law. Defense attorney Daniel Davis argued, "[E]ither they disobeyed the law, or they didn't believe that any child was molested." Davis cited state law which requires that anyone who works with children and suspects child abuse must contact authorities immediately, or as soon as practically possible, by telephone and shall prepare and send a written report thereof within 36 hours of receiving the information concerning the incident. Failure to do so was classified as a misdemeanor punishable by up to six months in jail and a fine of $1,000.[70]

MacFarlane defended her untimely reporting, insisting that she had made the videotaped interviews, files, and medical reports available to the police, had ongoing verbal communication with them as well as several face-to-face meetings, and referred every child the institute suspected was molested to the police.[71] MacFarlane insisted, "[I]t's a ridiculous attempt to focus attention on the forms themselves, rather than on the information that they contain, namely that hundreds of children were molested."[72]

Conflict Among Prosecutors

Something was awry in the DA's office. Various degrees of truth and conflict among the prosecution team had begun to emerge during late summer of

1985. Chief prosecuting attorney Lael Rubin had argued that all seven defendants should be prosecuted, while the two co-prosecutors believed that charges against five of the defendants should be dropped, or at a minimum the case should be re-evaluated at the conclusion of the preliminary hearing which, by October 1985 had entered its 15th month. The two co-prosecutors insisted that only Peggy McMartin Buckey and Raymond Buckey be prosecuted because the others were either innocent or their cases were too weak for successful prosecution. Due to the conflicts and disagreements among prosecuting attorneys, the Chief Deputy District Attorney Gil Garcetti announced that a new team might take over the prosecution.[73]

Though the original charges had been made two years earlier in August 1983, doubt about the defendants' guilt came after the prosecutors began watching videotapes of the interviews with the children. Apparently, up until the time of the preliminary hearing, the prosecuting attorneys had relied upon CII therapists for their knowledge about the child abuse and molestation, and had not reviewed or carefully studied the videotapes themselves. For two years the prosecution had slept on the job. "For a long time I believed that all seven of them were animals and should be thrown to the wolves," one of the prosecutors stated in 1985, "then I began to study the evidence."[74]

The lights finally went on in the district attorney's office. Outside the courtroom, one prosecuting attorney was quoted as saying that "Kee [Kathleen] MacFarlane could make a six-month old baby 'say' he was molested ...[and] knows as much about police interviews as I know about plastic surgery." "We heard stuff in court we'd never heard before—the kids were rewarded for telling things and they started embellishing," he stated. "Then they couldn't back down or they'd be liars. Now most of them have come to believe it and will go through life believing that that stuff happened to them."[75] Though this prosecutor believed that some of the children might have been molested, he admitted that, due to improper investigation, by whom would never be known.

Ira Reiner, the new district attorney who inherited the case from his predecessor, asked his aides for a "candid and complete evaluation" of the evidence in the case.[76] The breach of opinion among them had already widened into a gulf. It was reported that at least one of the prosecutors believed that charges against at least four of the defendants should be dropped because they were innocent. Other reports implied that two deputy district attorneys, Glenn Stevens and Christine Johnson, had begun to develop serious doubts about the prosecution's case, reasoning in part that the videotapes of the children sustaining the prosecution's case involved highly suggestive interviewing techniques, reinforced by rewards for the children.[77] The children no longer knew fact from fantasy. But due to the prosecution's unresolve, some of the defendants still had their freedom legally restrained.

Bail

While the district attorney changed personnel and procrastinated, Peggy McMartin Buckey was being held without bail on one count of molestation and $1 million bail on eleven other counts. Her attorney Dean Gits said that she had already spent nearly two years in the Sybil Brand Institute for Women, where inmates spit at her, called her unprintable names, and tried to set her hair on fire.[78]

Supposedly, the DA possessed some evidence that compelled them to keep her confined, but which the court sealed from public knowledge. California's Constitution specifies that a person cannot be held for punishment while raising money, but only for protecting public safety. The practice in California is that defendants can be held without bail in three different circumstances: (1) The person is charged with a capital crime; (2) the person is charged with a felony involving violence with the likelihood that release will result in great bodily harm to others; or (3) the person is charged with a felony that the judge determines is based on clear and convincing evidence that the person has threatened another with great bodily harm and there is substantial likelihood that the person would carry out the threat if released.[79]

Peggy Buckey was held under the last section, based on her alleged threats contained in 86 letters submitted by prosecutors in June, 1984.[80] According to information released by the prosecution, the letters, which were sealed by the court, said the defendants had threatened to kill the children and their parents by poison, bombs, drowning, or setting their houses on fire. The prosecution thus argued that the preventive detention was necessary because of the harmful effect her release would have on already traumatized children.[81]

Dean Gits countered by making a motion for her bail, arguing that only one of the original 15 indictment counts remained—concerning a 7-year-old boy who said that she had touched his penis. But the judge was rigid, saying that two of the alleged victims had testified that she had made threats. After taking the motion for bail under advisement, the judge then ruled, "I have considered the matter at very great length. I have reviewed the entire record in this case relating to the issue of Peggy Buckey's bail. I have reviewed the arguments of both counsel. After this review, I don't find sufficient grounds to modify the initial denial of bail by the Superior Court."

After more months in jail, without any change in the DA's allegations, in December, 1985, the court finally set bail for Peggy McMartin Buckey at $1 million. Her home was sold to pay legal costs for her son and mother. She gave her school property to defense attorney Daniel Davis to cover her own legal fees.[82] She was now both free and impoverished.

Dropping Charges

Public expectations for conviction of the McMartin Seven had been heightened by the press screeching the DA's high profile charges. But now there were allegations that the district attorney had over-charged the defendants to strengthen his political ambitions, and the factual basis for many charges seemed to collapse. In June, 1985, Judge Aviva K. Bobb thus dismissed more than 200 counts. In total, the judge dismissed 80 of 170 counts against Raymond Buckey, 33 of 45 counts against Betty Raidor, 15 of 22 counts against Babette Spitler, 16 of 20 counts against Mary Ann Jackson, and one of 25 counts against Peggy McMartin Buckey.

Predictably, the dismissals outraged parents and the public. "The ruling surely benefits the defendants in the immediate context of the McMartin prosecution." Two reporters pointed to the dearth of evidence. "It is, however, founded on an important principle of law, one that is absolutely essential to the fair operation of any legal system and helps to protect all of us against arbitrary and potentially vindictive government action."[83] Some counts were dismissed on the basis that the prosecution failed to present any evidence in support of the charges. Other charges were dropped because some children would not testify in person. Since the case had begun, a new law had been passed that allowed children to avoid testifying in person. But the judge ruled that the new law did not apply retroactively to the McMartin case, as *ex post facto* legislation was not binding; the relevant clause of the U.S. Constitution prohibits the retrospective application of rules that disadvantage a defendant in criminal prosecution.[84]

Despite the fact that the new law was not applied retroactively, with the judge disallowing children's testimony by closed-circuit television, prosecutors subsequently won a two-and-a-half month battle to allow several children to testify by closed-circuit television.[85] Some parents still hesitated, saying they would not allow their children to take the stand under any conditions. One father indicated that the family had gone through a lot of anguish, had moved, and settled where no one knew about their involvement in the case. Their decision left only four witnesses to testify in court.[86]

Several days later, two remaining child witnesses dropped out of the case. One 8-year-old girl had been re-evaluated and eliminated as a witness by the district attorney's office. The parents of a 10-year-old boy decided to withdraw their child for "confidential" reasons.[87] And the prosecution decided to go forward with the remaining two children.

It became obvious that prosecution's case was crumbling.[88] In attempts to rebuild it, they threatened to add 50 molestation counts against the defendants as a result of the testimony already presented by several of the 13 child witnesses. While the prosecution wanted to add these counts, the defense argued that Judge Bobb had ruled earlier that the preliminary hearing would only deal with the original charges.

The prosecution then announced that it would not call any of its remaining 28 witnesses. Among the reasons were that only five of them were willing to testify at all and then only by closed-circuit television. Six had dropped out because they were not comfortable even with videotaped testimony, and the remaining 17 had been withdrawn because parents would not subject their children to the lengthy cross-examination to which early witnesses had been exposed. Parents were particularly upset because they said that there had not been any communication between them and the prosecutors for months regarding the dismissal of charges and possible testimony by their children.[89] As of September 1985, of the original 41 complaining witnesses, 23 had either withdrawn or had been eliminated by the district attorney's office.[90]

The defense then asked that all charges be dismissed. Failing that, the attorney for Mary Ann Jackson argued that his client's trial should start immediately since charges against her were based only upon one child who had already testified at the preliminary hearing. Denying the motion, the judge ruled that splitting the case seemed inappropriate and that Jackson's trial would not possibly get underway before the conclusion of the preliminary hearing for the other defendants. As it turned out, this decision was an advantage to Jackson.

Dropping Defendants

Besides the dismissal of more than 200 counts against the seven defendants, in September 1985, there were rumors that the district attorney's office was considering dropping charges against five of the seven McMartin defendants.[91] *The Daily Breeze* in Torrance, California, had reported that some prosecutors questioned whether or not the supposed victims had had their accounts influenced and shaped by therapists who interviewed them. The DA thought that the children were too young to testify; some had begun to recant their charges. Other witnesses were being withdrawn by their parents.

Responding to the rumors, five parents petitioned the State Attorney General, John Van de Kamp, to investigate the Los Angeles District Attorney's handling of the case. The group also wanted him to re-investigate the evidence against the five defendants who were being dropped from the case. This followed a similar request by support groups for the McMartin defendants to Van de Kamp to investigate the handling of the investigation.[92]

Just before Christmas in 1985, the DA and a dozen of his top lawyers went into conclave for several days. They debated the strengths and weaknesses of the case, the possible degrees of guilt of the seven defendants, and whether to bring them to trial.[93] Members of the prosecution team recommended dropping charges against four of the defendants, bringing to trial only Raymond Buckey, his mother, and Betty Raidor. One prosecutor recommended that only Raymond Buckey and his mother be brought to trial; and one prosecutor argued that only Raymond Buckey be brought to trial.[94]

As consensus emerged, the district attorney decided that charges against five of the defendants would be dismissed because it was highly unlikely that they would be found guilty as charged.[95] In January 1986, charges were finally dropped against five of the McMartin defendants.

But not everyone agreed; several dozen angry parents converged on the courthouse to blast prosecutors for dropping the charges. Some of the parents were numb with shock, others were crying, one catcalling— "Reiner is chicken." "Why? Why? Why," staccato voices broke the bounds of orderly procedure. We "still feel those five people are guilty. We still believe our children," another parent said.[96]

Belief was one thing; convictability was another. District Attorney Ira Reiner said that though he empathized with the parents, he had little choice; his office had a moral obligation not to file criminal charges unless there was evidence.[97] Outside the courtroom, Reiner insisted that the interviews conducted at the CII were "blown massively out of proportion.... They would ask a kid if he had been touched in this yucky place by the bad teacher. If he said no, the therapist would say, 'all of your friends told us it happened, and you're just as smart as them,' and finally the kid would say it happened."

Defense attorney Forrest Latiner agreed, recounting that "these McMartin kids were playing a 'Can You Top This' competition among themselves.... If one kid said they slapped a rabbit, the next kid had the rabbit's ears cut off, and the next kid said the rabbit was cut up altogether."[98]

Co-prosecutor Glenn Stevens resigned, expressing grave doubts about the guilt of the McMartin defendants. Both Stevens and the district attorney's office denied that the reasons for his leaving were related to the McMartin case. Stevens stated that he had agreed with the DA to wait until the preliminary hearing was over before dropping charges against five of the defendants.[99]

On the day before Christmas, 1985, Judge Bobb rested the defense case, over their objections. The defense indicated that they had reduced their witness list, but needed several weeks for a defense medical expert to prepare to testify in the case. "Unless defense counsel is ready to proceed with the next witness, this court will deem the defense to have rested," the judge rested the preliminary hearing until after New Year greetings.[100]

Conclusions

Testimony in the preliminary hearings of the McMartin case ended in January 1986. Roger J. Gunson, of the district attorney's office, finally announced that unless there was a significant development, no additional charges would be filed against the defendants.[101]

Gunson also indicated that no further investigation would be made of Charles Buckey—father of two of the McMartin defendants and husband of Peggy McMartin Buckey—or of Rachid Aboufadel (also known as Ray Fadel), the Manhattan Beach grocer. Gunson also said that they would not prosecute three teachers at nearby Manhattan Ranch Preschool, noting that there was insufficient evidence to warrant criminal proceedings, although there was strong physical evidence of sexual molestation.[102]

The DA had yet to reveal any forensic evidence to support the incidence of child molestation at the McMartin Preschool. No adult witnesses of alleged crimes had surfaced. There were only child witnesses who testified that devils had been worshipped, animals mutilated, blood drunken, a live baby sacrificed in a church, and that they had been drugged and sexually molested.

The prosecution argued that the letter sent by the Manhattan Police Department requesting parents to ask their children about being molested by Raymond Buckey had alerted Buckey to the fact that he was being investigated, enabling him to destroy damaging evidence. Anthony Burnetti, the lead investigator for the Los Angeles District Attorney's office, testified that although the county had spent over $1 million since 1983, not one photograph of any McMartin children had been found.[103]

The case clearly demonstrated the difficulty for the prosecution to establish the fact of child abuse, while also protecting the rights of both victims and accused. Bizarre testimony and dubious court decisions only compounded the matter.

Fueled by the media and prosecution releasing unsubstantiated materials about the defendants, massive hysteria sustained the prosecution, strengthening their case on the frailest of evidence. Not only had the prosecution intentionally suppressed information on Judy Johnson, the first accuser, but the content of the videotaped interviews with alleged child victims and therapists was initially kept out of the defense's reach. The extent of the coaching and biased interview techniques was not revealed to the defense for critical assessment.

Similarly, the prosecutors had unfairly selected which persons to prosecute in the case. The prosecutor's charging power included virtually unlimited discretion to invoke public scrutiny and punishment, and therefore the power to control and destroy people's lives. Though child sexual molestation charges against five of the seven preschool teachers had been dropped, their professional reputation, social status, and property had been completely lost.

While the defendants lost, others hoped to gain. There were strong indications that the prosecution itself had been initiated for personal objectives, not the protection of the community. Some labeled the prosecution demagogic, beset with malice and evil intent. Ira Reiner publicly blamed his predecessor for turning over the initial interviews of the children to therapists who, he said, were "incredibly suggestive" in their interviews, building the case against the defendants on very weak evidence.[104]

The prosecution argued for—and the court exercised—considerable discretion in jailing the defendants without bail for an extended term. Raymond Buckey was detained without bail for the entire duration of the preliminary hearing—the longest in California history. The prosecution also held his mother, Peggy McMartin Buckey, for two years without bail. They were detained despite their community ties and solid personal backgrounds, despite the absence of any prior record, despite the Los Angeles Attorney's dismissal of the charges against five of seven original defendants.

Holding broad discretionary power to employ the full machinery of the state in scrutinizing the defendants and deciding what charges to bring, the prosecution brought far too many, considering the weakness of the evidence.[105] While excessive counts and charges later led to confusion and the defense's advantage, the child sexual molestation and conspiracy charges exploited by the media suffused community perceptions—destroying the personal and professional lives of all seven McMartin defendants and jeopardizing chances to select an impartial jury.

The costs also touched almost everyone within reach of the charges. At the close of the preliminary hearing, the case was estimated to have already cost Los Angeles County $4 million, financially ruined all seven defendants and possibly one defense attorney—and the end was nowhere in sight. In addition to financial losses, the preliminary hearing exacted a heavy emotional and physical toll from the defendants, children, their parents, attorneys, police, and judges. Yet the trial had not even begun. The first trial, verdicts, and their aftermath soon were to become the public shooting gallery for all who deigned to stand up for their rights.

Chapter 6

Pre-Trial Events:
Before the First McMartin Trial

Of the numerous, sensationalized charges that were made in the media, most were dismissed before the trial; five defendants were dropped from the case in January 1986, and cynicism began to emerge as the media began to question the validity and credibility of the prosecution's charges against the remaining McMartin defendants.[1] By the time the first McMartin trial began, only two defendants remained—Raymond Buckey and his mother, Peggy McMartin Buckey.[2]

Several weeks were spent selecting a judge, and after three judges were rejected for prejudice, court officials assigned Superior Court Judge William R. Pounders for the trial. Pounders had become a Los Angeles superior court judge in 1985 and possessed some positive strengths. He had good organizational skills and an extensive knowledge of the law, both enhanced by the systematic use of computers.

News also surfaced that several members of the prosecution team had serious doubts about the validity of charges against the defendants. A controversy emerged involving ex-prosecutor Glenn Stevens, who had his questions and doubts about the validity of the prosecution's charges taped by several film makers; and a second co-prosecutor, Christine Johnson, also had misgivings about the credibility of the prosecution's case. Meanwhile, with the death of Judy Johnson—the mother who originally alleged that her child had been molested—a critical link in the case was gone.

Several other controversies developed: (1) Denial of bail for Raymond Buckey; (2) motions to change venue and challenge the jury array; (3) the loss and then recovery of tapes made by then prosecutor Glenn Stevens; and (4) charges of discriminatory law enforcement and invidious pros-ecution. Before the case could be tried, then, a hornets' nest of stinging matters had to be salved and attended.

Charges of Discriminatory Enforcement and Prosecution

Defense attorney Dean Gits persuasively argued that Peggy McMartin Buckey was the subject of discriminatory enforcement and invidious pros-ecution. He insisted that there was no material difference between the released defendants and his client, only that she had to stand trial while five other defendants had been released.[3] He and the defense attorney for Raymond Buckey made identical motions to dismiss all charges. They were convinced that charges against the two remaining defendants had been made and were continued strictly for political reasons.

Judge Pounders ruled, based on a review of the available evidence, that it was sufficient and credible to justify the determination the district attorney had made to proceed against these two defendants and not the other five. He also added that for the district attorney not to proceed would have been an abuse of discretion on Reiner's part.[4]

One of the original prosecuting attorneys, Glenn Stevens, expressed doubts about the guilt of the McMartin defendants before leaving the district attorney's office in 1986. He was interviewed on tape for 30 hours by Abby and Myra Mann, Beverly Hill screenwriters and movie makers who wanted to produce a film based on Stevens' role in the McMartin case. Whatever role Stevens actually played, the story line was that he was an ambitious young prosecutor who was forced to give up his posi-tion because he had to obey the dictates of his conscience. Stevens said in the taped interview, "we had, through the tremendous power of our office, ruined their [McMartin defendants'] lives."[5]

Information from the taped interviews was given to both the defense and the State Attorney General's office just prior to the beginning of the trial. Though Stevens said that he had agreed to the taped interviews only because he thought that they would not surface until after the trial, the tapes were considered to be particularly important because they offered insight into the prosecution's case, much of it casting strong doubts from the start on the credibility of the child molestation charges.

After the Manns had reviewed the tapes, they became concerned with "vital materials" that had not been turned over to the defense as required by law. They showed some of the material to their attorney, former state appellate judge Richard Shauer, who told them to give the tapes to both the State Attorney General's office and the defense, or they could risk charges of obstruction of justice.[6] "We agonized over what to do," Abby Mann explained. "We knew that we would jeopardize our project if we turned over the tapes; however, two people's lives were at stake. And we realized that we had no choice."[7]

The taped interviews substantiated a number of defense contentions that the DA's office had intentionally withheld information from them. They had been particularly dismayed that the prosecution had unlawfully retained information concerning the mental instability of the McMartin preschooler's mother who had made the first complaint against Raymond Buckey. In the taped interviews, Stevens had also elaborated that the children "began embellishing and embellishing their stories." Therapists further contaminated the interviews by leading and suggestive questions, he said. Stevens also argued that the case was poorly investigated, the children's accounts were often contradictory, and "we had no business being in court."[8]

The Manns subsequently were hired as defense investigators, raising questions about their involvement in the case. Questions were also raised about Stevens as a former prosecutor working for the defense in the same case—a conflict of both interest and the attorney-client privilege. Stevens argued that the district attorney does not have a client, therefore the attorney-client privilege cannot be abrogated; some legal authorities said that a prosecutor does have a client—the state.[9] The California Business and Professional Code states that lawyers risk criminal misdemeanor charges and possible disbarment if, after prosecuting a case, they directly or indirectly advise the defense "as attorney or otherwise."

One other effect of the Stevens' tapes was that some children who had testified at the preliminary hearing "were stunned to find out that he might not believe them."[10] They felt that he had sold out for "30 pieces of silver," one parent explained. Stevens had received an initial $1,000, and a promise of another 5% of the project's profits which may still be considerable.[11]

Motion for Dismissal of Charges and the
Question of Prosecutorial Misconduct

On the basis of Stevens' disclosures, the defense claimed prosecutorial misconduct and moved to have the charges against the two remaining defendants dismissed. The defense cited a number of ways in which the prosecution had engaged in "outrageous governmental misconduct." The evidence the defense presented to the court, a 118-page document, contained information substantially derived from Mann's taped interviews of former prosecutor Glenn Stevens.

The defense motion to dismiss focused on prosecutorial misconduct, listing the following points:

(1) the defendants were held without bail on charges which the district attorney never intended to prosecute, with chief prosecutor Lael Rubin lying to the court in order to keep the defendants in jail for over two years;

(2) the prosecution intentionally suppressed evidence that might have exonerated the defendants—suppressed evidence including that the mother who initiated the McMartin investigation was mentally ill and that some of the molestations she alleged occurred when Raymond Buckey was already in jail;

(3) the prosecutors announced that they were ready to go to trial even though they were not, calling witnesses to court to fill time until the prosecutors were ready;

(4) the prosecution told parents of potential child witnesses that the children would never have to testify in front of the defendants;

(5) rather, these parents were told that the children would be able to testify by closed-circuit television, when in fact they would not be able to do so (though, eventually, one child did testify by closed-circuit television); and

(6) the prosecution prevented the defendants, mother and son, from having filial contact with each other in the jail facility.

The district attorney argued that the judge should reject the defense motion because the misconduct charges were based upon flimsy statements from people with a pecuniary stake in the trial's outcome, and were totally "lacking in substance and merit."[12] The prosecution thus argued that the defense motion was based upon unreliable, specious information provided by unreliable sources.[13]

Outright rejecting the defense motion, Judge William Pounders was firm: "I can't throw a case out like this based on the idea that they're [the prosecution] not being 100% truthful with every witness, at all times, over three or four years."[14] Even if evidence was withheld from the defense, the judge said that the charges did not warrant the case being dismissed. Judge Pounders also stated that "a lot of lives have been adversely affected. The public wants to know what the truth is. Why should I dismiss a case, bury the truth forever, rather than seek the truth in a trial?"[15]

The defense then made a motion to disqualify and dismiss prosecutor Lael Rubin because, like Glenn Stevens, she was privy to the same information, and because she had an "intense personal and emotional, as opposed to a merely professional, involvement" in prosecuting the case. This latter point was related to Rubin's alleged "romantic affair" with a Superior Court Judge, Alexander H. William III, whose child had attended the McMartin Preschool.[16]

The defense also attempted to have the judge of record, Roger W. Boren, disqualified on the basis that he was biased toward the prosecution. Defense attorney Daniel Davis asserted that Rubin had communicated with Superior Court Judge Williams about the case, and that Judge Williams in turn had discussed the case with Judge Boren. Judge Boren denied having discussed the case with Judge Williams and further disclaimed knowledge of any relationship between Williams and Rubin. "I deny I am biased or prejudiced against either defendant in this case for any reason or that a fair and impartial trial cannot be held before me," the judge averred.[17] Judge Pounders refused the defense motion, since to do so, he said, would disable the prosecution and create an unequal match between the prosecution and defense.[18]

The court's sense of fairness was then put in place. Ordering an evidentiary hearing to determine if the prosecutors had indeed engaged in discriminatory and invidious prosecution by proceeding against only two of the original seven defendants, Judge Pounders gave the defense two ways to obtain dismissal by showing that: (1) the prosecution pursued the case for political reasons, and (2) the prosecution's evidence against the dismissed defendants was the same as evidence against the two remaining defendants still standing trial, for this would be clear evidence of discriminatory prosecution.[19]

Withheld Evidence

As repeatedly mentioned, information casting doubt on the credibility of Judy Ann Johnson, the original complaining mother, was purposefully repressed and illegally withheld from the defense for ten months by Lael Rubin. Some of Johnson's statements were not given to the defense until June 1986, almost three years after the initial accusation of child molestation, and the statements were in the form of police reports that excluded the more bizarre statements Judy Johnson had made.

Indicating that the documents concerning Judy Johnson were "explosive" and their absence could have had an impact on the defense's case at the preliminary hearing, Judge Pounders faced a dilemma—to go backward to cure the DA's illegal acts, or to go forward with the prosecution of the case.[20] Accusatory and polemical, Johnson had complained that her child not only had been molested, but had been injured by a lion and an elephant while on a McMartin outing.[21] The withheld documents also revealed that Peggy McMartin Buckey allegedly drilled the boy under the armpits and that Raymond Buckey flew in the air. Also , the mother told prosecutors that McMartin teachers put staples in her child's ears, nipples, and tongue, and scissors in his eyes; further, she said her son was involved in a satanic ritual that involved human sacrifice and the drinking of a baby's blood.[22] The mother had also alleged that employees at a local gym had molested her son,[23] and charged that the boy's father—an AWOL marine—had sodomized their child and molested and beaten up their dog.[24]

A copy of the interview summary with the mother was found in the district attorney's office with a typewritten note attached that said "Confidential information. Not to be relayed to defense in McMartin Seven trial, per DA Lael Rubin."[25] Rubin testified that she did not give such an order. In fact, one of the documents in the file was written by Anthony Brunetti, the DA's investigator, indicating that Johnson's child was also unable to identify Raymond Buckey in a lineup, a fact in the interview summary which was also withheld from the defense.[26]

Several days after the documents became public knowledge, the chief prosecutor, Lael Rubin, took the stand and admitted that she waited ten months before giving defense attorneys the information that cast doubt on the credibility of the charges. The defense attorney asked "[Y]our negligence?" "That's correct," she replied.

Lael Rubin also testified that when she originally received the Johnson accusation document in July 1984, she did not believe it. Tim Tyson, a senior investigator for the Los Angeles County District Attorney's office, testified that he had never spoken with the woman's young son about the alleged incidents.[27] There was then no legal evidence to support the district attorney's original contention that a crime had been committed.[28]

Rubin, meanwhile, tried to offer explanations for her delay in turning the information over to the defense, a step she is legally required to take in order to allow the defense to make a proper presentation and evaluation during the preliminary hearing. She squirmed, telling the court she intended to temporarily delay turning over information about a public official who had been accused by Johnson, then contending that two key Johnson documents were inadvertently mislaid, and finally that she was negligent in waiting ten months before giving the defense attorneys the information.[29]

The question, however, involved whether or not withholding the evidence was a deliberate act—making it a crime. Rubin admitted in her testimony that she had deliberately delayed giving the defense information that Johnson had alleged that Roberta Weintraub—a Los Angeles school board member—had molested her son.[30] Rubin said that she considered the allegation against Weintraub to be ridiculous, though she did not explain why that allegation was ridiculous and Judy Johnson's other contentions against the McMartin defendants were not.

Glenn Stevens was also called to testify in a pre-trial hearing. Though he refused to answer most questions citing his right against self-incrimination, the defense attorneys asked that Stevens be granted immunity from prosecution.[31] Though both the defense and prosecution urged the judge to compel him to testify, Stevens refused to answer all questions, the judge ruling that Stevens had the right to assert the Fifth Amendment, his constitutional right against self-incrimination. In the interim, the State Attorney General decided not to file charges against Stevens for violating the California Business and Professional Code, referring the matter to Los Angeles City Attorney James Hahn for consideration of misdemeanor charges.[32]

Both the State Attorney General and the Los Angeles City Attorney finally asked Judge Pounders to grant Glenn Stevens immunity from prosecution. They argued that the potential significance of his testimony outweighed the potential prosecution of a misdemeanor charge against him.[33] They also noted that if he cooperated in testifying, he would not be prosecuted for conspiracy to obstruct justice, for unauthorized removal of a public record, or for advising the defense about a matter he formerly prosecuted.

Under a grant of immunity, Stevens testified that the entire prosecution team had suppressed evidence about the mental instability of Judy Johnson and that, although the prosecutors were under a court order to turn over all evidence they had to the defense, they told police to withhold evidence that they did not want the defense to have. Stevens also testified that Lael Rubin knew that the defense was entitled to receive the information immediately in 1984, but decided to wait, and that the prosecutors lied to the judge and over-filed charges to keep the defendants from being granted bail.[34] Similarly, the prosecutors withheld a letter written by Judy Johnson that said that she could not distinguish between fantasy and reality. Stevens stated that his motivation for disclosing information contained on the tapes was to bring out the truth showing that the McMartin defendants were innocent.[35]

Outside of the courtroom Rubin said that Stevens was lying.[36] Nevertheless, it was revealed in court that pertinent documents had indeed been withheld by the district attorney and, without them, the defense was not able to call Judy Johnson into court or otherwise cross-examine her about her emotional state—whether or not she was mentally ill.

Information about additional incidents of withholding evidence surfaced when it was alleged that Stevens himself had told investigators of other private schools in the area not to turn over evidence to the McMartin prosecution because they, in turn, would be legally compelled to give it to the defense.[37]

Deputy District Attorney Christine Johnson also testified that fellow prosecutors had intentionally withheld the statements made by Judy Johnson.[38] She added that such withholding of evidence and the conflict among the investigators about the defendants' guilt had led her to ask for reassignment to another case after the preliminary hearing. She also testified that Rubin knew about the mother's accusations that a school board member had molested her son, but that Rubin was determined not to turn the information over to the defense.[39] Obviously, her testimony contradicted that of Rubin's, who said that she only wanted to delay turning over the material for a few days and then forgot about it.[40]

From the very beginning, then, there were no grounds for the DA to believe a crime was committed. Judy Johnson's accusations were essentially charges of multiple sexual molestation of her child by numerous adults—charges that were not investigated, were not proven, yet were elaborated by the police and the print and electronic media, and infused in the minds of impressionable youngsters by police investigators, the district attorney's office, CII therapists, and the children's parents. The public at large was given their version of the truth.

After a three-month hearing, Judge Pounders determined that the prosecutors neither intentionally nor negligently withheld important information from the defense. "My conclusion is there was not intentional suppression of material evidence by anyone in the district attorney's office—with the exception of Mr. Stevens," the judge stated.[41] It seemed unfathomable that—despite two out of three deputy district attorneys previously assigned to the preliminary hearing now testifying that evidence had been purposefully withheld from the defense—the defense's charges of "outrageous conduct" were so brashly dismissed.

Death of Judy Johnson, the First Complaining Mother

The key accuser, Judy Ann Johnson, was found dead almost simultaneously with the motion of bail for Raymond Buckey. Foul play was suspected. Although there were no visible signs of trauma, because of Johnson's involvement in the McMartin case, Los Angeles County sheriff's homicide officers were asked to pursue an investigation into her death.[42] To the prosecution's surprise, the defense team said that her death would damage their clients' position. "It's a tragic circumstance all the way around," defense attorney Dean Gits said, noting that "[H]er death will hurt the defense much more than the prosecution because I believe she is the genesis of the allegations and the catalyst that perpetuated them." The prosecution argued that her testimony was not critical, involving only one of the 101 counts in the case.[43]

Though the first evaluation of Johnson's death was inconclusive, it appeared that she died of an internal hemorrhage. Subsequently, it was announced that she had died of liver disease associated with her addiction to alcohol.[44] This, the defense argued, was the source of her wild delusions and false accusations—both of which the prosecution and the CII possibly played upon and pursued in the name of convictions to protect the public.

Pre-Trial Defense Motions

Questions and doubts about the credibility of Johnson's initial accusations, however, no longer mattered for the two McMartin defendants. They still had to face a jury trial in a jurisdiction where the overwhelming majority of residents firmly believed in their guilt. The defense thus felt the need to delay the trial, getting more time to lessen the impact of the pre-trial publicity and prepare for the jury selection and the presentation of trial materials. The defense also thought that continuing disclosures of prosecutorial misconduct prior to the trial might generate strong doubts about the strength of prosecution's charges and possibly benefit the defendants' chance of receiving a fair trial. Pre-trial motions were one way to play for time.

Generally, pre-trial motions involving jury selection are important defense strategies to delay a trial, to cast doubt on the strength of prosecutors' charges, and to provide the defense counsel additional time to prepare for the actual trial. In the McMartin case, although defense counsel prepared a number of pre-trial motions, we only review three related to the issue of jury selection and defense strategies to secure a fair trial for the defendants: (1) a change of venue, (2) extended *voir dire* conditions, and (3) a challenge to the jury array. The following section evaluates how those pre-trial motions played important functions in the defense strategy to delay the trial, educate the judge and the public about defendants' difficulties in receiving a fair trial, and offer possible strategies to secure a retrial if the defendants are adjudicated guilty by the jury.

Motion to Change Venue

The defense first notified Judge Pounders in early January, 1987, that a motion was to be filed asking for a change of venue because extensive mass media publicity surrounding the case meant that the defendants could not receive a fair trial in Los Angles County. The defense motion specifically requested separate proceedings against two McMartin defendants in counties other than Los Angeles.[45]

Prior to the McMartin trial, the last time a change of venue was granted in Los Angeles County was in 1973, in a case involving the shotgun slaying of Joyce Ann Huff, a 4-year-old Hawaiian Garden girl. Los Angeles Superior Court Judge Julius Leetham ordered the trial moved from Norwalk to Redwood City in San Mateo County, near San Francisco, because of what he called "massive saturation" publicity about the case in Los Angeles. Three men charged with the child's murder were nonetheless convicted by the jury.

Most recently, a change of venue was granted in the infamous 1992 Rodney King beating trial, the judge ordering the trial moved from Los Angeles Central Superior Court to Ventura County, just north of Los Angeles County. While racial and ethnic minorities composed approximately 60% of L.A. residents over 18 years of age, whites made up nearly 80% of residents in the City of Simi Valley where the Ventura County Superior Court was located. Eventually a predominantly white jury tried and exonerated all four white L.A. police officers on assault charges for the beating of the black motorist. The acquittal brought into focus the anger of racial minorities, who had long criticized the Los Angeles Police Department (LAPD) for its use of excessive force against members of racial and ethnic minorities. The L.A. riot that followed resulted in nearly 60 deaths, 2,400 injuries, more than 14,000 arrests, 1,400 buildings damaged or destroyed, one billion dollars in property damage, and the loss of 11,500 jobs.[46]

The McMartin defense motion for a change of venue documented findings that the L.A. venue was worse than an alternative venue that the court could designate. The defense made additional surveys of other California counties and learned that a more impartial jury might be secured if the trial was moved out of the Southern California "media market" in the direction of San Francisco. The survey also found that Orange County, just southeast of Los Angeles, might be marginally better than Los Angeles or Ventura Counties.

The defense motion for a change of venue specifically stated the following:

[V]irtually all of the media reporting has been extremely negative toward the defendants, especially Raymond Buckey. The early coverage of the case was particularly negative setting the stage for what is known in the social psychology literature as a primacy or imprinting effect. As a result, it would take massive amounts of very positive coverage to overcome the initial imprint. This [initial] media coverage in itself would make a change of venue imperative ... based upon the media analysis and the results of the random sample survey of potential jurors, that both the general atmosphere and the specific prejudices against the defendant make a fair trial virtually impossible in this venue. Raymond Buckey has been prejudged to be guilty of a terrible crime—one for which there is widespread concern in Los Angeles ... and for which some people would impose harsh and unusual punishment. These conditions make a change of venue imperative for the selection of a fair and impartial jury.[47]

In March, 1987, Judge Pounders rejected the defense motion to move the trial to another county or jurisdiction, specifying that publicity had actually turned in the defense's favor, citing a Raymond Buckey television interview in which Buckey himself had judged that "the tide has turned." The judge also noted, after the charges were dropped against five of the defendants, the public's view of the case changed dramatically. "It caused a lot of people, myself included, to doubt the strength of the case against the remaining defendants," he offered.[48]

Prosecutor Lael Rubin called the judge's logic "astute and correct." Anticipating the judge's decision, the defense insisted that the decision would be appealed. Dean Gits noted, "all I have left is hope, I guess—hope that if the court of appeal won't look at this case, that we can find a jury that can somehow stand above the political pressures and the prejudice that I think is still in the county."[49]

Motions for Extensive Voir Dire *Sessions*

Even though the change of venue motion was denied, the defense effectively utilized the motion to persuade the judge to grant the defense extended *voir dire* conditions to screen potential jurors separately and individually by examining their biases, life conditions, and attitudes that might affect the outcome of the trial. Thus, the change of venue motion was strategically followed by motions requesting extended *voir dire* conditions. The former motion was designed to show that intense publicity made it almost impossible for the defendants to have a fair trial in a given jurisdiction. As it was denied, the defense then moved to point out the importance of instituting additional mechanisms to ensure that during *voir dire* biased and prejudiced jurors would be eliminated from serving on the jury.

The *voir dire* process is considered a fundamental guarantee of a defendant's Sixth Amendment right to trial by a fair and impartial jury. *Voir dire* examination is designed to elicit information about each prospective juror that will indicate her or his ability to serve in an impartial and unbiased manner—a process in which attorneys, or a judge in some courts, question a prospective juror.

Voir dire literally means "to speak the truth." Based on the answers offered, an attorney attempts to pick the most favorable jury for his or her client by using two types of challenges to remove potentially unfavorable jurors: (1) a peremptory challenge is a challenge of a prospective juror in which no explanation need be given for disqualifying a juror,[50] and (2) a challenge for cause is a challenge of a prospective juror in which an attorney must give the court legally cognizable grounds for disqualifying the juror, such as severe prejudice against either side.

While *voir dire* is considered to be a routine part of the jury selection process, many jurisdictions limit the extent of its usage. In California, for example, Proposition 115, which was passed in 1990, eliminated attorney-conducted *voir dire* and shifted the screening of prospective jurors to the presiding judge. Under the new system, attorneys are instructed to provide the judge with a list of potential questions that may be used to examine biases of prospective jurors during *voir dire*. However, the judge is not required to use all the questions provided by the attorneys. Similarly, while the judge is given the discretion to allow attorney-conducted *voir dire,* she or he can limit the length of *voir dire*. In *People v. Soto* (No. CR 5581, 1994), a capital felony case which took place in Santa Cruz County, California, for example, the judge allowed the use of attorney-conducted *voir dire*. However, the judge set the limit on the length of *voir dire,* and the defense attorneys were given a total of three hours to complete the *voir dire* process, in which 120 jurors were to be questioned and screened—spending an average of one and half minutes per juror.

Though the McMartin child molestation trial took place prior to the passage of Proposition 115, the judge still held similar discretion to expand or limit the extent of *voir dire*. The defense strategy attempted to expand the range of *voir dire* to give defense counsel wide latitude in *voir dire* questions, including: (1) the use of pre-*voir dire* jury questionnaires; (2) the inclusion of questions and information solicitations, covering a wide variety of socioeconomic, attitudinal, and behavioral measures as well as information about jurors' backgrounds so that potential biases and prejudice against child molestation and the defendants could be identified and examined; and (3) sequestered *voir dire* sessions in which potential jurors were to be questioned separately without the presence of other fellow jurors and the media.

In order to expand the scope of *voir dire* sessions, one of the most effective methods has been to alert the judge to potential biases that jury panels may have towards the defendants. Generally, a survey is considered an important tool to help the defense team educate the judge about the importance of expanding the *voir dire* in order to ferret out biases of prospective jurors assigned to the case.

The McMartin defense took the offensive, arguing that potential jurors in the jurisdiction were biased against their clients. Referring to the previous community survey findings, the defense contended that the expanded *voir dire* conditions were possibly the only means to select a pool of jurors with less bias and prejudice against the defendants. With the court's approval, critical examination of prospective jurors assigned to the case was thus seen as absolutely necessary for the defense to obtain a fair trial.

Selecting a Fair and Impartial Jury

The first step in understanding the difficulties involved in selecting a fair and impartial jury is a recognition that every prospective juror has biases and prejudices that are likely to affect one's ability to be impartial. These biases have been repeatedly documented in the context of criminal proceedings.

Surveys of prospective jurors conducted by the National Jury Project in jurisdictions throughout the country have revealed that from 23% to 58% of persons eligible for jury service would require a criminal defendant to prove his or her innocence, despite a judge's instructions to the contrary.[51] These survey results have been confirmed by other independent national studies. The National Center for State Courts commissioned a survey of 1,800 households nationwide and found that 37% of the population believe it is the responsibility of the defendant to prove his or her innocence in a criminal case.[52] The defense survey also showed that 47.1% of Los Angeles County residents and 38.3% of potential jurors in the Los Angeles Central Court jurisdiction believed that a defendant in a criminal trial should be required to prove his or her innocence.

Using these surveys, the defense argued that it was likely that a substantial proportion of prospective jurors would enter the courtroom holding opinions that do not conform to fundamental principles of the American criminal justice system. Further, these biases could not be compensated for by instructions from the trial court. It has been found repeatedly that even after service as a trial juror, a substantial proportion of persons are unable to correctly understand the principles of the presumption of innocence, burden of proof, and reasonable doubt. Even after trial, 50% of instructed jurors did not understand that the defendant did not have to present evidence of innocence. Jurors' average comprehension levels of trial instructions were 51% among 1,000 serving jurors in felony cases.[53] The subjects of both studies cited were actual jurors. Thus, prospective jurors enter the courtroom with problematic attitudes and opinions concerning the criminal justice system, law and order, and the role of jurors. These attitudes can have an effect on a juror's ability to comprehend and evaluate evidence.

If a fair and impartial jury is to be selected, these attitudes must be elicited, revealed, and probed during the *voir dire* examination so that prospective jurors whose attitudes and opinions will interfere with their evaluation of evidence can be excused. The McMartin defense thus considered the use of pre-*voir dire* questionnaires crucial, because the questionnaire might reveal jurors' backgrounds, attitudes, and potential biases as well as the extent to which they were influenced by the pervasive media scrutiny of the defendants and alleged crimes.

The defense counsel also considered it important for jurors to be sequestered during the *voir dire* session, creating proper conditions for extensive screening. While traditional and open *voir dire* proceedings involve the questioning of jurors as a group, the defense sought sequestered and individualized screening sessions to minimize media influence, as well as to limit possible "contamination" effects of having other jurors present in the courtroom.

Open *voir dire* is considered to be inadequate and poses special problems in highly publicized cases like the McMartin case. Dr. Craig Haney, an attorney and professor of psychology at the University of California, Santa Cruz, argued that prospective jurors enter the courtroom with biases and prejudices that are likely to affect their ability to be impartial in a given case, and that attitudes and behaviors are shaped and influenced by conditions in the courtroom. In one case, Dr. Haney's submitted affidavit argued for such sequestration and individuation. His affidavit was also made available to the McMartin defense counsel in requesting the extended *voir dire* conditions, which stated:

> During *voir dire,* a prospective juror's ability to reveal feelings or facts that may greatly influence the decision-making process is seriously inhibited by the prospective juror's needs to appear to be as good or as acceptable as other potential jurors.... *[V]oir dire* questioning of individual prospective jurors out of the presence of other panelists can help to minimize the impact of many of the social

psychological factors.... Individual *voir dire* minimizes those problems in several ways: (a) a smaller "audience" reduces prospective jurors' concern for their peers' opinions of them; (b) questioning of jurors individually minimizes opportunities for jurors to pick up cues from others about socially approved responses; (c) prospective jurors will be less able to contrive to be either seated or excused because they will not have the opportunity to observe others being questioned; and finally (d) questioning of jurors out of the presence of others eliminates the possibility that panelists will be exposed to or "contaminated" by the prejudicial statements or revelations of other prospective jurors.[54]

The conditions of extended *voir dire* were of particular importance to the defense because the prosecutors, the DA, and parents had already appeared on local and national TV programs and their opinions were freely circulated in the print media. CII interviewers and prosecutors attended many meetings held by parents and child abuse therapists, and it was possible that some prospective jurors might also have attended the meetings or had opportunities to talk with them, so that they may have been influenced by views shared by the prosecution, therapists, and parents of the alleged victims.

Thus, even though the change of venue motion was denied, the defense strategically tried to extend the conditions for *voir dire*. Defense counsel was able to educate the judge that the extent of media publicity made it almost impossible to obtain a pool of fair-minded, impartial jurors to try the defendants under the traditional jury selection method. Judge Pounders then considered the merits of the McMartin defense's arguments that the media had influenced the public's perceptions and had made it impossible to find a fair and impartial jury under the traditional and standard open *voir dire* session. The judge also considered the possible use of pre-*voir dire* questionnaires so that prospective jurors' biases and prejudices could be effectively evaluated and examined by the attorneys.

The judge finally granted the extended *voir dire* conditions, allowing the use of pre-*voir dire* questionnaires and sequestered screening sessions, with each defense counsel questioning and examining each and every potential juror assigned to the trial. The questionnaire was first drafted by the defense counsel with the help of the present authors, later evaluated by the judge and the prosecution, and finally accepted by the judge for use in the case. The questionnaire contained 118 separate questions and more than 200 sub-items to be answered by potential jurors. The judge, however, required that potential jurors' responses on the questionnaires also be made available to the prosecution.

Judge Pounders' decision to grant extended *voir dire* condition was not an anomaly. In many highly publicized trials in Los Angeles, including the Reginald Denny beating trial and the O. J. Simpson trial, L.A. superior court judges have granted defense requests for extended *voir dire* conditions. In the Reginald Denny beating trial, Judge John W. Ouderkirk even went one step further by assigning a private jury consultant to assist the defense in the jury selection process and to select the final jury. Judge Ouderkirk might well have felt that providing defense counsel expert jury consultation in selecting an impartial jury was an important step showing the court's concern for a fair and just trial for the black defendants.

Motion to Challenge the Jury Array

The defense also prepared a motion to challenge the jury array to obtain a fair and impartial jury for the defendants. Though defense counsel had planned to file the motion to challenge the jury array prior to jury selection, they did not notify the judge of the motion.

The challenge of a jury array motion is another defense strategy to delay the trial and provide a legal basis for possible judicial reviews by higher courts, if the defendants are adjudicated guilty in trial. Though the jury challenge motion was not submitted to the court, it is important to examine its content as well as the defense's strategy in later submitting such a motion to the court.

Following the defense motion to challenge the array, in a criminal case, if the defendant is then convicted by the jury, the appellate court may be requested to review whether or not the jury which convicted the defendant can be challenged on the following two constitutional grounds: (1) the jury pool or the specific jury panel failed to represent a fair cross-section of the community; and (2) the method of its composition is such that specific "cognizable" groups have not had equal opportunity to be part of the jury pool. These are due process and/or equal protection claims made through the Fifth, Sixth, and Fourteenth Amendments. The U.S. Supreme Court has given "cognizable" status to the following groups to be protected against discrimination in jury selection: blacks, Hispanics, women, and daily wage earners.[55]

In California, in addition to those four cognizable variables, age has also been considered to constitute an important factor in securing a community cross-section for fair and representative jury panels. For example, young people have generally been underrepresented on jury panels because of a number of logistical difficulties and institutional problems of jury selection processes. As the next chapter reveals, the community survey of residents in the McMartin court jurisdiction revealed that younger jurors were less likely than older jurors to assume that the defendants were guilty of child molestation.

So the McMartin defense sought to show that systematic exclusion of younger jurors from service led to a biased and partial jury that would lean more towards conviction. The defense motion challenging the array thus cut to the quick, arguing that Raymond Buckey's peers would be unfairly excluded from the jury itself:

> Raymond Buckey is a defendant in Los Angeles County Superior Court. He is charged with various counts of sexual molestation of children and conspiracy. He currently resides in County Jail without bond. Raymond Buckey is a white male, twenty-eight years of age, [of] lower middle class socioeconomic status with two years of college education.... Raymond Buckey's trial is expected to be inordinately long. As a result, an unusually large number of prospective jurors will be excused for economic hardship, pursuant to Rules of Court 4.5. These prospective jurors excused from economic hardship tend to be disproportionately young adults. Young adults, even for normal length trials, tend to be underrepresented on Los Angeles Superior Court jury panels. As a result, the Los Angeles County jury selection procedures will result in a significant shortfall of young adults in Buckey's array.
>
> Such a shortfall will completely strip Raymond Buckey of a critical constitutional right, under the United States Constitution, Amendment I, and the California Constitution, Article I, Section 16. Therefore, Raymond Buckey brings the instant motion to preserve a simple time honored right to a jury of peers ... [the] defendant respectfully requests that this court grant his motion to challenge the jury array.[56]

It was a powerful challenge to the array and the right to be tried by one's peers. The survey results showed that young adults, age 18 to 30, were underrepresented in jury panels by 53%, suggesting that more than half of young adults were systematically excluded from serving on the jury at Los Angeles Central Court. This disparity substantially exceeded the allowable underrepresentation, all jury panels being constitutionally deficient in young adults. Although courts rule differently on what constitutes significant underrepresentation, the Los Angeles County figures were in the same range as those accepted as unconstitutional in other major California and federal cases.[57]

Jury challenge cases in Los Angeles Central Superior Court had already shown that established law mandates change in the Los Angeles court system. Not only did the survey result show the deficits in young adult representation, but also many other jury challenges substantiated that the Los Angeles Central jurisdiction had suffered woefully from significant underrepresentation of racial and ethnic minorities, the poor, and women.[58]

The defense motion thus argued that as each day went by, for each trial conducted by juries selected from unrepresentative cross-sections, public confidence in the legal system was diminished, and the legitimacy of California courts was being undermined. The defense also contended that the significant underrepresentation of young adults might jeopardize the defendant's Sixth Amendment right to a jury of peers, assuming that young adults in defendant's age groups shared similar life experiences, distinctive outlooks, manners, roles, and behavior patterns, and thus might show greater understanding of and empathy with the defendant.

Though the defense jury challenge motion was not officially filed with the court, critical examinations of jury arrays in Los Angeles Central court had clearly assisted the defense to examine the unrepresentative nature of jury panels and prepare for scientific selection in choosing the McMartin jury. Thus, as the next chapter shows, the defense was able to rely on extended *voir dire* conditions and systematic jury selection methods to secure a larger proportion of younger adults for the jury.

Conclusions

Two of the three prosecutors who had been assigned to the preliminary hearing testified to prosecutorial misconduct in which the chief prosecutor, Lael Rubin, intentionally suppressed and hid information from the defense.

The testimony by co-prosecutor Christine Johnson and videotaped interviews by former prosecutor Glenn Stevens revealed crucial and important information which had been intentionally suppressed by the prosecution's office and was not given to the defense, including that: (1) Judy Johnson's child failed to identify Raymond Buckey in a lineup; (2) Johnson also lodged molestation charges against Raymond Buckey, as well as Roberta Weintraub, a Los Angeles school board member, Johnson's estranged husband, and employees at a local gym; (3) her child and family dog had been sodomized by her husband; (4) her child had been injured by wild animals including a lion and an elephant at the McMartin preschool; (5) Raymond Buckey was able to fly through the air; (6) Peggy

McMartin Buckey drilled Johnson's child under the armpits; (7) McMartin preschool teachers put staples in her child's ears, nipples, and tongue, and scissors in his eyes; and (8) her son was involved in a satanic ritual, saw human sacrifices, and was forced to drink a baby's blood.

Johnson's bizarre charges were very similar to the stories of many of the alleged child victims who were interviewed at the CII. At the preliminary hearing, children testified that they were forced to watch the killing of small animals, and some children said that they had drunk blood and engaged in satanic rituals. Is it possible that the children's accounts might have been adult renderings based on the original allegation of Judy Johnson? Further, is it also possible that Johnson's stories might have helped condition or pre-program CII personnel and, through them, the children's stories that were presented in court—even though Johnson's original charges regarding her son were never investigated, followed up, or evaluated?

We also need to ask some critical questions about the criminal justice system, the adversarial system that relies on a fair balance of opposing forces. Prosecutors are legally mandated to pursue justice, not simply convictions of those charged. Yet one of the greatest threats to rational and fair fact-finding in criminal cases comes from prosecutors' intentional withholding of evidence that might prove a defendant's innocence. Due to the superiority of law enforcement's investigative powers and resources, as well as their early access to crucial information and evidence, it is not unusual for prosecutors to become aware of information, or even proof, that might exonerate a defendant. While it is difficult to speculate on the motivation for the prosecutors intentionally withholding exculpatory evidence that might prove the defendants' innocence, such misconduct represents a powerful example of the abuse of power by the prosecution's office.

In order to effectively manage the problem of prosecutorial misconduct and to obtain a fair trial for the accused, the defense counsel filed a number of pre-trial motions with help from social and behavioral scientists. While the change of venue motion was denied by the court, findings used in the motion nevertheless persuaded the judge to acknowledge the significant media influence on the public's perceptions of the probable outcome of the case. The judge then carefully considered the defense motions requesting extended *voir dire* conditions and granted sequestered, individualized *voir dire* without the presence of other jurors and media. Similarly, the judge allowed the use of pre-*voir dire* questionnaires so that all prospective jurors assigned to the case were required to provide answers to many sensitive questions about their attitudes and perceptions about the McMartin case, their own sexual abuse experience, if any, and other sensitive issues relating to the case. The answers were used by the defense to assess potential biases and prejudices of prospective jurors.

The judge also granted extended attorney-conducted *voir dire* so that the attorneys were allowed to spend a considerable amount of time in questioning each and every prospective juror in a closed session. And though the defense did not formally challenge the jury array by a timely motion, the study of skewed jury pools in the court district allowed the defense to skillfully prepare for jury selection.

Chapter 7

Impaneling the McMartin Jury: Scientific Defense Jury Selection[1]

Pariahs, jailed with paltry evidence against them; frightened, vulnerable, impressionable children as their accusers; the McMartins stood practically alone. The vast majority of prospective jurors in the Los Angeles Central Superior Court District believed them guilty before the presentation of a shred of trial evidence. Selection of an impartial and fair-minded jury would be difficult, if not impossible. How to defend the heretics from a maddened public, their attorneys pondered. One way was to breach the tradition-bound methods of picking those who would judge these modern-day outcasts.

This meant going beyond the limits of previous jury selection practices. In the vast majority of trials, lawyers have traditionally selected juries based on inadequate information and ephemeral judgments. During the past several decades, however, some experts have begun to critically evaluate jury selection procedures and to assist in picking individual jurors using empirical information that is analyzed by sophisticated techniques. These experts have also helped develop effective *voir dire* questionnaires. Such methods have been developed and used in several well-publicized trials such as that of Black Panther Huey Newton in 1968 and the Harrisburg Seven in 1972, as well as in other trials that either touched on sensitive political and racial issues, or questioned the bounds of equity in certain death penalty cases.[2] Similar scientific methods have been used in trials with great pre-trial publicity, including the Angela Davis trial, the Vietnam Veterans Against the War case, the Attica Prison rebellion trial, the Wounded Knee trial of Indian activists, the trial of former U.S. Attorney General John Mitchell and Maurice Stans, the trial of Joan Little, the Rodney King beating trials, the trial of the Menendez brothers, and the media-driven trial of O. J. Simpson in Los Angeles.

Scientific jury selection is really a method of finding fair-minded peers of those charged with crimes. Jurors are sought not as peers of the public, of the judge, of the prosecutor, or of defense attorneys, but as peers of the defendants. As such, critical evaluation of prospective jurors is considered to be essential, especially in well-publicized criminal trials in which prosecutors have a great deal of leeway in deciding what charges against defendants will be brought, in regulating the extent of pre-trial information to be released to the media, and in deciding which regulations or laws apply.[3]

If fair-minded peers and impartial jurors are to be secured, how will they be shielded from influences that might jeopardize their independence of thought and will? The procedure of sequestration, for example, is sometimes used by courts to insulate jurors from publicity about the trial and to limit their access to inadmissible information about defendants. Sequestration requires all jurors to be housed in a hotel or motel for the duration of the trial to protect them from outside influences. While sequestration is a device used to enable the court to conduct a fair trial without putting limits on the freedom of the press, the hardships due to the loss of time and pay are likely to result in a jury that is itself very selective and thus not representative of the defendants' peers from the community where the alleged crime was committed.[4]

Due to the small compensation for jury service, the excluded and underrepresented are often persons in less-stable secondary labor markets, those in lower level positions receiving less pay, racial minorities, the poor, the young, and women with small children. The overrepresented in a sequestered jury are likely to be persons with high incomes, prestigious occupations, and a high level education. Thus, they may be more secure and less liberal, and may identify their attitudes about crimes and criminal justice with those of conservative judges and prosecutors. Research indicates that the resulting skewed jury representation exerts a significant influence on trial outcomes, increasing the likelihood of conviction.[5]

Compared with the great leeway and state resources provided to the prosecution, short of the millions spent in the O. J. Simpson trial, the defense typically has little to overcome such handicaps. Critical and scientific jury selection is one of the few options available for the defense to influence the jury composition. Though scientific jury selection methods have the potential for more frequent use in the future, particularly in criminal trials with extensive pre-trial media exposure or civil jury trials involving large multinational corporations with substantial economic resources, many questions remain about such techniques. Exactly what techniques can be legitimately used? Do they deserve the label "scientific" or not? Can they really make a difference in a jury's decision? Isn't this simply tampering with the jury to mold a favorable balance rather than an impartial jury?

In this chapter these questions will be reviewed using examples from the McMartin Preschool trial. The trial affirms that critical, scientific jury selection is particularly important when public exposure to preindictment and unsubstantiated materials plays an important role in shaping public perceptions of the defendants' alleged crimes and possible trial outcomes in well-publicized criminal cases.

With the public avidly following and being influenced by the effusive media release of "evidence" and interpretations of the McMartin case, the following questions arose:

> Would it be possible to find an impartial jury to judge the children's testimony and the available, though meager, forensic evidence against those charged in the McMartin investigation?
> Would it be possible to develop a trial jury composed of a fair cross-section of the community comprised of the defendants' peers where the alleged crimes were committed?

Defense attorneys thought not and attempted to marshal ways to overcome those handicaps by utilizing critical procedures to select the McMartin jury.

Social scientists were mobilized to devise statistical and observational methods to evaluate prospective jurors and examine their partiality. Techniques used in the McMartin trial were the product of the collaboration of defense attorneys with others, as well as the present authors' group of social scientists, who had previously been involved in jury selection in a variety of cases.[6]

Jury Selection: Community Cross-Section and Biases

To understand how a jury is drawn and composed, one has to take a broad view of the panorama of peers drawn into a trial setting. The logic of the jury selection process is based on screening—from a target population to those who finally enter the jury box. The purpose of the selection procedure is to choose a jury of peers that reflects a cross-section of a particular community where the alleged crimes have been committed by those charged. This is legally accomplished by a random selection of jurors from the geographic district in which a particular court convenes so that all qualified residents are given an equal opportunity to serve. Once the jurors are chosen, they are then viewed as being both impartial and qualified to represent the community's collective sentiments and interests.

The step-by-step process involves defining the population eligible for jury service, sending jury qualification questionnaires to randomly selected candidates, constructing a qualified juror's file of those who meet various requirements, assigning potential jurors to the court, placing those who actually show up for jury service on the jury panel, screening the jurors by *voir dire* to eliminate jurors who might be biased and unacceptable to both the prosecuting and defense attorneys, and final selection of specific jurors who will actually decide the case under consideration.[7]

Though the rationale of the jury system is to lend legitimacy to decisions through verdicts reached by a cross-section of the community, shortcomings of the process are well known. How closely the jury reflects a community's cross-section depends upon the success of the procedures by which jurors are chosen. At each stage of the selection process, there are many factors and informal filtering techniques influencing the fairness of jury participation and these can have a cumulative effect on the age, racial, ethnic, gender, economic, and political composition of a jury.

In California, one of the statutory regulations authorizing a *voir dire* challenge for cause is that the prospective juror has "the state of mind" preventing the candidate from acting with impartiality and without prejudice. Even so, there is evidence to show that, despite the explicit objective of revealing juror biases to identify and obtain impartial jurors, *voir dire* may elicit, accentuate, and even enlarge juror partiality. In criminal cases this is because the prosecution tends to look for prospective jurors with certain characteristics, such as middle-age, middle-class, and white. This type of juror is assumed to identify with the prosecution rather than the defendant and thus is more likely than other jurors to convict. By contrast, defense attorneys tend to seek jurors with certain qualities and views, who are least "offensive," who can approach a particular case with minimum prejudice against the defendant; or who look like, act like, or think like a defendant whose situation and life experience the juror can comprehend, empathize with, yet judge fairly. For both prosecution and defense, then, *voir dire* becomes a fight to enlarge the jury's bias toward one's position, thereby undermining jury impartiality and the statutory requirements for a jury representing a fair cross-section of the community—all of which raises the question of the possible fairness of a "scientific" method being used to select jurors.

Scientific Jury Selection

Scientific jury selection involves a number of strategic assessments of the socio-demographic, attitudinal, and behavioral background of prospective jurors. While the process may be undertaken by the prosecution, most often scientific jury selection is carried out by defense attorneys with the aid of consultants. In the McMartin case, the defense sought to impanel jurors with particular qualities, using both its peremptory challenges (i.e., those without cause) and challenges for cause to eliminate jurors with certain biases. Rather than using their own subjective and intuitive sense to evaluate prospective jurors to influence the jury composition, the defense attorneys mobilized social scientists and criminologists as jury consultants to prepare scientific questionnaires to be submitted to potential jurors in determining their preconceptions, biases, feelings, attitudes, and abilities to reason logically and "legally" about a hypothetical situation that approximated in broad outline the McMartin case.

More than simple community biases and media-influenced pathologies were at stake. The McMartin trial was to take place in the Central Superior Court Judicial District and its 20-mile radius located primarily in the City of Los Angeles—a zone of diverse racial and ethnic backgrounds.

In order to develop a profile of prospective jurors for the case, the community's demographics were mapped and analyzed. The comparisons of eligible juror profiles at several stages of jury selection revealed unique and significant demographic and socioeconomic differences among prospective jurors at the following junctures in the jury selection process: (1) the eligible population for the trial; (2) the prospective jurors who responded to a community survey of eligible jurors in the Central District; and (3) the potential jurors who actually appeared at the Central Superior Court and were assigned to the McMartin trial.

The 1980 U.S. Census information shows that 34.7% of prospective jurors in Los Angeles County are black and Hispanic. However, the population in the Central District is characterized by an even higher proportion of racial and ethnic minorities, containing 42.3% for the same groups.[8] It also differs significantly from the remainder of Los Angeles County in other demographic characteristics such as education and income. Thus, in the Central District, there is a larger proportion of prospective jurors with lower incomes, with less than a high-school education, and a smaller proportion of eligibles with a college education than for the whole county. This is probably because the higher concentration of a racial minority population with limited opportunities may have lowered the average educational attainment among potential jurors in the jurisdiction.

According to the survey findings on prospective jurors in the L.A. Central Superior Court jurisdiction as examined in Chapter 4, a group of potential jurors (who responded to the survey questionnaire) can be considered a proxy for those who responded to the jury summons and appeared at the courthouse, because two groups of the nonrespondents were already eliminated from the analysis, i.e., those classified as *undeliverables* and *recalcitrants*.

In comparing the survey results with the racial and ethnic composition of L.A. Central District residents, overrepresentation of white and black potential jurors is found in the survey, and thus the jury panel (+ 10.0% and 5.0% for whites and blacks, respectively). However, the proportion of Hispanics is significantly lower than the eligible population (−19.8%). Similarly, females were underrepresented, meaning that the majority of people in the jury panel was male. The jury panel also shows a significant underrepresentation of younger persons, especially those under 30 years of age. In addition, the underrepresented groups included those with a lower level education. For example, 34.1% of the eligible population in the community had less than a high-school education, while only 4.7% of the juror group in the panel had less than a high-school education. On the other hand, those with a college education were overrepresented in the jury panel. In fact, two-thirds of respondents had some college experience or had completed college—a surprising but hardly an unexpected finding.

Finally, survey data were collected from a court-distributed questionnaire administered to the 205 prospective jurors who were assigned to the case. Those prospective jurors who appeared at the courthouse and were assigned to the trial had somewhat different demographic and socioeconomic characteristics than those from Los Angeles County, the Central District, or from the community survey. The assigned potential jurors were more likely to be black, with fewer whites and Hispanics; and they were more likely to be male than female. There was a lower proportion of younger persons (under 30) among the assigned jurors than resided in the County or the District, and there was a disproportionately higher percentage of persons with at least some college level education.

Overall, then, both the community survey and survey of prospective jurors demonstrated that the group of jurors assigned to the McMartin trial did not reflect a fair cross-section of the community population in the jurisdiction. However, the discrepancy between the potential jurors in the community and assigned jurors was expected due to a number of legal and extra-legal factors influencing jury participation by different segments of populations in the community. The underrepresented groups included the poor, women, those with less education, and the young.

Impaneling McMartin Jurors: A Study in *Voir Dire* and Peremptory Challenges

Peremptory challenges that do not require cause to be stated and challenges for cause to eliminate jurors with certain biases were uniquely designed by the defense in seeking to impanel jurors with particular qualities. In choosing a fair-minded jury, McMartin counsel looked to several parameters that might disclose a juror's beliefs and biases. During the pre-*voir dire* screening sessions in the courtroom, to evaluate their suppositions and hidden prejudices, empirical and ethnographic information was gleaned by observing their behavior. This observed information was then given numerically assigned values, and almost simultaneously computerized by round-the-clock preparation for further use in empirical evaluation of potential jurors and their selection for the final jury.

These sources of information were also merged for further analyses to develop juror profiles from the combined results of the community survey, the pre-*voir dire* questionnaires, and observational data. For this merger, statistical and mathematical models included: (1) multiple regression analysis, (2) discriminant analysis, (3) logit regression techniques, and (4) factor analysis.[9]

Using the results from all of these sources and analyses, all 205 assigned jurors were given a numerical value and then rank-ordered from the least partial to the most partial, number one being the least biased and number 205 the most biased—using the standard of a prospective juror who had already decided upon a guilty verdict before the trial even began. The following section presents three different types of jurors' profiles: (1) socioeconomic profiles, (2) behavioral and attitudinal characteristics, and (3) observational assessments of prospective jurors assigned to the trial.

Socioeconomic and Demographic Dimensions of Juror Biases
The statistical analyses revealed that among many attitudinal variables, *race* of the prospective jurors was found to be one of the most crucial factors, distinguishing between those who said that the defendants were

guilty and those who were uncertain about the trial outcome—despite the massive media exposure. The survey findings were somewhat unexpected. The analyses suggested that both Hispanic and Native American jurors were more likely to have decided on guilt, but black, Asian, and white jurors were more likely to be unsure of the trial outcome.

While racial minorities were generally believed to be more sympathetic to the accused and less likely to identify with the prosecution, statistical analyses revealed that this was not necessarily the case. Two ethnic minority groups, Hispanics and Native Americans, were clearly more likely to render a pre-trial guilty verdict in the McMartin case than were other groups. This may be because the defendants did not share the same racial or ethnic background, or because child molestation and sexual experience might carry significant cultural and/or ideological meanings for some ethnic groups and not others. Additional studies are obviously needed to establish the causal relationship between the perception of child molestation and racial and ethnic background of prospective jurors to determine if this was an isolated instance or a general pattern.

On the surface, the issue of race did not appear to be a significant factor in the McMartin child molestation case. However, statistical analyses revealed that race, the social milieu surrounding the case, the defendants' socioeconomic backgrounds, and differential reactions by the community, police agencies, and the media, all exerted significant and varying impacts on the perception of the case and the potential outcome of the trial.

Recent jury research indicates that when a trial is highly publicized and contains evidence of possible prosecutorial misconduct and abuse of power, black jurors are more likely than any other racial group to apply greater scrutiny to the legal concepts of a presumption of innocence, a reasonable doubt, and the burden of proof in determining the potential outcome of the criminal trial.[10] Thus, in evaluating the potential deliberative performance of individual jurors, their racial identity could offer further insight into their views on the strength as well as the weakness of trial evidence in a very highly publicized trial.

Other important socioeconomic and demographic characteristics used to demarcate impartial and biased jurors in the case were as follows: (1) *age,* with older persons being more likely to believe that the defendants were guilty and younger persons more likely to believe otherwise; (2) *gender,* with females being more likely to render a guilty verdict than males; (3) *educational level,* with those with less than a high school education being more likely to believe the defendants to be guilty, while those with a college level education more likely to be unsure of guilt or innocence; and (4) *income,* with those with lower incomes more biased toward guilt and those with higher level incomes not sure or likely to judge the defendants not guilty. As indicated earlier, past jury research typically shows that potential jurors from a higher social class are more likely to be politically conservative and identify their attitudes about crimes and criminals with those in law enforcement authorities; thus they are more likely to lean towards convicting criminal defendants. However, the present findings showed that the same highly educated and affluent jurors in Los Angeles would be less likely to render a guilty verdict than their counterparts in the McMartin trial.

Behavioral and Attitudinal Dimensions of Juror Biases
In addition to using demographic and socioeconomic factors for judging prospective jurors' attitudes and biases, several behavioral and attitudinal variables differentiated those who were partial to a guilty verdict from those who were not. The following eight questions were asked of these possible jurors and explored the most important issues in the case.

(1) When you were a child, can you remember having any experiences you would consider sexual abuse?
(2) Do you feel that children can be trained to testify about things that really did not happen?
(3) Do you think that most of the children involved in the McMartin preschool case were sexually abused, or some of them were, or a few were, or do you think that none of them were sexually abused?
(4) Has a relative or close friend been a victim of child sexual abuse?
(5) Do you believe that the dismissed defendants [the five preschool teachers] were guilty or not guilty?
(6) How do you feel about law enforcement officials, the district attorneys, and defense attorneys who have handled the McMartin preschool case to date?
(7) Have you ever served on a federal or local grand jury?
(8) In a sexual abuse case, is medical evidence very useful in deciding whether a person is guilty or not guilty?

Those who said "yes" to the first and fourth questions and "no," to the second question, were more likely to have decided on a verdict of guilty. For the third question, assigned jurors who answered "most" were more likely to render a guilty verdict against the McMartin defendants. Potential jurors who said "yes" or "maybe" on the presumed guilt of five preschool teachers whose charges were previously dismissed were more likely to have decided on a guilty verdict.

The jurors who had previously served on a grand jury were more likely to vote guilty. Similarly, those who believed that medical evidence is very useful in deciding the defendant's guilt or innocence were more likely to have decided on the guilt.

With respect to the attitude on the investigation and disposition of the McMartin case by the prosecution and defense attorneys, those jurors who said "good" were also found to be more prone to a guilty verdict than those who said "poor."

Another series of questions focused on sexual abuse in order to identify those with a strong enough emotional response that convictions seemed inevitable; among these questions were:

- Exactly how would you define child sexual abuse?
- Are the laws of California adequate to deal with the problem of sexual abuse?
- During the past two years, have you heard or read about the subject of child sexual abuse?
- Do you have any opinion as to whether children (ages 2-5) can reliably describe things that actually happen to them?
- Do you believe that children never lie about sexual abuse?
- Do you think being exposed to sex or sexual acts at a *very* early age (two to ten years) has *any* effect on a child?
- Do you think it is possible that early exposure to sexual acts could have a benefit for a child?
- Has anyone ever made accusations about you relating to sexual misconduct?

To determine if the potential jurors' sense of equity and justice could overcome the emotion-charged issues surrounding the sexual abuse of children, a series of statements was utilized to gather information on their attitudes towards the adequacy or failing of the criminal court and justice systems. For each question, the jurors were asked to answer if they: strongly agree, somewhat agree, have no opinion/are undecided, somewhat disagree, or strongly disagree.

- If the prosecution goes to the trouble of bringing someone to trial, the person is probably guilty.
- Even the worst criminal should be considered for mercy.
- Regardless of what the law says, a defendant in a criminal case should be required to prove his innocence.
- The rights of persons charged with child sexual abuse are better protected than the rights of the alleged child victims.

- Too often people accused of serious crimes are treated lightly by the courts.
- If a person is allowed to get out of jail on bail, then that person is probably not guilty.
- Due to a great deal of media coverage, sometimes the public assumes that a person is guilty when in fact they are not.
- Sometimes political officials prosecute individuals for political gain.
- If a group of persons is charged with a crime and later charges against some of them are dropped, then those still charged are probably guilty.
- Children aged 7-11 almost always tell the truth about their sexual experiences that happened when they were ages 2-5.
- It is highly unlikely that a female would sexually abuse a child.
- Testimony by a child in sexual abuse cases should be confirmed by other evidence.

Since the media was highly critical of the defendants and the alleged crimes, it was important to determine the source-media from which the jurors obtained most of their information on the case. From the beginning, both KABC-TV (Channel 7) and the *Los Angeles Times* had been releasing negative news stories against the defendants. The questionnaire asked a series of items, examining jurors' access to the media and what types of topics or programs interested the jurors:

- Which news programs, newspapers, magazines or books did you see or hear over the last two years? (KABC-TV [Channel 7], KABC Radio [AM 790], *Los Angeles Times, Los Angeles Daily Journal, Los Angeles Magazine, People Magazine,* etc.)
- What are your five favorite television programs?
- How many hours a week do you watch television?
- Have you written a "Letter to the Editor"? If so, what publication and what was it about?

The answers to these questions were classified, given numerical values, and then rank-ordered to determine prospective jurors with the least biases and the greatest ability to fairly judge the defendants.

All of the evidence derived from the various facts and data gathering techniques, statistical analyses, and collective judgments was then utilized to assist in selecting the final jury and its alternates.

Observational Dimensions of Juror Biases

A view from the bridge, so to speak, often brings one closer to reality than all the statistically codified data about the landscape. In the selection of juries, this would be the view of the potential jurors themselves. Their verbal and non-verbal behavior may aid attorneys in assessing their potential biases. By structured observational methods, it is possible to examine and assess subtle assumptions or other biases of each assigned juror. Such observational methods are designed to produce empirical information appropriate for quantitative and statistical analysis. Typically, yielding qualitative data, observations are not easily reduced to numbers.[11] Therefore, in order to quantify the qualitative findings about prospective jurors, a number of personality characteristics were classified and then ranked from 1 to 5, 1 being the most acquittal prone and 5 for the most conviction prone.

The classified personality characteristics designated for the prospective McMartin jurors included the following: (1) empathy, (2) punitiveness, (3) analytic ability, (4) leadership, (5) authoritarianism, (6) gregariousness, and (7) "gut" reaction. These personality dimensions were designed to measure potential biases of each prospective juror through direct observations of his or her verbal and non-verbal behavior and responses to questions asked by both public prosecutors and defense attorneys. As noted for statistical analysis, those seven personality characteristics were rank-ordered in terms of their biases towards the defendants and their alleged crimes.

The nature of each criminal trial determines the importance of the various personality traits of prospective jurors. For the McMartin jurors, the prioritized order of personality characteristics were: (1) gut reaction, (2) analytic ability, (3) empathy, (4) gregariousness, (5) authoritarianism, (6) leadership, and (7) punitiveness. Gut reaction was considered the most important because of the observer's past experience and expertise in similar trials and the sensitive nature of the alleged crimes. The observer had to make critical interpretations of the prospective jurors' hidden biases and prejudices through verbal and non-verbal behavior. Thus, the observer's overall evaluation of the jurors' personality traits was considered to be the most important measurement of their hidden biases and prejudice to be used during the sequestered *voir dire* session.

Punitiveness was considered to be the least important in this case because the notion of retributive punitiveness was one widely shared by almost all potential jurors and it failed to differentiate prospective jurors according to their perception of the trial outcome. For example, both the community survey and the pre-*voir dire* questionnaire survey substantiated the importance of retribution to those who had actually experienced child sexual abuse in some way. The important question in the McMartin case was not about the attitude towards the imposition of punishment on criminals, but rather on the jurors' abilities to independently and objectively evaluate the credibility of children's testimony, material, and forensic evidence presented in court. Thus, the scale of punitiveness was considered to be less important than other measurements in gauging personal opinions and characteristics.

Completing the defense's preparations for *voir dire,* field notes and ethnographic information were prepared with full descriptions of empirical observations and overall assessments of each prospective juror. The empirical observations included jurors' appearance, their clothes, speech patterns, and other key verbal and non-verbal identification traits. This "reading" of jurors' intent included the selection, recording, and encoding of jurors' behavior in the courtroom.

The advantage of the structured observation lies in its greater control of sampling and measurement error. It also permits stronger generalizations and checks on reliability and validity of each item of personality characteristics. For example, a juror might exhibit some types of behavior or verbal/nonverbal responses that perhaps reflect his or her biases against the suspects accused of child sexual abuse. Once detected, it was then possible for the observer to judge whether to challenge the juror peremptorily or for cause. It was also possible to evaluate the juror's biases in conjunction with other objective scores and responses from the pre-*voir dire* questionnaire. With highly structured observation, it was assumed that the observational categories established by the researcher reflected the logic of the observed behavior and the potential intent of those observed.

Structured Observations and Assessments of Juror Biases

General observations and critical comments on all assigned jurors were based on the empirical data from a number of sources including: (1) the standardized scores of personality traits from the structured observation; (2) responses from the pre-*voir dire* questionnaire which incorporated the findings of the community survey in the L.A. Central Superior Court jurisdiction; and (3) the ranking scales of all assigned jurors which combined all three surveys as well as the empirical data.

In addition to the ranking scale of each prospective juror, a narrative evaluation was composed which served as an important base of information during *voir dire.* With this critical information of the ranking and evaluation, the defense attorneys were able to strategically assess their use of peremptory challenges and gauge the likelihood of prosecutorial peremptory challenges before the actual *voir dire* session.

To better understand the method of structured observations conducted by an experienced observer during a pre-*voir dire* session, it is important to distinguish it from casual and generic "scientific" observations. In contrast to casual watching, structured observation is planned, methodically carried out, and intended to extract meaningful interpretation. Structured observation thus differs from other forms of observation in two important ways: First, while the latter can involve direct observation, usually with the naked eye, structured observation can be both direct and/or indirect that characterizes respondents' report in questionnaires or interviews. Second, structured observation takes place in a laboratory or similarly contrived situation like a courtroom, not in a natural setting. Observations made in the field tend to be less structured than those made in a courtroom, and structured observations differ primarily in terms of the extent to which the researcher does not actively participate in the social setting being observed.

When the structured observation was utilized by the McMartin defense to extract meaningful interpretation of jurors' hidden prejudice and biases, it resulted in a narrative evaluation of each assigned juror and his or her potential partiality and impartiality vis-à-vis the defendants and their alleged crimes. The importance of such narrative evaluations can be seen in the following examples, as all of the jurors assigned to the McMartin case were asked to respond to the questions by prosecutors and defense attorneys during a pre-*voir dire* questioning session. Each juror was given a number so that he or she was assured of the confidentiality of their answers.

For example, the observations and narrative evaluation of sequestered juror #59 indicated the following:

> He practiced law until 1947 when he came to California. He said he wouldn't look forward to spending a year or so in this case. He was involved in real estate law. He used to play racquetball with Lou Watnick, DA. He anticipates questions based on his prior legal experience. Said he has never talked about pro's and con's of this case. He has gone to Manhattan Beach for business reasons.... He has heard that both Ira Reiner and Robert Philibosian have proceeded for political reasons. His legal background promotes an argumentative nature. "Children play games with imaginations. For the child it becomes very real." I think the DA will exercise a peremptory.

Interestingly, he was not peremptorily challenged and became one of six alternates for the trial. His empirical score was ranked as one of the highest on the impartiality scale among 205 assigned jurors.

Similarly, juror #156 was ranked high in terms of impartiality scales and the defense anticipated that the prosecution might exercise a peremptory challenge. The observation and final comments on this sequestered juror indicated:

> He is working on a masters program in education. He says that the media is slanted. He and his wife went to a marriage counselor. His niece is a secretary for the F.B.I. He is not the foreman in the case he served. He thinks that a defense attorney should use tact in cross-examining a child. He says that he could deal with being a juror in this case. This man doesn't smile at all. He thinks that psychiatric treatment is appropriate for child molesters. I think that DAs will exercise a peremptory on him.

Surprisingly, the juror was not peremptorily challenged by the prosecution and was accepted by both sides to become one of twelve initial jurors.

For juror #60, the narrative evaluation showed that the defense needed to exercise a peremptory challenge to exclude her from the jury. It was important for the defense to identify the individual jurors who had relied on the media and had extensive knowledge of the McMartin episode based on external media sources. Both statistical analyses and structured observations showed that this juror was one who already had anticipated the guilty verdict. The comments stated:

> She feels there *must be* some truth to the charges. She feels that some touching occurred at the school. She took a very long time answering Danny's [Defense Attorney Daniel Davis] questions about whether she thought Ray [Raymond Buckey] had molested someone. She was disturbed when she saw children's eyes blacked out on TV. *We will need to exercise a peremptory on this woman.* Danny challenged for cause—denied.

During *voir dire,* she was thus peremptorily challenged by the defense attorney.

Juror #33 had a prior criminal conviction. He was convicted of DUI in 1982 and pleaded guilty. The defense thought that the district attorney might exercise a peremptory challenge because of his prior conviction. The observation indicated:

> He thinks that media coverage is one-sided. Sometimes he has a hard time hearing—he listens with his right ear. He doesn't think

the death penalty is appropriate for child molestation. He would like to be a juror in this case because he is retired and would like something to do.... He lives in a mobile home park where no children are allowed. He said he has no experience about judging the credibility of a child witness. DA might kick because of prior conviction.

However, he was not challenged by the prosecutors and was accepted for the final jury.

Similarly, the final comments on juror #58 stated that the defense had to anticipate that the juror might be challenged by the prosecution because of his willingness to be open-minded and to apply objective evaluations of the materials presented in court. The sequestered observations and final comments stated:

His father was a lawyer in some criminal cases. "I have been brought up with a commitment for the search for truth." He says he hasn't really had any opinion about this case. He says he has no hardship.... I don't think that the DAs like this man.

Surprisingly he was not challenged by the prosecution and was selected to be one of the initial twelve jurors.

There were two other jurors, one with the highest personality characteristics' score. In fact, both of them indicated in the pre-*voir dire* questionnaire that the McMartin defendants were "probably not guilty." They were both black males, 56 and 35 years of age, respectively. The defense assessment of one of them, juror #150 (56 years of age), was the following:

He feels that Peggy (McMartin) was in charge of the school and not directly involved with the children and as such is probably not guilty. He feels that Ray was directly involved with the children but as such he has no opinion about his guilt or innocence.... He feels that most of the convicted molesters are repeat offenders because their sentences aren't long enough. *He sounds very fair.* He says he feels that the defendants should be able to give their side of the story. He has not been a foreman. He says that maybe some of the parents told their children these tales because they didn't like Ray. "The child would have been coached to say things they say on the stand." He doesn't particularly want to serve as a juror because he doesn't want to judge (biblical admonition).

The prosecutors identified both men as too biased against the prosecution, tried to eliminate them by challenge for cause, and successfully excluded both of them from the jury.

There were some jurors who initially believed that two McMartin defendants were guilty. They later reconstructed and reevaluated media information, realizing that the McMartin case might have been too sensationalized, and questioned the objectivity of the conventional news and reports on the case. Some of them made it to the final jury.

It was important to identify individual jurors who would be able to remain objective and evaluate information impartially. One of those jurors selected to serve on the McMartin jury was juror #48. The final comments on this juror indicated:

> He feels that papers tend to sensationalize [the McMartin case]. At first he thought that Ray and Peggy were guilty. He says that being raised in four different countries ... you must have an "open mind." He knows about the French legal system. "I'm a big boy—I can take care of myself." He is very eloquent and knows a great deal. He says American children are more pampered and that all testimony is questionable (adult and children).

His rank on the impartiality scale showed that he was one of the least biased among 205 jurors, and his average personality characteristics showed that he was capable of being objective and neutral in the assessment of testimony and evidence presented in court. No surprise, he later became the jury foreperson in the case.

Several jurors, like #161, had indicated great difficulties in separating their personal feelings about child molestation from their responsibility as impartial jurors. For a Hispanic male with a daughter, his rank on the impartiality scale showed very high bias, perhaps reflecting his strong parental and cultural ties with family and children. Statistical analyses also indicated the strong correlation between Hispanic potential jurors and their assumption of the defendants' guilt in the child molestation case. Final comments on him stated that:

> He says that little kids are so vulnerable and he feels that they should be protected. He will definitely side with the children! "Sympathy would affect a fair decision. It would be tough to watch little kids on the stand."... "I really can't do nothing"—his answer to Danny's question about what he would do to put aside his feelings about children. "I'll [be] seeing my daughter when the little kids testify. I won't be able to separate my feelings." He will have

a problem separating parental feelings from his responsibility as a juror.

The defense attorney then challenged him for cause, eliminating him as a juror in the case.

Juror #193 was also ranked very low in both the impartiality scale and the personality characteristics score. His daughter was molested and was going though counseling. He showed very strong feelings and emotions about child victims in the McMartin case and appeared to have already made up his mind that the defendants were guilty of child molestation. The general observation stated the following:

> He says he frequently hears about people saying that they have been improperly touched. Daughter was improperly touched three or four times and didn't tell her parents for quite a while because the molester threatened to kill her mother if she told. His daughter is seeing a therapist about once every three weeks. He has been to the beach in Manhattan Beach. *He is a very sinister individual who never smiles or changes his countenance....* We will need to examine a peremptory on this man.

He was peremptorily challenged by the defense during *voir dire*.

There were six potential jurors who believed that one or both of the McMartin defendants were "definitely guilty." Four of them were females; three were married and three were single. Three of the six potential jurors indicated that Peggy McMartin was definitely guilty. All of them, however, agreed that Raymond Buckey was definitely guilty. Subsequently, none of those six people was selected into the final jury box. Contrary to the assumption of guilt reflected in their responses in the questionnaire, some of those jurors appeared willing to exercise their impartiality, objectivity, and open-mindedness in making the final decision.

For example, juror #94 indicated in the questionnaire that Raymond Buckey was "definitely guilty," though she told the judge that she could be fair and unbiased in the trial. The general observation recorded:

> "I know of nothing that would bias me in any direction." This woman is a very intelligent woman who has not made any opinions about this case. She has a trace of a Bostonian accent. She knows three judges socially. Husband works for U.S. House of Representative's government committee. She seems fair but we need to know more about her.

While the observational assessment seemed to give every indication that she might be able to judge and decide on the case honestly and objectively, her rank on the impartiality scale was found to be very low and subsequently she was not selected to serve on the jury.

Often it is possible that the observer might be deceived by the jurors' style of self-presentation, his/her appearance, speech patterns, and statements made during *voir dire*. Thus, it becomes extremely difficult to uncover the hidden biases and prejudice against defendants based on observation alone. The jurors themselves may not even realize their own biases and hidden motives. The case of juror #94 illustrated the importance of additional objective evaluations by combining other quantified data and structured observational measurements.

Similarly, juror #174 indicated in the questionnaire that she had a personal interest in the McMartin child molestation case and that both McMartin defendants were "definitely guilty." While her responses in the questionnaire gave every indication that she was very familiar with the case and had already made up her mind on the trial outcome, she told the judge that she could be fair and impartial and knew almost nothing of the McMartin episode. Her case also offers another example of the difficulty the observer has in providing an objective interpretation of jurors' hidden biases and motives. For example, the observational note indicated that:

> She says she can be fair and impartial. She says she can't really remember much about the case. A friend told her about being sexually molested by her uncle. She is very soft spoken. She thinks that child molestation occurs frequently at preschools. She says she will only accept the judge's instructions which she agrees with. She wants to be a juror in this case. She doesn't feel that anything is wrong with male adults watching x-rated movies. She can't accept that the defendant has no obligation to prove innocence. She says she feels like she is honest. I don't think she is.

She ranked very low on the impartiality scale and her personality characteristics score was equally very low. She was not selected to serve on the final jury. Her *voir dire* performance seemed to reinforce the danger of relying solely on observational evaluations to judge jurors' impartiality, because jurors often provide very different pictures of where they are situated in terms of the conviction or the acquittal of defendants.

The cases of these two prospective jurors exemplify the problem of relying on one method to make the final inference. The above examples also show that the structured observational method is an extremely useful tool in extracting the meaningful interpretation of potential biases and prejudice. However, it is also important to note that, when combined with other statistical and empirical methods and knowledge, it may even become more critical in providing an overall, objective assessment of individual jurors.

Given the sensationalized publicity about the defendants and the alleged crimes, the selection of fair-minded individual jurors with abilities to objectively assess testimony and trial materials was considered to be an extremely difficult task. Among 205 assigned jurors, the pre-*voir dire* sequestered questionnaire revealed that only two jurors believed that the McMartin defendants were "probably not guilty." While there were other potential jurors with "Don't Know" responses on the question of the defendants' guilt, it was critical for the defense to identify clues useful to separate case-neutral jurors from those who had already decided on the trial outcome so that the final jurors and alternates might be able to rely on their ability to apply their judgment objectively.

The Final Jury and Alternates

Twelve jurors and six alternates were finally selected after the lengthy *voir dire* procedure. All the selected jurors met the basic criteria of expressing doubt about the potential outcome of the trial and appeared to be less influenced by the media's negative tone. All of the selected jurors and alternates indicated in the pre-*voir dire* questionnaire that they were uncertain as to whether or not both Raymond Buckey and Peggy McMartin Buckey were guilty of child molestation and would wait to decide until all evidence was presented before them.

What, then, were the jury's characteristics? In terms of racial composition, the initial twelve jurors consisted of six whites (50%), three blacks (25%), two Asians (16.7%), and one Hispanic (8.3%). There were seven males and five females; eight jurors were under 40 years of age and eleven of the jurors had at least some college education. Eleven members of the initial jury belonged to racial and ethnic groups that were found to be less prone to a guilty verdict—Asians, blacks, and whites. The age distribution of selected jurors also was skewed toward the young and middle-aged categories.

The six alternates had somewhat different characteristics: there were four whites (66.7%), one black, and one Asian. The alternates, however, were predominantly male—five out of six. Five of the alternates were under 50 years of age, all six had some college experience, and three had post-graduate education. With respect to attitudinal and behavioral characteristics, the overall profile of the alternates indicated greater impartiality than that of the twelve selected jurors.

Thus, the initial twelve jurors and six alternates met the basic demographic, socioeconomic, and attitudinal criteria that the statistical analyses indicated would make up an ideal jury for the defendants. The defense's scientific *voir dire* strategy had successfully selected a group of jurors who appeared to have greater abilities than the overall pool of 205 candidates to judge the testimony and court evidence in an open-minded and objective manner. The selection of alternates was also considered to be potentially more important and crucial than the selection of the initial 12 jurors. The defense team anticipated that the trial would last many months and that some alternate jurors might eventually become the final jurors as some of the initial jurors leave for various personal and economic reasons. Subsequently, it was a lengthy trial, and ultimately all six alternates became full-fledged jurors.

Past jury research revealed that the length of the jury trial had a significant impact upon the ultimate racial, socioeconomic, and political composition of the resulting jury. Because of the time commitment, personal sacrifices, and economic hardship imposed by lengthy jury trials, the resulting jurors typically are more likely to be white, highly educated, and from middle- to upper-social classes.[12]

The McMartin jury and alternates proved no exception. After two years and six months, four of the initial 12 jurors had asked to be released from duty and were eventually replaced by alternates. Two alternate jurors also asked to be released. The interesting aspect of the remaining jurors and their profiles is that the final jury was made up of jurors whose demographic, socioeconomic, and attitudinal characteristics (derived from the statistical analysis) were indicative of their greater willingness to evaluate the testimony and court evidence in an open-minded and objective fashion. The final group of 12 was composed of ten jurors who had at least some college experience, and three who had post-graduate education. Eleven of the jurors were under 50 years of age; eight were in their 20s and 30s, and eight were male. The final jury thus included a large proportion of jurors in a similar age bracket as defendant Raymond Buckey (66.7%).

Only one juror was in the ethnic/racial categories identified as being most prone toward conviction—Hispanic and/or Native American. He was originally selected to be one of the six alternates. While Hispanic potential jurors were identified as being conviction-prone, this particular Hispanic juror had stated in the *voir dire* questionnaire, as well as during the *voir dire* screening session, that both Raymond Buckey and Peggy McMartin Buckey were neither guilty nor not guilty, unless all the testimony and forensic and material evidence presented proved they were. During *voir dire,* he stated that his daughter had been sexually molested and received psychological counseling by his pastor. While he said that he was more hurt than angered over the incident with his daughter, he stated that "everybody's innocent until proven [guilty]." And all of the selected jurors had expressed doubt about the potential outcome of the trial and agreed to weigh the court evidence to render the final verdict.

Despite illness and financial pressures that caused four of the initially selected jurors to retire, the final jury's composition had almost the same racial/ethnic characteristics as the original twelve-member jury. Due to the high proportion of blacks and Hispanics in the L.A. Central Superior Court District, it is not surprising that racial minorities were substantially overrepresented on the jury. However, the average educational attainment of the jurors was substantially higher than that of the court jurisdiction. In addition to the demographic and socioeconomic dimensions associated with impartiality, the selected jurors also met basic attitudinal and behavioral characteristics that were found to be more associated with impartiality than prejudice on the trial outcome.

During *voir dire,* the prosecution also received the services of private jury selection consultants to help select jurors, in an effort to shape the jury towards one that would convict. They sat beside the prosecutors during the *voir dire* screening session, observed prospective jurors, assessed their responses to attorneys' questions, and evaluated the written-pre-*voir dire* questionnaires that were also shared with the defense counsel. Given the overwhelming presumption of guilt shared by the public, the jury consultants and the prosecution might have been over-confident about the defendants' conviction. They appeared to have relied upon intuitive and subjective selection criteria rather than the systematic and more critical methods of scientific jury selection procedures. With the assistance of scientific jury selection procedures utilized by the defense, the final jury was a well-balanced, neutral jury with a greater propensity to objectively and open-mindedly evaluate the charges brought against the defendants.

Once *voir dire* was completed, jurors and their alternates were assembled, and over the next two-and one-half years, they were put to the test. They listened to evidence, saw witnesses, heard testimony, watched as a blizzardd of documents was submitted.

The Final Jury's Backgrounds

Jurors who were to make decisions regarding guilt or innocence on each of the 65 charges were survivors from a number of panels summoned to the courthouse for the trial. These jurors and their alternates had a wide range of backgrounds, including a supermarket checker, a Pacific Bell telephone employee, a biomedical technician, a meat packer, an engineer, a mechanic, a federal government employee, and a stock clerk, among others.

With the limited biographical information made public, an overview of the jury nonetheless reveals great diversity.

Mark Bassett, a 33-year-old, white male, bachelor, was employed at a scientific computer company. He had an undergraduate degree from Princeton and a Ph.D. in chemical engineering from Cal Tech; he spent part of his spare time in Bible study, in Toastmasters, and providing tutoring and computer education to disadvantaged young people.[13] Clearly, he was a highly educated, moral person accustomed to dealing with both scientific and social problems. He was first chosen as an alternate but ultimately became a juror. Pressure on him intensified during the course of the trial when the company he worked for went out of business and he lost his job.

John Breese, a 51-year-old, white biomedical technician with five grandchildren. He became a widower during the course of the trial, remarrying while the trial was underway with many jurors attending as guests at the wedding. He had previous experience as a juror in another trial. During *voir dire,* he said that he remembered the media story that some of the children had their pets killed and buried them in the school yard. While he initially believed that the defendants were guilty as charged, he said that he soon changed his opinion, becoming neutral on the question of guilt or innocence of the defendants.

Luis Chang, an Asian-American electrical engineer, was chosen as foreperson and essentially guided jurors during the discussion of various charges. At the beginning of the trial, his daughter became the victim of a hit-and-run driver in front of her school. He had broad international experience and knew about the French legal system. He was given credit by the other jurors for making the process bearable.

Brenda Oliver (Williams), a 38-year-old black woman, a service representative with Pacific Bell telephone company, also married during the course of the trial. She voted for Ira Reiner during the 1984 election for district attorney of Los Angeles. She told the court that she did not see anything wrong with a young man working in a preschool and that children are good at making up stories to please their parents. During *voir dire,* she said that she could be a fair juror.

Barbara Celestine, a 49-year-old black mother of two, worked for the U.S. Air Force in nearby El Segundo. This was her first experience as a juror and she was one of the eight initially selected jurors who remained throughout the trial.

Henry Coleman, age 75, the oldest member of the jury, was a retired structural draftsman. He had completed a community college education, lived by himself in a mobile home park where no children were allowed, and was one of the initial eight jurors who remained in the jury box throughout the entire trial. He had served previously as a juror in a criminal trial. During *voir dire,* he stated that media coverage was one-sided. Though child molestation is a serious crime, he said that the administration of the death penalty was not appropriate in a child molestation case.

Sally Cordova, a white, single 27-year-old female, worked as a supermarket checker, and had never served as a juror prior to the McMartin trial. At the *voir dire* screening session she indicated that she had heard the McMartin case discussed by others and felt that their general opinion was that the alleged defendants were guilty as charged. She said that her employer would only pay for six months of jury duty and she was instructed by the judge to bring a letter from her supervisor, indicating the company's policy on jury duty.

Daryl Hutchins, a 28-year-old, white male, working for a Long Beach oil company, had never served as a juror. During *voir dire,* he stated that he was concerned about children testifying in court. He was initially selected as one of the original 12 jurors.

Danny Kindle, a 33-year-old black grocery store clerk, had attended postgraduate school and had previously been a juror in a criminal trial. At the beginning of the trial, he was working on a master's program in education. During *voir dire,* he stated that he believed psychiatric treatment was appropriate for child molesters.

Dante Ochoa, a 42-year-old, married man with two children, had completed four years of college education; he had never previously served as a juror. His father had served as a lawyer in some criminal cases, and he stated that he had been brought up with a commitment to the search for truth. During *voir dire,* he said that he had once been shot during a fraternity fight, though no charges were filed.

Julie Peters, a 47-year-old, white divorced woman with two children, had attended community college; she had previously served as a juror. During *voir dire,* she stated that her house was broken into five years ago, and that one night a week she went to a pediatrics ward and helped the children. She said that she saw the McMartin news coverage, wondered why such details were being given if they were important to the case, and wanted to be a juror in the trial. She was one of the initial eight jurors who remained in the jury box throughout the entire trial.

Michael Salazar, a 40-year-old Latino with three children who had attended a community college, was one of six alternatives who joined the final jury during the trial's proceedings. During *voir dire* screening, he indicated that he had never read or heard about the McMartin Preschool and told the court that "everybody is innocent until proven otherwise."

During the course of the trial of over two-and-one-half years, many unexpected pressures beset the 12 jurors and six alternates selected for the trial. Their number had been narrowed down to a jury of 12 persons, with no alternates left. By May, 1989, four jurors had been excused; two became ill, one had job troubles, and a fourth was inattentive—falling asleep in the jury box, And the trial was so long that several jurors even received summonses to jury duty for other cases.[14]

In their 30 months in court, the jurors also shared each other's lives. There were little groups that lunched together, other groups that chatted together in the hall during breaks. Bassett often ate in China Town with Luis Chang. These were people who understood that they were sharing an extraordinary experience.

When juror Breese, a bio-medical technician, became widowed during the trial and later remarried, a half-dozen jurors attended his wedding. When one juror suffered a stroke, some jurors visited him in the hospital. Later this juror dropped by the courthouse to say hello.[15]

As the trial progressed, strong feelings built among the jurors. Bassett indicated that each juror felt "a certain respect for the others for having gone though all of this." Still it was an arduous task to be a juror. During the second month of the trial, Judge Pounders reminded the jurors that they must stay awake during the proceedings and that they should be taking notes since the trial was expected to last for months if not years. The judge said that the jurors should ask for a break if they felt drowsy from lack of sleep or a big meal. The judge also threatened the jurors with dismissal (probably an idle threat), fines, or jail time if they were late, didn't stay awake during the proceedings, or didn't take notes.

The warning apparently took hold, as those jurors who ordinarily would be "given to yawning, shifting restlessly, sitting with eyes closed, chomping gum or keeping an eye on the clock seemed to take renewed interest."[16] So the final 12 jurors who rendered the verdicts in the McMartin case were survivors in more ways than one.[17]

Perceptions of Scientific Jury Selection in American Courtrooms

Scientific jury selection is derived from the nexus of the social sciences and the law; it attempts to add some quantifiable foundations to the stereotyping and intuition that, until recently, formed the basis for lawyers' selection of final jurors.

The jury plays a significant role in America's democratic and pluralistic tradition and is often seen as a bulwark of democracy. Approximately 80% of all jury trials in the world take place in the United States.[18] Many nations have only bench trials, where judges are given the power of adjudication, and have never had the jury trial as part of their judicial system. In the U.S., the infusion of laymen into the criminal justice system legitimizes the administration of justice and bolsters the belief in democracy. Jury participation in the administration of justice also "enlarges the human matrix of diffusion of responsibility through which people more easily make the difficult decisions that somehow must be made."[19] Similarly, jury service fortifies America's populist tradition. Unlike many elitist governmental bodies and bureaucratic systems, the jury panel is drawn from the community at large, and jury decision-making reflects the collective sentiments shared in the community and is, thus, "the voice of the people."[20]

Nonetheless, the use of scientific jury selection in highly publicized criminal trials in general, and civil product liability cases in particular, has come under increasing examination and assault. At first blush, the notion of scientific jury selection seems to undermine the basic values of our jury system. For example, it has been called "voodoo jury selection,"[21] and it is believed to foster a contradiction between the requirement that a jury be impartial and that it be composed of one's peers.

The Sixth Amendment calls for an impartial jury in a criminal trial, requiring both the impartiality of individual jurors as well as the process by which the jurors are selected. The Supreme Court has defined an impartial juror as one who is able to base a verdict on the evidence presented at trial, not on any preconceived notion or bias about the defendant's innocence or guilt.[22] The Supreme Court has also indicated that the notion of "peers" encompasses members of the defendant's community, and has defined "peers" to indicate "neighbors, fellows, associates, [and] persons having the same legal status in society as that which he holds."[23]

While there appears to be a contradiction between "impartiality" requirements and representation of "peers," the goals of achieving each can be viewed as compatible. For example, a peer may not be the one whose background is a mirror reflection of the defendant's, but rather one who is similarly stationed in life so that he or she is capable of assessing the defendant's act in context. An impartial juror may be able to judge a case on the evidence, rather than on a special understanding of the defendant's behavior.[24]

Similarly, while the Sixth Amendment may discourage both defense and prosecution from seeking an impartial jury, the adversarial climate of our legal system may lead to the eventual impaneling of an impartial jury. That is, although it may be possible that both the defense and prosecution aggressively seek out partial jurors with particular qualities and backgrounds, our legal system assumes that the adversarial struggle itself will foster the climate that produces impartial jurors at the end of jury selection.

We believe that the scientific jury selection procedures utilized by the defense in the McMartin trial undoubtedly assisted in obtaining a case-neutral and "impartial" jury to hear the evidence and to render a verdict. As we noted previously, compared to the great leeway given to the prosecution in most criminal trials, the defense has little to overcome such a handicap. Scientific jury selection is one of the few options available to the defense to influence jury composition and trial outcome.

Conclusions

As shown in the McMartin trial, massive media publicity and negative reportings influenced most of the general public and potential jurors to assume the guilt of the defendants. Selecting impartial jurors thus became a crucial aspect of the defense strategy. The community survey was carried out in the district from which actual jurors were to be chosen and their revelation of substantial belief in the guilt of the defendants obviously raised the prosecution's confidence in convicting the defendants. Nonetheless, the use of scientific jury selection procedures was quite effective in creating a ranking scale to assess jurors' impartiality and their ability to evaluate evidence rather than relying on the media as the source for judging guilt or innocence.

The McMartin trial was a historically critical case because it touched upon the sensitive issue of child sexual abuse that was transformed by massive media exposure and selective interpretations of pre-trial evidence. The defense attorneys initially sought jury consultants to pick a jury that would be more inclined to acquit the defendants. However, an overwhelming public presumption of the defendants' guilt changed the defense strategy from selecting the most *favorable* jury that would lean towards an acquittal to selecting an *impartial* and open-minded jury that would be more willing and open to evaluate material and forensic evidence and testimony.

There were, however, ethical questions involved in the use of scientific jury selection procedures, too. Specifically, "is it ethically permissible to use scientific techniques to influence the jury composition, thus the possible outcome of the trial?" As social scientists and participants in the trial, we struggled over this ethical issue during the jury selection process.

Many researchers justify their involvement in trials on the grounds that it is otherwise impossible for defendants to obtain a fair trial. No doubt, a large number of criminal defendants are more likely to be members of racial minorities, suffering under the weight of institutionalized forms of discrimination. Extensive research demonstrates that racial and ethnic minorities are substantially underrepresented on most state and federal jury pools.[25] However, scientific jury selection techniques hold hope for greater representation of various segments of the community and enable the defense to evaluate the proclivities of assigned jurors. Scientific jury selection seeks a fair-minded jury, not one that is simply capable of understanding a defendant's motives, comprehending the defendant's life condition, and possibly identifying with the defendant's gender, race, and socioeconomic background.

While some critics maintain that the legitimacy of the trial process and resulting verdicts can be undermined by the use of scientific jury selection procedures, the use of objective, evaluative means of jury selection is essential when a fair trial is perceived to be in jeopardy under traditional methods of jury selection. This is particularly true when there is massive pre-trial media publicity, or when there is an inadequate cross-sectional representation of the community on jury panels because of malfeasance by jury commissioners, benign neglect, or actual fraud in selecting persons to be placed on panels from which jurors are to be selected.

With these limits in mind, the defense sought and secured a body of fair-minded jurors to try the two McMartin defendants. Thus in chapter eight, a review of the trial begins by delineating testimony and evaluating evidence as presented by alleged victims, parents, and other witnesses— all of which the selected jurors would have to evaluate and examine.

Chapter 8

The First McMartin Trial

The first McMartin trial seemed almost an after-thought of the preliminary hearing. Once the jurors were carefully selected, with a series of pre-trial measures and legal motions overlapping, the trial finally got underway in July 1987. "We'll be celebrating next Christmas before the case is over," defense attorney Dean Gits said in December 1987; but the trial actually continued for a full two-and-a-half years.[1]

The trial was, in fact, a replay of the preliminary hearing, both the defense and prosecution reliving the roles they had already played. The waiting game had cut the prosecution's list of child witnesses, and thus the chances for conviction. At the beginning of the preliminary hearing, the case had involved 41 witnesses, seven defendants, and more than 200 counts of sexual molestation. By the time the trial actually began there were only 13 child witnesses, and approximately 100 counts of formal charges filed against two defendants. The prosecution called a total of 61 witnesses to testify, but as the trial progressed, only nine alleged child-victims testified, and charges were reduced by one-third.[2]

The trial involved many witnesses and experts in a wide variety of fields: children, parents, medical specialists on sexual abuse, child therapists, McMartin teachers including former defendants, a defense attorney, a woman who claimed to have had sexual relations with one defendant, and a jailhouse informant who declared that Raymond Buckey confessed about molesting and scaring children into silence. The key players of the trial also included Kathleen MacFarlane, from the Children's Institute International (CII), and Dr. Roland Summit, a psychiatrist at Harbor-UCLA Medical Center and a nationally known figure for his theory of the child sexual abuse accommodation syndrome, which holds that children never lie about molestation. He also worked with children and their parents and acted as a community liaison between the Los Angeles County Department of Mental Health and the local community. Dr. Michael Maloney, a key defense expert witness who was a clinical psychologist and professor of psychiatry at USC School of Medicine, criticized Kathleen MacFarlane's interviewing as misleading and traumatizing children, thus contaminating their responses and impairing the search for truth, and blamed Dr. Summit's theory for an avalanche of false accusations of sexual molestation by children.

The media was ready to cover every detail of the trial's progress. The judge had to act as the court's supreme officer and administrator in order to maintain order on a daily basis. As noted earlier, after a number of judges were eliminated and/or rejected by both the prosecution and the defense, Superior Court Judge William R. Pounders was finally appointed. He proved to be a responsive and effective judge in presiding over the proceedings, maintaining the decorum of the courtroom, and ruling on dozens of critical motions and objections by the defense and the prosecution attorneys.

After acknowledging that the first two child witnesses were emotionally and physically exhausted, for example, the judge announced that he intended to limit the length and form of cross-examination by the defense attorneys. The first young female witness had had a swollen, red face after four days of questioning. The second young witness also appeared to be exhausted, and her family reported that their daughter was emotionally and mentally drained.[3] Though his ruling might have clearly infringed on the defendants' constitutional rights to thoroughly examine prosecution witnesses, the limitation placed on testimony was considered to be important as the trial required vulnerable child witnesses to testify in court and be cross-examined by the defense attorneys.

The testimony was exhausting for everyone; tired and frazzled, several jurors appeared to be dozing during testimony, and the judge admonished their conduct. Some jurors arrived late and only a few were seen taking notes during the proceedings. For those jurors who continued to exhibit such behavior, Judge Pounders threatened dismissal, fines, or jail. The judge later dismissed one juror who had difficulty staying awake, immediately filling the empty place with one of the alternate jurors. On these and other occasions, the judge prevailed as the supreme officer of the court, responsive in presiding over courtroom proceedings, deciding questions of law, yet overseeing the welfare of the witnesses—often at the expense of the defendants.

Opening Statements

The trial finally began with the judge's instructions. Prior to the prosecution's and defense's opening statements, Judge Pounders gravely pointed out that "the opening statements are not evidence. It [sic] is a forecast of the evidence as it is expected."[4] The judge also admonished the jurors that "the American system of justice puts its trust in the jury system and you. We are confident you will reach a just and a fair verdict."[5]

All was not fair in the battle for the 12 jurors' emotions and thoughts, however. Procedure in jury trials is set by tradition and rules of evidence, with the prosecution making a first opening statement, outlining the case, and previewing what it proposes to prove and how. The defense then takes up the gauntlet, making its own opening statement. Long opening statements are common in jury trials, where prosecution and defense know that they will be presenting their cases before people unfamiliar with the facts and law, and the McMartin trial was no exception.

The mass media's unbridled scrutiny of the McMartin defendants, their alleged crimes, and child victims had continued unrelentingly almost daily over the previous four years. Thus, it was important for the prosecution—and most especially for the defense—to provide a preview of what would happen during the trial and to remain focused on important points they hoped to prove, using the technicalities of the legal process as a screen to both reflect and deflect the shadows of facts and fantasies.

The Prosecution and the Facts

The opening statements on July 14, 1987 found Deputy District Attorney Lael Rubin summarizing the case as a matter of trust that is held for all teachers, as well as those teachers of the McMartin Preschool and the betrayal of that trust. Rubin argued that the success of the state's case would depend on the believability of the children and their testimony and the acceptance of the medical evidence.[6]

The prosecution also elaborated that Raymond Buckey was being judged on 79 counts of molestation, his mother on 20, and both were being charged with one additional count of conspiracy. Lael Rubin then asked the jury to find Raymond Buckey and his mother, Peggy McMartin Buckey, guilty of sexually abusing 14 children.

Prosecutor Rubin detailed these abuses, arguing that the children had been penetrated with fingers and penis, forced to participate in oral copulation, cajoled into playing "naked games," threatened with death and bodily harm, and transported to other locations for "arousing of, appealing to and gratifying the sexual desires" of the defendants. Rubin also noted that a cell mate of Raymond Buckey would testify that Buckey admitted sodomizing the child who was involved in the initial charge of sexual molestation at the school, and having sex with other children. She further argued that these traumatic events were repulsive and embarrassing, and that they would be bolstered by medical evidence and testimony from parents who noticed physical and behavioral changes in their children while they were enrolled at the school.

The prosecutor admitted that the investigation might have been complicated by the intrusive actions of well-meaning parents, police, and interviewers at CII. However, Rubin argued, the children clearly remembered the incidents which happened when they were three to five years old, though now they were eight to 12. "This is a case about teachers who occupied a special position of trust," and who had exploited their opportunity to abuse.[7]

The major problems facing the prosecution were how to convince the jury that: (1) interviews carried out by unlicensed personnel of CII produced believable evidence; and (2) while no corroboration of any testimony by the children in the preliminary hearing was ever found, the two defendants were nevertheless guilty of the alleged crimes. In further attempts to bolster their case, prosecution investigators dutifully excavated the school grounds and an adjacent vacant lot, but again no corroborating evidence was found and later claims of tunnels discovered were not part of the evidence presented. The prosecution's opening statement attempted to sidestep and downplay these weaknesses.

The Defense and the Matter of "Reasonable Doubt"

In the defense's opening statement, attorney Dean Gits emphasized that the challenge for the jurors was to determine who "the bad guys, the enemy" were in the case. Gits stressed that his client Peggy McMartin Buckey, the children, their parents, the police, and the CII were all victims. He argued that the McMartin school had been a loving preschool for more than 20 years under the direction of Peggy McMartin Buckey. He noted that she had not been a perfect person—she talked too much and was nosy—but he countered she possessed a warm and kind heart. She did not molest children or kill animals, and did not deceive parents.

Gits elaborated that, despite charges made in the media by the prosecution, there were no photographs or movies, no traces of blood or semen found in the school, no buried animals, no hidden passageways or hidden tunnels beneath the school, and that there was no evidence corroborating any account of sexual abuse. Gits then put up a large sheet of posterboard for courtroom viewing, indicating a full-scale investigation by the prosecution. The posterboard showed:

Investigation
People Employed:
Three DA's full time
Five DA investigators, and as many as 14
Two full-time CII employees, and as many as 20
Twenty-two Sheriff's Task Force investigators who investigated 695 families about McMartin and four other pre-schools
One full-time Manhattan Beach Police Department detective and four others involved
Two full-time FBI agents and seven others
Searches:
Twenty-one residences
Seven businesses
Thirty-seven cars
Three motorcycles
One farm
Searched for:
Child pornography
Nude pictures
Records, diaries
Evidence of mutilated animals
Bank account records.[8]

Gits said, "All of these investigations came up negative.... They conducted surveillance of Ray Buckey, his family, and friends, which consumed 135 hours. They consulted with a satanic expert, U.S. Customs agents. They contacted pedophiles; they checked real estate records, utilities records, friends, associates of the Buckey family, other possible offenders, vehicles, uncharged suspects.... All of this cost more than one million dollars. The results? Zero. We believe the money was well spent.... Everything they investigated ... and found nothing ... is defense evidence. It was well worth it."[9]

Gits argued that shaping, coaching, and pressure by both adults and children contaminated what the children now said and believed that they had seen and heard; their accounts revealed confusion between fact and fantasy. Gits disclosed that while parents were filling out a nine-page questionnaire at the CII, interviewers took their children into a separate room and interviewed each child for more than an hour. The tapes of the interviews would show how coaching influenced the children's accounts of sexual molestation.

Making his opening statement, Raymond Buckey's defense attorney Daniel Davis said that Buckey would take the witness stand in his own "common sense defense." "He will provide information that hasn't been revealed in this case about why the charges may be false," Davis presented, adding that he would call as defense witnesses Glenn Stevens, the former prosecutor, some of the teachers who were once defendants, and the child who had started the entire case.

Davis argued that Raymond Buckey was a credible and sympathetic individual and a "normal human being," delineating a number of factors that he believed would cause jurors to have reasonable doubts about the prosecution's case against him. Among these, he pointed out, were that therapists who had interviewed the children had used suggestive techniques to put words in their mouths, leading children to believe that they had been molested; that the medical evidence was inconclusive; that the jail informant was not credible and had used his testimony in this and other cases to obtain better treatment and reduced sentences; that the children the prosecution said were molested may have been molested by someone else; and that Buckey was not teaching at the school when some of the children alleged that he had molested them.

Davis also likened the trial to the McCarthy era of searching for "pinkos" and the witch hunts of earlier times. With many children these days being cared for outside of the home, Davis argued that the opportunity for accusations by innuendo had been extended: Buckey was being falsely accused as a molester and was a scapegoat. Finally, Davis predicted that the children testifying would change their stories, in some instances backing down and in others adding new false charges.

Parents' Testimony

As the trial got underway, testimony rolled down like a mighty stream from the heights of parental anger and despair. Mostly hearsay, the parents' accounts supported the prosecution's case and acted as a foundation for their children's accounts.

In August 1987, the first parent to testify for the prosecution was the father of the first child scheduled to testify. He stated that after he had taken his daughter to the preschool, he had received a copy of a letter from the police announcing their investigation of Raymond Buckey. Though his daughter denied molestation at the preschool, he nevertheless took her to CII after learning that other parents had taken their children there. Having been told that his daughter was molested and believing the therapist was a qualified expert in child sexual abuse, he testified that he believed that his daughter was molested.

On cross-examination, however, he testified that no one had ever told him that his daughter denied on videotape that she had been molested. He said that he had filed claims for compensation in order to get help during the process at CII, and his wife filed a police report so that they would qualify for victims' assistance compensation to pay for their daughter's counseling. He also testified that he had attended the meeting in which Kathleen MacFarlane announced that the McMartin Preschool had been involved in mass molestation. The defense strategy was to make it clear that from the very beginning of the investigation that CII was in charge of the child, the parents, and police—prerequisites to obtain funding for the parents to get CII help for their children's counseling and treatment sessions.

The next witness was the mother of two children whose allegations accounted for 37 of the 100 formally charged counts. The children, a daughter aged eleven and a son aged ten at the time of the trial, attended the preschool when they were between the ages of two and five. The mother testified that after she had received the letter from the police department, she questioned her children if they had been touched, the children responded "no." She said that she continued to question them during the ensuing months because her close friends told her that their children had been molested at the preschool. Finally her daughter told her that she had seen Raymond Buckey put his hands inside a little girl's trousers.

She also testified that her daughter had had bladder infections while she attended the school, had nightmares, that her vaginal area was red and sore, and that she danced with few clothes on and masturbated a lot. According to her mother, her son looked pale and came home one day with clothes that did not belong to him.

Under cross-examination by defense attorney Dean Gits, she disclosed that she had been a very close friend of Virginia McMartin. She also said that she had some concern that a male teacher was at the preschool. She again affirmed that the children told her that they had not been touched. But after the children were interviewed at the CII, she became absolutely convinced that her children had been molested. Though she said that she never saw anything out of the ordinary at the school, she believed that the school's prohibition of parents picking up their children during naptime could have been a cover for molestation.

In order to find corroborating evidence of molestation at the preschool, she told the jury that her husband and thirty to forty other families had been digging in a vacant lot next to the preschool. She also attended a number of meetings organized to plan action to be taken against the defendants, the meetings also being attended by representatives of the DA's office and Kathleen MacFarlane from CII.

In November 1987, another mother testified that she initially did not believe that her son had been molested. Though she recalled making an entry in her diary that her son really liked the school, she finally had come to believe that he had been sexually abused by the defendants. She stated that she witnessed her son sitting on Raymond Buckey's lap on graduation day. She also testified that ten of the 14 children who were prosecution witnesses were now attending the same elementary school as her child. The defense examination raised the obvious implication of opportunities for both children and parents to talk about what might have happened at the McMartin Preschool.

Another prosecution witness was a mother who testified that she had brought her child to enroll at the preschool. She testified that she was troubled by her observation of how well-behaved and quiet McMartin children were at the preschool. However, she did not enroll her son, but placed him in another preschool.

The next prosecution witness was the mother of a young girl who, according to the mother, had nightmares, masturbated at least seven or eight times by inserting a tinkertoy into her vagina, and was observed " in the 69 position" with her sister while they were touching and licking each other's vaginas. The mother believed that molestation experiences eroticized her daughter beyond what would be normal for her age. Having received numerous telephone calls from a police detective prior to the letter sent by the police, she testified that she called Peggy McMartin Buckey, trying to find out what was happening at the preschool. The daughter denied that anything improper had happened at the preschool, but was taken to be interviewed at CII where her mother was told that her daughter had been molested.

On cross-examination, the defense discovered that the child was born with a yeast infection, causing a continual rash in the vaginal areas, and that sexual contact with her sister took place when she was not enrolled at the preschool. When asked about Kathleen MacFarlane and her role in treating her daughter, the mother stated that "prominent people reinforced my feelings" of her children being sexually molested by the defendant. The defense logically contended that nightmares were a perfectly normal occurrence in childhood, and adulthood as well.

A therapist at the South Bay Counseling Center, an organization with close ties to CII, also testified that her son had been molested at the preschool. She testified that when her son became angry with her, he pulled out his penis and pointed it at her. The son also drew pictures of men with large penises, and he refused to wear underwear. Her testimony revealed that although her son was examined by Dr. Astrid Heger and there were no physical findings of sexual abuse, Kathleen MacFarlane told her that her son had been molested. She also said that Raymond Buckey was a pedophile, although admitting she had never seen any such behavior by him.

Because she had been an outspoken advocate of the prosecution and she herself treated other McMartin children, defense attorney Daniel Davis argued that this witness had a strong conflict of interest. Besides her role in treating other children at the South Bay Counseling Center, which Davis called "the child abuse industry," the witness derived personal gain from the epidemic of child abuse cases. The defense also requested that the names of children interviewed by the mother be submitted to the defense. Ironically, the South Bay Counseling Center also operated a preschool that had had problems similar to those of the McMartin Preschool. Denying the defense request for the information, Judge Pounders ruled that the mother was allowed to testify only as a mother, and that the defense was not allowed to ask questions about her communications as a therapist.

The next prosecution witness was a mother whose child refused to testify in the trial. She testified that she believed that her daughter had been molested at the McMartin Preschool and that her then 4-year-old daughter had discussed this possibility with her prior to being interviewed by others and before extensive publicity.[10] The child had told her mother that Raymond Buckey had tied her up, touched her in the vaginal area, tickled her, and played "horsey" with her. Though the young girl did not testify, the prosecutor Lael Rubin argued that the mother's hearsay testimony was "very significant in rebutting [defense] inferences that statements were instilled by interviewers at Children's Institute International."

The defense strenuously objected to the girl's indirect testimony on the grounds that the mother's testimony was "hearsay" and speculative information, and that the prosecution was attempting to introduce the child's assertions without the child being cross-examined. The defense thus characterized the mother's testimony as "irrelevant, time-consuming, prejudicial, and a denial of the defendants' right of confrontation, and cross-examination."

Judge Pounders made the mother's hearsay testimony admissible, but cautioned jurors that they should not speculate on whether or not the child was actually molested. The judge also said that the chronology of this child telling her mother about potential molesting made clear that the external influence of the programming process was not carried out with all McMartin pupils. This assumes, of course, that the mother told the truth.

Another prosecution witness was the mother of the child who had made some of the most bizarre charges against the defendants and others, including a supermarket owner. Her testimony lasted five days. She testified that she had taken her son to CII shortly before the grand jury hearing and believed that her son was molested at the preschool. On cross-examination by defense attorney Gits, she testified that her son had said that nothing unusual happened at the preschool until he was interviewed at CII. She testified that she saw the CII videotape after her son's interview, but the tape had been fast-forwarded and she saw only brief excerpts. The defense examination tried to show that MacFarlane did not want her to see the leading questioning techniques used.

The prosecution's witnesses also included other mothers whose children had attended the preschool. Each said that she believed that her children had been molested by the defendants. One of them had observed that when she went into Raymond Buckey's classroom it was total chaos—children were climbing on him, sitting on him, jumping on him, and acting with a total lack of discipline. She testified that she did not like Buckey's teaching methods, but was told by Peggy McMartin Buckey that other children loved him, too. Another mother whose son attended the preschool testified that he refused to take off his underwear, stayed in the bathtub an hour or more, danced in his underwear, and was afraid of the dark. She said that her son sang the "Naked Movie Star" chant.

On cross-examination, all the mothers testified that they came to believe the sexual allegation only after their children were taken to CII. Some of them also stated that before the trial, both prosecution attorney Rubin and the DA's detective provided the relevant transcripts from the preliminary hearing, apparently trying to get their children's accounts to be consistent at the trial. Some parents also expressed their anger and strong emotions against the accused, especially when being cross-examined by defense attorneys. One mother shouted at the defense attorney to move away from Raymond Buckey so that she did not have to look at him. Another mother was overcome with emotion and began sobbing so loudly that Judge Pounders had to take a recess during the course of her testimony.

Children's Testimony

The first alleged victim, a girl now 12 years old, took the stand in early August 1987, testifying that she had been sexually abused by both Raymond Buckey and his mother, Peggy McMartin Buckey. She insisted that she was repeatedly forced to play a "Naked Movie Star" game while cameras clicked, and that Raymond Buckey threatened her and a class-mate into silence by sticking a knife into a dead cat. Prosecution ques-tions elicited from her the story that children were told to take off their clothes and pose for people taking pictures. She was not absolutely cer-tain, but thought that both defendants were also naked while the game was being played. This young girl testified that Raymond Buckey fondled her, "touched my vagina," and stuck his fingers inside of it; however, she could not remember how many times this occurred. She said that Raymond Buckey cut and killed a cat and told her that if she told anyone about the game that he would do the same to her and her parents. She also said that she was taken to a house where the naked game was played. Her testi-mony, however, changed from saying there had been no strangers to say-ing there were.

Under cross-examination, the witness was asked why she now testified that she had been penetrated by fingers in the vagina while previously she had not said so; her response was that only the recent use of tampons led her to recall this occurrence. She also testified that she did not ever re-member seeing Raymond Buckey at the preschool. Her response to the question "Did you ever see Raymond Buckey?" was "No."

Defense attorney Davis then elicited from the young girl that the prosecuting attorney had "tabbed" the preliminary testimony she had made. What were these tabs for? The girl witness responded that prosecutor Rubin told her these were smart answers. The defense contended that this witness had been trained to respond with smart answers to questions and that the witness in essence admitted that Lael Rubin told her "sort of" how to respond to questions. She also said that she had met with Lael Rubin six or seven times in sessions lasting as long as four hours, and that the interview included a discussion of "smart answers" to "tricky ques-tions." The young witness equivocated; she was now uncertain as to whether or not she had been drugged with a pink medicine that made her sleepy while at the school. The defense attorneys noted that if she had indeed been molested, she did not show any signs of anxiety or other symptoms of having been traumatized.[11] The defense also argued that if she had been really drugged, she would recall very little, certainly less than what she claimed.

Next on the court agenda was an 11-year-old girl. She was one of the key witnesses in the trial because, along with her younger brother, her testimony represented 37 of the 99 counts with which the defendants were charged. This young girl testified that "with the girls he [Raymond Buckey] put his finger and his penis in their vagina and their bottom. With the boys he put his finger and his penis in their bottom." She testified that she was taken to two houses, a farm, a car wash, and a market. At these places, people were there with cameras and took pictures of them as they played the naked game, and Raymond Buckey "put his finger and his penis in my vagina and my bottom." She said that he did not put his penis in her mouth. She also told of going to a car wash where he took off his clothes and she took off her clothes and again she said that he fingered her vagina and bottom.

Her testimony produced contradictory statements. She now recanted testimony given at the preliminary hearing that she had been sexually abused by former defendant Bette Raidor. Nonetheless, during the five days that she was on the stand, she continued to insist that she had been forced to submit to various sexual acts, and that Raidor only watched while "naked games" were being played.[12]

Outside of the courtroom, defense attorney Dean Gits stated that the young girl obviously was aware that Bette Raidor was no longer being charged and under coaching had changed her testimony. He also said that her testimony was contaminated and if she was mistaken about Raidor, she also was mistaken about Peggy McMartin Buckey.[13]

Next, the defense opposed the showing of videotaped testimony from a young girl who had testified in the preliminary hearing. The defense attorneys argued that it was unconstitutional not to be allowed to cross-examine a witness in a face-to-face confrontation when the witness was clearly available for testimony. The young girl told the judge that she was too scared to take the stand, and he thus ruled that the child was not legally available for testimony.[14]

The next child witness contradicted much of her earlier testimony and denied many of her mother's statements. After a week of testimony, the transcript revealed the same responses as the other child witnesses, with most of her responses, both to prosecution and defense attorneys, being "I don't remember" and "I don't know."

The prosecution then called an employee of the DA's victim-witness program to testify that the young girl was crying after testifying at the preliminary hearing because she had seen Raymond Buckey and was frightened by his presence. The defense contended that she was crying because her parents and Lael Rubin were mad and disappointed with her performance, because her testimony failed to live up to their expectations.

The defense seized this opportunity to show a videotape taken at the preliminary hearing at which this young witness consistently replied "no" to all questions about having being molested at the preschool by the defendants.

In the preliminary hearing, the following exchange took place:

Attorney: [D]id Ray [Raymond Buckey] threaten to shoot your mom and dad?
Girl: No.
Attorney: Did you hear that any other little girl was touched on the bottom?
Girl: No.
Attorney: Did you hear that Ray took pictures of kids naked?
Girl: No.
Attorney: Did Ray ever tell anybody to take their clothes off in the bathroom?
Girl: No.
Attorney: Did you see Ray naked at any time?
Girl: No.

Her trial testimony showed no direct contradictions to her statements in the preliminary hearing. To the details of molestation acts, she often stated "I don't remember" and "I don't know." Thus, her consistent denial to molestation questions surfaced during the preliminary hearing and the actual trial.

The 11-year-old son of a therapist at the South Bay Counseling Center was also called to testify in the trial. He charged that Raymond Buckey had put his penis in his mouth. The boy told the defense that he saw Raymond Buckey kill a horse with a bat. Defense attorney Davis quickly pointed out boy's contradictory statements in which the child had said in the preliminary hearing that he was sitting on the dirt when he was molested. In the trial, the witness said that he was sitting on the defendant's lap. In order to show apparent contradictions in the boy's accounts of alleged molestation acts, the defense sought to show the jurors the boy's interview videotape at CII. Judge Pounders denied the motion; however, the transcript was read into the record.

In trial, the following exchange took place.

Davis: Did Ray put his penis in your mouth?
Boy: Yes.
Davis: Did it happen more than once?
Boy: I had just one picture. I see Ray.
Davis: What is Ray doing?
Boy: He is sticking his penis up me.

In the videotaped interview at the CII with Kathleen MacFarlane, a different version of the exchange took place.

MacFarlane: Did anybody put something yucky in your mouth?
Boy: (No response)
MacFarlane: Can you remember?
Body: I'm not sure.
MacFarlane: How about a finger in your hole?
Boy: Yes.
MacFarlane: Boy! I bet it did! We'll see how smart you are. Did anything come out of Ray's wiener?
Boy: (No response)
MacFarlane: What did the stuff taste like?
Boy: He never did that.

By reading the transcript, the defense had managed not only to show the boy's contradictory responses, but also the apparent coaching and stage-settings for obtaining "smart answers" by the key CII interviewer.

In April 1988, a 13-year-old boy gave five days of graphic, detailed, and sometimes inconsistent testimony, including that he had been taken often to a "blue house" not far from the nursery school where he was forced to play the "Naked Movie Star" game on a brick hearth. The defense spent five days cross-examining this prosecution witness. Most of the defense cross-examination was spent pointing out contradictions between the boy's trial testimony and statements he had made at the preliminary hearing, during the grand jury hearings, and at CII.

Another prosecution witness was an 11-and-a-half-year-old girl who was only three when she attended the McMartin Preschool. She testified, "[W]ell, for little girls he [Raymond Buckey] was putting his penis in their vaginas. He was sticking his fingers in their bottom, and he did the same thing to me," she said.[15]

This time, the defense spent almost four days cross-examining the witness. The defense was able to point out a number of contradictory statements made by the girl. In the CII interview, the girl said that Buckey killed a rabbit with his finger, though in the trial she testified that he killed it with a knife. In the trial, she also stated that Buckey did not take his clothes off, while she said that he took his clothes off in the CII interview.[16]

The next witness, an 8-year-old girl, was the younger sister of the prosecution witness who had just completed her testimony. Her testimony was interrupted by several unexpected events, including the illness of both Peggy McMartin Buckey and one juror, and the prosecution's unsuccessful attempt to disqualify two jurors who had notified the judge that the girl's mother had been signaling to the witness with her hands, when to answer "yes" and when to answer "no." Prosecutor Rubin argued that the two jurors should not be allowed to remain on the jury because their observations were not objective, and they were no longer fair or impartial. Judge Pounders, however, dismissed the prosecution motion to disqualify the two jurors, ruling that the jury was entitled "to believe someone may have been coaching a witness. A jury cannot and shouldn't disregard that."

The defense also managed to show the videotaped interview of the witness at the CII, showing that MacFarlane repeatedly drew the girl's attention to the doll's genitalia, but got no response from her. Finally, the girl said, "time to go home." MacFarlane said, "no, not now ... I want you to help me figure things out." The girl responded, "I don't want to," finally being exhausted and lying on the floor. Her testimony produced many contradictory statements between the preliminary hearing and the actual trial.

Another prosecution witness was a 13-year-old boy, who testified that Raymond Buckey had taken him to a car wash in a van with a group of children and that the children were undressed, molested, and then dressed again while going though the car wash. His testimony also pro-duced contradictory statements. In CII interviews, he said that Raymond Buckey did not take his clothes off during the horsey game, but in the trial, he said that Buckey was naked. There was a long series of questions about a car wash and other alleged molestation acts, and almost all of the boy's answers were "I don't know" or "I don't remember."

Child Witnesses Refusing to Testify

Near the end of the prosecution's case, however, three young witnesses decided not to testify in court. A critical juncture had been reached. The statements of the children refusing to testify were the foundation of 27 of the 99 molestation counts. The prosecution then moved to demonstrate the counts by other testimony. This meant that these and three other counts would have to be dismissed unless they could be proven by means other than the children's direct testimony.

Though the prosecutors said that they would attempt to prove the charges, defense attorney Davis said that he would "vigorously" oppose such efforts to substitute any testimony other than that by the children.[17]

At the request of both the prosecution and the defense, 27 charges were dropped. The prosecution further requested that an additional eight counts be dropped because they had not proven the allegations. The de-fense reflected that the prosecution's case was "nose-diving," saying that though the move was "a face-saving device, ... it looks like major plastic surgery is going on."[18]

Davis told reporters that the accounts of those three witnesses were suffused with contradictions, more unbelievable than those of the other child witnesses who had already testified. As they were a liability to the prosecution, he argued that the DA decided not to let them testify. Whether Davis's accounts were true or whether intense defense cross-examinations of child witnesses contributed to children's refusal to testify, the prosecution finally had dropped nearly one-third of the original charges against the defendants. The defense team's reaction to the prosecution's case was one of obvious skepticism; defense attorney Davis remarked: "[I]t reminded me a little of yesterday's mashed potatoes, nothing new."[19]

Judy Ann Johnson's Son Refusing to Testify
Though the young boy whose allegations first began the McMartin case was going to be called as a defense witness, his father and prosecution experts tried to resist the defense subpoena. The father heatedly told reporters that his son would testify only "over my dead body."[20] The father argued that the boy had already been traumatized enough by the molestation, his mother's death, and the interviews. Edith Wolf, a psychologist at South Bay Counseling Center, testified that forcing the boy to testify in court might produce regressive behaviors such as nightmares and bed wetting—as he had already gone through significant emotional trauma including his parents' divorce and his mother's death. "It is my opinion that further questioning would only further exacerbate [the boy's] already stressful situation," she stated. Wolf also believed that the boy's testimony would be unreliable and inconsistent. She noted that the boy gave conflicting answers, attempted to give answers that he apparently felt would please her, and that about half of the time he wanted to testify because it would be fun and he would get attention, while the other half he was far too scared to testify.

Judge Pounders, however, ordered the boy be brought to court so that he could determine in a face-to-face conversation if the boy should be required to testify. Since the boy had previously also named his father as having molested him, the judge's potential decision to have the boy testify was a particularly important one for the defense. Unfortunately for the defense, the judge declared the boy legally unavailable for testimony and he did not testify in court; the boy's story was never told to the jury because he was never interviewed or videotaped by CII.

Because the judge determined that the child could not testify, several medical doctors examined him and testified as to whether he had been sodomized and molested by the defendant. Their testimony, however, was inconclusive and inconsistent. Other testimony was given by Manhattan

Beach Police Department officer Jane Hoag, who originally investigated the allegations by the child's mother. She testified that she questioned the boy and his older brother and was told that there had been some touching in the shower between the two boys. She admitted, however, that she did not explore the sexual touching between them and their possible connection to the initial accusation by their mother.[21]

Videotaped Testimony

The prosecution attempted to introduce seven and one-half hours of videotaped testimony of a young girl who had testified at the preliminary hearing but who now refused to testify in person. The child's mother had said that she was "too scared to testify and will not testify" at the trial. The testimony of this particular witness was considered to be important because her claims were the basis of three charges of sexual molestation by Raymond Buckey. Unless the girl was able to testify in person or by the use of videotapes, these counts would also have to be dismissed by the judge.

The prosecutors argued that this child's four days on the witness stand during the preliminary hearing were very traumatic. The child's mother filed a declaration that her child was adamant about not going through the same experience again. The judge indicated that he would talk to the girl privately in his chambers and if she did not want to testify again, he would not force her to. After interviewing her, the judge declared the girl legally unavailable for testimony. The prosecution criticized the judge's decision and blamed the defense attorneys for the child's refusal to testify in court. "It was not a fair decision," prosecutor Rubin was reported as saying. "It sends a message to defense attorneys that if you can intimidate a child at the preliminary hearing, you've got a sure way to prevent his or her testimony at a trial."[22]

Therapists' Testimony

Moving beyond child witnesses, another prosecution witness to testify was Kathleen MacFarlane, the key CII therapist. Defense counsel considered her cross-examination the significant and crucial juncture of the trial. As indicated earlier, survey findings indicated that the majority of eligible jurors in the court jurisdiction believed that children's accounts of sexual molestation could be easily influenced by interviewers.

Kathleen MacFarlane, Shawn Connerly, and Sandra Krebs conducted most interviews at the CII.[23] MacFarlane was not a licensed social worker and Connerly lied about her credentials.[24] Also, Dr. Astrid Heger—who testified as an expert—did some interviews of alleged child victims, as did Dr. Cheryl Kent at South Bay Counseling.[25]

MacFarlane spent five weeks on the witness stand, defending her interviewing procedures of the McMartin Preschool children. Judge Pounders concluded that "the central issue is what she [Kathleen MacFarlane] did and how it affected the children, whether it programmed them."

MacFarlane's testimony in the trial was similar to that in the preliminary hearing. She said that it was a long process, like putting together a jigsaw puzzle, to determine what actually happened at the school. She said that she took a "funnel approach," starting with open-ended questions and then becoming more specific, encouraging children to express themselves by using naked puppets and dolls with explicit sex organs. She told each child what other children had already told her had happened at the school, applied labels like "naked" and "yucky" to innocent childhood games, and encouraged young children to demonstrate what happened at the school. MacFarlane said that she doubted if she could "place" or implant a permanent erroneous image of having been molested in the minds of children or their parents.

When the jurors were not present, the judge confessed that he was becoming concerned about her credibility. "I've been concerned, and I want to be very candid about that, by the number of times that Miss MacFarlane has indicated in her answers that her answer depends upon definitions that don't seem to me to be very complex, and that she does not have a memory of a number of things that I would have expected her to remember. So in my view her credibility is becoming more of an issue as she testifies here."

On cross-examination, the defense asked if "[L]ooking at the videotapes that you employed with the children in this case, do you feel some of [your] techniques may have tended to induce the children to construct or fabricate a memory that was not reality?" Her answer, predictably, was "[N]o, I do not." She indicated that she believed that her interview method could never implant an image of sexual molestation in the minds of alleged child victims or their parents.

Because she used anatomically correct dolls during interviews, defense attorney Gits asked MacFarlane if they might suggest to the child that naked games were played at the preschool. Her response was "[N]o, I don't believe that." She also testified that CII interviewers worked hard on the male dolls to ensure they did not appear to have an erect stimulated penis, and that there was no research evidence that faulted the use of anatomically correct dolls in eliciting information from alleged child victims. Gits also asked a series of questions about her background, stressing that she was more of a grant writer rather than a therapist or an expert in diagnosing child sexual abuse.

Following Gits's cross-examination, defense attorney Davis also examined the validity and reliability of her interview techniques to draw information from the children. Davis asked a series of questions to establish that, in one of her interviews, the "Naked Movie Star" game was first mentioned by her, not the child. Relying on the interview transcript, Davis showed the jury that the child repeatedly denied ever playing naked games. MacFarlane responded that telling the child that she already knew about the naked games was designed to take any burden the child might have had about the repercussions of telling.

Davis also managed to show the jury some portions of her interviews on a television monitor in the courtroom. The following are typical excerpts from the transcript of videotaped interviews; Kathleen MacFarlane is interviewing an 8-year-old, former McMartin preschool pupil. The boy is holding an alligator puppet.

> MacFarlane: Mr. Monkey is a little bit chicken, and he can't remember any of the naked games, but we think that you can, 'cause we know a naked game that you were around for, 'cause the other kids told us, and it's called Naked Movie Star. Do you remember that game, Mr. Alligator, or is your memory too bad?
> Boy: Um, I don't remember that game.
> MacFarlane: Oh, Mr. Alligator.
> Boy: Umm, well, it's, umm, a little song that me and [a friend] heard of.
> MacFarlane: Oh.
> Boy: Well, I heard out loud someone singing, "Naked Movie Star, Naked Movie Star."
> MacFarlane: You know that, Mr. Alligator? That means you're smart, 'cause that's the same song the other kids knew and that's how we really know you're smarter than you look. So you better not play dumb, Mr. Alligator.
> Boy: Well, I didn't really hear it a whole lot. I just heard someone yell it from out in the—- Someone yelled it.
> MacFarlane: Maybe, Mr. Alligator, you peeked in the window one day and saw them playing it, and maybe you could remember and help us.
> Boy: Well, no, I haven't seen anyone playing Naked Movie Star. I've only heard the song.
> MacFarlane: What good are you? You must be dumb.
> Boy: Well. I don't know really, umm, remember seeing anyone play that, 'cause I wasn't there, when—I—when people are playing it.

MacFarlane: You weren't? You weren't? That's why we're hoping maybe you saw, see, a lot of these puppets weren't there, but they got to see what happened.

Boy: Well, I saw a lot of fighting.

MacFarlane: I bet you can help us a lot, though, 'cause, like, Naked Movie Star is a simple game, because we know about that game, 'cause we just have had twenty kids told us about that game. Just this morning, a little girl came in and played it for us and sang it just like that. Do you think if I asked you a question, you could put your thinking cap on and you might remember, Mr. Alligator?

Boy: Maybe.

MacFarlane: You could nod your head yes or no. Can you remember who took the pictures for the naked-movie-star game? That would be a great thing to feed into the secret machine [the video camera], and then it would be all gone, just like all the other kids did. You can just nod whether you remember or not, see how good your memory is.

Boy: [Nods puppet's head.]

MacFarlane: You do? Well, that's remarkable. I wonder if you could hold a pointer in your mouth, and then you wouldn't have to say a word and [boy] wouldn't have to say a word. And you could just point.

Boy: [Places pretend camera on adult male nude doll using alligator puppet] Sometimes he did.

MacFarlane: Can I pat you on the head for that? Look what a big help you can be. You're going to help all these little children, because you're so smart.... OK, did they ever pose in funny poses for the pictures?

Boy: Well, it wasn't a real camera. We just played....

MacFarlane: Mr. Alligator, I'm going to ... going to ask you something here. Now, we already found out from the other kids that it was a real camera, so you don't have to pretend, OK? Is that a deal?

Boy: Yes, it was a play camera that we played with.

MacFarlane: Oh, and it went flash?

Boy: Well, it didn't exactly go flash.

MacFarlane: It didn't exactly go flash. Went click? Did little pictures go zip, come out of it?

Boy: I don't remember that.

MacFarlane: Oh, you don't remember that. Well, you're doing pretty good, Mr. Alligator. I got to shake your hand.

There also were serious questions and doubts about the validity and objectivity of the interview techniques used by Dr. Astrid Heger. Below is an illustration of her interview carried out with a 6-year-old girl.

Heger: Maybe you could show me with this, with this doll [puts hand on two dolls, one naked, one dressed] how the kids danced for the Naked Movie Star.

Girl: They didn't really dance. It was just, like, a song.

Heger: Well, what did they do when they sang the song?

Girl: They just went around singing the song.

Heger: They just went around and sang the song?

Girl: [Nods her head]

Heger: And they didn't take their clothes off?

Girl: [Shakes her head]

Heger: I heard that, I heard from several different kids that they took their clothes off. I think that [first classmate] told me that, I know that [second classmate] told me that, I know that [third classmate] told me. [Fourth classmate] and [fifth classmate] all told me that. That's kind of a hard secret, it's kind of a yucky secret to talk of—but, maybe, we could see if we could find——.

Girl: Not that I remember.

Heger: This is my favorite puppet right here. [Picks up a bird puppet] You wanna be this puppet? Ok? Then I get to be the Detective Dog.... I know that we're gonna figure this out—— all this stuff out right now. We're gonna just figure it all out. Ok, when that tricky part about touching the kids was going on, could you take a pointer in your mouth and point on the, on the doll over here, on either one of these dolls, where, where the kids were touched? Could you do that?

Girl: I don't know.

Heger: I know that the kids were touched. Let's see if we can figure that out.

Girl: I don't know.

Heger: You don't know where they were touched?

Girl: Uh-uh. [Shakes her head]

Heger: Well, some of the kids told me that they were touched sometimes. They said that it was, it kinda, sometimes it kinda hurt. And some of the times, it felt pretty good. Do you remember that touching game that went on?

Girl: No.

Heger: Ok. Let me see if we can try something else and——.

Girl: Wheeee! [Spins the puppet above her head.]

Heger: Come on, bird, get down here and help us out here.

Girl: No.

Heger: [Girl/Bird] is having a hard time talking. I don't wanna hear any more no's. No no, Detective Dog and we're gonna figure this out.

The defense continued to question the credibility of these interviews and in particular those carried out by Kathleen MacFarlane. She noted that in her present position dealing with young children, it was not required that she be licensed. While MacFarlane was not licensed, she had a long record of work experience in child sexual abuse as well as having several publications.

After MacFarlane's testimony, jurors also watched other CII video-taped interviews, seeing for themselves interviewing techniques, interactions between the interviewers and children to determine if the prosecution could rely upon the interviews or if the defense was correct in arguing that the interviews were biased and that the children had been "brainwashed" into believing that they had been molested.

Medical Evidence

A major failing of the prosecution's case was a lack of corroborating forensic evidence.[26] Relying upon their medical evidence, the prosecution was fairly confident that some sexual abuse had taken place, but by whom and where was becoming increasingly more difficult to determine.

Similar to the preliminary hearing two years earlier, prosecution and defense experts interpreted forensic medical evidence differently, reciting the lines they had already scripted.[27] Dr. Astrid Heger again testified for the prosecution, stating that in ten of the children she found scars, tears, enlarged body openings, or other physical evidence demonstrating "blunt-force penetrating trauma" consistent with the repeated sodomy and rape that the children had described. Dr. Heger also testified that because sexual abuse often leaves no detectable signs she was surprised to find injuries, in some cases injuries indicative of severe trauma, in so many children. She documented physical findings in three boys and seven girls, explaining that five of the girls showed signs of having been penetrated both vaginally and anally. She added that dozens of some 150 former McMartin students whom she examined did not appear to have been molested.[28]

The defense initially indicated that they would call Dr. Robert ten Bensel of Minneapolis as their medical expert witness because he performed the preliminary examinations of the alleged abused children. But Dr. ten Bensel refused to come and testify for the defense because "the pressures brought on me were more than the price I was willing to pay. The ante was too high."[29] He stated that his department chair had received numerous calls from his colleagues, Los Angeles DA's office, and the state attorney general, and he faced the loss of state and federal funding if he testified for the defense. He admitted that being involved in the McMartin case was destroying his relationships with professional groups.

As a result, only one medical expert could be found who was willing to testify for the defense. Called to the stand was London city coroner Dr.

David M. Paul, who worked at the University of London Hospital, was a consultant on forensic medicine, and was not tied to the professional pressures at work in the American medical milieu. In replying to questions posed by defense attorney Dean Gits, he said that in his review of medical records and anatomical slides of the children, he found no evidence to suggest molestation. He testified that three of the five alleged victims he had questioned showed no physical signs of sexual abuse.

Dr. Paul characterized some slides, projected before the jury, as showing "perfectly normal" body parts, dismissing what appeared to be abnormalities in others as "of no significance." He took issue with the prosecution's medical findings and terminology, and testified that the prosecution's doctors were either mistaken, negligent, or inconsistent. He also criticized Dr. Heger's use of the colposcope, the camera-like machine that takes magnified three-dimensional photographs and renders objects abnormal in appearance.

Referring to the findings of two physicians who had examined the child whose mother's report triggered the investigation, Paul said, "I don't believe they're even consistent with sodomy." He said, however, there were medical signs that could be interpreted as evidence that the child had suffered lesser sexual abuse.[30]

After reviewing medical records, Dr. Paul testified that he found strong evidence of molestation in only two of the 11 alleged victims. His testimony was in direct contrast to the prosecution medical witnesses who said they had found physical evidence indicative of abuse in nine of the alleged victims. Dr. Paul also stated that there was disagreement among physicians about how to diagnose sexual abuse and admitted that, despite three decades of experience in the field, in many cases he could not tell either way. Dr. Paul's testimony, however, implied recent molestation of one young male victim because of fresh lesions, though this part of the testimony was not followed up by either the prosecution or defense.[31] Finally, Dr. Paul concluded, "[T]here is no physical evidence consistent [only] with abuse. Therefore my diagnosis neither confirms nor denies" molestation.[32]

Gits modestly concluded, "I am not a medical doctor, but I believe we've demonstrated throughout the testimony that these doctors don't agree among themselves. Even the prosecution doctors don't agree among themselves in terms of what they see."[33]

The Defense Expert Witness

The defense then called Dr. Michael Maloney to testify. His testimony played the central role in discrediting CII's interview techniques and criticizing Dr. Roland Summit's theory. Dr. Maloney, a clinical psychologist and professor of psychiatry at USC School of Medicine, testified that in addition to the McMartin children, he had evaluated hundreds of alleged victims of child sexual abuse.

The child sexual abuse accommodation syndrome, written by Dr. Roland Summit, was unanimously embraced by child abuse therapists as well as the prosecution. It had been a powerful weapon in the hands of prosecutors because it posits that children never lie when they say they have been sexually abused and that when they say they have not been molested they are "in denial," meaning that they are concealing molestation.[34] Perhaps the most important criticism of Dr. Summit's work is that it only focuses on cases where people have acknowledged they were molested but fails to focus on the issue of false allegations.

Dr. Maloney testified that after reviewing the CII interview videotapes, he concluded that the children were so contaminated by the process itself that, no matter what they said, their disclosure of sexual molestation was invalid and unreliable. Dr. Maloney observed that the CII interviewers were producing the vast majority of verbal output, creating their own blindspot:

> First ... there does not appear to have been any consideration from the [viewpoint of the] cognitive development of the children. Second, there is no consideration of the relative brightness of the children and the relative fluency of the children, the sex of the children. They are all considered, at least by implication, as a homogeneous mass that you must treat the same way.[35]

Dr. Maloney's criticism of the interview techniques also focused on the so-called "script," which he referred to as the "predetermined program" imposed on the children. Because the same interview script had been used for all the children, revelations of child abuse were underscored and pre-programmed in a way to generate similar responses from them.

> The very concept of using a program or a script in an interview of a child is wrong in the sense that it is putting in the interview situation material from the interviewer rather than obtaining spontaneous information from the child. The more that's done, the less you will be able to conclude about the child's behavior and statements.[36]

Dr. Maloney also criticized the systematic use of anatomically correct dolls to elicit information from the children, testifying that:

The primary problem with that is that the end result of this identifying body parts is to identify the sexual body parts.... At that point in the interview the child[ren have], typically, said zero about their own sexual experiences. But they have been directed to talk about genitalia and other so called private parts. Again, in doing that, you run the risk of stage setting.[37]

The use of the dolls got the McMartin children further away from their own spontaneous remarks about sex, Dr. Maloney testified. The children's responses were already expected and often supplied by the interviewers because of the way that the defendants were portrayed and identified. For example, Dr. Maloney criticized that Peggy McMartin Buckey had been identified by the fat doll, called "Miss Piggy." Raymond Buckey was identified by the black doll and introduced to children as a "bad person" who "needs to be put in jail." Thus, the CII interview was characterized as an "information-giving technique," in which interviewers had presented information to children, presented all the pieces to a puzzle, and told them things that had already happened at the preschool. The interview techniques motivated the children to solve the puzzle within the pre-programmed contexts presented by the interviewers, Dr. Maloney emphasizing that:

The motivation comes out of things like, "Are you smart or dumb?," "Are you a good detective?," "Are you going to please your mother and father?" And then, finally, it gives a vehicle for solution, which are these puppets, these dolls. So what you're doing is presenting a situation that you could take with any children, and not know why you got the results you got out of it, no matter what their experience was before that.[38]

Dr. Maloney's testimony was limited to only those children called by the prosecution as witnesses in the trial. However, the defense relied on his testimony to raise serious questions about CII interview techniques, including stage-settings, scripts, and the use of anatomically correct dolls.

Jailhouse Informant Testimony

Additional testimony was presented against defendant Raymond Buckey by George Freeman, who had shared a cell with Raymond Buckey in the Men's Central Jail. Freeman testified that Buckey had admitted to multiple child molestations both at the McMartin Preschool and at a preschool in San Diego. Freeman had contacted authorities after having shared the cell with Buckey to alert them to Buckey's alleged confession of sodomizing the child whose allegations triggered the massive investigation.

Freeman was the only adult to ever testify about knowledge of Buckey's alleged sexual abuse. According to Freeman, Buckey not only confessed to sodomizing the boy but also mentioned molesting several other children, having a long incestuous relationship with his sister, shipping pornographic photographs through a contact in Venice Beach to Denmark, and burying incriminating photographs of himself and youngsters in South Dakota shortly before his arrest. In addition to testifying about Buckey's alleged confession, he also testified that Daniel Davis, Raymond Buckey's defense attorney, had threatened to kill him. Lacking forensic or other evidence, Freeman's accusations became virtually unprovable.

Freeman, age 45, was a career criminal who had been convicted of at least nine felonies by the time of the McMartin trial. Subsequently, the prosecution revealed that Freeman might have perjured himself in a trial stemming from the Soledad Prison riots of 1979, when he said that he had witnessed a murder of an inmate, but later testified, "I didn't see nothing." He lied again in a 1984 Los Angeles murder trial and in the McMartin preliminary hearing when he testified that he had told the truth in the earlier case. As an admitted perjurer in a previous murder trial, Freeman also admitted that he had lied at the McMartin preliminary hearing. "We believe Mr. (George) Freeman may have lied under oath," prosecutor Rubin admitted to the judge, after asking the judge to appoint an attorney to advise him.

Judge Pounders ruled that Freeman would have to be cross-examined by the defense or that he would have to declare a mistrial.[39] Co-prosecutor Roger Gunson suggested that Freeman's testimony should be stricken from the record or that he could be given immunity from prosecution for testifying. Judge Pounders said that merely striking the man's testimony from the record would not remedy the situation. The defense argued that providing immunity would be a reward for perjury. "Lying under oath is a felony," Judge Pounders thus noted; "it goes to the heart of the believability of a witness who is testifying." If a mistrial were to be declared, the result would have been to sever the trials of the two defendants.[40]

Prosecutors were in a delicate position since they had admitted that they knew about Freeman's perjury in other cases, but did not initially disclose that knowledge to the judge and the defense. Against defense arguments, Judge Pounders nonetheless acceded to the prosecution's request to give Freeman immunity from prosecution for his testimony. During his initial testimony, Freeman had repeatedly said, "[O]n the advice of my attorney I refuse to answer and take the Fifth Amendment." After he resumed testifying, with immunity from prosecution, however, he explained that he had not told the truth when he had testified previously about a murder.

Subsequently, Freeman failed to show up in court to continue his testimony. He telephoned prosecutors that he had received a threatening phone call related to a murder that he presumably had witnessed (unrelated to the McMartin case). Judge Pounders issued a bench warrant for his arrest.[41] The defense contended that Freeman had left the country to avoid testifying. However, Freeman later returned to the courtroom and resumed testifying.

Freeman was asked by defense attorney Daniel Davis about a murder in 1979 and a tape in which Freeman allegedly confessed to the murder. Since Davis did not have the tape, Judge Pounders was furious at him for bringing up the subject and realized that he would have to deal with this problem during the next several days. The judge felt that Freeman's character had been destroyed.

Judge Pounders apparently did not believe Freeman's initial story but after interminable questioning by Davis, he came to believe that the conversation may well have happened.

Which side did Freeman's testimony help? The defense argued that Freeman, over the years, had curried special favors from prosecutors for perjured testimony, that this was just another instance of his past behavior, and that the district attorney's office was willing to trade perjury for special favors. The defense was particularly upset because Freeman had been allowed to testify, was then advised that he needed an attorney, and that he had done harm to the defense's case even though he may have perjured himself. Prosecutor Rubin did not deny that she knew of the previous perjury. However, after his testimony she said that she realized that it should have been brought to the court's attention.

Jailhouse informants who recount their fellow prisoners' "confessions" are often used by the state as witnesses in criminal prosecutions. A jailhouse informant is an inmate, usually awaiting trial or sentencing, who claims to have heard another prisoner make an admission about a case. The informant then reports the other prisoner's admission to the authorities in the hopes of trading his testimony for better treatment or leniency in sentencing. Because the informant's testimony may be completely fabricated, the use of jailhouse informants to obtain convictions may be one of the most abused aspects of the criminal justice system.

Despite criticism of this practice, its use is widespread. For instance, the Los Angeles District Attorney's office has used jailhouse informants to obtain convictions in at least 120 criminal cases between 1980 and 1990.[42]

The McMartin defense counsel discovered that the prosecutors had on their witness list not only George Freeman, but Leslie White and several other jailhouse informants known to trade perjury for leniency. In October 1988, the defense also discovered that Leslie White was employed by the Los Angeles District Attorney's office for more than ten years and that he was able to gather enough information about another unrelated crime to testify against a defendant at trial without ever having met the defendant.

White and several other informants regularly used by the Los Angeles District Attorney's office admitted to giving false testimony about various defendants' jailhouse confessions in order to obtain lenient treatment in their own cases. Though the district attorney's office was well aware of the unreliability of certain jailhouse informants, they continued to use their testimony in otherwise "weak" cases in order to obtain convictions.

The defense discovered that powerful incentives and rewards were promised to these informants in exchange for their testimony. For instance, in exchange for the testimony of one inmate informer, Los Angeles prosecutors reportedly relocated the informant, found him a job, and paid his rent for an entire year. George Freeman who had been convicted of felonies testified that the DA's office paid his first month's rent, approximately one thousand dollars. He also contacted the KABC TV station and Wayne Satz's investigator to make arrangements to appear on TV and make some money.

Freeman had falsely testified for the prosecution throughout his criminal career. When he had been charged with burglary and assault, officers of the Los Angeles Police and the Los Angeles County Sheriff's Office urged a judge to "go easy" on him and, subsequently, his sentence was reduced from three years in prison to one year in county jail.[43] When he was released, he was provided with a home, a job, and new identity by the DA's office. After months of failed investigation, unable to produce adult witnesses, photographs, or any other corroborating evidence to support the charges of McMartin child molestation, the DA's office placed Freeman in the witness protection program that paid his living expenses, and then placed him in Buckey's cell. In November 1987, after his court testimony against Buckey, Freeman was arrested for robbing a woman at gunpoint.

Leslie White also stated that he had received two seven-day furloughs from prison, while serving a twelve-month jail term for a parole violation. White was also transferred from county jail to a more comfortable suburban jail where privileges such as stereo-equipped cells and furloughs are easier to obtain.

One of the important issues raised by the use of jailhouse confessions is how to obtain a new trial for those convicted on the basis of perjured testimony. The logical solution is for the prisoner to file a petition for a writ of *habeas corpus* (a right to a new hearing) on the grounds that "false evidence substantially material or probative on the issue of guilt or punishment was introduced at trial." The writ would allow the prisoner to collaterally attack his conviction if he could present evidence that a purported jailhouse confession was actually fabricated by the prosecution's witness.

However, the road to obtaining a new trial is not easy and many prisoners remain behind bars. If the McMartin defendants had been found guilty, it would have been highly unlikely that higher courts would have reversed the conviction or remanded the case because of perjured testimony by the jailhouse informant.

Testimony of Daniel Davis

The first defense witness called was the defense attorney for Raymond Buckey, Daniel Davis. This was an unusual tactical move by the defense team, calling their own attorney to testify on the witness stand. Davis testified because he felt that it was important and necessary to restore his own credibility throughout the trial before proceeding further in the defense of his client. In responding to questions asked by his attorney Ed Rucker, Davis denied that he ever threatened to kill any of the witnesses including George Freeman. Davis also testified that Raymond Buckey had never admitted to him that he had sex with any of the children at the preschool.

His testimony was considered to be important in the following two ways: (1) to discredit the earlier testimony given by George Freeman and (2) to establish and restore his credibility that as Raymond Buckey's defense attorney, he was acting honestly in the best interest of his client.

The American criminal justice system assumes that the accused is presumed innocent until such time as guilt may be proven in a court of law. Even if an accused admits guilt to the defense attorney, it is the defense attorney's responsibility that the accused is still entitled to the full protection of the law, advice, and representation of counsel. Davis' testimony gave the assurance to the jury and the court that Buckey had never admitted the alleged sexual molestation to him either privately or publicly. His testimony sent the strong message that the defendant and his private counsel had nothing to hide.

Testimony of Peggy Ann Buckey

The first member of the Buckey-McMartin family to testify was Peggy Ann Buckey, who spent more than a month on the witness stand. Though the prosecution resisted having Peggy Ann Buckey testify as a defense witness, Judge Pounders insisted that she was an important witness and rejected the prosecution's motion.

Taking the stand, she testified about her early childhood and life. She insisted that she would not lie under any circumstances. She was adamant that she had never molested a child nor witnessed any such molestations by her brother Raymond Buckey or her mother, reiterating that she had observed nothing unusual at the school while she taught there. She said that the first time she heard of the "Naked Movie Star" game was on television.

Defense attorney Gits also revealed that Raymond Buckey's trip to South Dakota was planned and the tickets purchased well before he knew that an investigation was underway; that he was not teaching at the school when he allegedly was transporting children in a van being driven by Peggy Ann Buckey (when she was actually attending college in Irvine and Long Beach); that he was not teaching at the school when one child who testified against him and Peggy was enrolled. "If Peggy and Ray molested [the boy] in a secret room every day and at a supermarket, performed satanic rites and killed rabbits at a church, photographed and molested the kids at a house, filmed kids on a stage at a theater and killed horses with a sword at a farm, they must have really been busy," the defense insisted. These acts would have to had been accomplished in a 16-day period when both the child and Peggy Ann Buckey were at the school. Under cross-examination Peggy Ann Buckey continued to deny any unusual behavior by anyone at the preschool.

Gits argued that the artifacts seized during a search of the Buckey home were a graduation gown, gag underwear, and a toy that turned out to be a puzzle—all of which were used by the prosecution in "an attempt to create guilt by innuendo."

Outside the courtroom, Gits said, "[N]ever once did the [prosecution] focus on whether Peggy Ann Buckey molested a child or saw molestation.... Their only point was that she was there for more than five weeks, and we had to endure days and days of cross-examination for that purpose." The defense concluded that she had presented "a sense of what that family is and the love they have for each other." But according to the prosecution, Peggy Ann Buckey was quite another personality—"an unbelievable arrogant witness who lied."[44]

Testimony of Virginia McMartin

The original testimony of Virginia McMartin, Peggy McMartin Buckey's mother and Raymond Buckey's grandmother, was videotaped without the presence of the jury, in case she was unable to testify later. Her diaries were introduced into evidence by the prosecution, though they contained hearsay. One entry indicated that Peggy McMartin Buckey had seen a child touch Raymond Buckey's genitals. This was reported to the child's mother, who said that this little girl had a habit of doing it to her father and the mother apologized for the girl's behavior.[45]

During her testimony, she had an outburst directed at the judge for allowing the prosecutor to use hearsay evidence. She accused the prosecution of lying about Raymond Buckey, trying to indicate that she knew that he had a sexual problem with young children. The judge sternly told her to be quiet.

"I have been brought up a lady. I've been one all of my life and I expect to spend my senior years as a lady. You can speak to me respectfully," she retorted. For any more outbursts, the judge admonished, she could be sent to jail.

Prosecutor Rubin argued that the diaries also had an entry indicating that Raymond Buckey and his mother were counseled by Dr. Frank Richelieu of the Church of Religious Science. Outside of the courtroom, prosecutor Lael Rubin said that the counseling was for Buckey's sexual problems involving young children.[46] As he had stated at the preliminary hearing, both in and out of court, Dr. Richelieu categorically denied this allegation.

In her testimony, Virginia McMartin also denied having had any knowledge of why Peggy McMartin Buckey and her grandson had gone for counseling and specifically denied that he had a problem of touching children's genitals. She did acknowledge that one of her own granddaughters believed that her two children were molested at their preschool.[47] She attributed this to her granddaughter having been brainwashed by staff members from CII. And she continued to deny that she had ever molested a child or had seen the defendants do anything that might even be construed as molestation, that she was ever present or knew about "naked games," or that she touched any children in a manner that could be considered as molestation.

Testimony of Peggy McMartin Buckey

Almost six years after the original charges, Peggy McMartin Buckey finally took the stand for the first time. She testified that she had been teaching at the McMartin Preschool from its beginning. Over time, her mother Vir-

ginia McMartin came to rely upon her to run the preschool and she later
became the 50% owner.

She was asked specifically, "[D]id you ever molest any of those
children?" Her response was, "[N]ever." On a series of direct questions,
she denied ever touching any of them for the purposes of sexual
gratification, ever being naked in front of them, causing them to be naked or partially naked, permitting other adults to touch them, threatening them, molesting them, or ever seeing anyone else touch or molest
them. She defended her son working at the preschool indicating that he
had volunteered with children in San Diego and had received a certificate.
She felt that he had potential to be a good child care worker after he
took the courses.

Throughout her testimony, she denied that she had sexually assaulted
any of her students. She also denied the allegation that she and her son
had ever received sexually related counseling by Dr. Frank Richelieu, the
pastor of the Church of Religious Science in Redondo Beach, Los Angeles. She revealed that she had been sexually abused by a neighbor when
she was younger and told the court that she was religious and had been
involved in the Christian Science Church activities.

Testimony of Raymond Buckey

Two months after his mother testified, Raymond Buckey finally took the
witness stand, and media attention now reached its highest point.[48] After
six years of near-perfect silence since his arrest and detention, the print
and electronic media bridled to catch his every moment. As the media
greatly anticipated his testimony, Buckey was duly sworn in and took the
witness stand. The courtroom was completely packed; media reporters,
lawyers, and spectators hung silently in awe.

Meanwhile another scenario was at play. The judge became aware
that his court order had been violated when it appeared as though a witness' identity may have been revealed. As Daniel Davis, Raymond
Buckey's attorney, began to examine the defendant, Judge Pounders suddenly called a halt, instructing the jury to go into the jury room, admonishing that there had been recurring problems throughout the trial with
regard to people in the courtroom, other than court participants:

> We're constantly worried about news media video coverage, the
> cameras in the courtroom and the fact that as I've noticed with Mr.
> Davis and his client at the board, the camera, the TV camera cov-
> ered them, and behind them is the photograph of the child.

I have indicated before, and I'm not sure whether the news crew here is aware of it, that that is not to be photographed, and my only recourse is going to be if I ever see a child's photograph in any news media publications, wherever they are, I will never again allow video presentations in this courtroom on this case.

It is a punishment of all the news media for the error of one, but that's the only thing I know to do.

I'm not going to listen to each of you saying, but, judge, we followed your rules. There is nothing else I can seem to do, so I wanted to make sure that's understood.... I also know in another courtroom, in the Twilight Zone case where by accident one TV crew did close ups of the jury, the other TV stations felt it was appropriate to run those as well.

All I'm saying is the bottom line is the first time I see a child's photograph presented in any news media presentation, that will be the last time the cameras will be in this courtroom.[49]

Davis's questionings of Raymond Buckey then resumed. Despite the pall of media attention throughout his testimony, Raymond Buckey unstintingly denied all 53 charges of child sexual molestation. He stated, "[N]othing improper ever happened at the preschool." Each charge was weightedly read by the defense attorney Daniel Davis by asking, "[D]id you do that?" The answer was always, "[N]o." Buckey also testified that he had not even been at the school when many of the alleged victims had attended the school. He testified that he had never touched any child in any manner that could be construed as being sexual in nature.

Buckey admitted, however, that he sometimes did not wear underwear and that he used adult pornography for sexual gratification. He also testified that when the investigators visited his parents' home, he had attempted to flush some explicit adult photos down the toilet. Buckey's testimony also covered whether or not it was appropriate for a male to be working in a preschool, Buckey indicating, "I don't see anything inappropriate for a male to be working with children."[50]

Buckey also categorically denied ever having talked to Freeman about his sexual activities. During cross-examination by prosecution attorney Lael Rubin, he said that he did not dispose of the sexually explicit pictures he had carefully cut from magazines, despite advice from his lawyer's investigator to get rid of them, "because I still used them" for sexual gratification. Buckey said that it was not until the police started banging on the door of his parent's home just before his arrest that he had panicked and wanted to get rid of them. He testified that he had tried to flush them down the toilet but could not, so he threw them out the window.

Buckey's temper flared as Rubin hammered away at his lifestyle; he had admitted in his earlier testimony to skipping college classes to play volleyball, drinking heavily, being convicted of drunk driving, and showing a preoccupation with pictures of specific sexual acts—fellatio and cunnilingus—that he had kept under his pillow or mattress.

Aside from these specific pictures, Rubin asked, "Did anybody ever give you any advice about getting rid of or destroying any other piece of evidence?" Buckey took issue with the word "other."

"Is it your belief that those exhibits in front of you ... are not evidence?" Rubin asked Buckey. "Evidence of what? That I masturbate?" he responded. "Evidence, Mr. Buckey," Rubin countered. "I don't believe it's any relevant evidence at all.... What's that got to do with allegations of molesting children?"

"Are you asking me?" Rubin responded.

Unsure who was cross-examining whom, Judge Pounders then halted the heated exchange. Buckey then answered the prosecutor that he had no knowledge of any evidence being removed from his family's Manhattan Beach home or the nursery school just before the police search. He also testified that he had not been working at the school when some of his accusers attended and was seldom alone at the school. Most of the time he taught at the preschool, he stated, other teachers were there with him.

Buckey verified school records that documented that he had been the only teacher on duty the afternoon of August 11, 1983, the day that the first child reported that he had been molested, thus triggering the investigation. Buckey said that ten children had stayed for afternoon care and that all but two parents had picked up their children by 4 P.M. when the youngster left.[51] He testified that he had never molested or sodomized the boy and never touched the child in any sexual manner or way that could be construed as sexually abusive.

Miscellaneous Testimony Without End

There were other witnesses who were scheduled to testify, though not all of them appeared in the courtroom. One former defense investigator, Paul Bynum, committed suicide before he was able to testify about turtle shells and animal bones found at the McMartin Preschool. Judge Pounders informed jurors that the cause of death was not attributed to any criminal cause and that his testimony would be presented through other testimony and evidence.[52]

Among material evidence presented by the prosecution were boxes that contained "crumpled pages torn from pornographic magazines, canisters of film, cameras, a rubber duck and other toys, a black robe, a Robin Hood costume with bells, crayon makeup and three pairs of underpants—men's stretch bikinis—festooned with suggestive drawings and comments."[53] The robe was a graduation gown, the defense noted, the briefs were for adults rather than children, the film and negatives portrayed clothed children engaged in normal activities not nude or in sex acts, and the pornography from magazines only involved adults. All in all, the boxes of evidence produced no substantial impact other than waking up the jurors; *LA Times* headlines read: "Boxes of Evidence Enliven McMartin Trial."[54]

Several defense witnesses confirmed that Buckey had not even been at the McMartin Preschool during the time some of the molestations allegedly took place. Joseph Miles, Director of Northrup University's Institute of Technology, testified that Buckey was in class or lab during the period of October 23, 1978 to January 17, 1979. Miles indicated that it was highly unlikely that Buckey could have slipped away unnoticed to molest children at the preschool some ten miles away from the Institute.

Another witness, a former substitute teacher at the preschool, testified that she never saw children playing naked games, knew of no policy that had discouraged parents from visiting or coming onto the school grounds, and that she had never taken children from class. Further, she said that she had never seen Buckey at the school.

Ray Fadel—owner of Harry's Market, the scene of alleged molestations—and his employees also testified in February, 1988, denying any impropriety.[55] Similarly, other witnesses testified that they had not witnessed any sexual molestation—these including the owner and employees at the car wash, another supposed scene of sexual abuse, and the owner of the farm, where horses were allegedly killed and children were molested.

Another part of Buckey's defense was that, because he had had an affair with a woman, he could not be a child molester. A 37-year-old Montana woman, claiming she had had a sexual relationship with Raymond Buckey in 1982, also appeared in the courtroom and testified that there was no way he could be a child molester. Barbara Dusky Goles testified that she and Buckey had met in 1982 at a Las Vegas convention booth where both were selling pyramid power hats, and had spent several nights together. She also stated that she had visited the defendant in Manhattan Beach and observed that when he walked into the room at the preschool, the children came running with outstretched arms, and was amazed at the love that was exchanged between them. Now married, she testified that the prosecutors visited her home in Montana and had harassed her family for several weeks.

Deputy District Attorney Lael Rubin, after cross-examination, said that Goles' turnabout was more damaging to her reputation than if she had simply said that she and Buckey were just friends and stuck to her story. Rubin stated, "it's abundantly clear that the defense has gotten to her.... This lady is straight out of Central Casting. She is lying."[56]

Closing Arguments

The defense case was at a high pitch, still planning to call 40 more witnesses to invalidate the children's testimony and question the credibility of evidence presented by the prosecution. But Judge Pounders refused to allow the defense to call additional witness and ordered them to rest their case. Besides Dr. Maloney, the defense had planned to call other expert witnesses to further demonstrate the invalidity of the CII evaluations.

Under pressure to speed up the testimony and conclude more than two years of proceedings, which cost taxpayers millions of dollars, the judge ruled that additional testimony would be "irrelevant," "cumulative," and too time-consuming.[57]

The underlying reason was obvious. Given the lengthy trial, there were almost no alternate jurors left, and the judge would have had to declare a mistrial if he failed to maintain the 12-member jury. Thus, it was clear that the judge must have felt that additional testimony would risk the possibility of a mistrial.

The judge was particularly upset to learn that the defense had planned on calling additional medical experts, admonishing: "I would not have authorized an expenditure of $20,000 to bring Dr. David M. Paul [the defense sexual abuse expert] from England had not the defense contended that no doctors in this country were willing to touch the case."

The trial proper was coming to a close after more than two years and the appearance of numerous witnesses. In their closing arguments, the opposing lawyers presented a summary of their case to the jury, emphasizing the evidence most favorable to their side.

The prosecution's closing arguments focused on the children's silence about the alleged molestation. Initially the prosecution had argued that the children were silent because of threats to them and their parents; in closing, however, the prosecution now posed a countertheory that they had kept quiet because of the affection the children had for Raymond Buckey—a complete departure from the prosecution's earlier position. The prosecution also played the other flank, arguing that children could not be "brainwashed or programmed" to believe that molestation had taken place without it actually having had occurred. Following the supposition that the children were full of "denial," the prosecution argued that it was only through CII interviewers' and prosecution's efforts that they were able to overcome this denial. The prosecution even asked the jurors to believe the jailhouse informant, though he had been discredited in the courtroom.

In its closing, the defense told the jurors that they needed to utilize their "common sense" and be aware of the concept of "reasonable doubt." Defense attorney Gits argued, "Kee MacFarlane wasn't qualified to conduct the evaluations" she had carried out and that Dr. Astrid Heger was unqualified to carry out the medical examinations. Attacking the lack of scientific findings by the prosecutions' medical experts, Gits argued that Dr. Paul was a noted expert who had found virtually no indications of sexual abuse. Gits focused on the inconsistencies of the children's testimony and noted that their testimony defied "common sense." He also argued that the prosecution's case was filled with faulty evidence based on investigator incompetence and lacked soundness of judgment, logic, and legal foundation.

Taking six days to present his closing arguments, defense attorney Davis took another tack; he asked the jury to consider the question of the validity and credibility of CII interviewers, the children's testimony, medical testimony by child abuse experts provided by the prosecution, testimonial evidence that the two McMartin defendants had stated under oath that they had never molested children, and the additional witnesses who had testified that the defendants were not present at the preschool when alleged molestation took place.

He argued that the case was being used by those district attorneys "trying to win at all costs" and "trying to fulfill their career ambitions." Davis also played part of the CII videotapes once again, displaying how the children had been manipulated into saying that they were molested. He said that CII interviewers were like "used car salesmen" and that "[T]he truth never had a chance." Finally, he attacked the jailhouse informant stating that the prosecution, in desperation to use him, showed the lack of credibility of their charges. His final plea to the jurors was for them to "Keep your head.... Give both sides your fair, objective, and independent verdict."

After the closing arguments, the judge gave instructions to the jury, amounting to a minicourse in criminal law, including an explanation of the crime of child sexual molestation. The judge also reminded the jury that the McMartin defendants were considered not guilty and had to be acquitted unless the state had proved its case beyond a reasonable doubt. Finally, the judge provided the jury with procedural instructions about such matters as contacting the judge during deliberations if they had questions and the order in which they had to consider charges because the accusation included multiple charges of child sexual molestation.

And so on November 2, 1989, the jury of 12 retired to a private room to begin its deliberation.

McMartin Defendants Versus a McMartin Parent

While the criminal proceedings were underway, the two defendants had not been idle. They had filed a lawsuit against Robert Currie, a parent of a McMartin preschool child and former mortgage banker, for making a series of false, malicious, and slanderous statements against Virginia McMartin, her daughter Peggy McMartin Buckey, and her granddaughter Peggy Ann Buckey.[58] Although the young boy had not testified at the trial, Currie insisted that his son had been molested during the three years he attended the McMartin Preschool. Currie made slanderous statements on a variety of local and national talk shows, including "Geraldo," that the McMartins participated in satanic rituals and lewd acts with the children at the preschool.

In his own defense, Currie testified that he had been "seeking the truth" when he rented a backhoe to dig up the school grounds in search of tunnels and animal remains. He said that he believed that the children had been molested because of the allegations made by prosecutors, law enforcement personnel, and other parents.

Currie's defense attorney argued that the seven years of publicity endured by the McMartins made them "slander-proof" because they were public figures. A very peculiar and unjust argument indeed, as relay of such a falsehood is often considered a legal slander.

After a one-day trial, however, Superior Court Judge G. Keith Wisot awarded the three teachers only $1 each, saying that they had not proven that their reputations were damaged and that Robert Currie, the parent, had not deliberately set out to cause them emotional distress. Judge Wisot did say there was no proof that some of the things said by Currie were true; furthermore, the judge said that Currie was negligent for not verifying that what he said was true. The judge concluded that while Currie was guilty of spreading inaccurate information and defamed the three, such proof would not automatically result in punitive damages.

While the McMartins had asked for $500,000 in damages, Virginia McMartin was apparently satisfied with the $1 award because she said "I got what I wanted—the truth to come out. I didn't care a snip about the money. I wanted him to shut up."[59]

Bail for Raymond Buckey

Before concluding the trajectory of the first McMartin trial, this final section of the chapter presents the brief history on the defendants' lengthy
detention, Judge Pounders' decision on their bails, and his final decision
on the defendants' release from long incarceration.

Since his first arrest and detention in 1983, Raymond Buckey had
remained in jail. Though there had been numerous defense requests for
Buckey's release on bail, judges had rejected the defense motion. The
judges had also rejected similar requests for his mother's release.

Bail is a court-imposed requirement for the posting of security to
obtain release of a defendant pending disposition of a criminal case. The
Eighth Amendment to the United States Constitution provides there shall
not be excessive bail, though recent Supreme Court decisions have
affirmed the denial of bail to defendants deemed particularly dangerous
and charged with serious offenses, including child sexual molestation.
The Federal Bail Reform Act of 1984 also permits preventive detention
where "no condition or combination of conditions will reasonably assure
the appearance of the person as required and the safety of any other person and the community."[60] While preventive detention has been harshly
criticized as a deprivation of liberty for those whose guilt has not been
proved, the U.S. Supreme Court upheld the constitutionality of the preventive detention provision of the 1984 Bail Reform Act in *United States
vs. Salerno* (481 U.S. 739 1987), indicating that preventive detention was
not intended as a punishment but rather as a legitimate means of attempting to prevent harm to the community.

Similar standards had been applied to Raymond Buckey. When
Buckey was arrested for alleged child sexual molestation, he was originally denied bail. Only after he had spent nearly four years in jail, was
bail finally set for him at $3 million.

In January 1987, Judge Pounders indicated he would hear the defense
attorney's motion to release Raymond Buckey from jail where he had been
held since March, 1984.[61] Having now spent nearly three years in maximum
security in the County Jail, Buckey openly pleaded for bail, which had been
previously refused because of the repeated testimony of several child victims
that the defendants had threatened them. The release of other defendants did
not result in harm, so defense attorney Daniel Davis argued that Buckey should
also be released. Though the judge refused Buckey's request, he did say that
release "may be as close as the next turn of the cards."[62]

Though he previously had refused to allow bail, in December 1987,
Judge Pounders reversed course, reasoning: "It would be a travesty to

hold him without bail for five years" without determining his guilt or innocence. Prosecutors, meanwhile, argued that Buckey would carry out threats against his victims, molest other children, or flee to avoid a potential prison term of 71 years if convicted on all charges. Judge Pounders, however, concluded that there was "no substantial likelihood that he would carry out threats.... But I do think there is a concern about flight [so] I'm talking about a very substantial bail." To be released, Buckey would have to generate $300,000 cash or put up $6 million in real estate equity. Daniel Davis, his defense attorney, said that Raymond Buckey could live with him and that he would monitor his whereabouts around the clock. Davis said that he would seek a reduction in bail and that he would ask for Buckey's release when the trial was scheduled to resume.[63]

Over the objections of the prosecution, it was not until December 1988, 19 months after the trial began, that Judge Pounders reduced Buckey's bail by half to $1.5 million. The judge stated, "[I]t has been all year long a concern to me that Mr. Buckey is still incarcerated.... Is it reasonable to hold someone in jail for five years without determining his guilt?"[64] Yet this still required that $3 million in property be pledged to satisfy the lowered bail requirement for his release.

The defendant was finally released from jail on the $1.5 million bail in February, 1989 after having spent the full five years in jail.[65] He met the requirement of pledging twice that amount in real estate. The defense attorneys, Abby Mann, and friends of the Buckey family generously pledged their property for the bail.

In releasing him from jail, the judge required that he not contact any alleged victims or their families, not leave California without permission, give up his passport, that he not enter the cities of Manhattan Beach or Redondo Beach without permission, be kept under 24-hour guard, not consume alcohol, and not have contact with anyone under the age of 14 who was not a blood relative or accompanied by a parent.

"If you fail to return for trial," the judge warned Buckey, "the trial will take place in your absence, you'll be convicted in absentia and friends who posted their property will lose it."[66] For the first time in five years during the next court date Buckey walked into court a "free man"—although he was accompanied by Paul Baron, an armed defense investigator, and a second guard, under the terms of his bail.[67]

At the time of his release on bail, Buckey had not yet spent any time with his family and had expressed concern about the threats he had received. "I still realize there are people out there who have gone off the deep end," he told news reporters.[68]

Conclusions

This chapter detailed the first McMartin trial and prosecution and defense evidence heard by McMartin jurors. Emphasis was placed on evidence presented by both the prosecution and defense, the role played by the judge, defense tactics, DA's strategies including the use of a jailhouse informant, and bail for the defendants.

A particularly important issue was the question of the professional competence and independence of interviewers at CII, and specifically Kathleen MacFarlane who carried out most of the interviews.[69] The question of sufficient evidence to render a verdict of guilt also remained. The prosecution's case never adequately answered the dilemma of the great number of children claiming abuse, the lack of material or forensic evidence, and the absence of corroboration by adults. Though the CII had originally said that 369 children were molested at the preschool, only 12 testified before the grand jury, only nine eventually testified at the actual trial, and the other 300 or more simply disappeared without a trace from the legal scene. The prosecution's use of the children on videotape seemed to be clearly therapeutically-crafted, but strained the jurors' sense of credibility. The prosecution might have been better served by concentrating on forensic and medical evidence and other techniques to solicit the children's own unguided statements. But, rather, it had placed stress on suggestion-prone children, using leading questions that did much more than coax an unbiased answer.

Defense counsel called Dr. Maloney as their expert witness to present testimony to further discredit the CII interviews and evaluations. Dr. Maloney stated that the CII interview techniques were so unreliable and invalid that many of children's statements might have been generated by the examiners themselves, and that their accounts of child molestation were contaminated by many factors including pre-programmings, stage settings, scripts, anatomically correct dolls, and implicit and covert pressures to coerce children to "disclose" information of sexual abuse and molestation by the defendants.

CII interviewers followed Dr. Roland Summit's theory of children's sexual abuse accommodation syndrome in eliciting information of sexual abuse; and the child abuse accommodation syndrome has been excessively used to explain "denial," "recantation," and "disclosure" by children after they have spent months in therapy. The court had criticized his theory and questioned the reliability of elicited information and the testimonial evidence of child sexual molestation.

In 1990, for instance, the California Court of Appeal in the Second District finally rejected testimonial evidence of the child sexual abuse syndrome as not being generally accepted in the scientific community.[70] The court held that the admission of the testimony of Dr. Roland Summit, in regard to the scientific merit of the child sexual abuse accommodation syndrome and the admission of evidence of generic descriptions of various other uncorroborated acts of child abuse, constituted harmful error, reversing and remanding the case. In 1992, the Pennsylvania Supreme Court in *Commonwealth vs. Dunkle* also reversed the lower court and found that admission of expert testimony on this syndrome was reversible error. The Court ruled that the expert did not relate any of her testimony to the child in question. Finding that "abused children react in myriad ways and that abused and non-abused children often exhibit similar behavior problems," the Court found that "[T]he existence of a child abuse syndrome as either a generally accepted diagnostic tool or as relevant evidence is not supportable" and therefore inadmissible.[71] Similarly, the decision in *State v. Rimmasch* (Utah, 775 P.2d 388, 401 1989) excluded expert testimony concerning child sexual abuse syndrome, indicating that to allow such testimony was tantamount to permitting the expert witness to vouch for the victim's credibility.

Expert medical testimony was also often technical, contradictory, and confusing to jurors and others in attendance in the courtroom. Judge Pounders commented frequently on the credibility of both the prosecution and defense witnesses and made controversial rulings—most often in favor of the prosecution. If anything untoward happened at the McMartin Preschool, imagination had taken reality far afield, garbled it, and eventually most reporters who followed the trial believed that the children could not distinguish fact from fantasy in their elaborate trial accounts.

It was against this background that the jury was given instructions by the judge to decide the guilt or innocence of the two remaining defendants—Raymond Buckey and Peggy McMartin Buckey. It was now time for the jurors to decide if prosecutor Rubin was correct when she said, "[T]he success of our case depends upon the believability of the children and the acceptance of our medical evidence."

Chapter 9

The Jurors and Their Verdicts: The First Trial

After the judge's instructions to the jury were read on November 2, 1989, the jurors retired to deliberate, taking their places around an octagonal table in a room approximately 20-by-20 feet on the 15th floor of the building in which the Superior Court was located.

The first task the jurors agreed upon was the selection of a foreperson. The group polled themselves on prior jury service. Four jurors had had prior jury service and shared their knowledge of the methods to select a foreperson. Discussing the alternatives of oral vote or secret ballot, the secret ballot was ultimately agreed upon, with each person allowed to vote three names. After voting, one juror stood at a chalkboard to tally the votes, while another juror read the names from each ballot.

After the ballots were tallied, it was clear that Luis Chang had the majority vote. Defense observations during *voir dire* had rated him with strong leadership qualities. Similarly, he was evaluated with the best analytic abilities among the selected jurors crucial for sifting through voluminous evidence related to the large number of charges. He was also knowledgeable about legal processes because his daughter had been the victim of a hit-and-run car in front of her school, and that court action was pending.

He accepted the jury's vote and then proceeded to apologize to them for what he called his "rules." His concern was that the others might judge him too harshly because he wanted to establish guidelines from which they would embark upon deliberations.

The jury would have to discuss, evaluate, and render a verdict on each count. Jurors would also have to put aside whatever influence the media might have had on their judgment of guilt or innocence.

Though the defense's jury consultants held no direct control over the selection of the jury foreperson, there was a strong correlation between the final trial outcome and the demographic and ideological profile of a possible jury foreperson. According to earlier jury research, the jury foreperson in various trials had been found to exert significant control over the jury deliberation process and thus the final trial outcome, largely because the foreperson is given more opportunities to speak and articulate his/her opinions than any other members of the jury. Furthermore, as the leader of jury deliberations, the jury foreperson is more likely to exhibit the characteristics of an authoritarian personality during crucial moments of the decision-making process and has been found to be more successful in persuading other members of the jury. The jury foreperson is also more likely to be white, male, and highly educated, holding a prestigious job, and representing those of upper-social class backgrounds. Except for being Asian-American, Luis Chang met all the criteria for his position as foreperson.

Chang guided the jurors in reviewing long hours of testimony, examining exhibits, and evaluating other evidence. They generally gathered around 9:30 each morning and continued deliberating until 4:00 in the afternoon.

According to juror Mark Bassett, there was no single moment of enlightenment, but rather a long sorting out process. "There were times when things got heated, when people's tempers got short," juror Bassett observed.[1] Nonetheless, he said, "we started with the child who started the case, then requested all exhibits relevant to him and made a list of the testimony and discussed what was relevant."[2]

Eventually, Bassett concluded, "you could tell people were just kind of wearing down" as they repeated this procedure, day after day, child-by-child. Still, each juror tried to keep respect for the others for having gone through the trial.

The Verdicts

"For nearly 30 months, they sat together in the same box, mute participants in an exhausting, emotional legal drama," two journalists described the ordeal of the McMartin jurors in what is generally considered the longest and costliest criminal trial in American history. "They listened to more than a hundred witnesses, children, police officers, medical experts, the accused. Pounds of evidence—photographs, documents, diaries, checkbooks, even several pairs of underwear—were brought before them. Videotapes of children sharing their dark, sometimes bizarre accounts with counselors were played, rewound, and played again for their benefit. Throughout it all, the eight men and four women jurors in the McMartin Pre-School molestation case gave nothing away, surrendered no clues as to which way they might be leaning."[3]

"The verdict was a high mark, but not the final moment, in a lengthy and entangled legal saga," another pundit concluded.[4] It was three months after Raymond Buckey's testimony that the jury began deliberations; then it took the jurors nearly two and one-half months to render a verdict on each of the 65 counts against Raymond Buckey and Peggy McMartin Buckey, bringing the trial to a conclusion on most matters.

Jurors later said that they had entered the jury deliberation room with open minds, not only because the judge had so instructed, but also because the disjointed testimony had left them confused.

"When I went into the jury room I was as confused and uncertain as I was on the first day of the trial," said Brenda Williams, echoing the comments of the other jurors.[5] After hearing 124 witnesses that generated well over 60,000 pages of testimony, ten videotapes, and 1,000 exhibits, the jurors had retired without a clear sense of the events.

The jurors began deliberations by attempting to separate the facts and testimony in each child's case. They slowly and methodically reviewed each charge for each single child. They reviewed and debated each count, and went over the testimony and witnesses for each child, including that of parents, doctors, and on videotapes.

The first verdict was reached on the 13th day of jury deliberations, the decision remaining sealed for several weeks while the jury continued deliberating. This delay was an accommodation to defense lawyers, who objected to verdicts being released piecemeal, believing that the public's reaction might influence subsequent decisions by the jury. As jurors reached verdicts on each count, then heard of the judge's plan to unseal verdicts in batches, they told Judge Pounders that such a potential release was affecting their deliberations. A compromise allowed the jurors to sign, date, seal, and submit verdicts to the court clerk as soon as they were reached; but they were not to be read and affirmed in open court until all verdicts had been determined.

The 12 jurors finally agreed: It was impossible to convict the defendants on 52 of the counts charged; and on 13 other counts, they could only offer deadlocked votes. This meant the defendants were completely acquitted of 52 counts. With a split decision on 13 others, all deadlocked charges were against Raymond Buckey.

Superior Court Judge William F. Pounders then declared a mistrial on those 13 counts. "Any decision the jurors made was justified by the evidence they saw," the judge announced.[6] The acquittal meant that Peggy McMartin Buckey was a free and acquitted woman, while a DA decision was still left to be made about whether or not Raymond Buckey would face a second trial on the 13 deadlocked counts. With the acquittal of Peggy McMartin Buckey, six of the original seven defendants were now exonerated—either having their charges completely dismissed or having been acquitted by the jury.

Evaluation of Evidence

How did the jurors evaluate the evidence? How did the jurors deliberate and discuss the evidence? Was there need for developing consensus among 12 jurors during the jury deliberation?

Post-verdict interviews of the 12 jurors disclosed the difficulty of reaching unified opinions on each of 65 child molestation and conspiracy charges.

The jury's primary task was to evaluate evidence presented during the course of the trial, though at least one juror argued that the statute of limitations had expired for at least some of the older children. After the trial, some of the 12 jurors who gave public interviews stated that the prosecution's evidence was inadequate to prove guilt beyond a reasonable doubt. They were not there to decide abstractly the defendants' innocence or to simply convict, they said. Rather, the facts and testimony had to be carefully weighed.

Some unproven allegations cast aside, jurors indicated that they were still unsure if Raymond Buckey had told the truth. Yet, those speaking to reporters after the verdict held near-consensus on one point that led them to favor the defense: The prosecution's use of videotapes showing youngsters given anatomical dolls and—though the children at first denied abuse—being prodded and urged to show and say how they were molested.[7]

These jurors thought that the children were encouraged to invent. "I could not tell from watching the tape that the children were telling what actually happened to them or if they were repeating what they were told by their parents or other people ... and what they had heard their parents telling other people," offered juror Brenda Williams. "Children believe their parents. The parents did too much talking," she explained. "We would have believed the children's story a little more if there were no ... tapes." Yet, she insisted, "I believe the children believed what they were saying was true when they testified." "The key evidence that swayed me was the interview tapes," jury foreperson Luis Chang also said. "They were too biased, too leading. That's the main crux of it."[8] In themselves, the video-tapes helped seal the jurors' decision of innocence.[9]

"I tried to believe the children," offered juror Daryl Hutchins, saying that he believed in his heart that the children were molested, but on the basis of testimony before the jury, proving *where* and *when* was "a little shaky," Hutchins experiencing "a hard time picking fact from fiction."

Juror John Breese stated, "[W]e did not get in the children's own words their stories.... The interviewers asked leading questions in such a manner that we never got the children's story in their own words."

Some jurors felt that some of the children had been molested, but the main problems were a lack of concrete evidence and that the alleged victims who did testify did not show the emotion or fear that was expected.

Some jurors also were highly critical of the Manhattan Beach Police Department's decision to send out form letters to parents announcing the investigation and soliciting information.[10] "That right there almost wrecked the chances of the prosecution," one of them said, adding that he was convinced that no molestation had ever taken place. "There were incredible missteps that contributed to this big mess. That was a shotgun approach to gathering data."[11] "What kind of a police investigation is [it] when everyone knows what's happening?" another juror said of the original letter sent to 200 parents of McMartin preschool children.[12]

Still another juror recounted that he was determined to vote not guilty as soon as the testimony was over—especially where Peggy McMartin Buckey was concerned. "Look at it this way. Here's a woman that has been in this business for, what, 26 years? Isn't it incredible to believe she would do the things she was accused of doing? You just couldn't understand how she would get any pleasure out of such feelings."[13]

The bizarre nature of the children's testimony also led jurors to question other aspects of their accounts. Jurors were concerned that children could be trained to testify about things that did not really happen. During the post-verdict interview, some who voted for guilt on some counts told reporters that if they had known of the mental illness of Judy Johnson, the woman who launched the case, they would almost certainly have voted "not guilty" on all accounts.

Deputy District Attorney Lael Rubin concluded that "the interview techniques may have been overly leading but it was the only way to get them to talk," seemingly ignoring any influence such techniques had on the children's accounts.[14] Such were the important questions and improbabilities that the jury had to deal with in its deliberations.

Developing Consensus

While post-verdict interviews showed differing opinions on molestation and conspiracy charges against Raymond Buckey, how had the jury attempted to develop a unified consensus?

While the jury evaluated each charge for each child, if they were unable to reach a decision, they simply put that charge aside to come back to it at a later time. As they accumulated verdicts on each of the alleged charges, they considered another one. In the process, most debate centered around the degree of "contamination" of each child's testimony.[15]

Juror Mark Bassett said that "on determining that the evidence wasn't believable we decided 'not guilty' and turned the decisions in.... Usually we turned them in when we had finished going through the charges associated with a single child, sometimes we turned in blocks of charges for two children in one day."[16]

Sifting and winnowing this way, the process was as thorough as could be expected, resulting in consensus on 52 charges. Though there were still 13 counts upon which the jury could not reach total agreement, all of these charges involved Raymond Buckey, which meant that at least one or more of the jurors felt that he was guilty of that charge. With three of these counts involving one particular child, one juror noted that the videotaped interview with this young girl "gave what I thought was concrete information when she accused Ray of molestation. I believe her on those three [early] counts. I believe that Ray did it."[17]

One of the allegations also involved the conspiracy charge against Peggy McMartin Buckey. As 13 charges remained to be decided, the jury made a query of the judge if it was possible for them to find one person guilty of conspiracy and the other not guilty of the same count, since both were named in the same charge.[18] The answer appeared to be "yes" in this case; however, the defense asked the judge to discuss the matter before he gave the jurors a decision.

Most jurors apparently believed that the children who had testified had been molested, but they also said that the prosecution had failed to prove beyond a reasonable doubt that the defendants were the perpetrators.[19] Juror Sally Cordova concluded that "whether I believe he [Raymond Buckey] did it and whether it was proven are very different."

Part of the give-and-take in deliberations rested on the ties that had developed between the jurors themselves. After the trial, juror Brenda Williams said that "the jurors got along excellently, contrary to all the horror stories that we've heard about what happens [in a jury room].... I've made some serious friends. We get along together very well. John [Breese] and the others—they're great people. If it wasn't for the people in this jury, I don't think I could have made it."[20] While proceedings were long, tedious, and at times boring, jury members got along well together, and all of them apparently had great respect for the jury foreperson—Luis Chang.

Conclusions

At the post-verdict interview, the jurors stated that the McMartin Preschool case was botched from start to finish by investigators, psychologists, parents, and prosecutors.[21] The investigation process itself made it extremely difficult for jurors to separate truth from fantasy.

With these verdicts, the trial had come to a conclusion. Even the media reporters most critical of the defense agreed that "the case was hastily filed, and ... was flawed from the beginning."[22] The CII's use of untrained and unlicensed therapists to carry out videotaped interviews with the children using anatomically explicit dolls and leading and suggestive questions proved to be the prosecution's fatal flaw. These interviews were perceived by jurors as being forced, with children programmed to believe that they had been molested.

A major question that had to be dealt with by jurors was whether or not children could be trained or convinced to testify about things that really did not happen. Was this not a classic case of one rumor building on another, adults elevating innocent play school activities to be immoral and sexual, and children mixing fact and fancy with what they were told or instructed to believe? Was there undue influence on the children during the controversial interviews conducted by the unlicensed CII therapists? Or were the questionable interviewing procedures the only way to get them to talk, as prosecutor Lael Rubin insisted?

Post-verdict interviews substantiated that the jurors believed that many children had been led, coaxed, and programmed by the CII therapists to say that they had been molested when in fact they had not. Post-verdict interviews also supported the findings from pre-trial analyses of potential jurors that questions about the validity and credibility of children's stories in videotaped interviews would play an important role in rendering the final verdicts.

But not everyone agreed. One young girl and alleged victim, present at the moment of the final verdicts, said, "I know he [Raymond Buckey] is guilty. I don't understand how so many people could think that he is innocent." Yet the girl also said that the verdicts made her question whether any of the events she alleged really happened to her. "I don't know if it did. I don't remember that it happened. I can remember some things, but I don't know if they're true or not."[23]

The girl's parents lamented that "this tells child molesters that the more perverse and sick you are, the easier it is to get off." These parents also blamed the prosecution for mishandling the case. "We ultimately must respect the jury's decision even though I personally disagree with it," prosecutor Lael Rubin defended the DA's office, further commenting that the Buckeys "were lucky, and I hope to God that we don't hear anything about them in the future." District Attorney Ira Reiner also reflected, "Obviously I'm very disappointed. This was a very long road and it was not the results we hoped for."[24]

Judge Pounders concluded differently, stating, "I was not surprised by the verdicts. I would not have been surprised at any decision the jury made." He also noted that new legislation was needed to prevent such lengthy proceedings in the future. Asked if the defendants were owed an apology for the long trial, he said "no" because, according to his calculations, only 30% of the trial time was devoted to the prosecution.[25]

When jurors were released from service, they broke into shouts and applause. All jurors agreed that they had clear consciences about the verdicts they had reached after nine weeks of deliberations. "We did what we could with what we had on this case," offered one of the jurors who contributed to all of the innocent decisions and was instrumental in the deadlocked deliberations.[26] Apparently, Rubin had been correct when she said in her opening statement that if the jurors did not believe the children and/or the medical evidence, the defendants would be found not guilty.

Even though 13 charges could be pressed by the district attorney against Raymond Buckey, the criminal case was at last over for Peggy McMartin Buckey. Though the defendants were delighted with the outcome of the trial, Peggy McMartin Buckey was also saddened. "I've gone through hell and now we've lost everything.... If it can happen to seven innocent people, it can happen to you, too," she warned the public.[27]

She also insisted that she was not bitter. "I knew God would set my son and me free because we have done nothing." Her optimism was not matched by Raymond Buckey, who agonized that he "had fear, definitely" about what the jury would decide.[28]

She left the courthouse, as she had many times before, facing a jeering crowd of parents and children, some screaming lewdly, others giving her "the finger." When Peggy and Raymond Buckey left the building and reached the parking lot, many spectators shouted, "we're going to kill you, you are going to die." The Los Angeles Police Department made no arrests for lewd and lascivious behavior. "I did not look at their faces," Peggy McMartin Buckey said, turning her back to them, eyes welling, betraying a tear. "God forgive them. They know not what they do."[29]

Chapter 10

The Aftermath

The McMartin trial set limits on both child testimony and defendants' rights in molestation cases. But in doing so, was justice served? A reporter said that the McMartin trial forces us to ask the question—"What is expected from our criminal justice system?"[1] He argued that the decision rendered in the McMartin trial demonstrated that while the truth is desired, the public had to settle for court-rendered justice.

Certainly, those persons most intimately involved in the McMartin case—the children and their parents, defendants, and many others—would argue that justice was hardly served in the drawn-out proceedings. Both defendants had to spend long terms in jail, facing exorbitant bail, while being publicly denounced, convicted by most of the media for being guilty of what might have been nothing more than innocent play school activities.

There were other losers, too. The malleable children who mixed fact and fiction had been put through the trauma of police questioning, parental pressures, grand jury testimony, a long preliminary hearing, a grueling trial beset by promises and false expectations, and therapeutic debriefing that persuaded by using dubious methods of interrogation.

Jurors lost time on their regular jobs and in their personal lives. Six of the original 18 jurors and alternates had dropped out for health and financial reasons, leaving the minimum of 12. Without alternate jurors left, the case had teetered on the brink of a mistrial.

Judge Pounders found a county job for one juror to keep him on the jury. And during jury deliberations, the judge agreed to withhold reading verdicts in court until he had all 65, risking a mistrial if anything happened to even one juror. Judge Pounders also noted that the six-year-long case had poisoned everyone it had touched—children, parents, witnesses, litigants, judicial officers. On the day after the verdicts were announced, an editorial in the *Los Angeles Times* asked "whether there is anything in the record of the trial [that] could make even a sliver of the squandering of time and reputations worthwhile? The answer for most persons would have been a resounding 'NO'!"[2]

Finally, the case affected many others, even though from all possible indications they were not involved in any illegal or questionable manner with the defendants, the McMartin Preschool, or alleged victims. For after the investigation had widened, scores of "uncharged" suspects were questioned and nine South Bay nursery schools were ultimately closed. Thus, the impact of the case went far beyond those specifically involved in the trial.

The remainder of this chapter explores some of the devastation that followed the first McMartin trial. Public outcry over the verdicts are analyzed with respect to the jurors' evaluation of evidence. "Letters to the Editor" in numerous newspapers demonstrated the emotional overlay of childhood sexual abuse cases and why it is important to pick an impartial jury. Also, the media's response immediately after the verdicts and the soul searching by some members of the media are examined in some detail. A discussion of the jurors' evaluation of prosecution evidence illustrates the extreme difficulties of securing such evidence and how it was presented in the courtroom, suggesting substantial revisions are needed to protect and secure children, the accused, and others in future child molestation cases. Problems with the medical evidence are also discussed.[3] A review of the monetary, personal, and social costs illustrates the potential harm associated with child abuse cases.[4] And the final section of this chapter describes monetary costs and personal losses suffered by many actors in the McMartin episode, including children and their parents, defendants, a minister, and jurors. This section also discusses the impact of the case upon the criminal justice system and the so-called "child abuse therapeutic industry."

Public's Response

The alleged sexual abuse of the McMartin children captured the imagination and emotions across a wide spectrum of people, many who lived and still reside in Manhattan Beach. Defense attorney Walter Urban of Manhattan Beach still believes that "the community seems to be permanently polarized. This is a powerful historical event. A little town gets hit with something like this and it's not forgotten."[5]

Opinions differed sharply. There were those who said "kids don't lie," believed that the children were molested, and argued that "something has to be true out of all of the accusations that were made." There were those who were openly hostile to the defendants (and who undoubtedly remain hostile).[6]

Others in Manhattan Beach just refused to discuss the case. Friendships have been broken over the issue, while others maintain their relationships but carefully never discuss the case. As one news reporter noted, there is "an uncomfortable, albeit polite, quiet" in the city.[7]

There was some sentiment that the defendants were as much the victims as the children were. Kevin Cody, publisher of the major community newspaper *Easy Reader,* apparently started out believing that the defendants were guilty, but became convinced that there was no proof that molestation had actually occurred at the school.[8] So, too, there are parents who sent their children to McMartin who also believe that the defendants are innocent of any wrongdoing.

One of the deepest cuts of the McMartin case in Manhattan Beach, according to one parent, is that "there's no in-between here anymore." "These kids have been made to be deathly afraid of anyone who looks at them. What we're doing is raising paranoid kids." Another resident noted that the child-teacher relationship changed forever after McMartin. "It became very clear that people could not hug and touch kids. A lot of adults are very careful these days and they will be forever. And that's the great loss." Finally, one Manhattan Beach resident expressed the grief, "[E]very time I hug my nieces and nephews I think twice about it. Isn't that weird?"[9]

A Fox television call-in poll found that viewers by nearly a 7-1 margin believed that "justice was not served with the acquittal of Ray Buckey and his mother."[10] One writer in the *Wall Street Journal* "Letters to the Editor" section, called the "McMartin Trial a Legal Witch's Brew." While some letters to the editor published in newspapers were pro-McMartin defendants, most were against and strongly opposed the "not guilty" verdicts.[11]

Some writers to "Letters to the Editor," who regarded the McMartin decision unjust, focused on the jurors' skepticism about the credibility of the children's testimony. "To deny a child's evidence or allegations of such a serious nature would be most deleterious to our justice system and destructive to our youths' integrity," one argued.[12]

But not all letters were critical of the McMartin decision. One writer advised Los Angeles that: "[I]f Ray Buckey had killed a child in a drunken rage (manslaughter), he probably wouldn't have served more than five years in jail with time off for good behavior. Instead, he served five years without being convicted of anything. Guilty or innocent, his 'A' will never be removed." "The McMartin teachers are victims of media hype, ambitious politicos and crazed parents," this letter writer added. "They would have us believe child abuse has become a national sport. Anyone who works with children could be similarly put upon by the media and the courts. All it would take is one kid not telling the truth."[13] And another letter writer asked: "Has the press and television learned nothing over the years? Apparently not."[14]

Some also condemned the lawyers and doctor-psychiatrists involved in the decision, even harkening back to the nation's revolutionary origins, noting that "[T]he law is a filthy racket, not what we went to war for. If there is a need for graffiti, it should be used to cover the words around the courthouses reading 'equal justice.'"[15]

One point of reason that emerged was that new ways must be found to elicit and to incorporate children's testimony in child abuse cases. Reasonable or not, the McMartin trial also brought out strong public feelings that "public confidence in the U.S. judiciary system is low and ebbing fast,"[16] a critic offered, and that "public faith in the judicial system is fast eroding."[17]

After the verdicts were announced, many parents of the alleged victims were unhinged and outraged. In Manhattan Beach, ten days after the verdicts were announced, 500 marchers protested. They carried signs and had bumper stickers blazoned with "We believe the children." Tim Wheeler, father of two former McMartin pupils and an attorney in Los Angeles, told the marchers that "the crime that occurred in the courtroom was almost equal to the crime that occurred outside the courtroom."[18]

Within two weeks of the acquittals, parents and their allies were appearing on national television shows, holding press conferences, lobbying the Los Angeles County Board of Supervisors, collecting what they described as "6,000 letters of support," and even asking comedians to keep the issue alive by continuing to ridicule the McMartin verdict in their routines.

The campaign was joined by the families whose children had testified at the trial. Gathered in front of the downtown Los Angeles Criminal Courts building to express their views, on January 30, 1990, representatives of child abuse groups, including FOCOS (Families Of Crimes Of Silence), the Adam Walsh Center, Believe the Children, and the Hispanic Theatre Project, then moved on to the Hall of Administration where the County Board of Supervisors was meeting. There, following an emotional hour of testimony from McMartin parents and one former student, the board voted 4-1 to ask Attorney General John Van de Kamp to review the

60,000 pages of court transcripts as well as the comments of jurors to determine if the molestation prosecution was botched and if the 13 dead-locked charges should be refiled by the State of California.[19]

Soul Searching by the Mass Media

"Where Was Skepticism in Media?" the *Los Angeles Times* headline ironi-cally inquired the day after the McMartin verdicts of not guilty and 13 deadlocked counts were announced. A sub-headline pointed to "pack-journalism" and hysteria that marked early coverage of the McMartin case, criticizing that many journalists never stopped to question the cred-ibility and validity of the alleged charges.

Pack-journalism involves laziness, superficiality, cozy relationships with prosecutors, and jumping on the band-wagon in a media blitz—which made the McMartin case a *cause celebre*. There was intense competition to outdo each other with frantic searches to be the first with the latest, shocking allegation, "responsible journalism be damned."[20]

Highly critical of the mass media's coverage of the case, David Shaw of the *Los Angeles Times* penned a series of articles, noting that there had been a media feeding-frenzy: "the media seemed especially zealous—in large part because of the monstrous, bizarre, and seemingly incredible nature of the original accusations. Yet few journalists stopped to question the believability of the prosecution's charges."[21]

In the beginning, Wayne Satz's report shocked the public, triggering a kind of pathology in media coverage. KABC-TV seemed fixated on the case, systematically reporting that it would become "huger by far," and other television stations abidingly followed suit.[22] Local television report-ers were immediately under pressure to develop exclusives on the McMartin story to supplement or counter KABC-TV stories. "The story took on a life of its own," a reporter from another station noted. "We gotta get something new on McMartin; look how big this thing is getting."[23]

If truth went out the window, love and influence may have entered. As previously indicated, Satz had allegedly become romantically linked to Kathleen MacFarlane from CII. Later, it was charged that through his romantic interest, Satz had access to private information that she pro-vided.[24] MacFarlane transmitted information as well as certain suppressed evidence to him in defiance of court orders. Satz's competitors and even some McMartin parents believed that criminal charges might never have been filed, if it had not been for Satz's distorted programming.[25]

Collusion was also charged between Satz and the then District Attor-ney Robert Philibosian who was running for reelection. Competitors were well aware that Satz "continued to beat every reporter in town on the story for months to come."[26]

According to Michael Harris of the United Press International, early coverage of the case was "extremely slanted to the prosecution.... Everything they [the prosecution] said was reported as gospel."[27] Another Los Angeles area reporter, Barbara Salerno, said that the prosecutor was really hyping the case, adding, "I'm sorry I didn't ask more questions."[28]

Others argued that the media eventually swung the other way, although the evidence for this, other than the "60 Minutes" television segment, is slight. One co-prosecutor, Roger Gunson, argued that this was because the media was trying to overcompensate for not earlier reporting the defendants' side. Ignored in his view was the possibility that the media had finally begun to ask serious questions about the validity of the charges that had been filed by the prosecution.

Judge Pounders confirmed the reporting inaccuracies when he brought to the courtroom a news article that reported the wrong number of males and females on the jury the day after the jury was impaneled. "Not even on something so routine and obvious as their own sex" could the public rely upon the media for accurate information, he noted. Of course, the same point could have been made from the very beginning of the case—from the first arrest, from letters sent out by the police department, from various prosecution "plants" in the newspapers, etc. Pounders advised reporters that "they should pay attention only to what they would hear in the courtroom." From the *Los Angeles Times* desk, Shaw also noted that "the error seemed symbolic, in a sense, of the pivotal and sometimes distorting role the media had come to play [and would continue to play] in this remarkably complex and controversial case."[29]

What was important for the media, and especially the *Los Angeles Times,* Shaw criticized, was reflected "both by the stories they have published and broadcast and by the stories they haven't."[30] Shaw documented that in the early stages of the case, reporters and editors abandoned two of their most cherished and widely trumpeted traditions—fairness and skepticism. The media frequently plunged into hysteria, "a lynch mob syndrome."[31]

Perhaps most damaging was the process of carte blanche acceptance of the prosecution "allegations" that had never been officially charged— multiple charges of prostitution, child pornography rings, children being drugged and exchanged for sex, and even murder. None of these allegations was ever supported by evidence, and none of them ever became counts against the defendants or others identified in the media.

Notwithstanding some skepticism and questions raised, the press continued its sensationalistic *modus operandi* after the verdicts had been announced. Only a few reporters charged that the defendants had been assumed guilty by the media without a trial. Dean Gits, Peggy McMartin Buckey's attorney, stated that at the early stages the defendants were tried, convicted, and sentenced by the media—"all undeniably documented here and elsewhere."[32]

For six years, the *Los Angeles Times* had minimized and given late coverage to important trial developments that had raised questions about the validity of the prosecution's case—stories that other smaller local media promptly and prominently covered. For example, the swing in the media from being convinced of the defendants' guilt to possible innocence had first begun with several articles by Faye Fiore, a reporter who then worked for the *Daily Breeze* in Torrance.[33] Her report was the first to imply that the prosecutors were considering dropping charges against five defendants. Several months later that possibility became reality. Once questions were raised about the innocence of five of the defendants, suspicions began to emerge about the possible innocence of the remaining two. Videotaped interviews with children later shown to the jury also raised questions by both jurors and the media. Some media began to report that the case was nothing more than a series of sensational headlines.

"We all recognize how important the *Los Angeles Times* is," fired Walter Urban, who represented one of the defendants against whom all charges were dropped. "I think that had the *Los Angeles Times* done a major, long article, solid investigative work showing there was no child pornography, no child prostitution, no animal mutilation, maybe it would have stopped the case a lot sooner." But $15 million of "wasted" public monies later, the *Los Angeles Times* remained pro-prosecution, despite the strengthened defense and the press corps' perception of the *Los Angeles Times'* position as unalterably biased.

Though defense attorneys insisted that their clients had been tried and convicted by the media, what they failed to say was that, since their clients were acquitted by the jury, the media's efforts at conviction were less than effective.[34] In its final analysis of the trial, even the media ended up blaming itself for its failures in objective and unbiased reporting.[35] Journalists and editors stood accused of manipulating the public's vulnerability, with the McMartins paying the awful price.

Editors at the *Los Angeles Times* argued that their coverage was, "overall, fair and balanced." But defense attorneys and supporters, rival reporters, two prosecutors, and some insiders pointed to "flaws, large and small, in *Los Angeles Times* coverage that they say add up to unfairness and imbalance."[36] Prior to the announcement of the verdicts, criticism centered on three important areas: (1) the *Los Angeles Times* had published a number of stories, especially early in the case, that seemed to assume that the charges were true; (2) the paper published many stories that were heavily biased against the defense; and (3) there were never any major investigative stories examining the prosecution's allegations.

To these themes could be added that the newspaper also (1) neglected to compare the McMartin case with other similar cases throughout the country; (2) never published a detailed profile of Judy Johnson; (3) neglected to cover medical testimony in detail, and report the defense's difficulty in finding a medical expert willing to testify in the media-created milieu of hysteria; (4) neglected to report any part of testimony that was contrary to the prosecution's belief, or did so much later than other papers; (5) barely mentioned the tapes that Glenn Stevens made in a critical analysis of the prosecution's case; and (6) distorted and/or did not accurately portray other important events and developments in the trial.

Lois Timnick, the chief *Los Angeles Times* reporter on the case, was inexperienced in covering criminal justice system stories but had written articles about child sexual abuse prior to the McMartin episode. A number of subsequent evaluations of her articles were quite critical of her presentations; however, Norman Cousins, in a "Letter to the Editor" of the *Los Angeles Times,* argued that her reports were "balanced, fair-minded, comprehensive, and did great credit to your newspaper."[37] Similarly, Louis Joylon West, Professor of Psychiatry at UCLA, also argued that her coverage "was not at all biased."[38] Both of these "objective" observers argued that she deserved the Pulitzer Prize for her coverage.

This was much disputed by others. For example, one *Los Angeles Times* court and trial reporter, Bob Williams, became so concerned about the newspaper's bias that he wrote memos criticizing Lois Timnick's reporting assignments. While Williams was excited about the case, he had not been given the assignment.[39] So the question should be raised: Why wasn't Williams given the assignment when it was his beat? Williams left the newspaper several months later, convinced that the McMartin defendants were innocent.

Richard Barnes, *Los Angeles Times* city editor during most of the case, maintained that it is inappropriate for a newspaper to try to evaluate the legitimacy of a case once it has entered the criminal justice system. Believing the courtroom, and not the press, is the proper venue for evaluating a prosecution's case, Barnes argued that only law enforcement and the courts issue subpoenas and search warrants and compel testimony under oath, none of which a newspaper can do. Yet, clearly, newspapers can be biased in their presentation of prosecution and defense evidence.

While it has been pointed out that some of the media, especially the *Los Angeles Times,* was perceived by many people as being pro-prosecution, one newspaper reporter stated that "ultimately, just as it was the district attorney—not the media—that filed the charges, so it was the jury—not the media—that decided the case, [and] not a single McMartin defendant was convicted."[40] Ignored in this perspective was the possibility that the original charges may not have been filed at all except for the media exposure.

For the media-battered public, not much had changed after the trial. The November 2, 1986, national broadcast of the "60 Minutes" interview with Raymond Buckey and five of the other six original defendants had been sympathetic to their defense, but this was long forgotten on the day the McMartin verdicts were announced when some 87% of nearly 13,000 respondents to a Los Angeles television station still thought that the Buckeys were guilty—a drop of a few percentage points from the views of those surveyed before the trial began.

What were the lessons learned by the media in the McMartin case? An editorial in the *Los Angeles Times* suggested that journalistic skepticism is extremely important "when government officials make things so sensational as to be irresistible."[41] The same editorial, however, neglected to mention the very role that the *Los Angeles Times* itself had in perpetuating the mass hysteria in the McMartin case. Ultimately many members of the media became embarrassed by their own conduct and publicly acknowledged their misgivings.

Insufficient Evidence: Weakness of the Prosecution

The prosecution generally blamed the defense's strategies for the not-guilty verdicts and insisted that the defendants were still guilty. However, the prosecution's case itself was faulted by more than half the jurors, seven of whom said that though they were convinced that at least some of the children had indeed been molested, no persuasive evidence was offered that the crimes had taken place at the preschool or at the hands of the defendants. "I didn't vote innocent; I voted not guilty. It was not proved to me that [Raymond Buckey] did it," juror Sally Cordova was quoted as saying.[42]

Co-prosecutor Gunson acknowledged that the district attorney's office originally "vastly overstated" the case, but he ducked responsibility by stating that the media really never asked "real probing questions."[43] One news report quoting Deputy District Attorney Eleanor Bartlett said that there were "millions of child pornography photographs and films from McMartin." Either Bartlett was a loose canon on the DA's sinking ship, or the news media was rearing pathological reporters, because not a single sexually compromising photograph of any McMartin preschool child was ever found. A $10,000 award offered by McMartin parents for photographs never produced a single one, and no one had staked a claim.

Legal experts generally agreed that the case was bungled by the prosecution.[44] Terms such as "mishandled from the beginning," "a fiasco," and "worst case scenario" were attached to their criticisms.[45] Some jurors echoed these sentiments, and one noted, "in a story of children against adults, if Hollywood were doing the script, the children would win." But the McMartin case was not Hollywood, where action is quick and dramatic. "The escapades of Indiana Jones may sell tickets but in real life you can't tell 'an unbelievable story'" and expect to be believed, the juror observed.[46]

One nagging question in the case was the report by at least a dozen former McMartin pupils who had talked to prosecutors about a trap door, tunnel, or secret underground room at the school. Early in the case, the district attorney's office had the school searched; but the search turned up no passageways, trap doors, or any signs of disturbed floor tiles or concrete replacement.[47] Investigators utilized special sonar equipment in and around the buildings seeking "soft spots" that might indicate tunnels, passageways, rooms, or areas where dirt had been removed and perhaps replaced.[48] The sonar investigation also resulted in the conclusion that no such secret areas existed at the school site.

Parents refused to give up and obtained permission to dig from the new owner of the site who was going to build an office building. "I'm permitting these people to go on the property to find whatever they want and get it out of their system," he conceded.

Even though the official search found nothing that the parents sought, these parents still believed that the site had a story to tell, spending weeks watching a team of hired professional excavators digging through the site.[49] "We're not letting go because we want the children to be believed," Robert Salas, one of the parents, said.[50] "I don't expect anything we find here to turn the case around," Jackie McGauley, another McMartin parent added, "[W]e're doing this for our children and their credibility. That's the most important thing."[51] Still another McMartin parent, Jo Anne Farr, explained, "we weren't doing this for the court case. We're trying to validate what the kids said."[52]

Subsequently, archaeological investigations sponsored by the McMartin Tunnel Projects, an organization created by McMartin parents, alleged the presence of subterranean tunnels. The existence of McMartin tunnels was reported by Dr. Ronald Summit. Similarly, E. Gary Stickel reported in "Archaeological Investigations of the McMartin Preschool Site, Manhattan Beach, California: Executive Summary," indicating that:

> The failure of prosecutors to obtain even a single conviction in the McMartin trial has been taken by many as proof that the children's allegations were merely fantastic. Various journalists have demanded punishment of the professionals and parents who had chosen to believe them. Similar allegations arising more recently in other cases in the United States and abroad are tested against the McMartin standard, creating a prejudice against investigating or substantiating even remotely "bizarre" complaints. Parents in such cases feel triply betrayed: first with the dreadful discovery of abuse; second with their abandonment by law enforcement; and third with being blamed for imagining the abuse and fomenting public hysteria.
>
> One of the supposedly bizarre aspects of the McMartin case was the children's insistence that they were taken into underground tunnels. They explained that the tunnels led to an underground "secret room" where abuse occurred, as well as providing a route for subversive transport to off-site locations for sexual exploitation. These stories were apparently considered fantastic by investigators, who made *no attempt* to search beneath the building....
>
> The McMartin Tunnel Project confirms that a functional pattern of tunnels once existed under the McMartin Preschool, that the tunnels provided access outside the walls of the structure, that they must have been constructed after the structure was built in 1966, and that they were subsequently completely repacked with extraneous soil and implanted artifacts at some time prior to May, 1990. While this project had no way of determining who dug these tunnels, or for what purpose, the discoveries stand in stark contrast to the skeptical position that the children only imagined what they described as activities underground.
>
> If the stories of the children were bogus fantasies, there is no excuse for [not investigating existence of] the tunnels [purportedly] discovered under the school. If there really were tunnels, there is no excuse for the glib dismissal of any and all of the complaints of the children and their parents. [Emphasis added].[53]

There was little to validate the children, however. While a number of artifacts were found, none of them supported the parents' belief that subterranean areas existed at the school. The parents remained critical of the search carried out by the district attorney's office, too, explaining that they had dug down seven feet while the district attorney's office drilled down six inches. The district attorney's office, however, said that whatever was found during the excavations were unrelated to the case.[54]

As the school was being torn down one of the parents commented, "[G]etting rid of this school is like having a boil removed. They'll have to dig way down to remove it. It'll be painful. But, in the end, it'll be gone."[55]

Defense attorney Davis called the parents' efforts a "cathartic exercise to bury the issue once and for all. They refuse to even consider that maybe, just maybe they were wrong; that somehow they bought into a story that turned into a circus that has never been based upon fact." He further predicted that the parents' excavation would become part of the "witch-hunt folklore" surrounding the McMartin case. "It will become a paragraph or two in the voluminous story of the McMartin Preschool."[56]

Monetary Costs

The McMartin defendants were not the only parties to lose jobs, reputation, all of their life savings, homes, and other properties that they owned. Los Angeles residents also suffered a tremendous economic loss due to the long criminal justice proceeding and adjudication process in court.

Nationwide, lower county courts operate by tax revenues allocated from county budgets. In 1990, there were 2,449 state courts of general jurisdiction in the U.S., consisting of 9,250 judges, who heard approximately 28% of all trial court cases. Judges generally understand that certain limitations are established by both taxpayers and available county resources. Thus, the judges need to be concerned about the cost of trials and, in practice, evaluate the extent to which the length and cost of any trial may impose undue economic hardship on limited county resources.

Los Angeles County certainly enjoys considerable economic and financial resources by comparison to other jurisdictions. The Los Angeles District Attorney's office currently employs nearly 900 attorneys in 23 offices spread around the county, the largest in the country. The New York County District Attorney's office is the second largest agency with approximately 500 lawyers, followed by the Dallas County District Attorney's office with approximately 200 attorneys.[57] In large metropolitan areas where the vast majority of arrests occur, the DA's office is generally regarded as one of the largest employers of lawyers, hiring a battery of assistant district attorneys who are often recent graduates of law school.[58] Nonetheless, the cost of highly publicized criminal trials can lead superior court judges to "tear their hair," making rulings that shorten proceedings—however inequitable that may be for those charged with crimes.

McMartin litigation costs as of October, 1989, as reported in the *Los Angeles Times,* were as follows: (1) $6,228,914 for court-appointed defense attorneys and related costs; (2) $3,748,914 for district attorneys' costs; (3) $594,321 for Los Angeles Municipal Court preliminary hearing costs; (4) $121,837 to County Marshall's office (security); (5) $174,188 to the Public Defender's office; (6) $1,827,141 for the Sheriff's office, including investigative costs and Superior Court bailiffs; and (7) $397,171 for expenses of the L.A. Central Superior Court.[59] The total costs to Los Angeles County from July 1983 through October 1989 was $13,091,585. Additional county costs were also expected because the jury trial was still in progress when the running account was made. The total cost for the McMartin case was estimated to be approximately $15 million. These costs far exceeded the costs of the past two major criminal cases in Los Angeles County: the Night Stalker case which cost a total of $1.8 million, and the Hillside Strangler trial at an estimated cost of $1.6 million.[60]

The estimated $15 million, however, only represented the cost of criminal proceedings; not considered were the expectations of civil actions that would keep the case alive in the courts for at least the next decade. Eli Guana, representing Babette Spitler in her civil lawsuit against the county, concluded, "I'm convinced this case will never end. It will always be there, until everyone who was ever involved gets to old age and dies."[61] If financial losses had an impact on Los Angeles County, the other players in the case including the children, their families, and the defendants, all paid in turmoil, tension, and tears, their lives and their assets diminished.

Personal Losses

The Children and their Parents
The children and their parents were clearly victims of the legal process. In the U.S., considerable attention has been focused on the plight of child victims in the courtroom setting. Due to their unique vulnerabilities and their cognitive and emotional immaturity, their role as the most critical source of evidence in child sexual abuse cases can add terror and tension to the trauma they may have already experienced.

To alleviate the fear and stress on them when they testify, the federal government and many states have adopted laws to protect them. In the Victims of Child Abuse Act of 1990, the federal government provided a number of rights and protections for child victims and witnesses. Those protections included the following:

(1) alternatives to live in-court testimony, whether by two-way closed circuit television at trial or by videotaped depositions;

(2) presumption of children's competency as witnesses;

(3) privacy protection from public identification;

(4) closed courtrooms during children's testimony;

(5) victim impact statements from children;

(6) use of multidisciplinary teams to provide medical and mental health services to child victims; expert testimony; case management; and training for judges and court personnel;

(7) appointment of guardians ad litem to protect the best interests of child victims;

(8) appointment of a child's attendant to provide emotional support for children during judicial proceedings;

(9) speedy trial;

(10) extension of the statute of limitations for commencing prosecution of child sexual or physical abuse allegations until the child reaches the age of 25; and

(11) testimonial aids, such as dolls, puppets, or drawing.

While many of these reforms had already been adopted by state legislatures, children who have testified and directly confronted the accused during their testimony, as in the McMartin trial, are more likely to be terrified by their experience; and the negative impacts of the testimony may remain with the children for a long time. Similar emotional pain and suffering are also frequently observed among the parents of alleged child victims.[62]

It is not surprising, then, that distraught parents expressed shock and outrage that Raymond Buckey and Peggy McMartin Buckey were acquitted of molestation charges. Comments by parents and children demonstrated that they felt they had been betrayed by the district attorney's office, the judicial system, and the adjudication process.[63] Other parents blamed themselves for putting their children through the criminal justice process, which they said was designed for adults and not for children. When Judge Pounders was asked if the case was worth its costs, he responded, "[P]eople will be much more alert to the possibility of this type of offense taking place at preschools and schools. People are no longer dropping their children off and walking away blindly. They look back. They check things out more."[64]

When the "not guilty" verdicts were read, one of the children who had testified said, "[M]y stomach just hollowed out. I was beyond tears. Those words will stick with me probably the rest of my life. I'll never forget those two words."[65] A 15-year-old boy who also had testified said, "[W]e all know that we are telling the truth. No matter what the jury says, whatever anybody says, this is the truth. We were molested." The mother of one of the children said, "I guess maybe it's OK to [molest] kids. I can't believe this."

Other parents remarked that "[T]his is not justice," when the verdicts were announced. "Those jurors were brainwashed into believing the children weren't credible witnesses," one parent said. Still another parent said, "[L]ife is not fair. I tell my children all the time ... there is no such thing as fair."[66] Clearly, every contest by law and by lawyers that is designated to provide relief for some will produce pain for others—and cries of grief.

The Defendants

The defendants may have been exonerated, but their grief, tears, and losses seemed unfair and unbearable. "About the worst thing that can happen to a child is to be sexually molested," a McMartin trial reporter stated. "About the worst thing that can happen to an adult is to be wrongly accused of committing such a heinous crime."[67]

Defendants noted that they had received numerous death threats after the verdicts were announced, and that they were considering moving out of Southern California. Peggy McMartin Buckey stated, "My husband was threatened in court yesterday. They told him. 'You're gonna be killed.'"[68] Yet the police made no investigation; the DA brought no charges. Two defendants quickly moved offensively and filed a civil suit against CII and KABC. Virginia McMartin and Peggy Ann Buckey stated that beginning in 1984 and continuing periodically thereafter up to their dismissal of the criminal charges in 1986, they were "pushed, shoved, kicked and also hit and tripped by agents and employees of Defendants [CII and ABC Television Station in Los Angeles]."[69]

Raymond Buckey also "called the McMartin preschool trial a miscarriage of justice that destroyed my life and left children in torment."[70] "I saw what the system did. I saw how it treated children. I saw how it treated adults. It doesn't work very well," he bemoaned.[71] During a TV interview with Mike Wallace, Buckey said that "these poor children went through hell. And they did go through hell, but I'm not the cause of their hell, neither is my mother. Nothing that happened at that preschool is the cause of their hell. The cause of their hell is the product of the adults who took on this case and made it what it is."[72]

Mary Ann Jackson

Thrilled that the final two defendants were found not guilty, Mary Ann Jackson, who had been dropped from the case in 1986, said that her faith in the criminal justice system was nonetheless lost and that she was exhausted by the criminal justice process.[73] "To all of you, I would say, remember—please remember this case—remember the defendant, remember the embarrassment and bias on a daily basis, sometimes on an hourly basis over a period of six years, and remember we were innocent," she pleaded.[74] "This case should send a signal to [the] very heart of the justice system that there exists a lack of integrity and commitment to the truth," she expounded, adding that "it just snowballed. It was out of control." Though she said that she would like to substitute-teach again, she doubted if anyone would be willing to hire her.

Babette Spitler

Even when the final two defendants were found not guilty, Babette Spitler was still distraught. "I'm angry that it took so long—took six years for the outcome that we all knew was coming," she lashed out at the degrading ordeal the final two defendants had suffered.[75] During the two years that she had faced criminal charges, her two children had been taken first to be interviewed at CII without her permission, then placed in foster homes, and finally with relatives. The grandchild that she had been trying to adopt was also placed in a series of foster homes for more than two years. He still fears that every stranger is there to take him away.[76]

Spitler had asked her husband to divorce her so that he could have custody of the children; however, the dependency court told him, "He wasn't fit to be a parent either, because he should have known what a bad person I am, even though I hadn't done anything wrong." In addition to taking the children away from the family, the Spitlers were billed for foster home services and, as of July 1988, they were still paying the county $100 per month.[77]

After the charges were dropped against Spitler in 1986, in order to restore the custody of their own children, she and her husband decided to submit to a series of extensive psychological tests. The results were positive: They were finally allowed to have the custody of their two children and later legally were able to adopt their grandson.[78]

Yet, in addition to the loss of their home, huge debts incurred as a result of the charges, numerous death threats, the loss of jobs, and the stigma of the allegations. Spitler was extremely bitter about the way that the case was handled by both the prosecution and the media. She decried, "when they dropped the charges, they said they didn't have enough evidence to convict me. They never said that Babs Spitler is innocent."[79] "No one can give that time back to me," she railed after the jury verdict, "I'm bitter about that. I can't do anything about that. The time is gone."[80]

Peggy Ann Buckey

Peggy Ann Buckey applied for reinstatement as a teacher of deaf and learning-disabled high school students in Anaheim, California. Her initial appeal was rejected despite the dropping of all criminal charges against her; the denial was appealed and subsequently a full-scale hearing was held. In essence this hearing was a mini-McMartin trial, with a replay of many aspects of the main McMartin trial.[81]

The administrative hearings that would decide if she would be able to have her teaching credential reinstated took nearly three months, with some 39 witnesses called to testify. Testifying were young people who were former students at the McMartin Preschool. Several of them testified that they had never been molested at the school nor did they know anything about sex games, secret rooms, or tunnels.[82]

Deputy State Attorney Stephanie Wald and the attorney representing the school district, Kyle D. Brown, both admitted that Peggy Ann Buckey's performance at the school—where she had received excellent evaluations—was not in question, but that her moral character remained in doubt because of the McMartin molestation charges against her. Attorney Wald stated that because of these charges, "The state believes that Miss Buckey molested these five kids. That makes her unqualified to teach any children ever again." The prosecution wanted the hearing closed; however, the judge closed it only during the time children were testifying.[83]

In the civil procedure to which Peggy Ann Buckey was subjected, guilt and innocence were to be decided upon by the "preponderance of evidence," rather than "beyond a reasonable doubt" as in criminal cases. Also, it was up to her to disprove the charges, rather than for the state to prove them. Defense attorney John Wagner, representing Peggy Ann Buckey, characterized the hearings as "surreal." "It's theater of the absurd, straight out of a Kafka nightmare. The all-powerful state confronts my client with accusations that don't make sense, and she has to prove that there is some truth and meaning here."[84] Peggy Ann Buckey said, "It would be easier to give up and run away, but it's not fair to punish me, now even more with my career, when I didn't do anything wrong."[85]

The state had illegally changed some of the child witnesses, and defense attorney Wagner criticized this, saying that the state had also revised its list of allegations—including that Peggy Ann Buckey had personally killed a horse, which was an allegation never before made about her (but against her brother Raymond Buckey); and that several of the children, on the original and revised lists of alleged victims, were not enrolled at the school when Peggy Ann Buckey worked there and that one child had not even been born yet. Closing arguments by both the state and the defense were similar to those in the preliminary hearing and the main trial against her brother and mother.

Judge Ronald Gruen, the administrative judge in the hearing, ruled in favor of Peggy Ann Buckey and recommended that her request for a new teaching credential be granted. He stated that CII had done "incalculable damage" with a "pervasive use of leading and suggestive questions," and that the videotaped evidence "reveals a pronounced absence of any evidence implicating the respondent [Peggy Ann Buckey] in any wrongdoing and ... raises additional doubts of credibility with respect to the children interviewed or with respect to the value of CII interviewing techniques themselves." The next day, the state Commission on Teacher Credentialing met in Sacramento and voted, seven to six with one member abstaining, to endorse Judge Gruen's ruling and restore her right to teach.[86]

Minister John D. Eales

The impact of the McMartin case went far beyond those who had been charged with a crime. John Eales, Minister of St. Cross Episcopal Church, lived with years of extreme stress fighting rumors that satanic rituals had been performed at his church and taunting psychological pressure that forced him to seek disability retirement. Shackled with the McMartin charges, even though they were neither named as defendants nor ever charged, both minister and church had been denounced in the Manhattan Beach community. No evidence of blood on the altar was ever found, but following the charges, church attendance dropped drastically and the church-run preschool was forced to close.

Minister Eales recounted that he had received numerous threatening phone calls since the charges had been made; the harassment increased as the case moved towards a verdict; and the church and rectory were pelted with bottles and rotten eggs—a note was left stating that "THERE IS SIMPLY NO PLACE FOR SATAN WORSHIP IN THIS TOWN." The minister said that his health could not withstand the constant harassment and vandalization of the church. One young member of the church was dismayed and said, "We brought a good, strong man in here, and—well, this has ruined him."[87]

Since the McMartin case, there have been a large number of claims of ritualistic and satanic child abuse. However, the first empirical study of its actual prevalence suggested that these tales might have been figments of imagination. The first authoritative national survey of the subject, the 1994 survey conducted for the National Center on Child Abuse and Neglect, included 6,910 psychiatrists, psychologists, and clinical social workers, and 4,655 district attorneys, police departments, and social service agencies. While the survey found and investigated 12,264 accusations of group cult sexual abuse based on satanic rituals, the study could not substantiate a single case among them where there was clear corroborating evidence for the accusation of satanic ritual sexual abuse. The study also indicated that, although the survey found occasional cases of lone abusers who used ritualistic trappings, it found no substantiated reports of well-organized satanic rings of people who sexually abuse children.[88]

Jurors

The jurors spent two and one-half difficult years on the McMartin case. Their strongest emotion after the lengthy jury trial was one of relief, that the long ordeal that had disrupted their lives had come to an end. "It's been hard—very hard," one juror said, "there were some days when I thought I couldn't stand it any more. It will be real hard adjusting to the real world."[89]

Some of the jurors were parents, and they said that the painful, sometimes bizarre testimony given by children will remain with them forever. One juror cautioned that "It's always in the back of my mind. I watch my children a little closer." Also, he said, "Now I'm very cautious with other people's children because I'm aware of how easily something can be blown out of proportion and misinterpreted." Another juror said, "I think everyone was a victim. I don't think anyone came out of this case better or a winner. It's sad."

A bitter irony for the McMartin jurors was that after they had listened to all of the prosecution and defense testimony, they were chastised by friends, relatives, and complete strangers who pointedly asked, "How could you say they weren't guilty?" Juror Barbara Celestine said that since we found them not guilty, "Everyone wants to change the system. If we had found them guilty, no one would want to change anything. I have a problem with that. We did the best we could do."[90]

The jurors found very little public support for their verdict. Without identifying herself, Celestine asked a liquor store clerk what he thought of the verdict—his answer snapped back: "That's full of ... I think they were guilty."[91] Yet who knew more about the case than the jurors themselves?

Like other jurors, Mark Bassett had not been allowed to talk to anyone regarding the trial and children's testimony. He recalled that the trial was "very draining. You're dealing with extremely emotional issues. And there's no one in the whole world you can talk to and say, 'This is rough,' and why."[92] On the positive side, he said that the trial took him through all aspects of the human experience and gave him added self-confidence, knowledge about negotiation, and how to think critically.

Societal Costs

Igniting a nationwide panic about rampant sexual molestation of young children, the McMartin case focused harshly on child care workers and public sensitivities.[93] According to the director of the CII, sexual molestation became the number one concern of parents when it should be way down the list of concerns about education, diet, and play.[94]

A series of books and films about the general subject of childhood sexual abuse and the McMartin trial in particular are in process. The media not only helped to perpetuate the case, but is still on the *qui vive* in publicizing anything that revives it to boost circulation and viewers. The Manns, who assisted the defense, have an 800-page book manuscript planned and have produced a screenplay.[95] At least several other books are known to be in progress, one of which purportedly will be authored by Lois Timnick based upon her experiences covering the trial. One defense lawyer has been rumored to be working on a book, and others not yet known undoubtedly will emerge.

Several legal and ethical questions are now being examined in preparation for movie productions to be aired. One of the questions that needs to be resolved is: What is the story to be told, i.e., a story of justice done or justice denied? Abby Mann told a reporter that "unlike a documentary, it's hard to take an ambiguous position in a docudrama."[96] The ambiguities of the McMartin episode make it unresolvable as a metaphor of justice lost or won.

Nevertheless, movie directors Oliver Stone, Janet Young, Abby Mann, and Dianna Pokemy finally produced the HBO movie called *The Indictment: The McMartin Trial* which aired in May 1995. James Woods, who played defense attorney Daniel Davis, blamed the miscarriage of justice on an exploitative press and the abuse of due process of law by a press bent on profit and by the prosecution for its narrow political ends.

The Criminal Justice System

What impact the McMartin case will have upon the criminal justice system is difficult to assess. New approaches will likely have to be developed, if alleged childhood sexual abuse perpetrators and their alleged victims are both to receive equitable handling and a fair hearing in subsequent trials.

Past research indicates that victims often endure a status degradation or a second victimization in the criminal justice system at the hands of police and courts.[97] The privacy of alleged victims is violated, their credibility and character are often challenged, and frequently their reputations are put on trial as much as the charged offenders'. Inevitably, protecting the rights of all citizens from false accusations, false arrest, illegal search and seizures, and invasions of privacy places the task of legally acquiring evidence and the burden of proof on the prosecution, police, and victims. The rights of due process notwithstanding, victims themselves are often mistreated by being manipulated, coaxed, badgered, harassed, and dragged in and out of court at a moment's notice.

What factors lead courts to so insensitively treat alleged victims? As courts operate on their own norms, cases are processed as expeditiously as possible, especially considering the normal logjam of cases awaiting trial and the logistical limitations of jails, prisons, and police lockups. Victims are often seen as interfering, particularly when they demand that a prosecutor not plea bargain a case or that a judge not order bail instead of preventive detention. It was revealed after the case that the prosecution had attempted to allow the McMartin defendants to enter guilty pleas despite objections of the alleged victims' parents, in order to ensure conviction. The defendants refused the pleas. Similarly, even though parents opposed Buckey's release, Judge Pounders changed the defendant's status from unbailable to bailable, requiring the posting of $3 million bond.

Some crimes are also considered to be so common, e.g., burglary, larceny, disorderly conduct, and simple assault, that they are treated as "normal crimes" processed in a perfunctory manner with the victims perceived as almost superfluous to the court process. With the exponential increase of child sexual abuse accusations in recent years, victims are treated as incidentals, merely at the court's beckoned call.[98] Many parents and child victims thus have doubts about the seriousness and commitment of the prosecution in effectively handling child sexual abuse cases.

When children are victims or witnesses, the issue of their credibility is pushed to the limits by defense lawyers. Despite the research findings that sixth- to ninth-grade children perform as well as adults on tests of recognition, lawyers continually challenge a child's capacity for rendering the truth.[99] At the time of the trial, some witnesses were already in junior high school and considered to be old enough to provide the credible testimony based on their reconstruction of what had happened at the preschool.

Other research indicates that jurors tend to perceive older children's testimony less credible than that of younger children's which may seem more convincing and powerful. Many children who testified in the McMartin trial had grown considerably older since they had first attended the preschool, and jurors might have perceived their testimony as less credible and convincing.[100]

Victims sometimes have the last word during sentencing hearings, particularly capital felony cases, when the judge or jury may use victim impact statements to mete out punishment. The Supreme Court ruled in June 1991 that the families of murder victims could give testimony in death penalty sentencing hearings, and that the pain befalling family members could be considered aggravating circumstances related to the crime.[101] But victim impact statements have rarely been utilized in high-profile child molestation cases. As the prosecution often fails to convict defendants in many of these cases, they rarely reach the sentencing phase of the trial.[102]

In the quicksand of leveling charges, more than simply testifying was needed for the McMartin children to maintain their self-esteem. Attorneys are not usually child psychologists and fail to appreciate the fragility of young witnesses. At the moment charges were first brought, Robert Philibosian, Los Angeles District Attorney, had told a reporter that the McMartin child molestation trial had "set a national tone, so that [young] victims of child molesting have had the courage to come forward and tell their stories rather than have this crime hidden away."[103] However, much research will be needed to ascertain whether his statement accurately reflects the empirical reality experienced by children and their parents in child sexual abuse cases.

Child Sexual Abuse Rehabilitative and Therapeutic Industries

Since the early 80s, the dramatic increase of child sexual molestation cases in Los Angeles had overwhelmed the D.A.'s office, but the large case loads of alleged sexual abuse had also led to the expansion of so-called "child abuse rehabilitative and therapeutic centers and clinics." Many existing organizations specializing in treatment and offering diagnostic and counseling services to child victims and their parents had become the recipients of large government funds and private grants, and their businesses began to prosper.

Ever since the Federal Child Abuse Prevention and Treatment Act was passed by Congress in 1974, federal aid has supplemented state funding for child protection and similar family-oriented agencies that combat child abuse. The focus has been detection, prevention, treatment, and advocacy against child abuse. Specifically, through grants or contracts, the act made federal funds available for: (1) community education programs; (2) training of child protection and health care workers; and (3) technical assistance to the state for specialized intervention programs.[104]

Similarly, Congress enacted Senate Bill 140, more commonly known as the Children's Justice and Assistance Act of 1986, which established additional federal grant programs to reduce the trauma of child sexual abuse victims.[105] Various states also passed similar measures to protect abused children and to increase the successful prosecution of abusers. Consequently child treatment centers such as CII became beneficiaries of such federal and state funds in the Los Angeles area.

Since its first involvement in the McMartin case in 1983, CII has received multi-million dollar grants and funds from a variety of agencies, including the California state government, covered counties, federal agencies, and private organizations. The California Victim's Aid Fund was specifically made available to therapists who interviewed and treated McMartin children. In order to receive government funds for the treatment, the alleged victims had to file a police report and qualify for the victim-of-crime program. Interviewers often transmitted such information to alleged victims' parents, so that the children's CII and family treatment were together funded by the government program. If the children were unqualified, they were often asked if their insurance could cover the treatment. CII interviewer Sandra Krebs, for instance, testified that she told McMartin parents that filing a police report would help them to obtain funds to pay therapists because the state victim witness fund would then help them pay for the treatment.

Strong ties between the therapeutic industry and the state government also emerged. In 1985, the state government selected CII to establish the Southern California Training Center for Child Abuse Treatment, and in 1996, CII was still the only state-funded program providing the service in Southern California. The CII brochure describes their ever-increasing role in the area of child abuse:

> The number of abused children and families in crisis is growing—and so is CII's ability to serve. By adding a second location, ... CII will be able to help "heal the hurts" of 2,000 additional people each year. The new center is the only facility of its kind in south Los Angeles County....
>
> Dedicated to the goal of family preservation, ... (CII) is a private, non-profit organization specializing in the treatment and prevention of child abuse and neglect.... Children's Institute International provides a comprehensive social service delivery system to meet the needs of the children and families referred by the Department of Children's Services.

The propriety of the government's link to therapeutic industries was open to question so far as influencing and being influenced by the children's parents were concerned. The therapeutic industry was not simply linked to state funding, but became the cornerstone for providing the parents with police information, which the parents used to pressure the district attorney's office. The rehabilitative centers were able to work with alleged victims' parents through their therapists and physicians. As many McMartin children and their parents were CII's own clients, these parents were able to use their influence as successful and prominent professionals in the community. Including attorneys and a superior court judge, they mobilized their economic resources to create politically active organizations, which pressured the prosecution, influenced the media to deepen the investigation, and actively called for the reprosecution of the McMartin defendants.

With active support from CII and their therapists, the parents of the McMartin children created a networking and education group called "Believe the Children." A group of the parents gave a presentation on ritualistic child sexual abuse at the First National Conference on Child Victimization in New Orleans in May 1986. From this forum, an organization consisting of chapters across the nation was formed. This organization now serves as a clearinghouse on ritualistic child sexual abuse, has a speaker's bureau, and acts as a referral service to psychotherapists experienced in treating ritualistic abuse.

A group of McMartin parents also organized to lobby through the "Children's Civil Rights Fund," advocating closed-circuit television in the courtroom setting, so that an alleged child victim could be cross-examined without having to face the accused. This legislation was later passed in California, leading to even greater debates in the U.S. Supreme Court concerning the constitutional rights of an accused to confront his/her accuser in court.

Similarly, a support group, which included parents whose children had attended the nearby Manhattan Ranch Preschool, formed a legislative action organization called "Clout," which later lobbied the California legislature on child advocacy issues and succeeded in pressing passage of three pieces of legislation: (1) a prosecutor has the right to object to cross-examination questions that are not appropriate to a child's development level; (2) defense subpoenas must be submitted to the parents of child victims no less than 14 days in advance of testimony; and (3) judges must instruct juries that a child's testimony is no less credible than that of an adult.

McMartin parents, their therapists, and counselors often worked together and met regularly to discuss issues and procedures for dealing with their children's needs. They sought funding with the help of the California Community Foundation, submitted a research proposal, secured funding through the National Center on Child Abuse and Neglect, and published their findings on the subject of ritualistic sexual abuse.[106]

After the passage of mandatory reporting laws and large federal and state grants were allocated to diagnostic and treatment centers, the reporting of child sexual abuse increased dramatically. The nationally-reported 6,000 instances of child sex abuse in 1976 increased to 42,900 in 1980 and tripled to 138,000 in 1986—just before the McMartin trial began, annually rising thereafter. By 1988 there were an estimated 350,000 child sexual abuse cases reported.[107] In 1991 reports totaled 432,000, an increase of another 23%.[108] Over 85,000 sex offenders are now incarcerated in state and federal prisons, an increase of 48% in the two years from 1988 to 1990.[109] Though only about 10 to 15% of child abuse complaints are prosecuted, about 90% of these result in conviction. According to more recent figures, there were 2.9 million cases of suspected maltreatment of children below the age of 18 in 1992. Of these 2.9 million, approximately a half million involved sexual maltreatment and 128,556 were either "substantiated" or "indicated."[110]

Since 1985, however, it was found that nearly 65% of all child abuse reports nationwide proved to be unfounded. Similarly, 79% of the alleged cases of child sexual abuse in day care were unsubstantiated in 1990, and in 44% of all cases that resulted in arrest, the charges were dropped.[111] Originally, the reporting of child abuse was a duty imposed only upon physicians. As the problem grew, states expanded the duty to include other parties who had regular contacts with children such as nurses, teachers, social workers, and police officers.

The mandatory reporting laws have not required absolute certainty of abuse. They merely require that the reporter have a reasonable belief or reasonable cause to suspect that abuse has occurred. Immunity from civil and/or criminal liability has been designed to encourage cooperation in the reporting of suspected abuse especially in cases where no legal duty is imposed. Because the failure to report suspected cases may result in civil and criminal penalties, the system is so overwhelmed with unfounded reports that it endangers children who really have been abused and need help.[112]

The mandatory reporting laws and dramatic increases of reported child abuse cases have not only profited child sexual abuse diagnostic and treatment centers, but even some commercial firms as well. The Federation on Child Abuse and Neglect and the New York Chapter of the National Committee for Prevention of Child Abuse have utilized the telemarketers, Reese Brothers Inc., to establish a stable and continuing funding source to support their services, to make New York residents aware of the high incidence of child abuse in the state, and to increase use of the Federation's prevention programs.[113]

Today most preschools feel compelled to carry liability insurance for their clients due to possible civil lawsuit which may be filed against them by the children and their parents.[114] Since professional help is clearly needed for sexually abused children and their parents, there is an overwhelming demand for such treatment, which may cost $100 per hour or more for individual professional counseling.[115] Some sexual abuse victims develop such deep emotional problems that they may be unable to maintain jobs and must necessarily rely on resources provided by private health insurance or existing state funds for victims of violent crimes. In child sexual abuse cases, the preschool's liability insurance has become one of the few effective means of paying for the expensive, specialized treatment that the children may need.

However, many insurance resources available to preschools have begun to dry up, and insurance companies have stopped offering coverage for sexual abuse or set a price for coverage that is out of reach for most private and independent preschools.[116] A few insurance companies still offer a sexual-abuse rider but with a ceiling on limited coverage. Similarly, to cover potential liability, preschools often have to provide costly commercial policies and look to their business assets as sources of possible compensation.

As a result of such financial strain, many private nursery schools have been shut down and replaced by federally funded day-care centers operated and supported by the child-diagnostic institutes or treatment centers. CII, for instance, first established a facility for infant day care in 1976 and added a therapeutic day care center for infants and toddlers at risk of abuse and neglect in 1979. In 1984, the center was expanded to a 24-hour emergency shelter and assessment center. Nine independent preschools closed in the greater Los Angeles areas during the fearsome McMartin trial, and the government-funded agencies were able to replace them and offer services to many children and parents. The services were as much needed as the closed schools once were.

Conclusions

Legislative grants and intervention have now made it difficult, if not impossible, to defend against the allegation of sexual abuse. Legislative interventions, such as the Child Abuse Prevention and Treatment Act and mandatory reporting laws enacted by many states, were originally designed to help child sexual abuse victims. Ironically, the legislative programs have now led to an avalanche of federal and state funds to child sexual abuse therapeutic industries. Government-funded treatment and diagnostic centers were able to offer additional diagnostic services, education programs, and training sessions for child care workers. They also expanded their facilities to accommodate an influx of sexual abuse cases and offered assistance to the states for specialized intervention programs.

The McMartin case may be the last child molestation case where some semblance of defense can be balanced against the overwhelming funding power of the state and the district attorney's office in major metropolitan areas. The case ultimately cost the county an estimated $15 million, altered the lives and careers of almost everyone involved in the case, and provided a focal point for the issue of child abuse.

By the time the charges against the five defendants had been dismissed, the McMartin case was not yet the most expensive sexual molestation case in the nation's history. However, when the verdict was announced by the McMartin jury in 1990, the trial had become the longest and costliest criminal trial in history, undoubtedly damaging almost everyone within its reach. Yet, the "not guilty verdicts" and deadlocked counts did not satisfy the parents, the children, the defendants, or virtually anyone else associated with the case.

The exonerated defendants still suffered from the emotional trauma and economic devastation. Similarly, McMartin children and their parents have experienced deep personal and emotional pain. Though a successful defense had been mounted in the first McMartin trial, the personal, economic, and social injuries that were incurred were uncalculable. The end was not yet in sight. And, as the next chapter illustrates, in the second McMartin trial, Raymond Buckey was tried on the 13 charges on which the first McMartin jury failed to offer a unified judgment.

Chapter 11

The Second McMartin Trial

A number of issues were involved in deciding whether or not Raymond Buckey should be tried again on the 13 charges on which the first jury deadlocked. From a prosecutorial standpoint, a decision to go forward had to consider whether or not there was a reasonable expectation of conviction. Among these considerations was the extent to which the first jurors had voted guilty on various charges in the first trial. After the first verdict, Judge Pounders had said that in his opinion "the verdict could have gone either way."[1] The DA also had to balance the politics of possible exoneration when the case had already cost the taxpayers of Los Angeles County an admitted $15 million.

The DA's decision may have also considered retrying Raymond Buckey to appease the parents of McMartin Preschool children who were extremely active in pressing the media. An extensive campaign for a second trial was led by parents and child protection groups who rallied for public support. Their letter-writing barrage accompanied their lobbying of politicians, staging marches, appearing on television talk shows, and holding press conferences.[2] A few spectators of the McMartin episode even called for a second trial, knowing benefits might be showered on the "publicity-prone politician-prosecutor"—Ira Reiner—regardless of the financial and emotional costs.[3]

Not too surprisingly, Raymond Buckey stated that he had anticipated another jury trial, knowing the case had political overtones from its beginning.[4] District Attorney Reiner repeatedly denied that politics would play any role in his decision to retry Buckey, firmly stating, "This is not a political matter and is not going to be treated as such."[5] He also denied any political consideration in his bid for State Attorney General and said, "This is not a political matter but a matter of justice."[6] Yet few could believe his words, as the display of pomposity and deeds overwhelmed the public through the newspeak of Los Angeles press, radio, and TV.

Buckey, as expected, criticized the parents and their supporters who marched in rallies calling for a retrial. While he was sympathetic to their trauma and plight, he inveighed that "these people are not quite all in kilter." "Nothing that happened at the preschool is the cause of [the children's] hell," as he repeated his earlier refrain.[7]

Opposing a second trial, the defense raised legal argument about the violation of Buckey's constitutional rights to a speedy trial, his five years in jail without ever being convicted of a crime, the excessive bail, and that the ultimate outcome of a second trial undoubtedly would be the same as the first—another hung jury or an adjudication of innocence.

The Retrial Decision

After extensive lobbying of the district attorney's office by a variety of groups, consultation with parents of alleged victims, a review of evidence, and vigorous discussion with various members of the district attorney's office, District Attorney Ira Reiner finally decided to retry Raymond Buckey.

The decision to retry was based on four major issues: (1) seriousness of alleged offenses; (2) commitment of the families to go forward, with possible additional testimony by their children; (3) the feeling that the public was entitled to a resolution of the matter; and (4) the judge's assessment that, given the evidence presented, the verdicts could have gone either way.

The retrial was expected to last six months and to require at least $1 million in legal costs at approximately $169,000 per month.[8] Selection of a new jury was expected to lengthen the trial. The prosecution wanted the judge to interview all potential jurors, but the defense argued against that procedure. California proposition 115, which was later passed in the summer of 1990, prohibited attorneys from directly questioning prospective jurors during *voir dire*. While the proposal did not directly affect the second McMartin trial, it was designed to curtail the power of the defense to influence jury composition. Also, the defense expressed concern as to whether or not an impartial jury could be found that had not already been tainted by the publicity surrounding the case and the first trial.

When the decision was made to hold a second trial, the prosecution decided to drop one of the remaining charges against Buckey—the conspiracy charge—in an effort to strengthen the case on the remaining counts.[9] Another charge from the 13 undecided counts would also be dropped—the charge alleging sodomy of the child who had first triggered the case.[10] Despite the defense's belief that no child witnesses remained, prosecutors said that they would proceed with five child witnesses during the second trial.[11]

The mother of one of the children who would testify in the retrial said that she "was real shocked and surprised" by the jury verdict in the first trial, so her child's testimony in the second trial was "the right thing to do."[12] Though her daughter had previously refused to testify, she indicated that she would do so at the retrial. Another parent was skeptical of the second trial and the possibility of a conviction, saying that the parents would have to ask the question of whether they "really want to go through all of this again."[13]

But it began again, nevertheless. And nearly seven years after his arrest and three months after being acquitted of most charges against him, Raymond Buckey's second trial got underway. If convicted on the remaining counts, Buckey could be sentenced to 22 years in prison.

Was This a Valid Prosecution?

District Attorney Ira Reiner said that he knew the case was flawed "with serious evidentiary problems brought about by the early handling of the case. We have absolutely no illusions as to the difficulties of this case.... It will be an uphill battle." Yet Reiner stated that he and his colleagues felt that they had "at least an opportunity to get a conviction."[14]

When jurors from the first trial were interviewed, they expressed the view that without new evidence, a second jury could easily end up being divided on the same molestation charges.[15] Brenda Williams, a former juror, said that she believed that the charges were filed to satisfy the parents. "It is upsetting because it appears that everyone is hysterical," she thought. "No one seems to be dealing with this rationally. I thought once you are found not guilty of charges that the charges are dropped. But nobody seems willing to drop this."[16]

Former juror Coleman also stated, "I think they wasted enough money on that trial already. I think it's a mistake. I don't think they have any new evidence." First trial juror Ochoa also expressed similar concerns that another trial might add to the plight of the children. Obviously, many jurors from the first trial believed that a new jury would have the same problems and anticipated that new jurors would reach the same conclusion, i.e., a deadlock on the remaining charges.[17] On the other hand, former juror Kindle who voted guilty on several charges said that the parents had a right to another trial and, "I think it's up to the parents. If they think they can win their case, it's up to them to decide if they want to continue.... I think I would do the same thing."[18]

The Jury Selection

The trial jury was selected from a broad group, an array of 400 persons who were called into the courthouse. "The ideal would be to find 12 truly unbiased people," defense trial consultant Jo-Ellen Dimitrius told a reporter. "But in light of the international nature of the case, unless they have been living in a cave, it will be difficult to find anyone without some kind of bias."[19] Before the *voir dire* screening session, the prosecution and defense were each given ten peremptory challenges, an opportunity to reject potential jurors without any "cause" being specified.

In contrast to the first trial's three-month jury impanelment, the retrial jury was selected in just 13 days. The jury for the second trial of Raymond Buckey consisted of seven women and five men, including three blacks and one Asian. Half were college graduates, and half were also parents, a factor which may have favored the prosecution.

Trial

The second trial lasted only three months, with 43 witnesses appearing, in contrast to the first trial which took two and half years with over 120 witnesses. There was some speculation that charges might be reduced to five counts involving only two of the original 11 children.[20] The charges against Buckey were finally reduced to eight because prosecutors indicated that they were unable to proceed on the other five counts and felt that dropping these five charges would strengthen their case.[21]

So eventually, Buckey was retried on these eight counts of molestation—rape, sodomy, oral copulation, and digital penetration involving three children. In the second trial, all witnesses were girls. Toddlers at the time of the alleged incidents at the McMartin Preschool, two of the three young girls had testified at the first trial, while the remaining witness had not. One of the counts dropped involved the boy whose initial allegations began the case almost seven years previously. Through his father's efforts, the boy refused to testify at the retrial.

The prosecution team for the second trial consisted of Joe Martinez and Pamela Ferrero, who replaced the two first trial prosecutors, one of which—Lael Rubin—had been on the case since early 1984. Martinez was a former social worker and trial veteran who had spent 23 years in the district attorney's office, a former child abuse social worker with Catholic Charities of New York, as well as a former military officer. He had handled hundreds of cases including about three dozen murder trials and had a reputation for winning cases characterized as "sure losers" by other prosecutors. Co-prosecutor Ferrero was a Wellesley graduate who had majored in philosophy and was regarded as an accomplished trial lawyer by other attorneys. Yet the new prosecution team was unfamiliar with the finer details of the first McMartin trial.

In the retrial, the prosecution took only 13 days in presenting their evidence, in contrast to 15 months at the first trial. Similarly, instead of 61 witnesses, only 11 were called. Among these 11 witnesses were the three children, their parents, and a pediatrician who had examined them.

The second trial was delayed for a time because of defense attorney Davis's back injury. Davis had represented Raymond Buckey in the first trial. The judge threatened to remove him from the trial because both the prosecution and judge believed that his back ailment was only a ploy to delay the trial or to engineer a mistrial. Under such pressure, after a short remission, Davis recovered somewhat and continued to represent Buckey, moving the trial forward.

Judicial Assignment

The defense felt that the district attorney, the government, media, and other circumstances had placed Raymond Buckey in a vulnerable position. District attorneys in Los Angeles had traditionally aspired to higher office, so one of the defense's main concerns was that the second trial was undertaken largely for the political benefit of Ira Reiner who was now a candidate for state attorney general. Similar to previous efforts of District Attorney General of Los Angeles Robert Philibosian, the defense believed that Ira Reiner was elevating the McMartin episode to improve his political image and chance to win the upcoming election.

Judges in Los Angeles had also taken to glamorous self-promotion in the past. The defense was concerned about Judge Pounders' appearances on a number of national television programs such as "Oprah Winfrey," "Nightline," and "Good Morning America," expressing his views on the first McMartin trial and jury verdict. The defense contended that statements made by Judge Pounders on numerous TV shows indicated that he was biased against the defendant. In particular, Judge Pounders had said on "Good Morning America," "We are really set up to allow guilty people to go free." Davis said, "It's sacrosanct that judges do not discuss pending cases. I don't think we've ever seen a case where a judge has gone on national television opining [sic] about ... the nature of the evidence."[22]

Davis also contended that Judge Pounders was biased against him personally, citing the judge calling him "an ass," slashing the defense witness roster, excluding important defense evidence, and vowing to conclude the trial "even if it's over your dead body."[23]

Judge Pounders denied bias against the defendant or defense attorney Davis. He indicated that he had made public statements and appeared on radio and television shows only to explain legal issues and especially to praise the jurors and their dedication to the task of deciding guilt or innocence in the first trial.[24]

The defense did not believe him, and its first motion was to remove Judge Pounders from the second trial. Superior Court Judge Michael Hoff ruled that while Judge Pounders was not biased against the defendant, his broadcasts could become an issue in selecting new jurors who had not been tainted by post-trial publicity, and that the judge could be put into the awkward position of ruling upon his own actions taken during the initial post-trial period if he remained as the trial judge.[25]

Defense attorney Davis was delighted with the ruling excluding Judge Pounders from presiding at the second trial. "I'm finally free after three years and three months," Judge Pounders grandstanded. "I honestly was afraid I wouldn't live through it. Stress kills people and there was so much stress in the courtroom."[26] Nevertheless he also was quoted as expressing "disappointment" that he would not be able to see the case to its conclusion.[27]

In the following week, Superior Court Judge Stanley Weisberg was selected by the presiding judge to replace Judge Pounders.[28] Indicating that they had little knowledge about Judge Weisberg and that the prosecution attorneys had made no comment upon his selection, the defense team steeled their evidentiary armor. Judge Weisberg had been a prosecuting attorney for 18 years in Los Angeles County and served as a dependency court judge; he was elevated to the municipal court in 1986 and to the superior court in 1988. Judge Weisberg later became better known for his assignment to the first infamous 1991 Rodney King beating criminal trial in which the four white Los Angeles police officers were tried in the beating of a black motorist; he was generally considered to be intellectual, compassionate, and an efficient presider in the courtroom.[29]

Dismissal Request

In the second trial proper, the main concern was that the three young witnesses pleaded poor memories on events which were alleged to have occurred when they had been toddlers; two of them gave different versions of events from what they had presented at the first trial, and, in one instance, denied the specific acts with which Buckey was charged. Davis thus petitioned for acquittal on five of the eight counts and indicated that he might seek early rulings on the remaining three counts. He argued that, in the retrial, the same facts cited in the first trial must be presented, and that it would be unconstitutional to retry Buckey on counts not considered by the first jury.

Prosecutors acknowledged that details may have been somewhat different but that the essence of the charges remained and should be evaluated by the jury. According to the prosecution, all that mattered was that Buckey committed "a lewd and lascivious act with a child under 14," be it fondling or penetration.

After the prosecution presented its case, the defense moved for dismissal on grounds of double jeopardy and denial of due process. Judge Weisberg stated that the issues raised in the dismissal motion were not discussed before the court previously, and that he would have to take them under consideration.

Judge Weisberg then dismissed the defense motion, contending that defense arguments of denial of due process and double jeopardy were erroneous. The judge's decision was based on his belief that even though the children's testimony did not match the listed charges and departed from their earlier testimony, both earlier and later testimony came under the general heading of "a lewd and lascivious act with a child under 14."[30]

Dismissed Count—Refusal of Boy to Testify

Defense attorney Daniel Davis, in an unusual tactic, asked Judge Weisberg not to dismiss the one count related to the young boy whose mother had initially raised the charge of molestation at the preschool. Davis argued that to dismiss the count would prevent him from presenting evidence about the origins of the case.[31] Davis noted that the boy had implicated his father in molesting him, and that his mother had a long history of mental illness. Judge Weisberg denied the motion, but said that the defense would be allowed to present relevant evidence, effectively stopping Davis from calling the boy as a witness.

Plea Bargain Controversies

Another controversy also emerged during early phases of the retrial when Davis alleged that the district attorney's office had offered a plea bargain to defendant Raymond Buckey. Reiner, in campaign appearances, had repeatedly asserted that no such plea bargain had been made. However, a taped conversation between Los Angeles district attorneys and Davis demonstrated that the district attorney's office indeed had offered a "no-contest" plea with no additional time in prison.

Generally, by the plea of "no contest," the defendant admits criminal liability for purposes of the particular proceeding only. Such a plea has the practical advantage of avoiding implications of guilt in other proceedings, e.g., a civil suit for damages. It also provides the defendant with a face-saving mechanism because he/she can claim that there was no guilty verdict, even though the "no contest" plea results in a conviction and the defendant can be given the same sentence that would have resulted from a guilty plea.

For some types of crimes other than sexual molestations, "no contest pleas" are quite common. They constitute over half of the pleas for charges of driving while intoxicated, for instance. In Georgia, of the 61,622 charges of drunk driving, more than 50% (34,642) resulted in a plea of "no contest."[32] The legal community is divided over the usefulness of such "no contest" pleas. Though the plea is exercised in the state of California, it is not accepted in approximately half the states. Despite its widespread use, it is not known if the "no contest" plea in child sexual abuse cases provides adequate means of penalizing alleged child molesters.

The DA also discussed the so-called "West plea"—a defendant pleads guilty because the prosecution has offered a resolution that is too good to refuse. The taped interview revealed that Davis asked the prosecutors which counts they wanted Buckey to plead no contest to, the co-prosecutor answering, "[Y]ou can pick whatever sex act you feel most comfortable with." The taped conversation also revealed discussions about whether or not Buckey would have to agree to register with the state as a sex offender.

In response to defense allegations that a plea bargain had been offered, thus weakening the DA's assertion that crimes had been committed, the DA assigned an investigator to talk to Judge Weisberg about the allegations. Such contact is deemed highly improper during the course of a trial without written permission of all parties involved. District Attorney Ira Reiner denied that he or his office had done anything improper, only that he was attempting to straighten out the matter.[33] Others did not believe his story, the *Los Angeles Times* editorializing that "there is the question of [jeopardizing] justice for children who may have been molested, for a man who may have been falsely accused of heinous crimes, and a public which has a right to expect that their chief prosecutor puts their interests ahead of his own."[34] Raymond Buckey flatly rejected the plea, insisting that he be tried by a jury.

Child Witnesses

Again in the second trial, children were the central witnesses. The three young female witnesses (now ages 10 to 13) testified that they had been sexually abused by Buckey, often when they were playing "games," and that Buckey had threatened to kill their parents if they told anyone about the games.

One young witness, a 10-year-old girl, said that Buckey had urinated on her, sexually assaulted her, and threatened to kill her parents if she told anyone about it. She testified that Buckey had also "stuck a pencil in my bottom" and "took a pencil and stuck it in my vagina."[35] She said that she and other children were taken to a costume shop where they took bubble baths and went on an airplane ride. Though she testified during the preliminary hearing that Buckey was clothed during the incident, she now said that he was naked at the time of these alleged molestations.

The witness indicated that she could not remember part of the pencil episode, however; and when asked if she actually saw the pencil, she replied, "[W]ell, I can't see, can I, if my bottom is on one side of my body and eyes are on the other side."

Another young child witness testified that Buckey had a mustache and beard when he was at the school. Subsequently, a U.S. Customs inspector said that he had known Buckey for years, and had seen him running on the beach and noticed that he had grown a sparse mustache.[36] While the second child witness said that Buckey had a beard, Davis later said that Buckey "has never had a beard or mustache in his life."[37]

Another witness's testimony was graphic, sketchy, and inconsistent with previous statements. She testified that Buckey threatened to harm her parents and that he cut off a rabbit's ear with scissors to emphasize his threat. She also testified that both she and Buckey were naked, playing a game called "horsey." But her answers to questions were inconsistent with those given at CII during her first videotaped interview, those given at the preliminary hearing, and those given at the first trial. Her testimony did not add any new evidence to the alleged molestation charges, except that it indicated, as the defense alleged, coachings by CII's Kathleen MacFarlane. A close observer of the trial indicated that when the witness was asked whether statements by the therapist had made her believe that Buckey was a bad person, the child glared at the defendant, then looked back to defense attorney Davis and snapped, "I already knew he was a bad person."[38]

Similar emotional testimony was given by one of the parents of an alleged child victim. While testifying, the mother broke down on the stand when asked about the alleged molestations by Buckey. She glared at him and said: "I'm so angry at you, I could kill you right now."[39] No court-arrest for threatening a murder with intent aforethought was made.

Renewed Medical Testimony

Dr. Astrid Heger, who had testified in the first McMartin trial, also testified at the second trial. Her testimony was considered key prosecution evidence to demonstrate that the alleged molestations were not a figment of the children's imagination. She said that she found vaginal scarring in the three girls and anal scarring in two of them; she utilized photographs that had been taken at examinations six years earlier. She also testified that there were medical standards for diagnosing past trauma indicating sexual abuse and that she followed them.

The defense called Dr. David Paul who also had testified in the first trial. After going over the slides, the photographs, and Dr. Heger's written reports, Dr. Paul testified that there was no evidence of any tactile, sexual abuse in any of the children. In his testimony, he also said that he could find no signs of the witnesses having been raped or sodomized. Thus, once again, the conflict of medical testimony tested the jury's ability to render an equitable decision.

Kathleen MacFarlane and CII

In the first trial, Kathleen MacFarlane of CII had been called by the prosecution and spent five weeks on the stand being questioned by both the prosecution and defense. In the second trial, the prosecution did not call her as its key witness. Rather, the defense subpoenaed her to testify at the retrial. This time she spent only two days on the witness stand.[40]

The defense asked MacFarlane to explain her controversial methods in interviewing young children. She testified that she initially gave children an opportunity to volunteer information; if they did not respond with allegations of sexual abuse, she said that she brought such abuse up herself because "sexually abused children do not volunteer information and they try to avoid touchy topics."

Going on the attack, the defense pointed out that MacFarlane was not licensed to practice psychotherapy or to conduct interviews of alleged victims. Davis argued that she was a self-styled expert and a prolific grant writer, and her previous experience in the field of child sexual abuse was largely administrative and theoretical. With respect to her romantic relationship with Satz, the judge ruled that jurors could hear about it, though it could not be explored in detail. In the first McMartin trial, Judge Pounders disallowed the information to be presented to the jury.

The defense argued that MacFarlane leaked testimony and documentary evidence, which had been subject to protective orders in the criminal proceedings, to ABC Television Inc. and its news reporter Satz. The defense further argued that MacFarlane withheld, destroyed, and manipulated evidence, including information that discredited the mental stability and veracity of Judy Johnson.

Michael Maloney
The defense called Dr. Michael Maloney, the psychologist who also had testified in the first trial. He reiterated the more accepted model of interview techniques which involved getting the child to talk, keeping the child talking, getting the child to say what happened in his or her own words, and resolving inconsistencies of the child's responses. He testified that CII interviews were not appropriate because the interviewers had done most of the talking, stage settings were implicitly pre-determined, and the interviewers did not accept the children's reports of "no sexual contacts" at the preschool.

He said that the interview patterns were broken into subparts each with assumptions that implicated Raymond Buckey as the defendant, these including: drawing a person; presenting sexually anatomical dolls; naming parts on dolls; offering "sexual education"; "dolls help us figure it out" techniques; class photographs; introduction of other kids as having been molested; pressuring the older children in which they were told they had a duty to "disclose" in order to help younger, less verbal kids; calling attention to secret games; and the assumption that kids had been scared by the defendants. He testified that "dolls help us figure it out" techniques suggested to the children that there was something that needed to be figured out, and telling a child that other children had already "told secret stories" gave them additional social and situational pressures to make up more stories.

In both trials, Dr. Maloney's testimony generated much skepticism and controversy over the credibility of CII interview techniques. Furthermore, the defense pointed out that the prosecution refused to call MacFarlane as their key prosecution witness, creating even greater skepticism about her credibility. The defense strategy thus was effective in persuading the jury that the children's reports and accounts of sexual molestation had been coached and influenced by CII interviewers.

Virginia McMartin
The original defendants now took on the prosecution's case against Raymond Buckey. In her brief appearance, Virginia McMartin, now eighty-

two, testified that none of the alleged improprieties took place at the school, that actually the school was a caring place for young people, and that the young people there adored her grandson, Raymond Buckey.[41] Three hours of her earlier videotaped testimony was used in lieu of current testimony because she ignored the judge's instructions and talked directly to the jury. Thus the judge struck from the record many of her in person and videotaped remarks.

Babette Spitler and Her Children

Babette Spitler and her daughter and son testified as defense witnesses. Babette Spitler stated that her two children had attended the McMartin Preschool, and the defendant had been there when her son attended the preschool. She stated that her children had been taken away for interviews at CII, her daughter refused to be examined by Dr. Heger, and that she had lost custody of them for two years.

Wendy Spitler, Babette's daughter, also testified that she had attended McMartin as a preschooler and then came back with her mother to work as an assistant when she was older. Chad Spitler, Babette's son, then testified that he had never seen the defendant molest or touch children in any improper way. Spitler's children also stated that they had never seen the defendant with a mustache or a beard.

Peggy McMartin Buckey

Buckey's mother, Peggy McMartin Buckey, was subpoenaed by the prosecution. She testified that prior to the complaint by Judy Johnson, she had never received a complaint from any parent about Buckey's behavior at the school. She also testified that children often sat on her son's lap and that she had once checked to determine if he had an erection. She explained that she viewed running the school from a parent's perspective and was only doing her duty. She also noted that one parent did not want her child to have a male teacher.

Raymond Buckey

The last person to testify, among the original defendants who had previously appeared in the first McMartin trial, was Raymond Buckey. He took the stand to deny all charges against him and testified that ever since he was first accused, he had never been asked by any law enforcement officers whether he had molested a child. During his cross-examination, prosecuting attorney Ferrero asked him if it was normal for a then-23-year-old man to have an interest in children. She further asked, "[D]id you ever stop for a period of four hours [at a school yard] and stare at those children?" His response was, "no." Ferrero indicated that she planned on calling a private investigator who had testified at the first trial that Buckey stopped to watch children playing at a schoolyard for hours while ignoring young women who passed by.

What were Buckey's motivations, then? Buckey admitted that he sometimes did not wear underwear. "Did you dress to molest?" the defense attorney asked him. The answer given by a smiling Buckey was, "no." After his testimony, Buckey said, "I'm not the only person in the South Bay who doesn't wear underwear, but I was probably the dumbest person, not to have worn it at the preschool." He added, "I'm wearing it *now.*" [42]

Closing Arguments

The prosecution's closing arguments focused on circumstantial evidence that the DA believed supported the testimony by the three young female witnesses. It was weak both logically and legally. "I would not ask you to convict the defendant in this case based solely on the testimony of the children," Ferrero presented, asking jurors to also consider testimony of parents and the medical doctors who had examined the children. On the other hand, the prosecution noted, though some defendants may have been wrongly accused in the previous trial, the testimony by former teachers supporting Raymond Buckey also may have been tainted because they had "an ax to grind."

Admitting that some of the evidence might be flawed, the prosecutors argued that the total combination of events, behavior, and circumstances all led to the conclusion that Buckey was a child molester. "There are things that cannot be explained away," Ferrero argued, "I'm not conceding that leading questions lead to damaged testimony." In the final analysis, she said, "[T]his case boils down to credibility. If you believe the children, then we have proven our case beyond a reasonable doubt."

Prosecutor Martinez insisted that the children should be believed, despite inconsistencies. "If they fantasize, they fantasize within their experience," he offered a classic *non sequitur*. He then asked how they could have made up the graphic details of their alleged sexual abuse without any frame of reference other than Raymond Buckey. Martinez argued that Buckey did not have an interest in early childhood education but, he polemicized, "[T]he predator is always close to the prey." "These children were molested," Martinez nailed down his soliloquy, "these children have felt injustice for so long that they've come to you for help. Ray Buckey did this thing to them. Don't reject them."

The defense's closing arguments also sounded shrill—"the truth simply never had a chance" to emerge during the trial, Daniel Davis began.

"Where are the items that tie Mr. Buckey to a sexual act?" Davis told the jury that no physical evidence had ever been found linking Buckey with any of the witnesses or any other child from the McMartin Preschool. Davis pointed out that all the former teachers, who had been former defendants, testified that no sexual behavior ever took place at the preschool.

Davis also noted that one child witness even said that she did not recall or know anything about the specific acts Buckey was accused of having performed with her.[43] He argued that the children were pressured into making statements about events for which they had no memory—perhaps unintentionally—as a result of the "carpetbaggers and overnight experts" who had interviewed and examined them. Davis deftly referred to the CII interviewers and charged that the case turned on the false accusations of molestation using the medium of child therapy.

The appropriate decision by the jury would be to "stick it to the people [in the district attorney's office] if they didn't do their job," Davis referred to the botched investigation and what he called a parade of unreliable witnesses. The children should not be believed, he emphasized, because their stories had been contaminated by years of interviews and discussions and because their stories had changed dramatically over time. One young witness, he pointed out, when asked about the changed stories, naively replied, "[T]hat was then; this is now." Davis suggested that their stories about the former defendants would also change in the future, as they already had, and that their decision now might be righting what could be judged to be a wrong 20 years in the future.

Judge's Instructions to the Jury

Alert to an impending decision, the judge ordered Raymond Buckey to remain in the Criminal Courts Building until a verdict was reached, apparently expecting a quick verdict. He pressured the jury, too, warning them that they would be meeting six hours a day until they either reached a verdict or deadlocked on the issues.

The judge instructed the jury that they must not be influenced by "passion, prejudice, public opinion, or public feeling" in deciding whether or not Buckey was guilty or innocent. In addition, they were to base their decision upon "the facts and the law" alone, with the prosecution's burden "to prove beyond a reasonable doubt ... to a moral certainty that he [Raymond Buckey] was guilty before they could make that judgment."[44]

The judge also made certain that the jurors were to consider the testimony of children as neither more or less credible than that of adults, although they "may perform differently." Given their young age, they may have had a failure of recall, he explained, which is also true of witnesses of all ages. It was a tough call in the jury room—too little evidence to convict, too many factors implicating Raymond Buckey in acts he sharply denied.

Jury Deliberations

At the beginning of the second trial, the jurors agreed that they felt that Buckey probably was guilty, but as the parents, the children, and the defendant took the stand, uncertainty hovered. The CII interviews had led some jurors to believe that the children had been coached into describing sexual abuse that had not actually taken place. One juror said, "the [institute's] tapes were terrible."[45] Jurors also expressed concern that the few times children were making spontaneous revelations, they were cut off by "therapists."

The jurors also felt that they did not have enough information to reach a guilty verdict. There was a divergence of opinion about the medical testimony and the opinions expressed by opposing medical doctors regarding evidence indicating sexual abuse. One witness's own physicians had said that they found no evidence of molestation. The jurors also listened avidly to a reading of the entire testimony of Dr. David Paul, medical examiner for the city of London, in which he said that he could find no signs of the witnesses being raped or sodomized. The jurors reread testimony of one of the young girls who had said that she had gotten semen in her eyes. While jurors concluded the children had perhaps been molested, they were divided over *who was responsible for the abuse.* Most jurors expressed concern that no corroborating evidence implicated Buckey in the abuse.

"We had jurors who remained on both sides of the fence from start to finish," jury foreman Richard Dunham noted, "[S]ome jumped around as late as early [Friday] morning [the day of their verdict]."[46] The deliberations were "excruciating," in the words of another juror.

After two weeks of talk and argument, they reached a verdict on one of the counts, albeit later to be determined as a temporary decision, since the jury later changed its decision on one of the eight counts. After additional deliberations and another charge upon which they judged Buckey innocent, the jury told the judge that they were deadlocked on the remaining six counts.

Since they had reached a verdict on two counts but were deadlocked on the remaining six charges, the judge sent the jury back for further deliberations, hoping that they would be able to resolve their differences.

During these final hours of deliberation the judge offered additional instructions to the jury. They then asked for still further legal instructions, and the judge counseled them to continue their deliberations in an effort to overcome the deadlock.

The jury continued deliberating but found themselves further apart; and, in fact, after beginning deliberations once again, reversed themselves on the two counts upon which they had earlier reached consensus! "We went back to deliberate and went [in] the opposite direction. We got more hung than less hung," noted the jury foreperson. One juror said that during the last hours of deliberations, there was "an atmosphere of futility." Finally, another juror concluded, "We had to do the best we could, and that's really, frankly, not good enough—to be deciding the outcome of either side's life."[47]

The Verdicts

"Buckey Jury Deadlocks; Mistrial Is Declared," the headline screeched.[48] The charges made against Buckey in the second trial had ended in a hung jury. The jury reported that they were "hopelessly and irreversibly hung on all counts."[49] The jurors agreed unanimously that they were frustrated in their attempts to reach consensus. "We tried very hard. I feel disappointed ... like we failed," the jury foreperson conceded.

The jurors felt that there was not enough solid testimony and evidence to reach a definitive decision one way or another. One juror noted "[W]e got half a deck and had to play like we had a whole deck."[50] Reasonable doubt stirred their minds, resulting in their deadlock on all counts.

The jury ended up leaning toward a guilty verdict on only one count— the one in which the child volunteered during the CII interview that she had been anally penetrated by Buckey.[51] On another count the jury was split evenly, and on the remaining six counts the jury clearly leaned toward acquittal, casting votes that ranged from seven to five on one charge, to 11 to one on three others.[52]

The ultimate decision by this jury was almost identical to that reached by the first, although they were more sharply divided. Juror Isaacson concluded, "I don't think you could ever get 12 people together who could make a unanimous decision on this."[53] Judge Weisberg specified, "[I]t is clear to me that the jury will not reach a verdict in this case. Therefore, it is a legal necessity to declare a mistrial, and I do so."

As a result of the jury's deadlock and the declaration of a mistrial, District Attorney Ira Reiner had to decide whether or not there would be a third trial; but he opted out. In fact, prior to the verdict being announced he had made the decision that a third trial would not take place.

In the following week, all charges against Buckey were dismissed. Judge Weisberg finally declared, "[T]he case of the *People v. Raymond Buckey* is hereby dismissed and the defendant is discharged. All right, that's it. That completes this case."

Aftermath of the Second Trial

The McMartin embroglio was not really completed. While the aspects concerning the criminal charges might have been finished, the legal and human trauma was expected to continue for years into the future. The personal costs to the alleged victims and their parents, the defendants— especially Raymond Buckey—as well as others intimately involved in the case, opened the door to civil proceedings, ensuring that the "McMartin era" was only partially completed at best.

Parents

Anguished at the outcome of the second trial, the parents accused the prosecution of merely going through the motions to satisfy a politically-motivated decision to retry Buckey. Some parents called the proceedings a "sham trial for political purposes, an appeasement trial."[54] The prosecutors maintained that they had streamlined the case so that they could increase the probability of obtaining a conviction. Prosecutor Martinez told a newspaper reporter, "We put on everything that is relevant to getting a conviction. We avoided a lot of things that might confuse the jury.... All that matters is whether he molested these little girls."[55] Some parents were upset because, though many other children were anxious to testify as corroborating witnesses, they were not called. Some parents also said that direct confrontation with the accused was too much of a burden for their children. Many parents thus felt betrayed by what seemed to them a hurried, perfunctory trial.

Some tried to find merit in their continuing involvement in publicizing child advocacy issues. "The victory [for the families involved] may or may not come from the courtroom," one reporter quoted a parent as saying, "[T]he significant victories are that we found out our kids were molested and got the appropriate treatment for them, the case resulted in changes in the judicial system, and there is now a tremendous international awareness of child molestation."[56] Another parent, Marilyn Salas, explained, "People call us obsessed because we can't put it behind us. But we feel a certain responsibility: This is the only [molestation] case that has national attention, and a lot of people elsewhere have embraced it as their own. We're not going to stop even when this [trial] is over."[57]

Child Witnesses

With child witnesses expressing many fears about going to court, their most prominent fear was facing the accused. Their fears were manifest in having difficulty relaxing, falling asleep, or concentrating at school. Many children felt powerless to control their fears. Significant adjustments in their personal and court lives neither meshed nor bred tranquillity.[58] Children who feared the accused while testifying were less able to answer questions and more likely to say that testifying had affected them adversely. Girls expressed more fears than boys, in particular about their personal safety.[59]

In the second trial, the three child witnesses were young girls who had already testified and confronted Raymond Buckey in the courtroom. Fear and anger at their helplessness debilitated them on the witness stand. An 11-year-old who had testified at both the first and second trials said that she was "disappointed and really angry. I thought they'd believe me and say he's guilty. I sort of think it's just because we're kids, and people think all kids lie. But he deserved to be in jail. He knows what he did. He knows he's a bad person."[60]

Raymond Buckey

When the jury reported that they were hopelessly deadlocked, Raymond Buckey expressed conflicted relief. "I look at that I'm innocent until I'm proven guilty," he stated. "I don't think you can ever be free of something like McMartin. You can walk away from it and grow from it and not live in the shadow of it, but it affects everybody caught up in it."[61] "I've been through anger, I've gone through fear, and even a feeling of revenge for the people who have done this to my family," he solemnized. While he compared the trial to the Salem witch trials, Buckey said that he probably was not as bitter as the parents who believed that their children had been molested at the preschool. He offered that he still had a "real life" to lead outside of the courtroom.[62]

As a result of the failed prosecution, Buckey planned a multi-million dollar lawsuit against Los Angeles County and former District Attorney Robert Philibosian, the city of Manhattan Beach and its police department, the CII and Kathleen MacFarlane, and Capitol Cities-ABC and its reporter Wayne Satz. Scott Bernstein, representing Buckey in a civil lawsuit, said that "the main motivation is that after seven years of hell for this man and his family, perhaps they can pick up and put the pieces together and have a life of their own."[63]

Satz, meanwhile, argued that "all that ABC and I did was report with 100% accuracy what transpired—namely that kids made allegations, that

Ray Buckey was indicted, charged by two district attorneys, bound over to trial after a long preliminary hearing."[64] He lamented that legally pursuing ABC and himself was to go after the messengers, not the accusers.

The Public

Strong public reactions also followed the second McMartin trial, very similar to public responses to the first verdict. One "Letter to the Editor" said that as a child sexual abuse victim, she "was sickened and infuriated to hear of the jury deadlock on Ray Buckey. Buckey claims he is innocent. The true innocent are the dozens of helpless children and damaged families in the case.... My heart goes out to the children and the families of the McMartin case. To them I say, 'I believe you. I know that you are telling the truth.'"[65]

Some people who had had jury experience also expressed great concerns over the rights of children in court and their exploitation by predatory media reporters. One writer said, "I personally feel that these children were exploited by being exhibited on the talk show circuit and news conferences by their publicity hungry parents. This is child abuse at its lowest level."[66] Still another writer said, "I compare the McMartin trial with the Salem witch hunts. In those trials, long ago, there were politically motivated prosecutors, hysterical parents, absurd stories, and descriptions of fantasy."[67]

Others voiced concerns involving the cost of the trial: "The most disgusting part of the McMartin case is its unbelievable waste and inefficiency, as millions of dollars were flushed down the toilet on a case which was legally unwinnable. Our government should be held fiscally accountable and should make every effort to operate efficiently and to contain costs."[68]

District Attorney Ira Reiner

After the verdict of the first trial was announced, the media was critical of Ira Reiner and his prosecution team for their failure to convict the McMartin defendants. "DA Reiner Might Have Lost More Than a Case," the *Times* headline declared.[69]

The implication was that the acquittal of the McMartin defendants was the kiss of death in state politics for Reiner. Though Reiner was politically leveraged by the McMartin case in defeating then Los Angeles District Attorney Robert Philibosian, the acquittals now hurt Reiner's campaign against Arlo Smith of San Francisco in the California primary election for the democratic nomination for state attorney general. "The question is not whether this hurts Mr. Reiner's campaign for attorney general, it's whether he should resign immediately as District Attorney of Los Angeles County," Smith's campaign manager declared.[70] Arlo Smith also called for a grand jury investigation into Reiner's decision to retry Raymond Buckey, saying that the decision was purely political.

Asked to reflect if he would make the same decision to have a second trial in the case, Reiner said, "I may have paid a very serious personal price for it. If I had to do it over again, I'd tell you what the answer is. I'd hope that I would make the same decision. Obviously, when you take a beating from it, you're never sure if you would do it again, if you would be able to stand up there and do it. I think I would. I certainly hope I would."[71] Finally, he said, "When you are the district attorney, you have decisions that are sometimes no-win decisions. And clearly, that's what this case is. Obviously, it had a major political impact."[72]

Public consensus was that the case Ira Reiner had inherited from the former district attorney was a "political albatross," and it played a significant role in his defeat in the democratic primary election for state attorney general.[73] Reiner had been far ahead of Smith only a few weeks before the election, but he had fallen behind in the polls. In June 1990, Reiner lost the democratic nomination to Arlo Smith in the California primary election.

The end of Reiner's political and judicial career was nearing, too, for the failure in the Twilight Zone manslaughter trial, the acquittal of four white Los Angeles police officers in the Rodney King beating trial, and the subsequent Los Angeles riots. Reiner lost reelection for Los Angeles District Attorney and was replaced by Gil Garcetti, a former chief deputy district attorney, who gave the world the gala prosecution of O. J. Simpson. In 1994, to no one's surprise, the grand jury finally began investigating the effectiveness of the Los Angeles District Attorney's office, which had been accused of letting political patronage and flawed legal logic influence their policies. Often called "Buffalo Bills" of the West, the DA's office simply failed to win the "big ones."[74]

Conclusions

For Raymond Buckey, the last of the original seven McMartin defendants still facing criminal prosecution, the declaration of a mistrial in the second McMartin trial signaled the end of the criminal justice process.

A letter writer to the *Orange County Register* perhaps best stated the conclusion of the McMartin case: "After seven years, $15 million in court costs, and two trials without a verdict, a member of the district attorney's office said they will not retry the McMartin case, 'but that does not mean that he is not guilty.' Wrong, wrong, wrong. That is precisely what it means."[75]

For children who testified against Buckey, a well-defined method to try those accused of child molestation, when no evidence corroborates the accounts of young children, has yet to be found. Efforts to coordinate, streamline, and otherwise strengthen the investigation process will benefit both accused and alleged victims who become enmeshed in the criminal justice system and the criminal court process. The emotional impact may not dissolve, but a level of logical rationality may help offset the danger of future witch hunts and trials. Without deep-seated reforms, the most needy children will be the least likely to have their day in court and justice may not be served.

We now turn to constitutional questions involving child abuse victims and alleged perpetrators, discussing contemporary legal issues and court reforms in child sexual molestation cases.

Chapter 12

Constitutional Rights: Child Abuse Victims and Alleged Perpetrators

In the course of human history, in widely separated societies, historically determined mores, community traditions, and standards of acceptance of the relationship between adults and children have reflected material power, political puissance, religious and psychological "morality" and vigilance, and accepted rights, duties, and methods of enforced compliance.

Each society and social group holds to its own standards of what these relations should be, so that there is no way to compare societies in terms of what is right and what is wrong; what is in the best interest of the child or the parents; and how children must be raised. Though there is simply no universal standard for the relationship of child and parent or adult, hence no international standard for acceptable guidance, there is near unanimous agreement that if allegations in the McMartin case were true, they were beyond the pale of the social mores of contemporary American society. Saragin writes that:

> every society must set up norms for the regulation of sexual conduct. The first and most pervasive such norm in Western Society is that sexuality must be by mutual consent: the partners must be willing. Violent rape incites great outrage in our society. The anger is heightened only when the victim is a child.[1]

In the United States, the concept of mutuality of and "informed consent" to sexual relations relates to age, competence, and relationship.[2]

While "age of consent" varies from state to state—and the political battle of changing laws to raise or lower this age seems endless—in all states there is a concurrence of law and public opinions that it is "unnatural" or "immoral" for an adult to have sexual relations with someone under the age of 14. There is only a very small minority that claims that "such sexual activity is actually beneficial to children and helps provide them with a healthy introduction to sex and sexuality."[3] From both perspectives, the question of adult control over children and their sexuality is the central concern.

Virtually any sexual contact between a child and an adult has been escalated to possible criminalization in the United States. Though the categories of potential adult-child sexual encounters are innumerable, current legal lines of demarcation emphasize the following four types: (1) exhibitionism; (2) molestation; (3) statutory rape; and (4) violent rape. Exhibitionism usually consists of an adult exposing his/her genitalia in the presence of a child. By contrast, molestation involves some type of actual sexual contact between an adult and a child. In cases of rape, "statutory rape" does not involve force or violence but implies that consent was not given because child was under age and legally could not consent. Forceful or violent rape negates consent.[4]

Age and lack of consent was central in the McMartin case, testing the judicial system's ability to deal effectively and fairly with the emotionally laden issue of sexual abuse of children.[5] Bypassing strident feelings and public hysteria, one critic viewed the McMartin case as an illustration of the "shining example of the cornerstone of the American criminal justice system."[6] It was argued that the criminal justice system was fully operational in the McMartin trial, able to separate known facts from emotive and moralistic suppositions.

By contrast, other observers argued that the McMartin case represented the epitome of injustice and mishandling of the case by the prosecution. Some critics argued that the discretionary power of the prosecution allowed the prosecutor's office to ignore the criminal justice presumption of innocence. Deputy District Attorney San Sturla in nearby Orange County declared that the McMartin case "was like a natural disaster. I don't think any of us were prepared for an earthquake like that."[7] Clearly, the children and their families would agree that the system, subject to stress and emotional public pressures, was not operating as it should have been; they demanded the ultimate of guilty verdicts.

In the wake of the McMartin case, prosecutors nationwide appeared to pursue child molestation charges with greater caution; nevertheless, there were still cases that appeared to border on mass paranoia, contagion, and hysteria.[8] For example, in August 1991, the trial of Robert Kelly began in Edenton, North Carolina. Kelly, the owner of the now defunct "Little Rascals Day Care Center," had been charged with 183 counts of sexually abusing 22 children between 1986 and 1989. Much of the trial hinged on the testimony of day-care children, with an army of experts testifying as to whether children so young could know the truth after intense rehabilitative therapy for sexual abuse. Similarly, in Maplewood, New Jersey, 26-year-old nursery school teacher Margaret Kelly Michaels was convicted of 115 counts of sexual abuse against 20 three- to five-year-old children at the Wee Care Nursery School. Sentenced to serve 47 years in prison, she was released on bail after five years as a result of the Appeals Court of New Jersey that reversed her conviction. The prosecution appealed to the state supreme court which, however, ruled that if the prosecution were to decide to retry the case, they must first hold a pre-trial taint hearing, showing that despite improper interviewing techniques, children's statements and testimony were sufficiently reliable to admit them as witnesses at trial. In December 1994, the prosecution dropped all charges against the defendant.[9]

Despite the rise in the reports of child sexual abuse, in most instances there may have been a swing away from zealous prosecution, even though there have been some exceptions such as the Akiki trial in San Diego. The McMartin case has generated greater sophistication in the criminal justice system, but some argue that it engendered skepticism about both the criminal justice system and whether or not children can always or ever be believed. Perhaps personnel within the criminal justice system may now view their roles as being more balanced, with an increased awareness of the potential for harming alleged victims as well as assumed perpetrators.

Constitutional Questions

As observers of the McMartin case, we believe that child witnesses suffered during the workings of the criminal justice system. The system's failings included: (1) bringing charges and going to court, resulting in the children being thrown into a slow moving, impersonal criminal court system; (2) demanding the frequent and accurate recall of sexual abuse which was harsh, if not fearful, for many children; (3) exposing children to possible public stigmatization; (4) exacerbating feelings of shame, self-blame, guilt, and fear during cross-examination; and (5) imposing pressure from the police, prosecution, media, parents, and psychotherapists in and out of the courtroom.

The delays and slow pace of the criminal justice system have often proven to be very difficult for vulnerable children, especially the younger ones, who tire and often give up the will to fight.[10] While the second McMartin trial did not require extensive testimony of the child witnesses, during both the preliminary hearing and the first McMartin trial, some children stayed on the witness stand for as long as 15 days. Criminal court proceedings can try the best of witnesses, and in the case of children, the stress can prevent them from recovering their sense of control and well-being. Although testifying does not necessarily cause emotional disturbance in all child victims, it does appear to prevent children from healing both physically and psychologically.[11] Given the negative consequences of testimony on child witnesses, it is understandable that many parents decided not to let their children do so. With only a few child witnesses willing to testify, the prosecution's strategy was considerably weakened.

What recommendations are there to reform the system for taking children's testimony in abuse cases? The federal government endorsed a number of rights and protections for child victims and witnesses in the Victims of Child Abuse Act of 1990. While many of the reforms were not adopted in the McMartin child molestation trials, some state legislatures had already adopted many of them endorsed in the 1990 federal act. Some jurisdictions in California had been informally using them long before they were statutorily authorized, including the optional use of testimony via videotape or closed-circuit television and the admission of hearsay evidence.

Closed-Circuit TV Testimony
While closed-circuit TV had been used for only one child witness in the McMartin preliminary hearing, it is important to examine the merits and disadvantages of such testimony. The judge's ruling in the preliminary hearing, that children had to testify in court (with one noted exception), led to a dramatic decrease of potential testimony by children and parents.

With intent to shield the child from direct confrontation by the accused in court, the technique poses a serious threat to the Sixth Amendment to the U.S. Constitution, which guarantees every criminal defendant the right to confront his accusers face-to-face. The "Confrontation Clause" of the Sixth Amendment, made applicable to the states through the Fourteenth Amendment, provides that in all criminal prosecutions, the accused shall enjoy the right to be confronted by the witnesses against the accused. The central concern of the "Confrontation Clause" is to ensure the reliability of the evidence against a criminal defendant by subjecting the witness or medium to rigorous testing in the context of an adversarial proceeding, including physical presence, oath-taking, cross-examination, and observation of the testifying party's demeanor by the accused and the trier of facts. Trial courts have nonetheless experimented with techniques designed to protect sensitive victims from direct confrontation with the accused during their testimony.

In *Maryland v. Craig* (497 U.S. 836, 1990), the U.S. Supreme Court examined the right of an accused defendant to confront his or her accusers and ruled that closed-circuit television serves as the "functional equivalent" to live, in-court testimony. As of December 31, 1989, at the time of ruling, 31 states had already enacted legislation permitting the use of closed-circuit television and 36 had provided for videotaped depositions as alternatives to in-court testimony. Twenty-two states provided for both forms of alternative testimony and only seven states provided for neither.[12]

In the Maryland case, the defendant was tried on charges related to her alleged sexual abuse of a 6-year-old child. Before the trial began, the prosecution sought to invoke a state statutory procedure permitting a judge to receive the testimony of the child by one-way, closed-circuit television.

In Maryland, in a case of child sexual abuse, a court may order that the testimony of a child victim be taken outside the courtroom and then shown in the courtroom by means of a closed-circuit television. To invoke the procedure allowing one-way, closed-circuit television for testimony of an alleged child victim, however, the judge must first determine that testimony by the child victim in the courtroom will result in the child suffering serious emotional distress, such that the child cannot reasonably communicate.

Once the procedure is invoked, the child witness, prosecutor, and defense counsel withdraw to a separate room, while the judge, jury, and defendant remain in the courtroom. The child witness is then examined and cross-examined in the separate room, while a video monitor records and displays the witness' testimony to those in the courtroom. During the testimony, the child witness cannot see the defendant, who remains in electronic communication with the defense counsel, and objections may be made and ruled on as if the witness were testifying in the courtroom.

The law permits only the following persons to be in the room with the child when the child testifies by a closed-circuit television: (1) the prosecuting attorney; (2) the attorney for the defendant; and (3) any person whose presence may contribute to the well-being of the child, including a person who has dealt with the child in a therapeutic setting concerning the abuse.[13]

Reviewing this case, the Supreme Court held that "though we reaffirm the importance of face-to-face confrontation with witnesses appearing at trial, we cannot say that such confrontation is an indispensable element of the Sixth Amendment's guarantee of the right to confront one's accusers."[14] With respect to the Maryland procedure using the one-way, closed-circuit television, the Court also held that:

> We find it significant ... that Maryland's procedure preserves all of the other elements of the confrontation right: The child witness must be competent to testify and must testify under oath; the defendant retains full opportunity for contemporaneous cross-examination; and the judge, jury, and defendant are able to view (albeit by video monitor) the demeanor (and body) of the witness as he or she testifies. Although we are mindful of the many subtle effects face-to-face confrontation may have on an adversary criminal proceeding, the presence of these other elements of confrontation—oath, cross-examination, and observation of the witness' demeanor—adequately ensures that the testimony is both reliable and subject to rigorous adversarial testing in a manner functionally equivalent to that accorded live, in-person testimony.[15]

In a sharply divided 5-4 decision, the dissenting justices expressed the concern that use of alternative techniques may permit innocent people to be convicted by children who have been coached by malevolent adults and investigators; that the Confrontation Clause should apply to all criminal prosecutions; and that exceptions cannot be carved for child witnesses in the interests of public policy. Dissenting Justice Scalia disagreed with the majority opinion that the face-to-face confrontation with witnesses appearing in court is not an indispensable element of the Sixth Amendment's guarantee of the right to confront one's accusers, stating that:

> The Court makes the impossible plausible by recharacterizing the Confrontation Clause, so that confrontation becomes only one of many "elements of confrontation."... This reasoning abstracts from the right to its purposes, and then eliminates the right. It is wrong because the Confrontation Clause does not guarantee reliable evidence; *it guarantees specific trial procedures that were thought to assure reliable evidence, undeniably among which was "face-to-face" confrontation.*[16] [emphasis added]

Though one-way, closed-circuit television does not allow the defendant to confront the child witness "face-to-face," the Supreme Court ruled that if the state makes an adequate showing of necessity, its interest in protecting child witnesses from the trauma of testifying in the courtroom is sufficiently important to justify the use of a procedure such as closed-circuit television.

In California, Penal Code section 1347 authorizes the court in any criminal proceeding to order use of closed-circuit television to take the testimony of a minor alleged to be the victim of a sexual offense. In 1993, the California Supreme Court also ruled in *Dept. of Social Service vs. Armado* that closed-circuit television could be used in a civil proceeding and that the juvenile court had inherent power to order the use of one-way, closed-circuit television to take testimony of minors outside the presence of their parents to ensure truthfulness of testimony.[17] This case involved a father who had allegedly molested his daughters, who refused to testify in the presence of adults, including their parents and attorneys who represented the social service department. While the court acknowledged the right of the accused to confront and cross-examine witnesses, it concluded that closed-circuit television would adequately protect that right. Despite the encouraging opinion that allowed the use of alternative techniques at both state and federal levels, however, it appears that the alternatives to in-court testimony by child witnesses will remain the last resort.

Hearsay Evidence
A central concern in child witness testimony involves the admissibility of hearsay statements by children. In *Idaho v. Wright* (110 S. Ct. 3139, 1990), the U.S. Supreme Court ruled that a child's statement to a doctor lacked sufficient guarantees of trustworthiness to satisfy the reliability require-ment and could not be introduced as evidence in court. In this case, a child's response, made to a pediatrician, had been admitted after finding that the child was unable to testify in court. The doctor was permitted to testify to the child's statements made in response to his questions. The dissenting justices in the 5-4 decision argued that it is preferable to con-sider corroborating evidence because the evidence can be examined by the accused and the trial court "in an objective and critical way."

Though the Court denied the admissibility of out-of-court statements made by child victims who do not testify, the judge in the McMartin pre-liminary hearing allowed the hearsay statements made by children and their parents into evidence. The parents of the McMartin children had been called by the prosecution to disclose their children's statements that they had been drugged and sexually molested at preschool, though there was no corroborating material evidence of drug use or molestation.

In California, the State Supreme Court has recently ruled that pros-ecutors may present expert testimony that parents often hesitate to report child sexual abuse crimes out of "fear, shame, or embarrassment." *In re Clara B.* (25 Cal.Rptr.2d 56, 1993), the California appellate court ruled that out-of-court statements indicating a child's fear of a parent would be admissible as relevant non-hearsay evidence. In this specific case, a 4-year-old child made the statement outside of the courtroom that she was afraid of being molested by her father if left alone in the bathroom. On interviews with the girl, the Department of Social Services in San Diego County filed a petition in juvenile court, alleging that she was a child in need of juvenile court protection because her father had sexually abused her. A clinical therapist testified that the girl told her that she had been molested by her father. The medical expert also testified that there was undisputed medical evidence that the girl had been sexually molested.

While her father argued that the hymen injury was caused by an accidental fall, the medical expert testified that there was a 99% chance that it had been caused by some type of object attempting to penetrate the hymen. The father also stated that such testimony was of little value and should not have been admitted at the trial. His defense attorney argued that this made it extremely easy for the prosecution to convict anyone when they have these types of allegation, and that unless there was legislation passed, there were going to be large numbers of innocent people sitting in jails just because some suspicion had been pointed against them. Yet the court ruled that in addition to the strong medical evidence, such out-of-court statements indicating the child's fear of a parent would be admissible as relevant non-hearsay evidence.

While these laws certainly protect the alleged child victims, some critics of closed-circuit television testimony continue to argue that it is unconstitutional under the Sixth Amendment by denying defendants the right to confront their accusers. As stated previously, such confrontations are especially important because the possibility exists that innocent persons may be accused and ensnared in childhood sexual abuse cases. There are those who intentionally seek to destroy the reputations of innocent people, and there are hundreds of instances of such unmeritorious charges being made in divorce custody cases.[18]

Prosecutors' Abuse of Power

In examining the constitutional rights of the defendants in the McMartin trials, few have acknowledged the discretionary misuse of power by the prosecution's office at various phases of the criminal process. In and out of the courtroom, the prosecution often failed to provide crucial information which might have indicated the possible innocence of the defendants. Many times during the extended legal process, the prosecution intentionally suppressed access to vital information from the defense and the jury. Some information was reluctantly revealed only after the defense and/or judge made repeated requests and demands.

The prosecution also exercised discretionary control over the release of pre-indictment materials to the media, thereby influencing the public's general perception of the possible outcome of the trial. It is no wonder that a community opinion survey conducted a year before the actual trial found that well over 90% of Los Angeles residents firmly believed that the defendants were guilty.

To what extent, then, was there an actual abuse of power by the prosecutor's office and, given such abuse, did it lead to new charges jeopardizing the defendants' constitutional rights to equal protection and due process? To better understand the issues at stake, it is essential to acknowledge and examine similar abuses of prosecutors' discretionary power in other felony cases.

Exonerating Evidence

In theory, the adversarial legal system relies on establishing a fair balance of opposing forces. However, one of the greatest threats to rational and fair fact-finding in criminal cases comes from a prosecutor's misfeasance in hiding evidence and information that might prove a defendant's innocence. Any misuse of discretionary power by the prosecution denying crucial evidence to the defense impairs the ability of the adversary system to function properly. It also undermines public confidence and respect for the public prosecutor's office, because many criminal defendants are unjustly convicted, with the consequent loss of their liberty, property, and even their lives.

One possible prosecutorial misuse of power occurs with the withholding of exculpatory evidence. In the general course of an investigation, pre-trial preparation, or even during a jury trial, prosecutors often become aware of information that might exonerate a criminal defendant. In view of the superiority of law enforcement's investigative resources and its early access to crucial evidence, it is not unusual for the prosecutor to have access to or possession of such evidence.

Did the DA's access to evidence which it withheld in the McMartin case shape the way in which the defense mobilized for trial? The first accusations of the child molestation at the McMartin Preschool had pointed at Raymond Buckey, Roberta Weintraub (a Los Angeles School Board member), the accuser's husband and victim's father, and employees at the local gym, among others. Yet information casting doubt on the credibility of statements made by the accuser, Judy Ann Johnson, was purposefully with-held and successfully kept out of reach of the defense counsel. Beyond these allegations, Johnson's bizarre accusations and stories were known by CII, and likely helped condition and pre-program their personnel in inter-viewing the children about molestation that supposedly took place at the preschool. The children's stories were then presented in the preliminary hearing and the trial, even though Johnson's original charges regarding her son were never followed up, proven, or corroborated by witnesses or by forensic or medical evidence. The police, CII personnel, and prosecutors working in concert also had illegally kept evidence from the defense that the initial accuser's son had failed to identify the defendant in a photo lineup and, in fact, had pointed out someone else.

The chief prosecutor also released confidential information to a *Los Angeles Times* reporter, including an unsubstantiated allegation that Buckey had had sexual problems and sought private professional help. The chief prosecutor also allegedly had a romantic love affair with the *Los Angeles Times* metropolitan editor, who kept running prosecution-oriented stories, setting the tone of the newspaper's negative coverage of the McMartin defendants. In addition, the prosecution's office used Raymond Buckey's cell mate as an informer to "substantiate" allegations of sexual molestation with Johnson's 2 year-old son, though it became evident that the informant had testified against Buckey pursuant to an agreement with the prosecution that rewarded him financially and miti-gated other criminal charges against him—and that the DA knew that he had previously given perjured testimony in other unrelated trials.

Case Studies of Prosecutorial Misconduct

In reference to the McMartin prosecutors' misconduct, here we briefly review three recent court rulings on comparable misconduct that led courts to vacate convictions, and free the defendants who had been wrongly indicted by the grand jury, convicted and sentenced to death by criminal trial juries. While these cases involve capital felony charges, many struc-tural aspects of the cases and the incidences of prosecutorial misconduct mirror those of McMartin prosecution.

In the criminal cases of (1) Randall Dale Adams in Texas, (2) James Joseph Richardson in Florida, and (3) Joseph R. Brown in Florida, pros-ecutors were found to have intentionally falsified evidence, exploited false testimony, and suppressed crucial evidence that would have proved these defendants' innocence.

In 1977, Randall Dale Adams was convicted of the murder of a Dal-las police officer and was given the death penalty. Based on the original testimony, a Dallas police officer was shot and killed by the driver of an automobile that the officer and his partner had stopped for failing to have its headlights turned on. In the trial, the prosecution largely relied on the testimony of two witnesses: (1) David Harris, a passenger with Adams and 16 years old at the time of the offense, who had a long criminal record and had made a secret deal with the prosecutor to implicate the defendant; and (2) a female eye-witness who was at the scene of the killing. As he originally confessed and later acknowledged, David Harris actually murdered the policeman.[19]

During the criminal trial, the prosecutor intentionally withheld information about the deal with Harris, the key witness in the case, as well as successfully kept from the jury knowledge of his lengthy criminal record. At the time of the trial, Harris had pending against him two burglary cases, an aggravated robbery case, as well as a motion to revoke his juvenile probation. The court later learned that Harris had testified against Adams during the original trial because of promises made to him by the prosecutor. Though the prosecutor denied such promises, all of the charges against Harris had miraculously been dismissed and disappeared from the record after his 1977 testimony.[20]

The court also learned that the prosecution knowingly suppressed the evidence that the key eye-witness in the case had failed to identify Adams in a police lineup and that a police officer advised her that she had not identified the defendant and told her which person she should have identified. Further, Adams' conviction was based on the same witness testifying outside the presence of the jury that she had identified Adams in a police lineup.

Though the jury imposed the death penalty, Adams' sentence was subsequently overturned due to the unconstitutionality of the capital punishment statute then in use by Texas. The court ruled that because of the prosecution's misconduct and perjured testimony, Adams' rights to due process and due course of law had been violated.[21] Adams' conviction was set aside and he was finally released in 1989.

Convicted and condemned to die for poisoning his seven children to death in 1967, *James Joseph Richardson*'s original trial turned on the prosecutor's claim that Richardson, a poor farm worker, killed his children to collect insurance. The victims included his stepdaughter along with six younger children, three of whom were Richardson's natural children. The evidence report showed that all seven children died after having ingested large quantities of the poison parathion that had been placed in the food, which the children had eaten for lunch. But the court later found that the prosecutor had purposefully withheld evidence that would have shown the defendant's innocence.[22] Undisclosed evidence included the prosecution's knowledge of perjured testimony, the suppression of exculpatory evidence by the prosecution, and the recantation of a prosecution witness. Specifically, the withheld information included "a sworn statement from the children's babysitter that she had killed the youngsters; a sworn statement from a cell mate of Richardson's that the cell mate had been beaten by a sheriff's deputy into fabricating his story implicating Richardson; statements from other inmates contradicting their claims that Richardson confessed to them; and proof that Richardson had never purchased any insurance."[23]

After Richardson was sentenced to death by the original jury, he came within hours of being executed, when his death sentence was commuted to life imprisonment by the decision in *Furman v. Georgia* (408 U.S. 238, 1972). Luckily for Richardson, volunteer counsel eventually succeeded in unearthing critical evidence. In 1989, his conviction was overturned based on judicial findings of suppressed evidence, and he was released after having spent 21 years in a Florida prison.

Joseph Green Brown was convicted in 1974 for robbery, rape, and murder. He received a death sentence on his murder conviction and two consecutive life sentences on the robbery and rape convictions. After pursuing state remedies, he filed a petition for *habeas corpus* in 1983. The court later found that the prosecutor "knowingly allowed material false testimony to be introduced at trial, failed to step forward and make the falsity known, and knowingly exploited the false testimony in its closing argument to the jury, in violation of the due process clause of the Fourteenth Amendment."[24]

The prosecutorial misconduct included the perjured testimony of a key prosecution witness, who falsely denied that a deal had been made with the prosecutor, and the prosecutor's misrepresentation of that fact to the court.[25] The key government witness testified on cross-examination that he had not received any promises that he would not be indicted if he would testify against Brown, and in his closing argument, the prosecutor told the jury that the witness did not receive any promises for his testimony. However, the court later found that the witness had been offered "favorable consideration" in the murder and another unrelated robbery case for which he had only been given probation.[26] Similarly, the prosecutor informed the jury that ballistics evidence proved the defendant's guilt, even though the prosecutor knew that the FBI ballistics report in evidence indicated that the bullet that killed the victim could be neither chambered nor fired by the defendant's pistol. This point was linked with the contention that the prosecution had made the FBI agent who had prepared the report unavailable as a witness for the defense.[27] Brown's murder conviction was reversed by the Eleventh Circuit when he was only fifteen hours away from being electrocuted and his execution was stayed.

Disclosure is the "one area above all else that relies on the prosecutor's good faith and integrity."[28] Abuses most frequently occur in connection with the prosecutor's power to bring charges, to control the information used to convict those on trial, and to influence juries. The Supreme Court, however, has defaulted in dealing with this important area in which the prosecution's good faith, fairness, and integrity are so dramatically put to the test. The Court has indicated that the prosecutor's good or bad faith in secreting evidence is irrelevant. It is the character of the evidence that counts, not the character of the prosecutor. Yet even if a violation is deliberate with an intent to harm the defendant, the courts will still not order relief unless the evidence is so crucial that it would have changed the verdict. Thus, there is no real incentive for prosecutors to disclose such evidence now or in the future.

Civil Rights Violations

The charge of the sexual abuse of children has often resulted in the violation of the civil rights of the alleged perpetrators. These civil rights violations have usually stemmed from the misapplication and misinterpretation of the law, as well as by misguided use or purposeful misuse of legal structures.

In general, the basic premise of America's legal ethos is that a person is innocent until proven guilty. This legal principle has often been ignored in the allegations of the sexual abuse of children. Instead, various community standards are applied, and children's accounts are relied upon even when adult witnesses and/or forensic and material evidence are lacking. The media is often all too ready to misrepresent the record and selectively interpret evidence, imposing further emotional stress upon the alleged perpetrator (not to mention purported victims). The police and media together have exhibited a tendency to disparage the reputations of alleged perpetrators, creating the milieu for grand juries to bring formal charges, often restraining and incarcerating those charged before any guilt has been proven.

To assist parents and others who feel that they have been unjustly accused, two organizations currently operate on the cutting edge of child abuse cases. VOCAL (Victims of Child Abuse Legislation), headquartered in Orangevale, California, is very active with chapters in many states. VOCAL, for instance, provided both moral and organizational support to McMartin defendants. The organization was created in the wake of the highly publicized, ill-fated multiple victims case in Jordan, Minnesota. The organization provides parents and others who have been falsely accused of child sexual abuse and neglect with support and referrals to legal counsel and expert witnesses. With chapters operating nationwide, VOCAL has been successful in lobbying state legislatures to pass protective legislation, securing individual rights in child sexual abuse cases. Another group, the Family Rights Coalition headquartered in Crystal Lake, Illinois, serves as a clearing house for information on cases of unwarranted and unjust actions against families by government agencies.

Certainly there are many cases where over-zealous prosecutors and unskilled and untrained police and social workers have done irreparable harm to both victims and those innocent of any intentional crime. For example, in 1984 a father was convicted of pornography for taking photos of his naked daughters following their bath. A drug store clerk who saw the negatives turned him in, and he was arrested and investigated for child sexual abuse. A trap had been set for those meeting an offender profile, designed by the so called "therapeutic state," critiqued by an opponent in stark, frightening prose:

> The police often strike at night. Your children are seized and taken to a secret location. They are placed in the hands of state doctors who strip them down and give them a thorough examination, focusing attention on their genitalia. Meanwhile, you are hauled into court to face an inquisitorial hearing into your character. Your accusers enjoy complete anonymity and full legal protection. Your guilt is essentially assumed. Many standard rules of evidence are tossed out, including the hearsay prohibition. Also unavailable to you are ancient privileges such as husband-wife and patient-doctor confidentialities. Even among those who, against all odds, manage to prove their innocence and recover their children, many escape only by agreeing to state-directed psychological counseling, where therapists work to restructure one's mind and values.... Over the last twenty years, legitimate concern over the complex social problem of violence within the family has been translated into a witch-hunt, with devastating consequences for the Constitution and for thousands of innocent families who have their lives shattered by the minions of the therapeutic state.[29]

While the prosecutor's office is the legitimate place to report suspicions of possible child sexual abuse, allegations may well be false and, following investigation and possible indictment, often lead to emotional and economic devastation for those accused.

The alleged child sexual abuse case in Jordan, Minnesota, also illustrates the calamity of being falsely accused of being active participants in a child sex ring in the community. The history and circumstantial evidence in Jordan were very similar to those of the McMartin child molestation case. In 1983, James John Rud, a trash collector and babysitter, was arrested for allegedly molesting two small children. After being taken into custody, he struck a bargain with the prosecution in an exchange for a short jail term by disclosing his participation in a child sex ring composed of many of the parents in the community. With virtually no further investigation, the police immediately arrested the newly accused and seized their children. The children, put in the care of welfare authorities, were forcibly examined by medical experts and repeatedly interrogated by police investigators. But they vehemently denied that any sexual abuse had taken place.

The first couple tried was acquitted by the jury. Before the other trials were to begin, James Rud admitted in a radio interview that he had lied about the sex ring. Yet the prosecution's office blindly insisted that the defendants were guilty of child sexual abuse. Once the prosecution realized that there was absolutely no corroborating evidence supporting the alleged crime, the DA offered plea bargains to the defendants in exchange for testimony against other defendants. The plea bargains included the offer of relocation, a new identity, and monetary rewards. All the defendants rejected the offers, insisting on being tried by a jury.[30] Only the intervention of the Minnesota Attorney General's Office brought this reign of terror in a small town in Minnesota to an end.

A witch hunt by another name, this case illustrates one more example of over-zealous prosecution and the misuse of discretionary power by its office, even though it seems apparent to the lay population of Jordan, Minnesota, that all defendants were innocent. Following this well-publicized multiple-victim case, VOCAL (Victims of Child Abuse Legislation) was created to assist falsely accused victims of child sexual abuse and molestation.

Reputations of Alleged Perpetrators
It is not always so that the truth alone shall rain freedom upon those who suffer. For those charged in child sexual abuse cases the consequences are often devastating. The personal lives of those who are found innocent

are thoroughly ruined; they are stigmatized as child molesters in their community; their families are destroyed; their personal and professional reputations are lost.

Ann Landers printed several letters illustrating part of the problem associated with unproven accusations of child molestation. "I know you can't help us, but perhaps printing this letter will help demonstrate that an accusation does not prove guilt," one letter writer said. During therapy, the letter recounted, a young woman suddenly "remembered" that she had been molested by her father between the ages of 2 and 11. The father vehemently denied such acts, bitterly dividing the family.[31]

Another letter demonstrated the problem of untrained persons telling youngsters that no one should "touch their body." A grandfather playing "pattycake, pattycake" with a grandchild was accused by the child and mother of sexual molestation. As this grandfather noted: "Some of these young nursery school teachers are glorified baby sitters trying to play psychologist. They don't know how to present sensitive information to young children and these amateurs give kids the wrong idea." The grandfather went on to write that there was now a terrible strain between his daughter and himself because of this unfortunate "world" view that had been taught to his granddaughter.[32]

Another emerging problem is the blurring of the distinction between rehabilitative therapy and the determination of possible guilt or innocence by a trained investigator, leading to innocent people being not only accused, but sent to jail for years awaiting trial. Although there may be no evidence and the accused adamantly denies the charge, the child's version of a story still holds the key to prison. There are, then, those who spend time in jail even though they have never been found criminally guilty of a child molestation charge.

Children and the Criminal Justice Process

The McMartin defendants might paraphrase Shakespeare—those who steal my purse might steal trash, not my reputation—but once stolen surely penury follows.

The McMartin case stole other things as well. "If the children were not robbed of their innocence by sexual abuse, it was stolen from them by a legal system that took six years to bring this case to a conclusion," a columnist bemoaned. "One child witness was four when the abuse allegedly occurred, seven when she first told a social worker about it, eight when she told her story to a grand jury, ten when she told it to a judge, and eleven when she finally told it to the jury that rendered a verdict."[33] Obviously the length of decision-time must be shortened if there is to be meaningful justice in child abuse cases.[34]

Taking a longer view, what other reforms are suggested by the McMartin case? Judges, prosecutors, and defense lawyers have agreed that the criminal justice system and its various agencies have not adapted very well to the needs of young people who may have been sexually abused. Children lack vocabulary to express what they know and have experienced.[35]

By the time their remembrance jells with word descriptions, their vision may have been blurred or shaped by other influences. And the legal time-clock may have run its course. Parents of the McMartin Preschool children and others nonetheless believe that the six-year statute of limitation on child molestation charges should be changed. They argue that several of the children were very young when the alleged abuses took place and too young to testify; by the time they were old enough to testify, the statute of limitations would have expired.[36] One father of a former McMartin pupil said that as a result of the statute, "Those kids don't have any civil rights. It's the perfect crime because no one can testify against you."[37] One hopes the California legislature is listening.

The Mass Media

In 1910, G. K. Chesterton observed that "there exists in the modern world, perhaps for the first time in history, a class of people whose interest is not that things should happen well or happen badly, should happen successfully or happen unsuccessfully, should happen to the advantage of this party or the advantage of that party, but whose interest simply is that things should happen." When that "class of people" comprise a massive bureaucracy that stylizes the news into those things that should happen and plays such events emotively to the public, those things that *should happen,* according to the media as both messenger and herald, are those things that do happen. This is the essence of media creation: A massive event pictured by the media as having actually taken place—in other words, a monstrous distortion.

As a stylized, media-heralded event, the McMartin case may illustrate the worst of what can happen when the bureaucratized media loses the journalistic skepticism and the goal of objective investigative reporting. Presuming the guilt of those charged, their reportings were designed to convict the defendants without a trial, alleging guilt by association of many others in addition to the seven accused of criminal violations.[38]

While the media in general used its constitutional First Amendment rights of free speech and press to report what it zealously selected as McMartin news, it also created a climate of hysteria that helped jeopardize the defendants' Fourth Amendment rights to security against unreasonable searches and seizures of their persons, houses, papers, and effects; made almost impossible their Sixth Amendment right to a fair trial by an impartial jury of peers; and weakened, if not limited, their Fourteenth Amendment right to due process of law depriving them of liberty and property. The media held court, reporters brought charges, testified to partial truths, and crafted evidence, so that the public might judge the defendants unfairly, if not avariciously, with emotions and furor.

But they seriously over-reached their bounds, causing Judge Pounders to remark, "[W]hen the reporters decided to be investigators as well as reporters, a lot of people didn't want to come in and testify," noting in some instances that witnesses were contacted by the media before they were scheduled to testify.[39]

Court Mechanisms to Limit the Effect of Prejudicial Materials

Before concluding the examination of constitutional questions in child sexual abuse cases, the final section of this chapter presents a number of possible court mechanisms and strategies to limit the effect of prejudicial materials on the accused and the alleged crimes.

From the start, the McMartin case was a media event. In a highly publicized case, it is difficult for the court to limit access to and dissemination of prejudicial materials by the print and electronic media. The court has followed two basic strategies. The first method is proactive and attempts to limit the availability of potentially prejudicial material to the media. The second is reactive and seeks to limit the effects of material after it has been disseminated by the media. Since the court has utilized both proactive and reactive mechanisms to control the media's access to court proceedings and evidence, it is of great importance to discuss some of those strategies employed in the McMartin child molestation trial and their applicability to other highly publicized trials.

Proactive Mechanisms in the McMartin Trial

Under the first, proactive strategy, if a court deems information to be prejudicial, it acts to restrict either media access to the information or publication of the information. This approach, however, directly clashes with the First Amendment protection of freedom of the press and has been most vigorously resisted by the media. It has also not been a favored strategy of the courts, either, shown in test cases in which the U.S. Supreme Court has been more stringent in reviewing appeals where the proactive strategy has been employed.

The proactive strategy includes the following three mechanisms to limit the availability of prejudicial information about the defendant and the alleged crime, each mechanism utilizing a court order, restraining to varying degrees the ability of the media to report a criminal case. Those mechanisms include the following: (1) court closure isolating a judicial proceeding from outside attendance; (2) restrictive orders preventing the media from printing or broadcasting information; and (3) protective, gag orders in which a trial judge proscribes statements made outside the courtroom by court participants because they are usually the most common source of prejudicial information.

Closure was not employed in the McMartin trial, perhaps a wise move by the court. In *Gannett Co. v. DePasquale* (443 U.S. 368, 1979) the U.S. Supreme Court had ruled that members of the general public, and, by extension, the media, have a constitutional right to attend a pre-trial hearing. In this case, the media claimed a public right of access to criminal proceedings based on the right to a public trial as provided in the Sixth Amendment. While the Court held that the public trial provision of the Sixth Amendment exists solely for the benefit of the defendant and does not confer any constitutional right of access on the media or the general public, the justices failed to specify standards for the use of closure. With respect to the right to trial access, in 1980, the Supreme Court also ruled in *Richmond Newspaper v. Virginia* (448 U.S. 555) that the media and the public have a right of access to trials and that access cannot be closed arbitrarily and without cause. Furthermore, the court placed the burden of proof on the party seeking closure, to show that media access would result in the loss of Sixth Amendment due process protections.

The second mechanism of a proactive strategy, a restrictive order, was designed to prevent the media from printing or broadcasting information. Current judicial support for restrictive orders originated in *Sheppard v. Maxwell* (384 U.S. 333, 1966) in which the Supreme Court made trial judges directly responsible for controlling the media during proceedings. The position that restrictive orders are acceptable only in rare circumstances was reinforced in *Landmark Communications v. Virginia* (435 U.S. 829, 1978) and in *Smith v. Daily Mail Publishing Co.* (443 U.S. 97, 1979). Both Supreme Court decisions overturned lower court restrictive orders because of a lack of clear overriding need for such orders. Moreover, more recent court decisions on the free use of restrictive orders have not been encouraged, and the Supreme Court favored the media, generally opposing the restrictive order mechanisms.[40]

Thus, lower courts had looked more to closure of proceedings and to the less contentious reactive mechanisms, which are aimed at limiting the effects of information already reported. In the McMartin case, the judges in both the preliminary hearing and the jury trial asked the media not to release any information that could be used to identify child witnesses, including their photographs. While it was one form of censorship, the judge generally did not exercise restrictive orders regarding information on the defendants and their alleged crimes.

The third judicial mechanism to limit the availability of prejudicial information is the protective order. The legal rationale for allowing court-participants' speech to be restricted is that they possess privileged information regarding a criminal case and no longer have the same First Amendment right to speak as does the public at large. It is currently easier for a trial judge to restrict the speech of trial participants, excluding defendants, than to close a proceeding or to restrain the media from publishing prejudicial materials and statements.[41] The McMartin court utilized protective orders to protect prejudicial information from reaching the print and electronic mass media. Unfortunately, some participants, such as a CII interviewer and the district attorneys, released information, despite protective orders issued by the court. Although the Supreme Court currently views protective orders in a better light than restrictive orders, uncertainty still remains as to whether a trial court must first exhaust other, less contentious measures such as reactive strategies before resorting to a protective order.[42]

Reactive Mechanisms in the McMartin Trial

The trial court also can invoke a number of reactive mechanisms to limit the effects of potentially prejudicial information by the mass media. Generally, reactive mechanisms have been preferred over proactive measures, because they do not directly limit activities of the mass media and thus do not undermine First Amendment rights to freedom of the press. The reactive mechanisms rest on the premise that even though the public may be influenced and biased by prejudicial information and reports by the media, unbiased juries may still be assembled and unbiased trials conducted.[43]

The reactive mechanisms by the court to limit the effect of published prejudicial materials and information include the following five strategies: (1) *voir dire* with more freedom to exclude prejudiced jurors from sitting in the jury box; (2) a change of venue; (3) continuance; (4) sequestration of jurors for the entire duration of the criminal trial; and (5) special instructions to the jury to counteract the effect of publicity on jury deliberations. Some of those strategies were actually used in the McMartin trial, though their effectiveness was still questioned by the defense.

During *voir dire,* attorneys can prevent jurors from serving on the jury either through challenges for cause, where attorneys must state a valid reason for eliminating a juror, or peremptory challenges that do not have to be supported by a reason.[44] *Voir dire* only identifies jurors who admit knowledge and prejudice about a case and is based on the premise that jurors will recognize themselves as biased and admit it. As noted earlier, in two McMartin trials, the individualized and sequestered *voir dire* session allowed the defense attorneys to critically assess the biases of assigned jurors through direct questions and written responses to pre-*voir dire* jury questionnaires.

Another reactive mechanism is a continuance which is a delay in the start of the trial until pre-trial coverage and its effects are thought to have subsided enough to allow an unbiased trial for the defendants. The practice is based on the premise that media interests in the case will wane and that jurors are expected to forget details of past media reports on the case. While the advantage of the continuance is the greater possibility of assembling more unbiased jurors, the disadvantage is that it may be inconsistent with the defendants' right to a speedy trial and that some witnesses and evidence may not be available at a later time. Given the nature of public hostility surrounding the issue of child sexual molestation in Los Angeles, the continuance may not have been an effective reactive measure to minimize the effects of prejudicial materials and information on the McMartin defendants and their alleged crimes. Greater Los Angelenos may well have gone on an emotive rampage.

A change of venue is another mechanism to limit the effects of published prejudicial materials. A change of venue occurs when a trial is moved from a location in which the case has received heavy media coverage to one in which it has received less coverage and thus potential jurors are assumed to be less biased. A change of venue has been granted in several well-publicized cases because venue changes were deemed necessary. For example, the 1991 initial state trial of four white police officers in the Rodney King beating case was moved from Los Angeles to Ventura County. The Vincent Chin civil rights trial in the late 1980s was also moved from Detroit to Cincinnati. In the McMartin trial, the defense requested a change of venue because survey findings showed that well over 90% of those people interviewed in Los Angeles thought that the McMartin defendants were guilty as charged. Though the survey was conducted one year prior to the actual trial, the petition for a change of venue was denied. While the effectiveness of a change of venue still can be debated, such a reactive judicial mechanism might have benefited the defense in securing a pool of more impartial and unbiased jurors.

Sequestration is still another reactive measure to control the effects of prejudicial materials by the media. It involves the isolation of a jury to control information that reaches it. This method can be effective if the jury has not been exposed to prejudicial materials and information prior to the jury trial. Sequestration is costly in monetary terms as well as in personal sacrifice. In the second McMartin trial, jurors were sequestered for several months and had limited contacts with their families and loved ones. Thus, sequestration is extremely costly and disruptive to jurors, and in certain cases generates animosity toward the accused.[45]

Jury instructions are perhaps the least expensive judicial mechanism that can be invoked to limit the effect of prejudicial materials on defendants by the media. Instructions consist of telling jurors to ignore media reports of the trial and not to discuss the case with anyone. Standard warnings concerning the media and outside sources of information have commonly been given as a matter of course in many trials that have received extensive media scrutiny and coverage. The McMartin trial was no exception. Past research has suggested that the standard jury warnings do not completely eliminate publicity biases, and studies also show that jurors do discuss prejudicial and biased information about the defendants and their alleged crimes despite instructions.[46]

While there are various proactive and reactive court mechanisms to control the media's access to trial evidence and limit the effects of prejudicial materials, the effectiveness of such strategies is still questioned by both prosecution and defense attorneys.

As reactive methods can more easily be applied than proactive methods in highly publicized cases like McMartin, it is of great importance to evaluate the usefulness and effectiveness of both reactive and proactive judicial mechanisms in order to control the media's access to potentially prejudicial materials and limit the dissemination and negative effects of prejudicial information by the media.

Conclusions

Given the notoriety of the McMartin case, it is uncertain whether or not it provides a road map for future handling of allegations of child sexual abuse. Prosecutor Lael Rubin has said that the case broke new legal grounds, insisting "We are the pioneers. We are beginning to learn what to do, how to recognize the needs and rights of children and balance them against the rights of the defendants."[47]

Both alleged victims and alleged perpetrators probably would vehemently disagree with her. But clearly the McMartin case has influenced procedures used in the criminal justice system. Alleged sexual abuse cases are now treated differently than they had been in most places. One child abuse prosecutor in Oakland, California has said, for example, that instead of being referred to regular police detectives, most charges now go to investigators educated in how to put sensitive questions to toddlers. Interviews are taped at the outset so they can answer counter claims that a child was coerced or coached.[48]

Mike Hertica of the Torrance Police Department, who has been actively involved in child abuse cases, suggested that investigation of such cases should be carried out by the police department with investigators who are trained for that purpose, not by the district attorney's office. Also, such outside agencies such as the CII usually may not have the training that allows "evidence" they generate to be utilized effectively in court proceedings and to be considered as serious testimony.

Hertica was also critical of the lack of preparation by the McMartin prosecution team. "Typically, no one involved in this case will admit that there were any errors made. Common sense dictates otherwise. Hopefully, with what we have learned, however, we will never find ourselves in this situation again."[49]

The McMartin case also illustrates that more attention needs to be paid to one of the fundamental principles of procedural justice in the United States—a person is considered innocent until proven and adjudicated guilty. Although child molestation is almost universally frightening and traumatic for children abused, the constitutional rights of alleged perpetrators must not be trampled upon if justice is to be served. Similarly, a number of court-instituted judicial strategies and mechanisms must be considered in order to limit the effects of published prejudicial materials on the defendants and their alleged crimes.

There are undoubtedly various motives of both children and adults influencing them to make false charges of sexual abuse. Thus there needs to be constant vigilance and a recognition that such charges may be false; yet there must also be mechanisms in place to protect the child who actually has been sexually molested. It is obvious that there is a need for better-trained professionals in the investigative and prosecutorial process, so that they can best understand how to find the truth among conflicting stories in child sexual abuse cases.

One close observer of the McMartin case has argued that if the charges of sexual molestation and various aspects related to it—such as McMartin defendants killing a horse with a bare hand and a baseball bat—are disproved, then the child should be indicted and jailed for perjury.[50] Furthermore, he believes that if a parent abetted the child in such false accusations, then this parent should also be indicted for perjury. If the court then establishes that parent and child are making false statements, at least the parent should suffer the consequences of possible incarceration. With a few well-publicized sentences or imprisonment of parents along with "therapists," social workers, and unscrupulous attorneys in the DA's office, it may be possible to see a speedy end to possible miscarriages of justice.

As a close relative of the two main defendants noted during the early phases of the case: "It is a shame that the McMartin trial is destined to continue, and an even greater shame that those responsible for this massive hoax cannot receive just punishment for the evil they have created. That would be justice well served."[51]

Chapter 13

The Rights of Victims and Alleged Perpetrators: Possible Recipe for Reform

Currently, little research has been done to develop an adequate theory explaining and defining child molestation and abuse. Nor is there a way to account for its recurrence in everyday life in the United States. Most perspectives focusing on child sexual abuse concentrate on the family situation, the pathology of those taking liberties with children, the immediate milieu or environment of the child, and the so-called opportunity structure that leads to molestation. The resulting diagnosis is usually anecdotal, with individual accounts catalogued as a sort of resource encyclopedia of the phenomenon; and subsequent experiences of adult-child sexuality and abuse are then treated as their own internal proof that "explain" such precedents.

Such a dictionary-like summation and retrieval system acts as its own impediment, however. It rarely cuts beneath the facade of police investigations, social worker reports, vague and convoluted accounts rendered by children to rehabilitation "experts" and therapist-coaching specialists, and the procedure-bound process of courts blinded by their own arcane rules and legalisms.

It is obvious, however, that any initial inquiry must first be able to define sexuality, sexual abuse, abuse of child, and then address the problems of forensic evidence or other proof corroborating abuse. To oppose abuse remains a safe political response and repose. Representative Patricia Schroeder (D-Colo.) has noted that "you don't need to convince people [that] child abuse is bad. It's not like cigarette smoking, which at one point was socially acceptable. There's no place in America where it's socially acceptable to be a child abuser."[1] However, despite political agreement on the issue and a declaration that it is "a national emergency," as delineated by the U.S. Advisory Board on Child Abuse and Neglect, there has been little progress toward finding legal and logistical solutions to combat the problem.

In our contemporary society, child sexual abuse has become a matter of mass media attention and politics. Child abuse expert Gelles has concluded that:

> Twenty years of discussion, debate, and action have led me to conclude that there will never be an accepted or acceptable definition of abuse, because abuse is not a scientific or clinical term. Rather, it is a political concept. Abuse is essentially any act that is considered deviant or harmful by a group large enough or with sufficient political power to enforce the definition. Abuse is a useful term for journalists who want to capture the attention of their readers or viewers. It is a useful political term because it carries such a pejorative connotation that it captures public attention. Unfortunately, there is no one set of objective acts than can be characterized as abusive, and what is defined as abuse depends on a process of political negotiation.[2]

These negotiations take place in a society where there is no longer a reliable safety net. The erosion of traditional family ties, institutional support networks, community organizations, churches, and schools reflects changing social standards. The increasing mobility of families displaces children, allowing them to be placed in day-care centers or become latch-key self-providers, which produces the consequent opportunity for them to be exposed to abuse and sexual mistreatment.

These are all part of the larger background picture of the McMartin Preschool case, in which interlinked social, personal, and community pressures bred what a journalist stylized as: "Nightmares, fears, shadows on the nursery wall. Imprisonment and bankruptcy. Suicide. Exploitation. Careers and friendships destroyed. Childhoods lost. A cloud over the sun-drenched beach town that spawned the largest molestation trial in history."[3] These, at least, were what one parent reported as being a "seven-year walk through hell."

Nor will the McMartin episode easily fade into the portraiture of contemporary America.[4] The children of the McMartin embroglio may have suffered more than anyone else involved. Indeed, children may suffer most by being saved. False accusations often lead to the needless placement of innocent children in foster care as well as exposure to a largely unsympathetic and non-understanding legal system.[5] "The step toward finding real solutions is to apply the 'common-sense test' to the pronouncements of child savers."[6]

There are other lessons to be learned from the McMartin case. Perhaps the most important one which has been overlooked is that parents, therapists, and prosecutors assume that only perpetrators can threaten, confuse, and otherwise manipulate young children. If the assumption that children can be manipulated by wrongdoers is correct, undoubtedly they also can be manipulated by well-meaning therapists, police officers, and prosecutors. Given these possibilities, it should be clearly recognized that future charges of child abuse should be handled in a way that exalts reason above emotion. Without an increasing awareness of child sexual abuse and an expanding knowledge of the need to develop new techniques to adequately investigate child sexual abuse allegations, undoubtedly in the future more persons who are alleged child sexual abusers will be brought to trial. As many of them may be exonerated, undoubtedly there will be more and more countersuits filed in the courts.

Countersuits

The first section of this chapter presents the synopsis of the original defendants' countersuits, evaluations of their charges, and courts' rulings. The countersuits against prosecuting authorities reveal an interesting panorama of decisions by a variety of judges. In the McMartin saga, all of these decisions have so far exonerated the media, parental and child accusers, therapists, investigators, the police, and prosecuting attorneys. Each decision made by judges has assumed "good faith" by all of the accusers and prosecutors, though this assumption of good faith has been questioned by the defendants as well as by close observers of the episode.

Virginia McMartin and Former Defendants

In April 1986, Virginia McMartin, Peggy Ann Buckey, and Babette Spitler filed claims against Los Angeles County asserting that their lives were ruined when they were unjustly prosecuted for molesting children at the McMartin Preschool. Though the charges against them were eventually dropped, it did not make up for the loss of Virginia McMartin's professional reputation, her school, and her oceanfront home to pay for attorneys' fees.

In May 1986, Superior Court Judge Warren Derring ruled that the suit alleging false arrest, invasion of privacy, and slander was beyond the statute of limitations, and that the plaintiff had not shown by competent evidence any excuse for their failure to file their claims within 100 days after the alleged wrongful conduct.[7] To the extent such conduct fell within 100 days of their filing the claims, however, they could litigate the claims in their suits against defendants. Their petitions were then denied on the merits.

The point of contention was the moment that the statute of limitations expired. The prosecution—now defendants in this suit—argued that time began when defendants were first arrested, while the defendants—now plaintiff accusers—argued that time began running when all charges were dismissed. There appears to be an unresolved relationship here between false accusations and the Bill of Rights mandating the right to redress grievances against the government.

The law seems relatively clear that defendants cannot sue the prosecution while criminal charges are pending, but does require them to file within a 100-day deadline for filing claims after the trial or dismissal of charges. Such requirements are specified in California's Davis Amendment to the Government Code Section 945.3. Despite the filing of the suit within these legal guidelines, the judge dismissed the charges against the defendant—on the basis that the McMartin plaintiffs did not file their suit within the correct legal time limits. Nevertheless, they were still able to file a suit for conspiracy and civil rights violations.

Similarly, other defendants and their families filed a petition for relief from the government tort-claim-filing-statutes pursuant to the Davis Amendment. For example, in March 1986, Babette Spitler, Donald Spitler, and their children, Chad Spitler and Wendi Spitler, filed claims with the County of Los Angeles alleging injury due to tortious conduct by the district attorney's office, namely negligent police investigation and unconstitutional police action. Babette Spitler claimed injury due to malicious prosecution continuing from March 1984 through January 1986. Donald Spitler filed similar claims with the County of Los Angeles, as did his two children with the City of Manhattan Beach.

Among the charges were that the prosecution decided to launch an investigation without a reasonable factual basis and material evidence and did not follow appropriate investigative procedures; that evidence was developed by improper agencies including CII, which relied on an unlicensed psychoanalyst to conduct videotaped interviews with the children; and that KABC-TV demonstrated "outrageous conduct" by manipulating, distorting, and exaggerating McMartin news stories. As a consequence, the plaintiffs argued that they suffered "loss of employment and earnings, humiliation and severe emotional distress in that [they] endured embarrassment, public obloquy, unemployment, financial destitution, strained familial and social relationships, loss of self-esteem and permanent impairment of earning capability."[8] All of them sought to file claims against the County of Los Angeles and the City of Manhattan Beach. The petitions, however, were denied.

As to the Spitler children, their petitions were denied without prejudice. In January 1987, the plaintiffs then moved to strike the notices of ruling on the ground that they did not correctly reflect the court's decision or, in the alternative, for reconsideration based upon additional new evidence. The motions to strike were denied. The motions for reconsideration were also denied on two grounds: (1) they were not timely, and (2) no new facts were presented which could not have been presented at the original hearing with the exercise of reasonable diligence.

They appealed, but the California Court of Appeal in the Second District upheld the original ruling on October 12, 1988. The court held that: (1) the Davis Amendment, which requires notice of claim to be filed within statutory limits, even though a civil action cannot be filed because of pending criminal proceedings, does not deny equal protection to claimants whose claims arise out of criminal proceedings; (2) the Davis Amendment does not violate the Fifth Amendment privilege against self-incrimination; and (3) the petition failed to establish that delay in filing claims was not attributable to themselves.[9]

Peggy Ann Buckey

After her mother and brother were acquitted, Peggy Ann Buckey sued the Anaheim Union High School District for five years' back pay—the time she was not allowed to teach because of the unsubstantiated McMartin charges.[10] Using legal "logic" one judge refused to grant $223,000 in back pay, even though she had been reinstated and rehired to teach after a battle with the State Board of Education. The judge who denied her request stated that, even though she was not given a hearing before her teaching credentials had expired, she had *voluntarily* allowed her teaching credential to expire. Though she finally regained her teaching certificate, her economic loss and professional reputation have not yet been fully recovered.[11]

Peggy Ann Buckey also filed a law suit that asked for $10 million for wrongful prosecution. The defendants included Los Angeles County, CII, its therapist Kathleen MacFarlane, the City of Manhattan Beach, television reporter Wayne Satz and his television station KABC, prosecution medical expert witnesses Astrid Heger and Bruce Woodling who had examined the children, former District Attorney Robert Philibosian, Sheriff

Block of Los Angeles County, and others who had helped to sensational-ize the McMartin sexual allegations.[12] Peggy Ann Buckey complained that she had lost her job teaching deaf children at a high school in Orange County and that she had lost her teaching certificate and life savings be-cause of the "witch hunt."[13] Her petition was, again, summarily dismissed.

Peggy McMartin Buckey and Raymond Buckey

Soon after the jury verdicts were announced on January 19, 1990, Peggy McMartin Buckey also filed a multi-million dollar federal lawsuit in the Los Angeles Federal Court District to recoup her losses, naming everyone within reach as defendants, including the city of Manhattan Beach, whose police department had sent the original letters to 200 parents; Los Angeles County and its former District Attorney, Robert Philibosian; Capital Cities-ABC and former reporter Wayne Satz and its Los Angeles ABC station.

Peggy McMartin Buckey's suit alleged that her civil rights had been violated because of the romantic attachment of Wayne Satz and Kathleen MacFarlane—which led MacFarlane to provide information prior to the indictments that Satz used on broadcasts over KABC-TV, resulting in public outrage and an over-zealous prosecution.[14]

Almost immediately after the second trial, Raymond Buckey also filed a multi-million dollar suit that was similar to his mother's. The dis-trict attorney's office argued that it was "for the best" to dismiss these charges to end the seven-year ordeal that had shattered lives and strained the legal system.[15]

Two days after Raymond Buckey had filed his suit, however, a fed-eral judge ruled that Peggy McMartin Buckey could not sue prosecutors because a jury had acquitted her. She then appealed to a higher court.

Peggy McMartin Buckey also alleged that several of the defendants named in her complaint had had improper motives that led them to pur-sue the McMartin case despite the lack of factual foundation for doing so: In the early 1980s, the CII needed to unearth a scandal to save its busi-ness from bankruptcy; Philibosian needed ammunition for an upcoming election battle; Capital Cities/ABC wanted to sell a sensational story and was willing to go beyond the bounds of responsible journalism, and there-fore created, rather than simply reported, the news; and that all of the defendants were in a conspiracy to disclose the McMartin affair prior to Buckey's indictment.[16]

On February 19, 1992, Judge Richard A. Gadbois of the U.S. Court of Appeals in the Ninth Circuit dismissed her suit because he ruled that the police and prosecutors had had sufficient cause to arrest and try her, though the judge did not indicate that she could sue if she had been found guilty.[17]

The judge had followed a long-established doctrine that gives prosecutors, who reputedly have sufficient cause to file charges, immunity from civil suits. What this ultimately means, of course, is that no prosecutor, no matter how spiteful or incompetent, can ever be charged with malicious prosecution. This also implies that, as Buckey had charged, a shoddy, biased investigation by police, prosecutors, and others who damage reputations and cause economic loss will never have to answer for their deeds.

Other Countersuits

One of the most important purposes of the lawsuits was to restore the reputation of the former defendants and to reiterate the fact that they were no longer charged with child sexual molestation, and had been declared legally not guilty, and thus proclaimed their innocence.

The lawsuits themselves continued the awkward and awful strain of events that had burdened those charged with child sexual abuse. They seemingly had no recourse in California because state law requires that child care workers must report any suspicions of abuse, and the law also protects those making accusations from any liability. Law enforcement officials are similarly protected from both civil and criminal liability for potential harm that they may have caused the accused. Past Supreme Court rulings have indicated that people who work with law enforcement officials cannot be held liable.

In August 1989, a state appeals court dismissed the list of complaints filed by the McMartin defendants and affirmed the original order of dismissal by Los Angeles Superior Court Judge, Kurt J. Lewin. Virginia McMartin and Peggy Ann Buckey then appealed to the higher federal court. The review, however, was denied by the Federal Court of Appeal in the Second District in November 1989.

The plaintiffs supported their claims of wrongdoing against the defendants based on the following facts:

(1) the CII was retained by the City of Manhattan Beach and the County of Los Angeles to interview, examine, interrogate and evaluate the alleged victims of child abuse, and to report to the city and county whether child abuse had occurred and who the perpetrators were;

(2) CII was acting through its duly authorized officers and agents, including defendant Kathleen MacFarlane;

(3) CII reported to the city and county its conclusions that numerous acts of child abuse had occurred at the McMartin Preschool,

and that plaintiffs were perpetrators or probable perpetrators, although CII had no contact with plaintiffs nor specific knowledge about plaintiffs at the time such report was made;

(4) CII violated substantially all standards for interviewing alleged child abuse victims;

(5) CII's therapists engaged in these improper activities because it was to their personal advantage to do so;

(6) as a result of CII's conduct, plaintiffs were wrongfully indicted and subjected to a preliminary hearing on charges of child abuse;

(7) MacFarlane leaked testimony and documentary evidence which was subject to protective orders in the criminal proceedings to ABC Television Inc. and its news reporter; and

(8) MacFarlane and others suppressed, destroyed, and manipulated evidence such as that discrediting the mental stability and veracity of Judy Johnson, the initial complaining witness against the plaintiff in 1983.[18]

Appellate Court Judge Rowen, however, held that:

(1) CII as a nonprofit corporation and its employees had absolute immunity from civil liability under the child abuse reporting statute;

(2) their privilege was not waived in court;

(3) the CII corporation and its employee could not be held liable in contribution or equitable indemnity to McMartin day-care workers with respect to any damages which McMartin workers might be required to pay in civil lawsuits brought against them by parents;

(4) the CII corporation and its employee were entitled to immunity in performing quasi-prosecutorial functions in reporting their observations of children to authorities;

(5) McMartin workers did not state a cause of action under the Racketeer Influenced and Corrupt Organizations Act; and

(6) McMartin workers were not given leave to amend their complaint.[19]

The court also ruled that while members of the general public who voluntarily report incidences of child abuse are protected by law, their immunity from civil or criminal liability is not absolute. They may not be protected if they make a report with knowledge of its falsity or with reckless disregard of its truth or falsity. The court, however, stated that CII and its employees were protected under the absolute immunity provision because CII is "a California non-profit corporation which holds itself out to the public as an independent, professional and objective organization that is expert at the task of assessing whether in fact child abuse has occurred, ... and MacFarlane is identified as its duly authorized officer and agent." Further, the court noted, in response to MacFarlane's lack of proper licenses to conduct interviews, that "a child care license is simply not a prerequisite for the shield of immunity."[20]

Both state and federal courts thus failed to rule on the merits of the McMartin case and the Federal Court of Appeal simply upheld the state of California law providing blanket immunity to the CII, as a non-profit organization, as well as to the TV station whose reporter first released the information.[21]

Recipe for Reform

The not-guilty and hung-jury verdicts ended years of nightmares for the defendants, but could hardly undo the emotional and financial ruin inflicted over seven years of a lurid investigation and trial. When the preposterousness of the prosecutors' charges and evidence and the techniques of the prosecution's child therapists all stood revealed, it was said that the lessons of the McMartin case would prevent such cruel fiascoes from recurring.[22] Though others throughout the country apparently could see the damage done to the McMartin defendants, those most involved in the local arena seemingly could not.

The McMartin case thus illustrates structural dilemmas that call for possible future reforms of the court and judicial system in child abuse cases. We propose several specific reforms in order to ensure a fair trial in well-publicized cases that touch upon sensitive issues. These suggestions are of critical importance since the prosecutorial handling of the case and the decision to selectively disclose pre-indictment and unsubstantiated materials exerted—and could again exert—significant influence on public perception of guilt and innocence of defendants.

Thus we offer the following reforms.

(1) In highly-charged and emotion-laden situations, police investigations should proceed using a professional code of ethics and methods without political interference from the district attorney's office or other governmental organizations utilizing the media to stylize the news against potential defendants.

(2) The case should proceed to the grand jury only if there are adult witnesses, strong forensic and material evidence, reasons to believe that a

felony has been committed, and that those suspected have in fact perpe-trated the crime. State law or federal legislation should explicitly make it a crime for a district attorney or other governmental agency personnel to use the office for political and/or personal gain in criminal matters.

(3) The media should not be contacted by either police investigators or the district attorney's office before grand jury hearings have been con-vened to consider both the evidence and basis of charges leveled against those suspected of commission of a crime. Laws thus need to be passed making it a felony for a district attorney or investigators to build their case by manipulating the media to justify bringing charges, indict the suspects, and act as judge and jury in convicting and sentencing.

(4) In cases of the district attorney and media violating the rights of the accused, the defense should be legally empowered to move successfully to change the venue of the trial. Because every development of the McMartin child molestation trial had been continuously covered by the media, it is important to consider a way to make the trial fair for the defendant, and the change of venue is one of few options left for the defense with possibilities to select impartial and unbiased jurors to try the defendant.

(5) Other court mechanisms such as disclosure, restrictive orders, and protective orders need to be considered and applied in child sexual abuse cases in order to control the media's access to evidentiary information, limit the dissemination of potentially prejudicial materials, and increase the opportunity for the defendants to receive a fair trial.

(6) The defense should also be funded by the court in such cases to: (a) to carry out community surveys to find unbiased population sectors that might act as qualified and impartial jurors; and (b) for such purposes to design a three-tier system by: (i) expanding the geographic district by including areas from neighboring jurisdictions from which potential, unbiased ju-rors are sought; (ii) making it legally obligatory for judges to grant a change of venue if unbiased jurors do not reside in areas within the juris-diction of the court; and (iii) allowing the further random selection of qualified jurors on the basis of more sophisticated sampling procedures to eliminate the selection of biased jurors, such as cluster sampling with probability proportions to size (PPS) being mandatory once smaller areas have been selected.[23]

(7) In child molestation cases, the defense should be legally empowered: (a) to have access to and use of pre-trial discovery of the district attorney's records, to review any and all forensic and material evidence, confessions, or any other relevant or confidential information related to the case and

child testimony; (b) to have the judge review forensic evidence and child testimony before presentation to the jury; (c) to immediately sequester the jury to insulate it from the media, the public, and district attorney's office; (d) to move successfully for mistrial if child testimony is *not* corroborated by adult testimony, forensic evidence, or other circumstantial proofs; and (e) to have the judge review the merit of scheduled expert and/or jailhouse informant testimony before they appear before the jury.

(8) The defense should be legally empowered to use extensive *voir dire* methods and systematic scientific jury selection techniques in high profile criminal trials, so that they will be able to evaluate the pool of prospective jurors and assess their potential biases and prejudice against the defendant and alleged crimes. Due to the massive publicity on the defendant and the alleged crimes, it becomes extremely difficult to select potential jurors with abilities to view the case impartially and without prejudice. Extended *voir dire* conditions should thus be required in well-publicized trials to give the defendant the opportunity to receive a fair trial by a pool of unbiased and impartial jurors.

(9) In assessing the validity and credibility of alleged child victims, more systematic and scientific uses of validity assessment techniques should be used and perhaps mandated. Both the court and legislature need to evaluate the utilization of such methods and consider their adaptation in obtaining more credible and reliable information from alleged child sexual abuse victims. Without systematic applications of more scientific methods for obtaining credible and reliable data and statements from children, the broad discretionary power of those who interview alleged child victims may influence the outcome of the trial and thus the fate of alleged perpetrators. Similarly the court will be in a position to violate the defendant's due process and equal protection rights.

Conclusions

Lawsuits, counterclaims, films, books, and the inconclusiveness of two jury trials have meant that there will never be a complete resolution of the McMartin case. Our examination of the McMartin case demonstrates that it is likely that this will always remain so. Even today, many who have virtually no knowledge about the case are willing to condemn the defendants as guilty, while others remain unmoved in their belief in their innocence.

Our examination of the case also implies that some of the children who attended the McMartin Preschool may have been sexually molested. However, despite seven years of testimony and millions of dollars expended, serious questions remain: If these children were molested, *where were they molested, and by whom?* There has never been any conclusive forensic evidence that any molestation took place at the school and/or by anyone connected with the school. Thus, those most intimately aware of the evidence—the jurors in the two trials—came to the same conclusion that we did.

Unexamined, so far, is the fact that the American legal system was designed with the testimony of adult witnesses in mind. The recent rise in child sexual abuse cases has challenged the ideal of the adult witness system to accept and accurately interpret testimony of child witnesses and to incorporate their special needs. Since children have become frequent visitors to the witness stand, it is becoming increasingly important for legislation and court practices to promote the most accurate and complete testimony which will lead to the fairness of trials.

Similarly, frequent prosecutorial misuse of discretionary power has proven to be detrimental to the ideal of a fair trial for the accused. Certainly this appears to have been so in the McMartin case. Although the prosecutor's charging power includes the virtually unfettered discretion to invoke or deny punishment and thus the power to control and destroy people's lives, the prosecutors are still not personally held liable for engaging in any legal misconduct. The prosecutors are further shielded from any civil liability that might arise due to their misconduct, and immunity provides no deterrent to prosecutorial misconduct.

It is thus important to focus on the availability or adequacy of possible penalties that might be imposed on prosecutors in the event of egregious misconduct. Certainly, an appellate court can punish a prosecutor by cautioning him or her not to act in the same manner again, reversing the case, or, in some instances, identifying by name the prosecutor engaged in misconduct. While such punishment may not be sufficient to dissuade prosecutors from acting improperly or unethically, the appellate court should be empowered to provide significant disincentives to deter prosecutorial misconduct. Unfortunately, as far as the McMartin case was concerned, the appellate court failed to show significant resolve to end future prosecutorial misconduct. And the California civil courts have lifted the blinders of justice guaranteeing fairness from their eyes and tipped the scale of justice to favor both prosecutors and "therapeutic" clinics which have engaged in legally questionable practices harming the accused, the children and their parents.

Chapter 14

Epilogue

The search for "justice" can sometimes lead to tyranny. Small particles of evidence dredged up from a larger, accusatory terrain do not in themselves fill in the pieces of a judicial puzzle resulting in sufficient proof of guilt. Such evidentiary patchwork becomes a search for "things," usually leading to the search for the people who are more or less associated with these things.

The lens may be fogged, too, so much so that ambiguity becomes the dominant pattern in the uncompleted mosaic of "evidence." Relying on such an ambiguous assortment of things to track down and accuse people in the name of the pursuit of justice may indeed produce much political and emotional smoke and mirrors—but it may also lead to a form of legal tyranny. Believing such possibilities for injustices, thus did this study emerge.

Since the End

Since the end of the last McMartin trial in 1990, the key players have begun to fade from the public eye.

Chief Deputy Prosecutor Lael Rubin was transferred from the Los Angeles Central to the Santa Monica division, hardly a career promotion for a deputy prosecutor in the largest district attorney's office in the country.[1]

Wayne Satz, whose McMartin reports ignited mass hysteria in 1983, died in December 1992 at the age of 47.[2]

Three years later, in December 1995, Virginia McMartin, one of the original McMartin Seven and co-founder of McMartin Preschool, passed away at the age of 88—a faithful Christian Science follower, she refused hospitalization for her ailing physical condition.[3]

Kathleen MacFarlane quit the CII in 1990, and began working on another controversial issue—children who sexually molest other children. Similar to satanic ritual abuse allegations, the subject of children-who-molest is highly debatable and of uncertain scientific merit.[4] Right after the first trial, MacFarlane and Toni Cavanagh Johnson, who began working with MacFarlane in 1985, presented their work on children-who-molest at a professional conference in San Diego.[5] As in the satanic-ritual-abuse scare, they claim that the problem is enormous, while admitting "[S]o far, relatively few have come to our attention."[6]

And in 1995, a couple who had been accused of sexually molesting McMartin preschoolers along with the McMartin Seven, secured a civil trial. The jury finally awarded them $10 million.[7]

* * * *

In the early 1980s, efforts to protect children from sexual abuse received supportive and extensive media coverage. This attention followed on the heels of heightened public awareness, increased public funding to child protection, and the adoption of new statutory authority mandating reporting of suspected instances of abuse. The print and electronic media largely encouraged greater support for victims and for increased funding and other resources in response to the perceived epidemic. The circle was almost completed by the massive publicity generated by high profile child sexual assault cases such as McMartin, leading the public to believe that America was indeed in the grip of an epidemic of child sexual assault.

Toward the end of the 1980s, however, as public perception changed, the media coverage of the "child-protection-system" became increasingly negative and skeptical.[8] Some writers even asserted that this network was pursuing a baseless witch hunt similar to the Salem witchcraft trials of 1692.[9]

The zig-zag pathway that has marked the trail of awareness of abuse and protection is fairly clear. Although child sexual abuse was initially "discovered" in the early 1960s, it was not until the late 1970s that it began to be perceived as a social problem requiring immediate national and international protection.[10] A scholarly organization, the International Society for Prevention of Child Abuse and Neglect, was not even founded until 1977, along with its journal, *Child Abuse & Neglect: The International Journal.* A decade later, in 1987, the American Professional Society on the Abuse of Children was also formed. And since then awareness of the sexual maltreatment of children has escalated, becoming part of a growing, national emergency movement to protect children.

By the mid-1980s, moreover, criminal courts in several jurisdictions had begun to handle child sexual abuse cases differently. Previously, most abuse cases were managed exclusively through family courts, primarily because abuse was perceived as part of family law, with "family problems" encompassing harm inflicted by parents and other caretakers.[11] The most popular reform in handling children's sexual assault cases placed a renewed focus on criminalization, prosecution, and strict adjudication, quite unlike approaches taken to combat other forms of child maltreatment. The main legal reforms and innovative approaches adopted in the 1980s included: (1) special government child abuse prosecution units; (2) elimination of state mandatory competency requirements for child testimony; (3) court use of closed-circuit television or videotaping of child testimony; (4) expert legal testimony concerning the typical behavior of child sexual abuse victims; and (5) court allowance of exceptions to the rules of hearsay in special child abuse cases.[12]

Government Abuse and Misconduct

A growing and vocal public fear emphasized the need for prosecution, fast trials, and extended criminalization; it also generated controversies over the integrity of the criminal justice system. Heavy-handed prosecutorial actions became common, accompanying the nation's social crisis and extending the opportunity for abuse and misconduct by government officials involved in criminal matters.

The logic of the new milieu demanded new approaches. After the early 1980s, public opinion had gradually begun to shift support from the traditional due-process-oriented criminal justice model to one emphasizing crime-control and -prevention. The emboldened prosecutor emerged as the central figure with training and experience to "get-tough on crime."[13] Cooperating in this new effort, the judiciary relaxed constitutional protections such as due process as well as those embodied in the exclusionary rule for evidence obtained under certain circumstances, and began to broadly interpret statutory and evidentiary rules in the prosecution's favor. The courts also made it much easier for prosecutors to win convictions, even in cases that involved their misconduct.[14] "By their increasing deference to prosecutorial discretion in every form, the courts have stimulated a law enforcement mentality that the 'end justifies the means,'" one legal authority has declared, adding "the prosecutor has become the most dominant figure on the question of who will live and who will die for crimes committed."[15] This dramatic enlargement of the prosecutor's power and prestige over the past few decades has made them increasingly immune to ethical restraints on their conduct.

The new prosecutorial ethos is also reflected in the most recent state and national child-protection efforts. Some state activities, for instance, reflect a tougher law enforcement code. For example, Washington state's enactment of a series of statutes commits offenders to institutions for long-term treatment, even after their prison terms have ended.[16] New Jersey now requires police to notify the community, house-by-house, that a high-risk former child molester is being released into the neighborhood.[17] Called "Megan's Law," the New Jersey statute was enacted after 7-year-old Megan Kanka was kidnapped, raped, and killed by a twice-convicted sex offender, who had moved in across the street from her residence, concealing his identity and prior convictions.

On December 20, 1993, President Clinton signed the National Child Protection Act of 1993 into law, enhancing the criminal-history record-keeping system of the FBI. Later, in May 1996, Congress passed a bill that allows law enforcement officers to notify residents that a sex offender is living in their community, giving officers greater discretion to disclose information about a sex offender, if it would protect the public or serve another legitimate law enforcement purpose.[18] These approaches illustrate the current ethos that tougher law enforcement, in the form of legalized, community surveillance of known sex offenders, is the most effective way to deal with child sexual abuse.

Heavy-Handed Prosecutors

The hand of justice that is most in public view is the one extended by the public prosecutor. There to protect the public interest from crime and criminals, that heavy hand is often laid on those charged with crimes that violate deep cultural values held by the community. Whenever, at any cost, overzealousness to win conviction besets child sexual assault cases, the prosecutor's near-unlimited authority has often been characterized as a modern mechanism able to set a witch hunt in motion.

Troubling and injurious, such pursuits are often not only a double injury to abused children themselves, but to the integrity of the criminal justice system and criminal court proceedings. They tend to emphasize overbearing intervention linked to public reporting, extensive investigation, and biased prosecution of the accused, rather than timely protection and treatment of abused children.[19] Though there has been a renewed focus on taking a so-called child-friendly approach—such as emphasizing a close working relationship among criminal justice, mental health, and child protection and welfare systems—the dominant measures in sexual abuse cases still remain heavy-handed intervention and prosecution.[20]

This ethos of prosecution is the backdrop of the McMartin case. Whether or not the McMartin experiences have led to just and lawful prosecution of other child sexual assault cases is explored in the first section of this chapter. One child sexual assault case centered in San Diego was begun while the McMartin trial was still underway. It involved physically handicapped Dale Akiki, who had been accused of molesting children while he taught at a church-run preschool as a volunteer. Because of the proximity and close working relations among prosecutors and child protection agencies in Los Angeles and San Diego, the case revealed that the McMartin experiences had not yet awakened California's law enforcement agencies to proceed cautiously in handling child sexual abuse cases that entwine political prosecution and investigatory misconduct.

Amidst continuing controversies surrounding the Los Angeles District Attorney's office, the DA failed to secure a conviction in the highly-publicized and scrutinized O. J. Simpson trial, thereby making possible a critical comparison with the McMartin trials. As summarized in the final section, aggressively and egregiously steeped in the misconduct of their investigators, prosecutors in McMartin and Simpson held the upper hand in leveling charges in these criminal cases. Their ultimate authority and autonomy raise the issue of the defendants' ability to secure a fair trial in a media-impacted, sensationalized atmosphere, and create the concurrent necessity for the accused to have access to the shield of scientific jury selection methods to obtain a representative jury of peers.

A Dismal Path Ahead

What is the path ahead in handling and prosecuting other child molestation cases? In sensationalized, high-profile cases, legal action often appears to be a political football, rather than a focus on the best interest and welfare of the child.[21] Ethical codes mandate that prosecutors and other government officers must seek justice, not merely convictions, but it is no surprise that district attorneys continue to vehemently deny that they are engaged in political prosecution or have a motive to unfairly prejudice a defendant's rights to a fair trial.[22]

Obviously the McMartin episode was not the only case of alleged child molestation in Los Angeles or elsewhere during the past decade. In the Los Angeles area during the course of the McMartin trials, for example, a South-Central Los Angeles elementary school teacher was charged with multiple misdemeanor counts of child molestation, including sexual intercourse with a 12-year-old. The person charged resided in Redondo Beach, a town located near the McMartin Preschool in Los Angeles County.[23]

In September 1990, 20 felony molestation charges were leveled against a former Los Angeles Court Children's Services Supervisor who pleaded no contest. Known for his liberal views about children and sexual experience, he wrote: "It is time to acknowledge that our norms for non-violent, erotic experiences of young people in this society fail to reflect actual practices." Writing to supervisors and other officials about his views, he also apparently practiced them as well.[24]

To fight a perceived satanic threat in the late 1980s and the early 1990s, both Los Angeles and San Diego, in close proximity and with working relations, established ritual-abuse task forces. The Los Angeles task force, consisting largely of therapists, was formed in 1988 by the Los Angeles Commission for Women. The San Diego group, modeled after the one in L.A., was formed in 1991 by the county's Commission for Children and Youth. The San Diego force went into action when molestation was reported at a preschool that enrolled many children who were predominantly white and from a local upper socioeconomic class. From the start, the prosecution handed the child abuse investigation to child psychologists and therapists, not law enforcement officers. Known as the San Diego model, this approach was based on the assumption that an interdisciplinary team of child specialists can elicit honest and accurate information from young victims, more so than law enforcement officers.

Interlinked personnel, prosecutors and therapists in San Diego and Los Angeles established a close network with a common ideological outlook. Harry Elias was the head of the district attorney's child abuse unit when an accused child care worker, Dale Akiki, was arrested. Elias, who was preoccupied with a national child abuse conspiracy as well as satanic ritual practices in San Diego, later married Kathleen MacFarlane, who was by then a key witness testifying in Congress about the alleged national child abuse conspiracy, the prevalence of satanic cult rituals, and the importance of establishing a child protection system against children's sexual maltreatment. In a co-authored article, he firmly stated that: "[As] a result of dramatic increases in the number of reports of suspected child abuse and neglect in the United States in the past decade, many professionals have been called on to respond. Interdisciplinary teams have begun to work together to improve investigations, with a shared goal of maximizing protection of children."[25]

Nevertheless, as the Akiki case illustrates, San Diego officials had learned very little, if anything, from the McMartin episode. As the jigsaw puzzle of gossip, media intervention, and legal machinery was being pieced together by community "leaders," the image that emerged showed that Akiki fit the criminal type that they themselves might had deftly created.

The first allegations against Dale Akiki arose in August 1989, when the McMartin trial was still underway. Akiki was born with a rare genetic disorder called Noonan's syndrome which left him with droopy eyelids, an enlarged head, and a concave chest. He also suffered from hycirocephalus and had had nine operations since childhood, including one to insert a brain shunt to drain fluid into his bloodstream.

Akiki worked as a civilian clerk at the Navy installation in San Diego. On Sunday evenings for one year—from April 1988 to April 1989—he volunteered as a teacher's aide in a bible class for preschoolers at his church, Faith Chapel in suburban Spring Valley. In April 1989, he was dismissed from minding children during a 90-minute Sunday evening church service because several parents complained that his odd appearance was causing their children to have nightmares and to wet their beds.[26]

After intensive questioning by her mother, one 3-year-old said that Akiki had exposed himself in class. Although he firmly denied the allegation, Akiki was asked to leave the church, and a formal investigation was launched. Assigned to the case, San Diego Sheriff's Deputy Kathy Dobbins started asking other children about Akiki; and one 4-year-old boy told Dobbins that Akiki had dropped his pants five times in class. The children's claims were then announced to several thousand worshippers during the next church service.

By the fall of 1989, a dozen Faith Chapel children had been interviewed by psychotherapists or social workers. In their initial videotaped interviews at Children's Hospital Center for Child Protection, most youngsters denied that Akiki had abused them. Through extensive therapy sessions, however, the children later said that Akiki had killed live rabbits, a chicken, a turtle, a puppy, several babies, an elephant, and a giraffe in the classroom; and further, that Akiki and his *fiancée* drank the animals' blood afterward. Some of children also stated that Akiki used a Freddy Krueger mask to terrify them into silence.

The charges included accounts that Akiki sneaked groups of children out of Faith Chapel, took them in a van or truck, brutally abused them with objects including curling irons and toy firetruck ladders, and returned them to class within a 90-minute timeframe. Others said that Akiki had urinated on them and forced them to drink blood and eat feces.[27] Although Akiki could not drive any vehicle because of his handicaps, he nevertheless faced 52 counts of kidnapping, child abuse, and molestation.[28]

Almost identical to the McMartin case was the powerful influence of the children's parents on the prosecution to keep the case alive, and their close working relationship with therapists, social workers, and prosecutors. Thus, in February 1990, Faith Chapel members Jackson and Mary Goodall met with San Diego District Attorney Edwin Miller to discuss their concerns about the leisurely way the case was being handled. The Goodalls—owners of Foodmaker, Inc., the parent company of the Jack-in-the-Box restaurant chain, and part of the San Diego Padres baseball team—had two grandchildren in Akiki's class as well as close relations with the child who had disclosed the sexual abuse.

Mary Goodall, in her pre-trial testimony, stated that she personally knew of children who had been "tortured, sodomized, raped, forced to participate in oral copulation, locked in and beaten. I told Mr. Miller [San Diego District Attorney] about a 17-month-old baby whose diapers were removed so she could be raped."[29]

One of the original prosecutors, Sally Penso—who later testified that she had "a log of concerns about the merits of the case"—had been quickly removed by Miller, who replaced her with Mary Avery, one of the co-founders of San Diego's Child Abuse Prevention Foundation—an organization in which Jack Goodall served as board chairman and Edwin Miller as an honorary board member.

Mary Avery had established herself in the field of child sexual molestation cases by publishing an article in which she asserted that children rarely lie about abuse. She echoed the testimony of Dr. Summit on the child sexual abuse accommodation syndrome.[30]

Mary Avery and Mary Goodall were also affiliated with the San Diego Ritual Abuse Task Force. The task force, which has since disbanded, alleged the existence of numerous satanic cults that were said to have "sophisticated suppliers of sacrificial persons, from kidnappers through 'breeders'"—women supposedly bearing children intended for sexual abuse and sacrifice.[31]

As the group of people involved in the accusations grew, so did their personalities. Avery had appointed Linda Walker, a clinical social worker and one of the San Diego Ritual Abuse Task Force co-founders, as her consultant in the case. Walker referred many children to therapists, including some to a colleague and task force member, Pam Badger. The therapists received $500,000 from the Faith Chapel and $350,000 from California's Victims of Crime Prevention.[32] Also, Walker and Faith Chapel parents helped author the task force's 1991 handbook,

Ritual Abuse: Treatment, Intervention and Safety Guidelines, which was patterned after one written by a similarly controversial Los Angeles Ritual Abuse Task Force, including theories and warnings about sophisticated secret cult networks.

These connections were designed to skewer Dale Akiki, even though the investigation came at a time when research, decisions by appeals courts, and the debunking of satanic myths by the press might have been logically linked to ease the hysterical atmosphere surrounding child molestation cases. Though Akiki's 1993 trial lasted seven months and was the longest and one of the most expensive criminal trials in San Diego history, costing an estimated $2.3 million, the jury took only seven hours to acquit him on all charges.

Spending two-and-half-years in jail without ever being convicted of any crime, Akiki quickly filed a law suit against the city, seeking $110 million in damages for false arrest and imprisonment, defamation, and violation of his civil rights.[33] Ken Bourke, 52, one of Akiki supporters throughout the trial, declared, "In Los Angeles, more than $15 million was spent on the McMartin preschool case. The same situations apply to this case—therapist involvement, impressionable children, irate parents and stubborn, stupid prosecution. No win is possible. So why can't they see that?"[34]

After receiving sharp complaints about misconduct and perjury by therapists and social workers in the Akiki case, the San Diego County Grand Jury finally decided to launch a series of investigations of the Child Protective Services (CPS) and their ability to fairly protect children and their families. The grand jury subsequently spent nine months in an intensive study of the case. Their investigation became the basis for a movement to restructure the Department of Social Services (DSS) and CPS systems in California.

A letter sent from the San Diego County Grand Jury to John Burton, Assemblyman and Chair of Public Safety Committee in the California State Assembly, disclosed the abuses and unethical conduct by investigators and prosecutors, declaring that the grand jury had seen evidence indicating that the social workers were so obsessed with molestation scenarios that they were unable to maintain any semblance of objectivity. This verbatim grand jury letter revealed that it had:

(1) seen repeated episodes of social worker perjury in court reports, and, indeed, even in court testimony;
(2) heard testimony by attorneys and court-appointed therapists that social workers had threatened to remove them from court-ap-

proved lists if they failed to adhere.to social worker recommendations;

(3) heard testimony that social workers had threatened to remove additional children from families who failed to exactly follow social worker's recommendations, even when there was no issue regarding that child;

(4) heard testimony that even repeated adverse reports by professionals about individual social workers have resulted in a failure to discipline;

(5) heard testimony by attorneys that when faced with the most blatant abuses of power, there are still no remedies available to their clients;

(6) heard therapists testify that social workers have threatened to ruin their careers, with a report that they have "accommodated the denial" of a client, or questioned a "true finding";

(7) seen documented evidence of social workers conspiring to place children for adoption with their own family members even while reunification with natural families was in process;

(8) seen evidence of social workers placing children in particular foster homes which would render the opportunity to reunify nonexistent;

(9) heard testimony of social workers lying to adoptive parents about the past history of the children available for adoption;

(10) heard testimony of social workers misrepresenting to natural family members, in order to gain their necessary consent to an open adoption, that they will be able to have a permanent role in the life of the child when the law does not guarantee that right;

(11) seen evidence of social workers placing children with an unfit parent in apparent reprisal against the other parent;

(12) read numerous Social Study reports written by social workers and filled with innuendo, half truths and lies....

This can not be totally rectified by this legislation but it will mean some accountability among the line social worker and every Department head. It will allow the system to purge itself of the social worker who abuses power and leave in place those who are willing to live within the standards of law. This highly sensitive and very vulnerable area of social service is not the place for the abuse of power.[35]

The conclusion? Armed with their unrestrained use of discretionary power, social workers and prosecutors intimately involved in the investigation of Akiki's child molestation charges had become the source of great controversies that had an impact on the administration of justice. The grand jury had warned that, when there is absolute immunity for social workers and prosecutors who promote and cause societal damage, it is essential to block them from deploying the same types of pressures and manipulations, thereby removing their barriers to change.

The power of incumbency also eroded in the wake of Akiki's prosecution. Edwin Miller, a twenty-four year incumbent San Diego District Attorney, lost by a landslide in the subsequent primary reelection after receiving a scant 11% of the votes.[36]

Fair Trial in Jeopardy: The O. J. Simpson Trial and L.A. District Attorney's Office

Continual controversy over the Los Angeles DA's office provides a broader focus on the same jurisdiction and courthouse. The glory and accolades of a media feeding frenzy have drawn the district attorney's office to repeatedly offer the media confidential information in exchange for a forum to grind its ax, often making it extremely difficult for an accused to receive a fair trial. As this study emphasizes, the McMartin episode immediately attracted media coverage locally and nationally, prompting defense counsel to ask the court for an order restricting media publication of information because of the threat it posed to the defendants' right to a fair trial. The O. J. Simpson ordeal was *deja vu*.[37]

Los Angeles District Attorney Gil Garcetti—who was a chief deputy district attorney at the time of McMartin—displayed his preference for intense media coverage that bordered on the absurd when an estimated 70 million television viewers, many watching thenlast minutes of the 1994 NBA final championship game, suddenly were compelled to watch Los Angeles police pursuing Simpson in a low-speed freeway chase in Los Angeles. Handsome and articulate, Garcetti appeared on TV, suggesting that Simpson would use a "Mendendez-type defense" to charges he had murdered his former wife, Nicole Simpson, and her friend Ronald Goldman.[38] Garcetti, seeking to endear himself to his constituents, also effectively used the Simpson case as a springboard to talk about his special concern for domestic violence. He said that he had instituted procedures, before the murders, for handling domestic violence felonies by assigning a team of lawyers to work solely on such cases from preliminary hearing through trial.[39]

Garcetti threw the legal dice, keeping himself centered in the public mind as both protector and accuser. Like his predecessors Philibosian and Reiner, when asked for his pre-decision for a retrial if the Simpson jury was hung 11-1 in favor of acquittal, he announced early in the trial at a press conference that the case would be retried.[40]

In the face of media intensity easily comparable to and ultimately surpassing that of the McMartin trials, defense counsel for O. J. Simpson relied on private jury consultants to select prospective jurors and to successfully argue for extended *voir dire* with sequestered conditions as appropriate to select the jury.[41] Perhaps too confident of securing guilty verdicts, Garcetti declined jury selection advice from his pro bono consultant, Donald Vinson, of DecisionQuest in Torrance, California.[42]

The need for an honest, thorough investigation was obvious. Before jury selection took place, the defense proceeded to survey approximately 1,600 Los Angeles residents by random-digit dialing telephone methods, soliciting and examining opinions and attitudes towards the defendant and the trial evidence. One important survey finding was that black females were much more neutral on the issue of abuse and domestic violence than were white females. The survey also showed that constant public scrutiny made it impossible to impanel impartial jurors without individualized sequestered *voir dire* screening conditions, quite similar to the conditions and needs in the McMartin jury impanelment stage.

Prior to *voir dire,* the defense also drafted a 75-page questionnaire which was distributed and filled out by all potential jurors assigned to the Simpson case. Modeling the questionnaire after the McMartin's, the pre-*voir dire* questionnaire asked a series of socio-demographic and attitudinal questions including some about potential jurors' perceptions on the probable trial outcome: "As a result of what you have seen or heard or read about this case, do you think O. J. Simpson is: (1) not guilty; (2) more likely not guilty than guilty; (3) more likely guilty than not guilty; (4) guilty; or (5) no opinion."

Other attitudinal measures in the questionnaire also included the following:

- Does the fact that O. J. Simpson excelled at football make it unlikely in your mind that he could commit murder?
- Based upon your feeling toward O. J. Simpson, are you inclined to believe him not guilty of the crimes with which he has been charged?
- Have you purchased, or otherwise obtained any commercial item relating to this case? (For example, a T-shirt, book, video or trading card.)
- After you learned that the defendant was charged with the mur-

ders of Ronald Goldman and Nicole Brown Simpson, did your feelings about him change?

Other measurements designed to examine jurors' views on domestic violence and use of force also included:

- Have you ever experienced domestic violence in your home, either growing up or as an adult?
- Have you ever had your spouse or significant other call police on you for any reason, even if you were not arrested?
- Have you ever known anyone who had problems leaving an abusive relationship?
- Male professional athletes who participate in contact sports are more aggressive in their personal lives than other people. Strongly agree? Agree? No opinion? Disagree? Strongly Disagree?
- Male professional athletes who participate in contact sports are more aggressive towards women. Strongly agree? Agree? No opinion? Disagree? Strongly Disagree?
- How do you feel about interracial marriages?
- How would you feel if a close family member or relative married someone of a different race?

Since the Simpson case raised questions of racially biased investigative methods and prosecution, the questionnaire posed the following questions to assess jurors' attitudes towards law enforcement and criminal justice systems:

- Have you had a good or positive experience with any law enforcement agency, including the Los Angeles Police Department?
- Has any member of your family or any acquaintance had a good or positive experience with any law enforcement agency, including the Los Angeles Police Department?
- Have you or has any family member ever had occasion to use the services of the district attorney's office, for such services as the Family Support, Consumer Fraud, or Victim-Witness division?
- Will you hold the prosecution to a higher standard than is legally required because the defendant is African American?
- Have you ever experienced fear of a person of another race?
- How big a problem do you think racial discrimination against African Americans is in Southern California?

- Have you ever been a victim of a crime? If yes, do you feel the job the police did on it was: Satisfactory? Unsatisfactory?

Among the findings were that 75% believed Simpson was unlikely to murder because he excelled at football; 42% thought that it was acceptable to use physical force on a family member; 42% said that they or their family members had negative law enforcement experiences; and 100% said that they did not regularly read newspapers.

Another defense concern in the selection of the Simpson jury was the track records of past jury decisions in criminal cases that involved minority defendants and white murder victims. Structural analyses of the Simpson affair provided the worst case scenario for a racial minority defendant accused of murdering whites. Past research indicated that black defendants accused of murdering whites were more likely to be found guilty and sentenced to death than white defendants accused of killing blacks.[43] Besides evidence pertinent to the case, the two principal factors for sentencing disparities involving interracial crimes remain the prosecutor's charging discretion and the composition of the jury.[44]

In the past, prosecutors have sought the death penalty disproportionately against black defendants as distinguished from white defendants. Thus, of 455 men executed for rape since 1930, 405 (89%) were black and, in the vast majority of cases, the complainants were white.[45] In Georgia alone, prosecutors sought the death penalty in 70% of the cases involving black defendants and white victims, and only 19% of the cases involving white defendants and black victims.[46]

Such past tendencies had an impact on the Simpson case. The prosecution used code words for a black man's rage, bursting forth with charges of Simpson's use of a stiletto, a death-dealing instrument most whites believe is the black man's signature trait. The prosecution alleged that the double murder had been committed with a large, razor-sharp knife, that the assailant had purposefully inflicted multiple slash and stab wounds on the victims, and that the murder acts were performed at close range, with the brutality of the attack indicating the accused's special animus. Thus, the prosecutor's decision to not seek the death penalty against Simpson was clearly inconsistent with the particular circumstances, the nature of the crime, and history of interracial cases.

So history was not the only guideline. In September 1994, well before the beginning of the Simpson trial in January 1995, Garcetti announced that he would not seek the death penalty.[47] While Garcetti's decision might have reflected the DA's concerns about potential threats of social unrest in and around Los Angeles, his choice illustrates the prosecutor's enormous degree of latitude and discretion in deciding whether or not to seek the death penalty in capital cases. Similarly, in view of the many ways in which racial discrimination continues to manifest itself in capital cases, it facilitates an understanding of why there is overwhelming statistical proof of racial disparities in capital sentencing based on the race of victims and defendants.[48]

Garcetti also could have chosen the precise trial site in Los Angeles County where the murders occurred—Brentwood, an exclusive enclave of upper-class white residents. According to the 1990 U.S. Census, in the city of Brentwood, blacks constituted a total of a mere 63 individuals— 0.83% of community residents.[49] Garcetti evidently preferred a trial in downtown L.A., however, where the likelihood that the jury would include racial minorities was greater, again illustrating prosecutorial calculations and discretion.[50]

After the Simpson jury was chosen, moreover, both electronic and print media remained sharply critical of the jury selection procedure resulting in the "overrepresentation" of racial minorities. In fact, among the 12 final jurors and 12 alternates, there were 15 blacks (62.5%), 5 whites (20.8%), 3 Hispanics (12.5%) and 1 Native American (4.2%). What the media failed to mention, however, was that these racial and ethnic minorities already constitute the majority of residents in both the city and county of Los Angeles (57.2% and 55.0%, respectively, according to the 1990 U.S. Census). Similarly in East Los Angeles which is only a few miles away from the courthouse, white populations constitute only 3.7% of residents over 18 years of age (93.0% are Hispanic). In Inglewood City, south of Los Angeles, blacks also account for 51.9% of residents over 18 years of age. In other words, the majority of residents in neighboring areas adjacent to the Garcetti-picked downtown courthouse were members of racial and ethnic minorities.[51]

Racial minorities' overrepresentation in the Los Angeles Superior courthouse does not reflect the reality of racial makeups in other superior and municipal courtrooms in Los Angeles County. And many logistical problems and procedural deficiencies of the jury selection system still eliminate a large proportion of racial minorities from serving on juries.[52] One significant factor that leads to unrepresentative juries is the jury selection method specifically employed by the Los Angeles Jury Commissioner's Office, called the "bull's-eye method," which further skews racial representativeness. This is because Los Angeles County has more than thirty superior and municipal courts and overlapping court jurisdictions. The bull's-eye selection system was specifically designed to draw prospective jurors based on their residential proximity to each of the individual courthouses in the county.

This jury selection procedure is both tortured and inequitable. Los Angeles Central Superior Court first draws available potential jurors who live closest to the courthouse, and then draws on residents from concentric circles moving outward from it. Since the central courthouse is located in the heart of downtown where blacks and other ethnic minorities are predominant residents, racial minorities have dominated jury pools here.[53] The deficiencies of the bull's-eye method have been well-known and empirically substantiated and documented: The distance-based selection system leaves a very small number of racial minority jurors available to all the other remaining superior and municipal courts in Los Angeles, creating significant deficits in the representation of racial minority jurors.[54]

As a result, the bull's-eye system has been criticized and challenged numerous times in court, though none of the jury challenges have been successful in repealing the system so far. Other methods have been proposed, including the cluster-sampling technique that relies on random sampling of census tracts to cover large geographical areas rather than residential distance from courthouses.[55] Such selection methods are, however, yet to be adopted by Los Angeles or other large metropolitan jurisdictions.

The biases of jury selection methods, then, leave almost no other choice in future criminal cases in Los Angeles, other than for racial minority defendants to work vigilantly to bring their cases to be heard and tried in the Central Los Angeles Superior Court. Otherwise, they will face juries that do not reflect a balance of their own peers or that do not reflect a cross-section of the community. Though the DA's office may select the trial site for different racial groups of defendants, there is still no guarantee that minority defendants will be tried by predominantly minority juries.

Conclusions

What lessons can we draw from this study?

For the past decade, the media has been intensely focused on the issue of child sexual assault, and media coverage and scrutiny have been overwhelming—coming almost daily from newspaper articles, magazine reports, television programs, movies, celebrity confessions, and repressed memory cases of alleged child molestation. Such dramatic attention has also periodically backfired, however, raising questions of personal, social, and economic devastation to those accused of sexually molesting children and casting serious doubt on the integrity of the criminal justice system.

For the McMartins, the underlying post-trial "crime" against them is that, though they and their colleagues have been cleared of criminal charges, they remain indigent and suffer both socially and emotionally from the past trauma of incarceration and societal condemnation.

The public has not exonerated them because the media and police continue to mis-identify the episode as the *apogée* of the sexual mistreatment of children. The past decade has also witnessed the strengthening of forces fighting against the sexual abuse of children. Yet there has been a negative side, best summarized as the empowerment of the prosecutors to raise their public image and political ambitions by leveling unfounded accusations without a proper evidentiary foundation. Once the line is crossed between sufficient evidence explicating the guilt of those charged and a lack of such evidence, the accusatory framework for lawless order is set.

We believe that the McMartin case illustrates the worst aspects of what can happen to those accused of child molestation, effectively undermining the legitimacy of the criminal justice system and criminal court proceedings. In our opinion, the McMartin case would have been a minor matter, possibly an insignificant event, if not for the media and the prominence of crucial players in the case—especially the *Los Angeles Times* and *KABC* reporters, the district attorney, and some of the parents of McMartin children. Yet the case and its garish publicity congealed national consensus in supporting prosecution and court proceedings, leading to a rise in accusations of those suspected of child sexual abuse.

Will the McMartin experience provide an important lesson to prosecutors handling future sexual abuse cases? Can prosecutors' overzealousness be curtailed—to seek justice, rather than simply to win convictions?

As far as the Akiki case is concerned, the answers to the above questions would be a resounding "no."

What, then, can any of us do to ensure future equity and fairness in such matters? As long as adequate evidence for prosecution is lacking or so suspect as to call in question the methods of its gathering, the quality of its substance, or its corroborative nature, prosecutors need to be regulated by some higher civil authority. Limits on the power of prosecutors are essential.

There is a moral component, too. To understand the human calamity of the former McMartin defendants accused of atrocious crimes, we conclude this account with the simple plea of Mary Ann Jackson, one of the original defendants during the preliminary hearing, who read the following statement prior to the judge's decision:

> I was brought up to believe that my country and its laws were designed to protect the innocent.... What I have witnessed, through these many months of court procedure has not been a search for truth and justice, but a continuous theatrical display. I have been accused, persecuted, prosecuted, maligned, threatened, badgered, harassed, tried, and found guilty due to media-hype. We, the defendants, have been pushed to the limits of our endurance, and in this extremity we have learned what few people ever face—that of our very survival. Several of us have read books and diaries of concentration camp survivors which have given us courage and hope.... The truly heroic figures in this tragic marathon are the defendants and time will some day declare this to be true.[56]

We believe that that day, so long delayed, is finally arriving for the McMartin survivors.

Notes

Chapter 1

1. Narina Nunez Nightingale, "Juror reactions to child victim witnesses: Factors affecting trial outcome," *Law and Human Behavior* 17 (1993): 679–694. See also Meridith Felise Sopher, "'The best of all possible worlds': Balancing victims' and defendants' rights in the child sexual abuse case," *Fordham Law Review* 63 (1994): 633–664; Wendy Anton Fitzgerald, "Maturity, Difference, and Mystery: Children's Perspectives and the Law," *Arizona Law Review* 36 (1994): 11–111.
2. California law also defines sexual battery as touching "an intimate part of another person while that person is unlawfully restrained." See California Penal Code, Section 243.4.
3. John Doris, *The Suggestibility of Children's Recollections* (Hyattsville, MD: Copies from APA Order Dept, 1991). For further discussion, see also Michael R. Leippe, Andrew P. Manion, and Ann Romanczyk, "Discernibility or discrimination? Understanding jurors' reactions to accurate and inaccurate child and adult eyewitnesses," in Gail S. Goodman and Bette L. Bottoms, eds., *Child Victims, Child Witnesses: Understanding and Improving Testimony* (New York: The Guilford Press, 1993).
4. See L. M. Duggan III, M. Aubrey, E. Doherty, P. Isquith, M. Levine, and J. Scheiner, "The Credibility of Children as Witnesses in a Simulated Child Sex Abuse Trial," in S. J. Ceci, D. F. Ross, and M. P. Toglia, eds., *Perspectives on the Child Witness* (New York: Springer-Verlag, 1989), pp. 71–91; G. S. Goodman, B. L. Bottoms, B.B. Herscovi, and P. Shaver, "Determinants of the Child Victim's Perceived Credibility," in Ceci et al., eds., *Perspectives,* pp. 1–22. See also Michael Quinn Patton, *Family Sexual Abuse: Frontline Research and Evaluation* (Newbury Park, CA: Sage Publications, 1991); Joel Best, *Troubling Children: Studies of Children and Social Problems* (New York: Adaldine De Gruyter, 1994). For the McMartin children as research subjects, see Jill Waterman, Robert J Kelly, Mary Kay Oliveri, and Jane

McCord, *Behind Playground Walls: Sexual Abuse in Preschools* (New York: Guilford Press, 1994); Debbie Nathan and Michael Snedeker, *Satan's Silence: Ritual Abuse and the Making of a Modern American Witch Hunt* (New York: Basic Books, 1995). See also Lucy McGough, *Child Witnesses: Fragile Voices in the American Legal System* (New Haven: Yale University Press, 1994).

Chapter 2

1. Roxane Arnold and Cathleen Decker, "McMartin case: A community divided," *Los Angeles Times (LAT)*, April 29, 1984.
2. Ibid.
3. Dorothy Townsend, "Judge will not free McMartin teacher," *LAT*, May 30, 1984
4. The very same Glenn Stevens later resigned the position of Deputy District Attorney, joined the defense team, and acted as one of the defense attorneys.
5. Lois Timnick, "New Suspect in McMartin case named," *LAT*, August 3, 1984.
6. Arnold and Decker, "McMartin case."
7. Ibid.
8. Ted Rohrlich, "93 new charges filed in McMartin child abuse case," *LAT*, May 24, 1984.
9. There were important political ramifications of the case. At the particular time that Los Angeles District Attorney Robert Philibosian leveled charges against the Buckeys, he was facing a bid for re-election and his campaign was not going well; nonetheless, Philibosian denied any political motives for the arrests. Later, in 1984, Philibosian lost the election in 1984 and was replaced by Ira Reiner.
10. As future events evolved, it became ironic that the *LAT* advocated that the hearings should be conducted openly in the interest of accurate and objective reporting. Also ironic is that this particular day's report in the *Times* was done by Lois Timnick who later was charged with biases against the defendants in her reporting.
11. Robert W. Stewart, "McMartin suspects face added counts," *LAT*, May 18, 1984.
12. Ted Rohrlich, "30 more probed in McMartin case," *LAT*, July 11, 1984.
13. Lois Timnick and Victor Merina, "9 new areas raided in molestation case," *LAT*, July 17, 1984.
14. Ibid.
15. Lois Timnick, "McMartin parents group offers reward for photos," *LAT*, November 13, 1984.
16. Lois Timnick, "A town that no longer trusts itself," *LAT*, July 29, 1984.
17. Ibid.
18. Alexander Cockburn, "The McMartin case: Indict the children, jail the parents," *Wall Street Journal (WSJ)*, February 8, 1990.

19. Mark Arax, "Officials search lot for abuse evidence," *LAT,* March, 18, 1985.
20. Ibid.
21. Ted Rohrlich, "McMartin case raid yields rabbit ears, black robes," *LAT,* February 19, 1985.
21. "Preschool aide faces trial on 35 molestation charges," *LAT,* December 14, 1984.
22. Carol McGraw and Paul Feldman, "Children were swapped for sexual abuse, state alleges," *LAT,* August 4, 1984.
23. Lois Timnick, "Aide charged in molestation at another beach preschool," *LAT,* June 27, 1984.
24. "Preschool," *LAT.*
25. McGraw and Feldman, "Children were swapped."
26. "Preschool," *LAT.*
27. Timnick, "Aide charged."
28. Timnick and Merina, "9 new areas." For the official search by the prosecution and parents, see Mark Arax, "Officials search lot for abuse evidence," *LAT,* March 18, 1985.
29. McGraw and Feldman, "Children were swapped."
30. "Suspect in molestation surrenders on warrant," *LAT,* June 17, 1994.
31. Ibid.
32. Dorothy Townsend, "Conflicting court actions cloud bail status in McMartin case," *LAT,* June 2, 1984.
33. Ted Rohrlich, "Warrant issued for McMartin Pre-School teacher," *LAT,* June 16, 1984.
34. Gene Blake, "McMartin teacher released by judge," *LAT,* June 5, 1984.
35. "Suspect," *LAT.*
36. "Spitler freed after posting $400,000 bail," *LAT,* June 20, 1984.
37. Ted Rohrlich, "Attorney seeks to disqualify D.A. in McMartin case," *LAT,* May 25, 1984.
38. Townsend, "Judge."

Chapter 3

1. Scott Harris, "Trial finale is only the beginning of TV deals," *LAT,* January 21, 1990.
2. Dorothy Townsend, "Details in preschool case remain sealed," *LAT,* May 19, 1984.
3. "Closed session to be sought in sex case," *LAT,* May 3, 1984.
4. "Judge prohibits TV in molestation case," *LAT,* June 15, 1984.
5. Lois Timnick, "McMartin case will have open hearing," *LAT,* August 14, 1984; Lois Timnick, "Court orders McMartin hearing opened," *LAT,* September 11, 1984; Lois Timnick, "McMartin hearings reopened to public," *LAT,* October 2, 1984.

6. Robert Lindsey, "Reporter's notebook: 6 months of California case," *New York Times (NYT)*, February 13, 1985.

7. Ibid.

8. Thomas B. Rosenstiel, "Lurid news: Are victims exploited?," *LAT*, May 11, 1984.

9. Ibid.

10. Ibid.

11. Ibid.

12. *McMartin v. Children's Institute International,* 261 Cal.Rptr. 437, 1989.

13. Morgan Gendel, "KABC plans to preempt '20/20' show," *LAT*, December 24, 1984; Peter W. Kaplan, "ABC station rejects a '20/20' report," *LAT*, December 27, 1984.

14. Robert W. Stewart, "Reporter claims '20/20' can get McMartin tapes," *LAT*, May 10, 1984; "Protective Order" by Superior Court Judge Roger W. Boren, February 28, 1986.

15. Gendel, "KABC plan."

16. Howard Rosenberg, "'20/20' takes a limited view of McMartin case," *LAT*, January 2, 1985.

17. Ibid.

18. Ibid.

19. Paul Eberle and Shirley Eberle, *The Abuse of Innocence: The McMartin Preschool Trial* (Buffalo, NY: Prometheus Books, 1993), p. 91.

20. David Shaw, "Times McMartin coverage was biased, critics charge," *LAT*, January 22, 1990

21. An Orange County judge, however, decided that the George did not need to be disqualified. See also Robert W. Stewart, "McMartin aids attorney criticizes tape," *LAT*, May 11, 1984.

22. *The Notice of and Motion to Disqualify District Attorney, Statement of Facts, and Memorandum of Points and Authorities,* filed by Daniel Davis, on May 24, 1984.

23. "Judge prohibits," *LAT*.

24. Robert W. Stewart, "Attorney calls for D.A.'s ouster in McMartin case," *LAT*, June 14, 1984.

25. David Finkelhor, Linda M. Williams, and Nanci Burns, *Nursery Crimes: Sexual Abuse in Day Care* (Newsbury Park, CA: Sage Publications, 1988), p. 238.

26. Ibid.

27. The figures are based on the 1990 U.S. Census information.

28. Howard Rosenberg, "McMartin case as media spectacle," *LAT*, June 20, 1984.

29. Ann Landers, "Abuse fears carried too far," *San Bernardino Sun,* April 29, 1991.

30. Stewart, "McMartin aids."

Chapter 4

1. The information in this section is based on the national telephone opinion survey conducted by the *LAT.* The survey was coded as the *LAT* poll No. 98.
2. Lois Timnick, "Educator's study stirs new McMartin controversy," *LAT,* November 11, 1986
3. Hiroshi Fukurai, Edgar W. Butler, and Richard Krooth, *Race and the Jury: Racial Disenfranchisement and Search for Justice* (New York: Plenum Press, 1993).
4. Ibid.
5. Ibid.
6. Don A. Dillman, *Mail and Telephone Surveys: The Total Design Method* (New York: Wiley, 1978).
7. Fukurai et al., *Race and the Jury.*
8. Timnick, "Educator's study."
9. Those two articles are the following: Lois Timnick, "22% in survey were child abuse victims," *LAT,* August 25, 1986; Lois Timnick, "Children's abuse reports reliable, most believe," *LAT,* August 26, 1986. It may be possible that Timnick felt that it was legitimate for both her and the *Times* to carry out a survey on childhood sexual abuse but that others should not, especially if the information might be used by the defense.
10. The information was based on the *KABC Evening News* report aired on November 13, 1986.
11. Despite criticism by Timnick of the *Times,* unsolicited responses by several respondents suggested that the questionnaire was constructed in such a way to maintain neutrality and the questions in the questionnaire were designed to be objective and unbiased.
12. Responses from the survey respondents included in this section were only corrected for spelling errors.
13. Selected responses to questions asked in this survey are further examined in Chapter 7 along with discussion of scientific defense jury selection used in the McMartin trial.

Chapter 5

1. "Chief McMartin prosecutor fined $200 for contempt," *United Press International,* November 18, 1984.
2. Carol McGraw, "McMartin seeks to act as own attorney," *LAT,* May 24, 1985.
3. Carol McGraw, "Virginia McMartin in courtroom outburst," *LAT,* May 25, 1985.
4. Lindsey, "Reporter's notebook."
5. Lois Timnick, "McMartin case: Delays may drag it on until 1987," *LAT,* September 17, 1984.

6. Ted Rohrlich, "Judge limits access to interview tapes of McMartin pupils," *LAT,* May 23, 1984.
7. "McMartin defense tape order stayed," *LAT,* August 4, 1984.
8. Rohrlich, "Judge limits."
9. Marcia Chambers, "Judge's ruling stops defense in abuse case," *LAT,* December 27, 1985.
10. See *Cal Jur 3d [Rev] Criminal Law* 2076–2079.
11. *Transcript,* p. 19, September 12, 1984.
12. Lois Timnick, "McMartin case will have open hearing," *LAT,* August 14, 1984.
13. *Transcript,* pp. 6–7, September 18, 1984.
14. Ibid.
15. *Transcript,* pp. 5–6, September 18, 1984.
16. Ted Rorhlich, "Court hears first parent testify in McMartin hearing," *LAT,* June 27, 1984.
17. Timnick, "McMartin case."
18. Lois Timnick, " McMartin children drugged, D.A. says," *LAT,* August 9, 1984.
19. Marcia Chambers, "Sex-case defense assails therapists," *NYT,* December 15, 1985.
20. *Transcript,* p. 22, September 18, 1984.
21. *Transcript,* p. 23, September 18, 1984.
22. Timnick, "McMartin case: Delays."
23. See, for example, the court transcript on January 14, 1985.
24. *Transcript,* pp. 12–17, January 14, 1985.
25. *Transcript,* p. 62, January 14, 1985.
26. A. Couch and K. Keniston, "Yeasayers and naysayers: Agreeing response set as a personality style," *Journal of Abnormal and Social Psychology* (1960): 151–174; D. Crowne and D. Marlowe, *The Approval Motive* (New York: Wiley, 1964); John H. Freeman and Edgar W. Butler, "Some sources of interviewer variance in surveys," *Public Opinion Quarterly* 40: 79–91, 1974.
27. *Transcript,* pp. 3–54, September 7, 1984.
28. *Transcript,* p. 23, September 7, 1984.
29. *Transcript,* pp. 24–25, September 7, 1984.
30. Kee MacFarlane and Jill Waterman, *Sexual Abuse of Young Children* (New York: Guilford Press, 1986), pp. 87, 99–100.
31. Chambers, "Sex-case defense." The credibility problem was illustrated in one instance by videotaped testimony in which one alleged victim testified that Raymond Buckey didn't take pictures during the naked movie game, while in court she testified that he did. See, for example, Carol McGraw, "Child witness questioning limits asked," *LAT,* May 12, 1985.
32. Note that the United States Constitution, Sixth and Fourteenth Amendments, state that an accused in a criminal trial has the fundamental right to confront witnesses against him/her. The so-called confrontation clause in the child sexual molestation case is examined in detail in Chapter 12.

33. Robert Lindsey, "Boy's responses at sex abuse trial underscore legal conflict," *NYT,* January 27, 1985.

34. Ironically, an article in *LAT* was entitled "First witness sticks to his story" which appeared on January 24, 1985. The article was written by Lois Timnick, a principal reporter of the McMartin episode for the *LAT.*

35. Lindsey, "Boy's responses."

36. Robert Lindsey, "Boy in sex case describes mutilation threat," *NYT,* February 20, 1985.

37. "Grocer joined sex games, McMartin witness says," *LAT,* February, 16, 1985.

38. Lois Timnick, "McMartin witness claims grocer watched sex games," *LAT,* February 7, 1985.

39. Lindsey, "Reporter's notebook."

40. Carol McGraw, "McMartin pupil, 10, tells of bizarre rite: Forced to drink blood witness claims," *LAT,* February 21, 1985.

41. Timnick, "McMartin witness claims."

42. Lois Timnick, "Court sees videotape of a therapy session for McMartin witness," *LAT,* March 6, 1985.

43. Lois Timnick, "Lies admitted by McMartin case child," *LAT,* March 12, 1985.

44. Carol McGraw and Lois Timnick, "Witness, 9, gives detailed account of alleged abuse," *LAT,* March 14, 1985.

45. Carol McGraw, "Saw McMartin movie sold, boy testifies," *LAT,* March 15, 1985.

46. Lois Timnick, "McMartin witness, 5, holds to tale of rape and sodomy," *LAT,* April 5, 1985.

47. Carol McGraw, "Girl, 5 tells of abuses, threats by Ray Buckey," *LAT,* March 27, 1985.

48. Carol McGraw, "Judge questions the credibility of latest witness in McMartin case," *LAT,* April 13, 1985.

49. *Transcript,* pp. 20–21, April 23, 1985.

50. Carol McGraw, "'Awful lies," McMartin screams in courtroom," *LAT,* April 16, 1985.

51. "'This cult stuff is nonsense,' figure in McMartin case says," *LAT,* February 20, 1985.

52. Carol McGraw, "Macabre cemetery rites told by McMartin witness," *LAT,* April 25, 1985.

53. *Transcript,* pp. 62–64, April 24, 1985.

54. *Transcript,* pp. 18–69, May 3, 1985.

55. *Transcript,* pp. 11–19, May 20, 1985.

56. Robert Lindsey, "Boy, 7, is witness in California child abuse case," *NYT,* December 23, 1985.

57. Ibid.

58. Lois Timnick, "New snag in McMartin case: Parents won't let child testify, even over TV," *LAT,* September 5, 1985.

59. *People v. Kelly,* 130 Cal.Rptr. 144, 1976.

60. Lois Timnick, "Testimony ends in McMartin child-abuse case," *LAT,* January 9, 1986.
61. "McMartin: Anatomy of a witch-hunt," *Playboy,* June (1990): 45, 49.
62. *Transcript,* pp. 159–160, January 9, 1985:
63. *Transcript,* p. 48, January 9, 1985.
64. *Transcript,* p. 48, January 10, 1985.
65. John B. Williamson, David A. Konk, and John R. Dalphin, *The Research Craft* (Boston: Little, Brown, 1977).
66. Chava Frankfort-Nachimias and David Nachmias, *Research Methods in the Social Sciences* (New York: St. Martin's, 1992).
67. Rohrlich, "McMartin case raid."
68. Carol McGraw and Lois Timnick, "'This cult stuff is nonsense,' Figure in McMartin case says," *LAT,* February 20, 1985.
69. Ibid.
70. Lois Timnick, "McMartin case attorney charges illegal delays," *LAT,* November 23, 1985.
71. Ibid.
72. Ibid.
73. Lois Timnick, "New D.A. team may take over McMartin case," *LAT,* October 13, 1985.
74. Ibid.
75. Ibid.
76. Marcia Chambers, "Questions raised on coast molestation case," *NYT,* October 22, 1985.
77. Ibid.
78. Lois Timnick, "A plea for bail: Lawyer calls it unfair that his client is 1 of only 2 McMartin defendants still in jail," *LAT,* November 17, 1985.
79. See the California Constitution, Article I, 12.
80. Timnick, "A plea for bail."
81. Ibid.
82. Lois Timnick, "County's expense in McMartin case above $4 million," *LAT,* December 29, 1985.
83. Noel M. Ragsdale and William J. Genego, "The McMartin bombshell: Necessary, fair—and brave," *LAT,* June 16, 1985.
84. Ibid.
85. Timnick, "New snag."
86. Ibid.
87. Lois Timnick, "Two more McMartin witnesses out: Dropping of children to eliminate 18 TV testimony counts," *LAT,* September 7, 1985.
88. Carol McGraw and Lois Timnick, "50 new counts sought in the McMartin case," *LAT,* June 14, 1985.
89. Ibid.
90. In October, 1985, however, an 8-year-old child did testify by closed-circuit television.

91. Edward J. Boyer, "Deputy D.A. allegedly considered dropping 5 of 7 McMartin cases," *LAT,* September 28, 1985.
92. Janet Rae Depree, "Five McMartin parents call for state probe of D.A.'s office," *LAT,* October 20, 1985.
93. Ted Rohrlich and Lois Timnick, "McMartin flaw: Gaps in evidence," *LAT,* January 27, 1986.
94. Michael Reese, "A child-abuse case implodes: Absence of evidence," *Newsweek,* January 27, 1986.
95. Ted Rohrlich and Lois Timnick, "McMartin flaw: gaps in evidence," *LAT,* January 27, 1986.
96. Roxanne Arnold, "'Why? why,' Distraught parents ask; seek inquiry," *LAT,* January 18, 1986.
97. Ibid.
98. Debra Cassens Moss, "Are the children lying?," *American Bar Association Journal* 58 (1987): 1–17.
99. Lois Timnick, "1 of McMartin case prosecutors resigns: Deputy D.A. had expressed doubt that most defendants were guilty," *LAT,* January 1, 1986.
100. Ted Rohrlick, "Judge in McMartin Pre-School hearing rests defense case," *LAT,* December 25, 1985.
101. Timnick, "Testimony ends."
102. Ibid.
103. Chambers, "Sex-case defense."
104. Moss, "Are the children lying?," pp. 1–17.
105. Marc Miller, "Pretrial detention and punishment," *Minnesota Law Review* 75 (1990): 335.

Chapter 6

1. Lois Timnick, "Trial judge may not achieve goal as McMartin case enters fifth year," *LAT,* December 28, 1987.
2. Michael Reese, "A child-abuse case implodes: Absence of evidence," *Newsweek,* January 27, 1986.
3. Lois Timnick, "Bias in prosecution of Peggy Buckey charged," *LAT,* February 5, 1987.
4. Lois Timnick, "Decision to try two in McMartin case upheld," *LAT,* February 18, 1987.
5. Marcia Chambers, "Prosecutor's film story snags molestation case," *NYT,* November 30, 1986
6. Marcia Chambers, "Screenwriter says ex-prosecutor made a deal in child abuse case," *NYT,* November 17, 1986.
7. Chambers, "Prosecutor's film."
8. Ibid.
9. Ibid.

10. Ibid.

11. Chambers, "Screenwriter says."

12. Lois Timnick, "D.A. urges rejection of dismissal motion in the McMartin case," *LAT*, December 6, 1986.

13. Marcia Chambers, "Prosecutors in child molestation case ask judge to start trial," *NYT*, December 6, 1986.

14. Marcia Chambers, "Judge won't dismiss preschool molestation case," *NYT*, December 9, 1986.

15. Ibid.

16. Lois Timnick, "McMartin attorneys charge misconduct, seek case dismissal," *LAT*, November 13, 1986.

17. Lois Timnick, "Judge won't quit McMartin school case," *LAT*, November 15, 1986.

18. Timnick, McMartin attorneys charge,"

19. Marcia Chambers, "Judge declines request to halt sex abuse case," *NYT*, December 10, 1986; George Hackett and Janet Huck, "Child abuse or adult paranoia?," *Newsweek*, December 15, 1986.

20. Marcia Chambers, "Lost document discussed in sex abuse case," *NYT*, December 16, 1986.

21. Hackett and Huck, "Child abuse."

22. Lois Timnick, "Judge grants new delay in McMartin school trial," LAT, January 12, 1987.

23. Lois Timnick, "Withheld facts in McMartin case—ex-prosecutor," *LAT*, January 21, 1987.

24. Lois Timnick, "Data held from McMartin defense, ex-prosecutor says," *LAT*, January 13, 1987; Lois Timnick, "Lost McMartin tape surfaces, court thrown into Pandemonium," *LAT*, January 24, 1987.

25. Timnick, "Withheld facts." See also Eberle and Eberle, *Abuse*, p. 32.

26. Marcia Chambers, "Negligence on evidence admitted in abuse case," *NYT*, December 18, 1986.

27. Eberle and Eberle, *Abuse*, p. 34.

28. Ibid., p. 176.

29. Judge Pounders stated that the absence of the documents could have had an impact on the defense's case in the preliminary hearing. See also Chambers, "Negligence."

30. Timnick, "Judge grants."

31. Lois Timnick, "Ex-McMartin prosecutor refuses to answer most questions at hearing," *LAT*, January 10, 1987.

32. Ibid.

33. Lois Timnick, "Immunity sought for McMartin case figure," *LAT*, January 14, 1987.

34. Eberle and Eberle, *Abuse*, p. 33.

35. Ibid., p. 34.

36. Marcia Chambers, "Abuse hearing is told of withheld evidence," *NYT*, January 21, 1987.

37. Marcia Chambers, "Prosecution an issue in abuse case," *NYT,* January 19, 1987.
38. Timnick, "Data held."
39. Ibid.
40. Ibid.
41. Lois Timnick, "D.A. didn't withhold evidence from McMartin defense, judge rules," *LAT,* March 10, 1987.
42. Lois Timnick, "Key McMartin case accuser found dead," *LAT*, December 20, 1986.
43. Lois Timnick and Carol McGraw, "McMartin figure's death cause unclear: Mother's complaint triggered molestation investigation," *LAT,* December 21, 1987.
44. Chambers, "Abuse hearing."
45. Timnick, "Ex-McMartin prosecutor."
46. Hiroshi Fukurai, Edgar W. Butler, and Richard Krooth, "Rodney King Beating Verdicts," in Mark Baldassare, ed., *The Los Angeles Riots: Lessons for the Urban Future* (Boulder, CO: Westview Press, 1994), pp. 73–102.
47. The motion was signed by John B. McConahay on December 4, 1986, and submitted to the court in January 1987.
48. Lois Timnick, "Judge rejects defense bid to move McMartin trial," *LAT,* March 27, 1987.
49. Ibid.
50. *Swain v. Alabama,* 380 U.S. 202 1965.
51. The figures were based on survey data compiled by the National Jury Project and utilized as the basis of its *Amicus Curiae* brief in *People v. Williams,* 29 Cal.3d 392 1981.
52. "The public image of the courts: Highlights of a national survey of the general public, judges, lawyers, and community leaders" (paper prepared for the National Center for State Courts by Skelley Yankelovich and White, Inc., March 1978), p. 6.
53. D. Strawn and R. Buchanan, "Jury confusion: A threat to justice," *Judicature* 59 (1977): 478: B. Sales, et al., *Making Jury Instructions Understandable* (Charlottesville, VA: Michie Company, 1981)
54. See Craig Haney, "Affidavit of Dr Craig Haney in support of defendant's motion regarding *voir dire* procedures," *Maryland v. Sails* (Circuit Court, Prince Georges County, Md, No. 80–352, 1982).
55. Fukurai et al., *Race and the Jury.*
56. The declaration to challenge the jury array was prepared by the present authors.
57. The figure is based on a comparative disparity computation. See *People v. Alexander,* 163 Cal.App.3d 1189, 210 Cal.Rptr. 306 (1985) (34.5%); *Kleifgen v. United States,* 557 F.2d 1293 (9th cir. 1977) (27.1%); *United States v. Vutera,* 420 F.2d 564 (1st Cit. 1970) overruled on other grounds; *Barber v. Ponti,* 772 F.2d 982 (1st Cir. 1985) (32.7%).
58. Fukurai et al., *Race and the Jury.*

Chapter 7

1. The first earlier draft of this chapter was reported in "Sociologists in action: The McMartin sexual abuse case, litigation, justice, and mass hysteria," *American Sociologist* 25: 44–71.
2. For a review of some of these cases, see Fukurai et al., *Race and the Jury.*
3. Ibid. See also James Levine, *Juries and Politics* (Pacific Grove, CA: Brooks/ Cole Publishing Co., 1991).
4. Fukurai et al., *Race and the Jury.*
5. Jon M. Van Dyke, *Jury Selection Procedure* (Massachusetts: Ballinger Publishing Company, 1977), pp. 181–183.
6. Hiroshi Fukurai, Edgar W. Butler, and Jo-Ellan Dimitrius, "Spatial and Racial Imbalances in Voter Registration and Jury Selection," *Sociology and Social Research* 72 (1987): 33–38; Hiroshi Fukurai, Edgar W. Butler and Richard Krooth, "Where did black jurors go? The theoretical synthesis of racial disenfranchisement in the jury system and jury selection," *Journal of Black Studies* 22(1991a): 196–215; Hiroshi Fukurai, Edgar W. Butler, and Richard Krooth, "A cross sectional jury representation or systematic jury representation? Simple random and cluster sampling strategies in jury selection," *Journal of Criminal Justice* 19 (1991b): 31–48; Hiroshi Fukurai and Edgar W. Butler, "Organization, labor force, and jury representation: Economic excuses and jury participation," *Jurimetrics* 32 (1991a) : 49–69; Hiroshi Fukurai and Edgar W. Butler, "Computer-aided evaluation of racial representation in jury selection," *Computers, Environment and Urban Systems* 16 (1991b): 131–155; Hiroshi Fukurai and Edgar W. Butler, "Sources of racial disenfranchisement in the jury and jury selection system," *National Black Law Journal* 13 (1994): 238–275.
7. Fukurai et al., *Race and the Jury,* pp. 39–80.
8. Those figures are based on the 1980 U.S. Census because the 1990 Census information was unavailable during the McMartin trial.
9. For discussions of four statistical methods, see Fukurai et al., *Race and the Jury,* pp. 202–203.
10. Hiroshi Fukurai, "Is O.J. Simpson verdict jury nullification? Legal concepts, racial acquittals, and jury performance in a racially sensitive case" (paper presented at the Academy of Criminal Justice Sciences meeting in Las Vegas, Nevada, March 1996).
11. Royce Singleton, Bruce C. Straits, and Margaret Miller Straits, *Approaches to Social Research* (New York: Oxford University Press, 1993), pp. 260–277.
12. Fukurai et al., *Race and the Jury,* pp. 159–160.
13. Beverly Beyette, "A juror's trials: Mark Bassett thought jury duty might be a lark. After the McMartin trial, he knew better," *LAT,* February 1, 1990.
14. "Making history—of a dubious sort," *U.S. World News & World Report,* May 1, 1989; Jay Mathews, "After 33 months, return to 'real world' a problem for jurors," *Washington Post,* January 19, 1990.

15. Beyette, "A juror's trials."
16. Ibid.
17. "Mistrial seen near in preschool molestation case," *NYT,* July 25, 1989; Lois Timnick, "McMartin case closer to mistrial," *LAT,* September 1, 1989.
18. Fukurai et al., *Race and the Jury.*
19. Michael J. Saks, "Blaming the jury," *Georgia Law Journal* 75 (1986): 702.
20. For a brief history of the jury, see Levine, *Juries,* pp. 22–39.
21. Shirley S. Abramson, "Justice and juror," *Georgia Law Review* 20 (1986): 257–259. For the critique of scientific jury selection, see also Jeffrey Abramson, *We, the Jury: The Jury System and the Ideal of Democracy* (New York: BasicBooks, 1994), pp. 143–176.
22. *Irvin v. Dowd,* 366 U.S. 717 722 1961.
23. *Strauder v. West Virginia,* 100 U.S. 303 1880.
24. Jeremy W. Barber, "The jury is still out: The role of jury science in the modern American courtroom," *American Criminal Law Review* 31 (1994): 1225–1252.
25. See, for example, Fukurai et al., "Where did black jurors go"; Fukurai and Butler, "Organization"; Fukurai and Butler, "Computer-aided evaluation."

Chapter 8

1. Timnick, "Trial judge."
2. Lois Timnick "More charges in McMartin case dropped," *LAT,* October 13, 1988.
3. Lois Timnick, "McMartin judge tries to speed up proceedings," *LAT,* August 23, 1987.
4. *Transcript,* p. 14954, July 13, 1987.
5. *Transcript,* p. 14975, July 13, 1987.
6. *Transcript,* p. 14977, July 13, 1987.
7. Ibid.
8. Eberle and Eberle, *Abuse,* p. 42.
9. Ibid., pp. 42–43.
10. Lois Timnick, "McMartin mother's testimony disputes talk of 'brainwash,'" *LAT,* March 30, 1988. See also Daniel Goleman, "Study casts doubt on claims of satanic ritual abuse," *San Francisco Chronicle (SFC),* November 11, 1994.
11. Timnick Lois, "1st McMartin witness steps down—tired but unshaken," *LAT,* August 9, 1987.
12. Raidor later stated under the cross-examination that she had never penetrated the child with her fingers.
13. Lois Timnick, "Girl, 11, recants some molestation testimony," *LAT,* August 18, 1987.
14. Lois Timnick, "McMartin judge bars tape of girl's testimony," *LAT,* July 21, 1988.

15. *Transcript,* p. 17478, July 1987.
16. *Transcript,* p. 17480, July 1987.
17. Lois Timnick, "3 child witnesses in McMartin case refuse to testify," *LAT,* August 9, 1988.
18. Lois Timnick, "More charges in McMartin case dropped," *LAT,* October 13, 1988.
19. Lois Timnick, "'Trust, betrayal cited as McMartin trial opens," *LAT,* July 14, 1987; "After long, costly preliminaries, California sex abuse case opens," *NYT,* July 14, 1987.
20. Carol McGraw and Lois Timnick, "Raymond Buckey to testify in McMartin preschool molestation trial, lawyer says," *LAT,* July 22, 1987.
21. *Transcript,* pp. 15187–15188, July 21, 1987.
22. Lois Timnick, "McMartin judge bars tape of girl's testimony," *LAT,* July 21, 1988.
23. *Transcript,* p. 15184, July 21, 1987.
24. *Transcript,* pp. 15185–15188, July 21, 1987.
25. *Transcript,* p. 17350, July 21, 1987.
26. Ted Rohrlich and Lois Timnick, "McMartin flaw: Gaps in evidence," *LAT,* January 27, 1986.
27. Ibid.
28. *Transcript,* p. 14969, July 13, 1987. Three other medical doctors also testified and their findings varied.
29. Eberle and Eberle, *Abuse,* p. 307.
30. *Transcript,* p. 56630, August 18, 1989.
31. *Transcript,* p. 56631, August 18, 1989.
32. Ibid.
33. *Transcript,* p. 14750, July 8, 1987.
34. Dr. Roland Summit's theory has been criticized by his peers. See Lee Coleman, *Reign of Terror* (Boston, MA: Beacon Press, 1984).
35. Dr. Maloney further stated that:
I watched probably forty or fifty tapes of different children and developed what I have referred to as a *script....* The reason I called it a script is that in interviewing children the focus is on the child. The opposite of following the child is following some kind of predetermined program. I used the word, "script" for that—to refer to that program, but I also use the word, "script" because even word usage by the various examiners with the various children was very close. It was as if they were reading a script.... [emphasis added]
36. Dr. Maloney also stated that there was something basically and inherently wrong with using a script in any type of evaluation interview.
37. Chapter 11 focuses on the validity and the admissibility of the testimony of children whose responses were obtained by the interviewer though the use of anatomically correct dolls.
38. Dr. Maloney finally concluded that the CII interview thus presented information to the children so that nobody knew if children did or did not

have it before, thus making children's elicited information unreliable and invalid.

39. Lois Timnick, "McMartin case faces mistrial, judge says," *LAT,* October 6, 1987.
40. Ibid.
41. Lois Timnick, "Warrant in McMartin case issued, *LAT,* October 9, 1987.
42. Clifford S. Zimmerman, "Toward a new vision of informants: A history of abuses and suggestions for reform," *Hastings Constitutional Law Quarterly* 22 (1994): 81.
43. Ibid.
44. Lois Timnick, "Bias in prosecution of Peggy Buckey charged," *LAT,* February 5, 1987.
45. Lois Timnick, "Raymond Buckey known as molester, D.A. says: Virginia McMartin's diaries put in evidence," *LAT,* September 11, 1987.
46. Ibid.
47. Lois Timnick, "McMartin judge blasts defense's 'improper' question," *LAT,* October 21, 1987.
48. Lois Timnick, "Buckey denies all 53 charges against him," *LAT,* July 28, 1989.
49. *Transcript,* pp. 54372–54373, July 27, 1989.
50. Interestingly, Lois Timnick, the *LAT* reporter who had been covering the case, reported that "The tenor of most of [Raymond] Buckey's testimony under direct examination was straightforward and subdued." See Timnick, "Buckey denies."
51. Ibid.
52. "McMartin case witness is an apparent suicide," *LAT,* December 11, 1987.
53. Lois Timnick, "Boxes of evidence enliven McMartin Trial," *LAT,* April 30, 1988.
54. Ibid.
55. His testimony revealed that the boy who stated that molestation took place at Fadel's market had previously been accused of stealing by Fadel. See Eberle and Eberle, *Abuse.*
56. Lois Timnick, "Woman testifies that she had sex with Ray Buckey," *LAT,* August 22, 1989.
57. Timnick, "McMartin case closer to mistrial."
58. Richard Beene, "Father of McMartin ex-student is hit with suit alleging slander," *LAT,* February 8, 1990.
59. Carol McGraw, "McMartin figures win $1 in civil trial," *LAT,* May 8, 1991.
60. See Section 18, pp. 3141–3150.
61. Lois Timnick, "After 4 years in jail, Buckey has bail set at $3 million," *LAT,* December 18, 1987.
62. Ibid.
63. Ibid.
64. Lois Timnick, "Judge halves bail to $1.5 million for Raymond Buckey," *LAT,* December 7, 1987.

65. Lois Timnick, "Buckey makes his 1st trial appearance as free man: 'still numb,'" *LAT,* February 17, 1989.
66. Nielson Himmel, "Buckey freed on $1.5-million bail after 5 years in jail," *LAT,* February 16, 1989.
67. Timnick, "Buckey makes."
68. Ibid.
69. Similarly, the information on other possible collaboration and intimacy among key players in the McMartin case was not given to the jury.
70. See *People v. Leon* (214 Cal. App. 3d 925, 263 Cal.Rptr. 77 (Ct.App.1989), another sexual molestation case in Los Angeles. Prior to the *People v. Leon,* the California court generally held that the use of expert testimony on the child sexual abuse accommodation syndrome was reversible error. See *People v. Jeff* (1988) 204 Cal.App.3d 309, 251 Cal.Rptr. 135 and *In re Sara M.* (1988) 194 Cal.App.3d 585, 239 Cal.Rptr. 605. In *Sara M.,* it is stated: "If the syndrome was not developed as a truth-seeking procedure but as a therapeutic aid, it cannot be used for a different purpose, i.e., to prove molestation occurred." See also *People v. Roscoe* (1985) 168 Cal.App.3d 1093, 215 Cal.Rptr. 45 [inadmissible under Bledsoe] and *In re Amber B.* (1987) 191 Cal.App.3d 682, 236 Cal.Rptr. 623 [reversed because use of anatomically correct dolls was a new scientific method and no Kelly-Frye foundation was laid].
71. In 1992, the Pennsylvania Supreme Court in *Commonwealth vs. Dunkle* (604 A.2d 30) reversed the lower court and found that admission of expert testimony on this syndrome was reversible error. The Court in *State v. Rimmasch* (Utah, 775 P.2d 388, 401 1989) found that the expert's testimony concerning the reasons abused children delay reporting an incident of abuse to family members—why children omit details of the abuse and why a sexually abused child may be unable to recall dates and times of abuse— were "not beyond the realm of the average layman" and, thus, were inappropriate subject of expert testimony.

Chapter 9

1. Fukurai et al., *Race and the Jury,* pp. 71–74.
2. Beverly Beyette, "A juror's trials: Mark Bassett thought jury duty might be a lark. After the McMartin trial, he knew better," *LAT,* February 1, 1990.
3. Tracy Wilkinson and James Rainey, "Tapes of children decided the case for most jurors," *LAT,* January 19, 1990.
4. Carol McGraw, "McMartin lawsuits may go on for years," *LAT,* January 20, 1990.
5. Lois Timnick and Carol McGraw, "Justice: The jury's findings close the longest and costliest criminal trial in history. No decision has been made on retrying Ray Buckey on 13 undecided counts," *LAT,* January 19, 1990.

6. Rick Oriov, "Judge says evidence was enough for jury to decide either way," *Los Angeles Daily News,* January 19, 1990.
7. Lois Timnick and Carol McGraw, "Justice."
8. Ibid.
9. Jim Tranquada, "Mistakes marred case from the start, jurors say," *Los Angeles Daily News,* January 19, 1990.
10. Timnick and McGraw, "Justice."
11. Wilkinson and Rainey, "Tapes of children."
12. Tranquada, "Mistakes marred."
13. Wilkinson and Rainey, "Tapes of children."
14. Ibid.
15. Ibid.
16. Ibid.
17. Ibid.
18. Lois Timnick, "McMartin jurors resume deliberations after holiday break," *Los Angles Times,* January 3, 1990.
19. Timnick and McGraw, "Justice."
20. "Jurors relieved trial is over, anxious to get on with lives," *Los Angeles Daily News (LADN),* January 19, 1990.
21. Tranquada, "Mistakes marred."
22. Timnick and McGraw, "Justice."
23. Linda Deutsch, "McMartin pair acquitted: Jury deadlocks on 13 counts in longest trial," *Orange County Register,* January 19, 1990.
24. Ibid.
25. Ibid.
26. Tranquada, "Mistakes marred."
27. Deutsch," McMartin pair acquitted."
28. Timnick and McGraw, "Justice."
29. Deutsch," McMartin pair acquitted."

Chapter 10

1. Robert Safian, "We All Wanted the Truth, But Must Settle for Justice." *LAT,* January 19, 1990.
2. "A verdict in a very sad case," (editorial), *LAT,* January 19, 1990.
3. See the following California Supreme Court reviews involving litigation by the McMartin defendants: 249 Cal.Rptr. 57 1988; 261 Cal.Rptr. 437 1989; 14 Cal.Rptr.2d 197 1992.
4. Ibid.
5. Allan Citron, "McMartin remains a festering, open sore in Manhattan Beach," *LAT,* November 19, 1989.
6. Ibid.
7. Ibid.

8. Ibid.
9. Ibid.
10. James Rainey, "McMartin jurors feel ire of public over their verdicts," *LAT,* January 20, 1990.
11. "Letters to the editor—McMartin trial a legal witch's brew," *WSJ,* February 28, 1990.
12. Ibid.
13. Ibid.
14. "Letters to the editor—McMartin preschool trial," *San Bernardino Sun* (SB Sun), February 3, 1990.
15. Ibid.
16. "Letters to the editor," *WSJ.*
17. "Letters to the editor," *SB Sun.*
18. Marc Lacey, "500 Marchers protest verdict in McMartin case," *LAT,* January 29, 1990.
19. Lois Timnick and Frederick M. Muir, "Parents, abuse groups push for retrial of 13 McMartin charges," *LAT,* January 31, 1990.
20. David Shaw, "McMartin verdict: Not guilty: Where was skepticism in media?," *Los Angles Times,* January 19, 1990.
21. Ibid. See also David Shaw, "Reporter's early exclusives triggered a media frenzy," *LAT,* January 20, 1990; David Shaw, "Media skepticism grew as McMartin case lingered," *LAT,* January 21, 1990; David Shaw, "Times' McMartin coverage was biased, critics charge," January 22, 1990.
22. Shaw, "Reporter's early exclusives."
23. Ibid.
24. *Virginia McMartin et al., v. Children's Institute International,* 261 Cal.Rptr. 437 442, 1989.
25. Shaw, "Reporter's early exclusives."
26. Ibid.
27. Shaw, "Reporter's early exclusives."
28. Ibid.
29. Ibid.
30. Ibid.
31. Ibid.
32. Ibid.
33. Shaw, "Media skepticism."
34. Al Martinez, "The news media did it again," *LAT,* January 20, 1990.
35. Ibid.
36. Shaw, "Times' McMartin coverage."
37. Norman Cousins, "Lois Timnick," *LAT,* February 23, 1990.
38. Louis Joylon West, "Times' coverage of McMartin case," *LAT,* February 8, 1990.
39. Shaw, "Times' McMartin coverage."
40. Ibid.
41. Shaw, "Times' McMartin coverage."

42. "Prosecution tempers loss with calls for reform of system," *Register,* January 19, 1990.
43. Shaw, "McMartin verdict."
44. Ted Rohrlich, "Legal experts believe case was bungled," *LAT,* January 19, 1990.
45. Ibid.
46. Beyette, "A juror's trials."
47. "McMartin parents search site," *Associated Press (AP),* April 30, 1990.
48. Steven R. Churm, "Parents dig persistently for evidence," *LAT,* June 5, 1990.
49. John M. Glionna, "Last-ditch search: Crew looks for clues below McMartin school site," *LAT,* May 28, 1990.
50. "McMartin parents," *AP.*
51. Glionna, "Last-ditch search."
52. Lois Timnick, "McMartin Pre-School reduced to rubble," *LAT,* May 30, 1990.
53. The executive summary of the archaeological investigation by E. Gary Stickel has not been published. The present authors obtained the copy of the report from Dr. Roland Summit in February, 1995.
54. Timnick, "McMartin Pre-School."
55. Glionna, "Last-ditch search."
56. Churm, "Parents."
57. Freda Adler, Gerhard Mueller, and William Laufer, *Criminal Justice* (New York: McGraw-Hill Inc., 1994).
58. Ibid.
59. Carol McGraw, "McMartin lawsuits may go on for years," *LAT,* January 20, 1990.
60. Ibid.
61. Ibid.
62. Helen Dent and Rhona Flin, *Children as Witnesses* (New York: John Wiley and Sons, 1994).
63. Rene Lynch, "Parents still believe children were molested," *Los Angeles Daily News,* January 19, 1990.
64. Timnick and McGraw, "Justice."
65. Ibid.
66. Lynch, "Parents still believe." With many of the parents still refusing to believe that their children were not molested by the defendants, one of the most prominent among them was found in early May 1995 telling a militia rally that "unnamed demonic sources within the [U.S.] Government blew up the federal building in Oklahoma City." See John J. O'Connor, "McMartin Preschool Case: A Portrait of Hysteria," *NYT,* May 19, 1995.
67. Margaret Carlson, "Six years of trial by torture," *Time,* January 29, 1990.
68. Lois Timnick,."McMartin case defendants sues for millions," *LAT,* January 20, 1990.
69. *McMartin and Buckey v. Children's Institute International et al.,* 261 Cal.Rptr.437 443 fn6, 1988.

70. "Buckey says justice system failed," *AP*, March 5, 1990.
71. Ibid.
72. Quoted in *AP* (March 5, 1990).
73. James Anderson, "'Remember we were innocent,'" *Register*, January 19, 1990.
74. Ibid.
75. Ibid.
76. Bob Williams, "Trial by hearing: Ex-defendant in molestation case wants to teach again," *LAT*, July 12, 1988.
77. Bob Williams, "Picking up the pieces: A freed ex-McMartin Pre-School teacher still haunted by her family's shattered life," *LAT*, July 17, 1988.
78. Ibid.
79. Ibid.
80. Anderson, "Remember."
81. John Kendall, "Peggy Ann Buckey hears self described as victim, molester at hearing for credential," *LAT*, November, 11, 1988.
82. Ibid.
83. Bob Williams, "Buckey teaching credentials issue spawns another long proceeding," *LAT*, June 20, 1988.
84. Ibid.
85. Williams, "Picking up."
86. Moss, "Are the children lying," pp. 1–17.
87. Shawn Hubler, "McMartin fallout takes its toll on minister," *LAT*, January 22, 1990.
88. Goleman, "Study casts doubt." See also Jeffrey Victor, *Satanic Panic* (Chicago, IL: Open Court, 1993); Nathan and Snedeker, *Satan's Silence*.
89. Oriov, "Judge says evidence."
90. Rainey, "McMartin jurors."
91. Ibid.
92. Beyette, "A juror's trials."
93. Shaw, "McMartin verdict."
94. Ibid.
95. Harris, "Trial finale."
96. Ibid.
97. R. Lynch, "Improving the treatment of victims: Some guide for actions," in W. McDonald, ed., *Criminal Justice and the Victim* (Beverly Hills, CA: Sage, 1976), pp. 165–176; Roberts (1982); T. Miethe and D. McDonald, "Contextual effects in models of criminal victimization," *Social Forces* 71 (1993): 741–759; C. Widom and M. Ames, "Criminal consequences of childhood sexual victimization," *Child Abuse & Neglect* 18 (1994): 303–318.
98. Freda Adler, Gerhard Mueller, and William Laufer, *Criminology* (New York: McGraw-Hill, Inc, 1994).
99. B. Marin, D. Holmes, M. Guth, and P. Kovac, "The potential of children as eyewitnesses," *Law and Human Behavior* 3 (1979): 295–305; Duggan III, et

al., "The credibility of children as witnesses in a simulated child sex abuse trial," in Ceci et al., eds., *Perspectives,* pp. 71–99; G. S. Goodman, B. L. Bottoms, B. B. Herscovi, and P. Shaver, "Determinants of the child victim's perceived credibility," in Ceci et al., eds., *Perspectives,* pp. 1–22; John C. Yuille, Robin Hunter, Risha joffe, and Judy Zaparniuk, "Interviewing children in sexual abuse cases," in Goodman and Bottoms (eds.) in *Child Victims,* pp. 95–115.

100. Nightingale, "Juror reactions," pp. 679–694.

101. See, for example, the U.S. Supreme Court decision in *Payne v. Tennessee* (501 U.S. 808, 1991)

102. Lynch, "Parents still believe."

103. Deutsch, "McMartin pair acquitted."

104. Section (b) of the federal act outlines the following eligibility criteria: states must (1) have a law in effect addressing child abuse; (2) provide for reporting of known and suspected abuse; (3) provide for investigation upon receipt of a report; (4) demonstrate that the state has procedures, rules, and professionals available to respond to abuse; (5) have the means to protect confidentiality of records; (6) provide for a cooperative working system between law enforcement and social service agencies; (7) provide for appointment of guardians ad litem; (8) provide for dissemination of information to the general public; (9) if possible give preference in awards to family agencies; (10) assign any funds received to the respective organization within 18 months of receipt; and (11) not reduce their funding below the amount of state contributed funds in 1977.

105. The purpose of the Children's Justice Act was to "encourage States to enact child protection reforms which are designed to improve legal and administrative proceedings regarding the investigation and prosecution of child abuse cases." (Children's Justice Act, PUB. L. NO 99–401, 100 Stat. 903 (1986)).

106. A number of articles and books came out of the research funded by the National Center on Child Abuse and Neglect. One assumption shared by those researchers is that interviewed children in their sample were assumed to be sexually abused. For example, when analyses focused on McMartin children, more than 300 children were classified as victims of sexual molestation perpetuated by McMartin defendants. See Waterman, et al., *Behind the Playground Walls.*

107. Carlson, "Six years."

108. Adler et al., *Criminology,* pp. 241–243.

109. Ibid.

110. Carlson, "Six years."

111. Terese L. Fitzpatrick, "Innocent until proven guilty: Shallow words for the falsely accused in a criminal prosecution for child sexual abuse," *University of Bridgeport Law Review* 12 (1991): 175.

112. See Douglas J. Besharov, "An overdose of concern: Child abuse and

overreporting problem," *Regulation* 9 (1985): 25–28.
113. Martina Millot, "Telemarketing helps prevent child abuse." *Telemarketing Magazine* 11 (1993): 28–29.
114. The McMartin Preschool had liability insurance of one million dollars per child. If the defendants were convicted, the parents had created groups to sue the insurance companies for many millions. See, for example, Paul Eberle and Shirley Eberle, *The Politics of Child Abuse* (Secaucus, NJ: Lyle Stuart Inc., 1986), p. 61.
115. John B. Mitchell, "What would happen if videotaped depositions of sexually abuse children were routinely admitted in civil trials? A journey through the legal process and beyond," *University of Puget Sound School of Law* 15 (1992): 261. As of March 1995, at CII, individual counselings currently cost parents $90 per session and $54 for a group session.
116. Ibid.

Chapter 11

1. Timnick and Muir, "Parents, abuse groups."
2. Lois Timnick and James Rainey, "Ray Buckey to be retried on 13 counts," *LAT,* February 1, 1990.
3. Virginia M. Donohue, "Times' coverage of McMartin case," *LAT,* February 8, 1990.
4. Lois Timnick and Edward J. Boyer, "Murder trial veteran will prosecute Buckey," *LAT,* February 1, 1990.
5. Timnick and Rainey, "Ray Buckey."
6. Ibid.
7. Quoted from a Mike Wallace "60 Minutes" television interview.
8. Dawn Webber, "McMartin retrial likely to be long, costly," *LAT,* February 5, 1990.
9. Dawn Webber, "Prosecution to drop one charge against Raymond Buckey," *LAT,* March 1, 1990.
10. Timnick and Muir, "Parents, abuse groups."
11. "Conspiracy count against Buckeys will be dropped," *LAT,* March 1, 1990.
12. Timnick and Rainey, "Ray Buckey."
13. Ibid.
14. Ibid.
15. Ibid.
16. Ibid.
17. Once a decision had been made by District Attorney Ira Reiner for a second trial on the charges for which the jury could not come to agreement, controversy emerged. As one letter writer put it—"Certainly, when this new trial turns into another farce, Reiner can no longer slough off the blame onto his predecessor. How much will we have to pay for all of this?" See Allen R.

McMahon, "Times' coverage of McMartin case," *LAT*, February 8, 1990.

18. Timnick and Rainey, "Ray Buckey."
19. Lois Timnick, "Retrial for Ray Buckey on 8 counts set today," *LAT*, April 9, 1990.
20. Norma Meyer, "McMartin judge removed from retrial," *LAT*, February 22, 1990.
21. Lois Timnick, "8 counts remain against Buckey," *LAT*, March 7, 1990.
22. Meyer, "McMartin judge."
23. Lois Timnick, "Judge Pounders is taken off Buckey's retrial," *LAT*, February 22, 1990.
24. Lois Timnick, "McMartin trial judge denies bias, rebuts defense accusations," *LAT*, February 16, 1990.
25. Meyer, "McMartin judge."
26. Ibid.
27. Timnick, "Judge Pounders."
28. "Judge selected for retrial of child-molestation case," *Associated Press*, February 27, 1990.
29. Fukurai et al., "Rodney King," pp. 73–102.
30. Lois Timnick, "McMartin a talkative witness for grandson," *LAT*, June 6, 1990.
31. Timnick, "8 counts remain."
32. Adams Gelb, "Georgia's DUI scandal," *Atlanta Journal and Constitution*, November 4, 1991, p. 1.
33. Paul Feldman, "Reiner says judge 'misunderstood' action in call on McMartin case," *LAT*, May 25, 1990.
34. "Reiner and the art of setting priorities," *LAT*, May 23, 1990
35. Carol McGraw, "Girl, 10, recounts alleged molestation by Buckey," *LAT*, May 25, 1990.
36. Lois Timnick, "Key witness plays lesser role in second McMartin trial," *LAT*, June 2, 1990a; Lois Timnick, "Parents call it 'sham' as Buckey prosecution rests," *LAT*, June 2, 1990b.
37. McGraw, "Girl, 10."
38. Lois Timnick, "Child says Buckey raped her at pre-school," *LAT*, June 1, 1990.
39. Ibid.
40. Timnick, "Key witness."
41. Timnick, "McMartin a talkative."
42. Lois Timnick, "Buckey's defense rests case," *LAT*, June 27, 1990.
43. Lois Timnick, "Case for, against Buckey recapped," *LAT*, July 3, 1990.
44. Lois Timnick, "Follow law, not feelings, judge orders Buckey jury," *LAT*, July 10, 1990.
45. Carol McGraw, "In the end, jury gave in to confusion," *LAT*, July 28, 1990.
46. Ibid.
47. Ibid.
48. Lois Timnick, "Buckey jury deadlocks; Mistrial is declared," *LAT*, July 28,

1990.
49. McGraw, "In the end."
50. Timnick, "Buckey jury."
51. McGraw, "In the end."
52. Ibid.
53. Ibid.
54. Timnick, "Buckey jury."
55. Ibid.
56. Timnick, "Follow law."
57. Timnick, "Buckey jury."
58. Gail S. Goodman and Beth M. Schwatrz-Kenney, "Why knowing a child's age is not enough: Influences of cognitive, social, and emotional factors on children's testimony," in Dent and Flin, eds., *Children as Witnesses.*
59. Louise Dezwirek-Sas, 1994. "Empowering child witnesses for sexual abuse prosecution," in Dent and Flin, eds., *Children as Witnesses;* see also Joel Best, *Troubling Children: Studies of Children and Social Problems* (New York: Aldine de Gruyter, 1994).
60. Timnick, "Buckey jury."
61. Terry Pristin, "A philosophical Buckey expresses relief his 7-year ordeal is ending," *LAT,* July 28, 1990.
62. Ibid.
63. Lois Webber, "McMartin teacher to file suit," *LAT,* July 31, 1990.
64. Lois Timnick, "Charges against Buckey dismissed," *LAT,* August 2, 1990.
65. "Letter to the Times—2nd Buckey trial ends in deadlock," *LAT,* August 8, 1990.
66. Ibid.
67. Ibid.
68. Ibid.
69. Keith Love, "D.A. Reiner might have lost more than a case," *LAT,* January 19, 1990.
70. Ibid.
71. Paul Feldman, "Reiner decided earlier against a third trial," *LAT,* July 28, 1990.
72. Ibid.
73. Ibid.
74. Ron Curran, "Garcetti on trial: An LA grand jury probes the DA's criminal prosecution record," *California Lawyer* July (1994).
75. Earl W. Sasser, "The McMartin debacle," *LAT,* August 7, 1990.

Chapter 12

1. Edward Saragin, *Current Perspectives on Criminal Behavior: Essays on*

Criminology (New York: Alfred A. Knopf, 1981), p. 203.

2. A. W. Burgess, A. N. Groth, L. L. Holstrom, and S. M. Sgroi, *Sexual Assault of Children and Adolescents* (Lexington, MA: Lexington Books, 1978); Florence Rush, *The Best Kept Secret: Sexual Abuse of Children* (Englewood Cliffs, NJ: Prentice Hall, 1980); Holly Smith and Edie Israel, "Sibling Incest: A Study of the Dynamic Impact of 25 Cases," *Child Abuse and Neglect* 11 (1987): 1001–108.

3. Richard J. Gelles, "Child Abuse: An Overview," in Robin E. Clark and Judith Freeman Clark, eds., *The Encyclopedia of Child Abuse* (New York: Facts on File, 1989), p. xvi.

4. Saragin, *Current Perspectives,* pp. 203–204.

5. Lindsey, "Reporter's notebook."

6. Safian, "We All Wanted."

7. Donna Ware, "Lessons affected OC cases," *Register,* January 19, 1990.

8. Ann Hagedorn, "Prosecution of child molestation cases grows more wary in wake of acquittals," *WSJ,* April 15, 1991.

9. "Judge drops more charges in Carolina sex abuse case (charges against Robert F. Kelly Jr. are dropped in Little Rascals day–care center case)," *NYT,* December 18, 1991; "Some charges dropped in sexual abuse case (Robert F. Kelly Jr. of the Little Rascals Day Care Center in Edenton, North Carolina)," *NYT,* December 12, 1991; "Abuse trial hears ex-day care worker (Robert F. Kelly Jr. trial in Farmville, North Carolina)," *LAT,* August 21, 1991.

10. Sas Dezwirek, "Empowering child witnesses for sexual abuse prosecution," in Dent and Flin, eds., *Children as Witnesses.*

11. J. F. Tedesco and S.V. Schnell, "Children's reactions to sex abuse investigation and litigation," *Child Abuse and Neglect* 11 (1987): 267–272; D. K. Runyan, M. D. Everson, G. A. Edelsohn, W. M. Hunter and M. L. Coulter, "Impact of legal intervention on sexually abused children," *Journal of Pediatrics* 113 (1988): 647–653.

12. Debra Whitcomb, "Legal reforms on behalf of child witnesses: Recent developments in the American courts," in Dent and Flin, eds., *Children as Witnesses.*

13. See *Maryland Cts. & Jud.Proc.Code Ann.,* Section 9–102, 1989.

14. 497 U.S. 836 849 850, 1990.

15. Ibid., 497 U.S. 836 851, 1990.

16. Ibid., 497 U.S. 836 862, 1990.

17. *Dept. of Social Services v. Armando,* 19 Cal.Rptr.2d 404, 1993. See also Spencer and Flin, 1990; G. S. Goodman, M. Levine, G. B. Melton, and D. W. Ogden, "Child witnesses and the confrontation clause: The American Psychological Association Brief in Maryland v. Craig," *Law and Human Behavior* 15 (1991): 13–29.

18. False accusations are most likely to occur in divorce and custody related matters. As the number of child sexual abuse reports increased, the number of sexual abuse accusations in family court also increased. See Nancy Thoennes and Jessica

Pearson, "Summary of findings from the sexual abuse allegations project," in E. Bruce Nicholson with Josephine Bulkley, eds., *Sexual Abuse Allegations in Custody and Visitation Cases: A Resource Book for Judges and Court Personnel* (Washington, DC: American Bar Association, 1988). According to a study of sexual abuse allegations, "in most courts approximately two percent to 10 percent of all family court cases involving custody and/or visitation disputes also involve a charge of sexual abuse" (Thoennes and Pearson, "Summary," p. 4). Recent statistics show that in California, the percent of child abuse accusations in custody disputes is much higher. A survey conducted by the Office of Family Court Services showed a 24% increase in the number of child custody mediation cases between 1988 and 1990, with 26% of the 1700 custody disputes involving physical or sexual child abuse ("Custody battles increase sharply," *LAT,* November 10, 1991). According to Ralph Wakefield and Ralph Underwager (*The Real World of Child Interrogations,* Springfield, IL: Thomas, 1991), 80% of the allegations of child sexual abuse made during divorce custody and visitation disputes are blatantly false.

19. What can be fairly certain is that courtroom maneuvering may result in exactly what the California Penal Code attempts to avoid—psychological harm to children. Constitutional guarantees should not be overlooked simply because charges involve sexual abuse and children, either. "There is a broader social issue here," asserted William Powell, Jr., attorney for Mary Ann Jackson. "The issue is that in child molestation cases innocent people should not be terrorized by the incorrect handling of such highly emotive testimony as a child's testimony" (*LAT,* May 11, 1984).

20. *Harris v. Texas,* 784 S.W.2d 5, 1989.

21. *Adams v. Texas,* 768 S.W.2d 281 284, 1989.

22. Ibid., 768 S.W.2d 281 286 287, 1989.

23. *Richardson v. Florida,* 546 So.2d 1037, 1989.

24. *Brown v. Wainwright,* 785 F.2d 1457, 1458. See also Moran Malcolm, "Tainted verdicts resurrect specter of executing the innocent," *NYT,* May 3, 1989.

25. *Brown v. Wainwright,* 785 F.2d 1457, 1458.

26. Ibid. See also Barry Siegel, "Sentencing the wrong man to die (case study; examination of criminal justice system)," *LAT,* May 10, 1987; Joseph M. Giarratano, "To the best of our knowledge, we have never been wrong: Fallibility vs. finality in capital punishment," *Yale Law Journal* 100 (1991): 1005–1011.

27. *Brown v. Wainwright,* 785 F.2d 1457, 1461.

28. See generally, Bennett L. Gershman, "Abuse of power in the prosecutor's office," *The World & I,* June 1991, pp. 477–487; Bennett L. Gershman, "The new prosecutors," *University of Pittsburgh Law Review* 53 (1992): 393–458.

29. See the article by Allan C. Carlson, "Family abuse," in the 1986 May issue of the magazine, *Reasons.* The account resembles the experience of Babette

Spitler, one of the original McMartin defendants, whose two children were taken away from her home by authorities, interviewed without their parents' permission by the CII staff for possible child sexual abuse, forcibly examined by medical experts, repeatedly interrogated by the police and welfare workers, and finally placed in foster care.

30. For detailed information, see "Man says his charges of sex abuse were false," *NYT*, November 29, 1984; "Figure in child sex case is sentenced to 40 years," *NYT*, January 19, 1985.

31. Landers, *LAT*, December 17, 1990.

32. Ibid.

33. Carlson, "Six years."

34. Judge Richard P. Byrne of the Los Angeles County Superior Court in 1989 has said that undoubtedly "lessons in how to expedite complex criminal cases can be learned from the McMartin case." However, he also insists that despite time, a defendant's rights have to be protected, and that guilt or innocence must be determined in a court of law by a jury of peers. "That's the way our jury system should and does work—regardless of how much time it takes." See also Timnick and Muir, "Parents, abuse groups."

35. Marcia Chambers, "Procedures in child abuse cases challenge the legal system," *NYT*, February 11, 1986.

36. Dupree, "Five McMartin."

37. Ibid.

38. The reputation of KABC-TV proved its mettle not only for the McMartin case but in other instances as well. One *LAT* reporter has said that KABC-TV "is known for resorting to almost anything in the cause of ratings." See, for example, Howard Rosenberg, "Channel 7 doesn't hear the voices of dissent," *LAT*, February 26, 1991.

39. Rick Oriov, "Judge says evidence was enough for jury to decide either way," *Los Angeles Daily News*, January 19, 1990.

40. D. Apfel, "Gag orders, exclusionary orders, and protective orders: Expanding the use of preventive remedies to safeguard a criminal defendant's right to a fair trial," *American University Law Review* 29 (1980): 456–459.

41. See the case of *Buckey v. County of Los Angeles et al.*, 957 F.2d 652, 1992.

42. Apfel, "Gag orders," pp. 439–484.

43. Ibid.

44. *Batson v. Kentucky*, 106 S.Ct. 1712 1986. Jurors cannot be peremptorily struck based on race and gender.

45. D. Pember, *Mass Media Law* (Dubuque, Iowa: William C. Brown, 1987).

46. Valerie Hans and Neil Vidmar, *Judging the Jury* (New York: Plenum Press, 1986); G. Kramer, N. Keer, and J. Carroll, "Pretrial publicity, judicial remedies, and jury bias," *Law and Human Behavior* 14 (1990): 409–438.

47. Chambers, "Procedures."

48. "The child-abuse trial that left a national legacy," *U.S. News and World Report*, January 29, 1990.

49. Mike Hertica, "Letters to the *Times,* 2nd Buckey trial ends in deadlock," *LAT,* August 8, 1990.
50. Cockburn, "The McMartin case."
51. Virginia J. Ostrander, "The McMartin farce" (letter to the editor), *Herald-Express,* August 5, 1987.

Chapter 13

1. Marlene Cimons, "No new federal funding seen to combat child abuse," *LAT,* April 17, 1991.
2. Gelles, "Child Abuse," p. xvi
3. "Trial may be over—but McMartin will never end," *LAT,* July 29, 1990.
4. Ibid.
5. Richard Wexler, *Wounded Innocents: The Real Victims of the War Against Child Abuse* (Buffalo, NY: Promethus Books, 1991a).
6. Ibid. See also Richard Wexler, "Child-abuse hysteria snares innocent victims, *WSJ,* June 4, 1991b.
7. *McMartin et al., vs. County of Los Angeles, et al.,* 249 Cal.Rptr. 53, 1988.
8. Lois Timnick, "3 ex-McMartin defendants file suit for millions," *LAT,* May 30, 1986.
9. *McMartin et al., vs. County of Los Angeles, et al.,* 249 Cal.Rptr. 53, 1988.
10. "Figures in molestation case regains teaching credential," *NYT,* January 7, 1989.
11. David Greenwald and Marilyn Kalfus, "Attorney plans federal civil-rights suit," *Register,* January 19, 1990.
12. Lois Timnick, "3 ex-McMartin defendants file suit for millions," *LAT,* May 30, 1986.
13. "Figures in molestation," *NYT,* January 7, 1989.
14. Greenwald and Kalfus, "Attorney plans."
15. "Buckey case ends: He files suit," *Associated Press,* August 2, 1990.
16. *Buckey v. County of Los Angeles, et al.,* 957 F.2d 652 653, 1992.
17. Ibid., 957 F.2d 652, 1992.
18. *McMartin and Buckey v. Children's Institute International et al.,* 261 Cal.Rptr. 437 439 440, 1989.
19. Ibid., 261 Cal.Rptr. 437, 1989.
20. Ibid., 261 Cal.Rptr. 437 441 442, 1989.
21. For media reports of countersuits, see David G. Savage, "High court refuses to hear McMartin suit on civil rights," *LAT,* March 27, 1990; Dawn Weber, "US Supreme Court says no to McMartin defendant's lawsuit," *Los Angeles Daily News,* March 27, 1990; Marita Hernandez, "Civil rights lawsuit by Mrs. Buckey dismissed," *LAT,* August 7, 1990; "Peggy Buckey files suit for malicious prosecution," *LAT,* September 27, 1990.
22. Dorothy Rabinowitz, "Parents and children on trial," *WSJ,* May 6, 1991.

23. For more discussions on cluster sampling with probability proportionate to size (PPS), see chapter 7 in Fukurai et al., *Race and the Jury,* pp. 165–192.

Chapter 14

1. Eberle and Eberle, *Abuse,* p. 361.
2. Kenneth Reich, "Wayne T. Satz: TV reporter who broke the McMartin story," *LAT,* December 26, 1992.
3. David Stout, "Virginia McMartin dies at 88: Figure in case on child abuse," *NYT,* December 19, 1995.
4. Judith Levine, "A question of abuse," *Mother Jones,* July/August (1996), pp. 33–70.
5. Ibid., p. 36.
6. Ibid. p. 36, quoting Kathleen MacFarlane's 1996 book, *When Children Abuse.*
7. Gail Diane Cox, "L.A. abortive abuse case leads to $10 million award: jury awards compensation, feels for two couples 'caught' in the McMartin frenzy," *National Law Journal,* v17: A11, May 9, 1995. On April 12, 1995, the civil jury in Norwalk branch of Los Angeles Superior Court ordered the county to pay $7.4 million in compensatory damages to two couples arrested in 11 years ago on molestation charges that were dropped for lack of evidence. Attorney fees remained to be assessed, but as of 1990, a court set them at $2 million. Timothy and Helen O'Keefe and their neighbors, Jose Valentin and Myrna Malave, were targets of a raid in early April 1994, just six weeks after the child abuse indictments in the McMartin Preschool case caused a world wide sensation. Based on the testimony of children who later recanted, the four were accused of luring at least 11 boys and girls into their houses, sodomizing them and having oral sex with them.
8. Shaw, "Reporter's early exclusives."
9. See, for instance, Nathan and Snedeker, *Satan's Silence.*
10. Lloyd deMause, *The History of Childhood: The Untold Story of Child Abuse* (New York: P. Bedrick Books, 1988); Erna Olarson, David L. Corwin, and Roland C. Summit, "Modern history of child sexual abuse awareness: Cycles of discovery and suppression," *Child Abuse and Neglect* 17 (1993): 7–24.
11. Ellen Gray, *Unequal Justice: The Prosecution of Child Sexual Abuse* (New York: Free Press, 1995); Gregory J. Skibinski, "The influence of the family preservation model on child sexual abuse intervention strategies: Changes in child welfare worker tasks," *Child Welfare* 74 (1995): 975–989.
12. See chapters 11 and 12 for extended discussion.
13. Gray, *Unequal Justice.*
14. Bennett L. Gershman, "The new prosecutors," *University of Pittsburgh Law Review* 53 (1992): 393–458.
15. Ibid., p. 394.
16. "Sex-offender laws pushed by Reno," *SFC,* April 8, 1995.

17. However, a federal judge in March 1995 ruled unconstitutional New Jersey's "Megan's law" requirement that law enforcement authorities notify the public when a convicted sex offender is released into a community. But the ruling applies only to those offenders whose crimes were committed before Megan's Law was enacted in October 1994. See "New Jersey's sex offender law is unconstitutional, judge rules." *SFC,* March 1, 1995.

18. Tyra Lucile Mead, "Senate panel to take up bill on notifying sex offenders' neighbors," *SFC,* May 9, 1996.

19. Roger Levesque, "The sexual use, abuse and exploitation of children: Challenges in implementing children's human rights," *Brooking Law Review* 60 (1994): 959.

20. Roger Levesque, "Prosecuting sex crimes against children: Time for 'outrageous proposals'?," *Law and Psychology Review* 19 (1995): 59–91.

21. Ibid.

22. Gray, *Unequal Justice.*

23. The *LAT* article discussing this case was placed next to the McMartin report for that day. See McGraw and Feldman, "Children were swapped."

24. During the 1980s and 1990s, other cases similar to the McMartin case emerged and were widely reported in Los Angeles and other neighboring counties: individuals being allegedly abused by principals, by teachers, by baby-sitters; and by fathers, stepfathers, and other family members. See "Principal now faces 14 charges of molestation," *LAT,* May 3, 1984; Mark Landsbaum and Jeffery A. Perlman, "Orange County D.A. abandons molestation case against teacher," *LAT,* May 24, 1984; Terry Pristin, "Teacher accused in molestation of students charged with 21 felonies," *LAT,* August 4, 1987; Tim Waters and Lois Timnick, "Baby-sitting service under probe," *LAT,* March 23, 1985; Sheryl Stolberg, "Girl, 7, recants: D.A. calls off abuse probe of foster father," *LAT,* August 11, 1990.

25. Patricia A. Toth and Harry Elias, 1991, "Gathering legal evidence," in Kathleen Murray and David A. Gough, eds., *Intervening in Child Sexual Abuse* (Edinburgh: Scottish Academic Press, 1991).

26. Michael Granberry, "Ex-school volunteer acquitted of child abuse charges," *LAT,* November 20, 1993.

27. Jason Fine, "Seeking evidence: The hell of prosecuting satanic ritual abuse," *California Lawyer* July (1994).

28. A few church members, however, came forward after Akiki's trial began to claim that they remembered seeing him drive, information that they never revealed during a four-year investigation.

29. Fine, "Seeking evidence."

30. Mary Avery, "The Child abuse witness: Potential for secondary victimization," *Criminal Justice Journal* 7 (1983): 1, 10–13.

31. Fine, "Seeking evidence."

32. Ibid.

33. Ibid. In 1994, San Diego County rejected a claim filed by Akiki. On June 1,

1994, however, a San Diego grand jury issued a report criticizing the prosecution's handling of the case, stating that "The parents were urging children to provide more and more allegations that could be used for trials.... There is no justification for further pursuit of the theory of satanic ritual child molestation and prosecution of child abuse cases."

34. Michael Granberry, "Is a trial of church volunteer accused of abusing children a witch hunt?," *LAT,* June 28, 1993.
35. The letter written by the San Diego County Grand Jury, April 20, 1992.
36. Granberry, "Is a trial of church."
37. Prior to the Simpson trial, a five-month investigation by an advisory committee of trial lawyers from the Los Angeles County Bar Association evaluated trial assignment proceedings, morale, and training—finding that the Los Angeles District Attorney's office provided insufficient training for its attorneys. See Cindy Collins, "More training recommended for L.A. district attorney's office," *Lawyer Hiring and Training Report* 12 (1994): 8. Part of a comprehensive report prepared by the committee, it advised the DA's office to assign a training supervisor to each branch to evaluate the deputies' performance. But the recommendation was almost ignored.
38. Charles B. Rosenberg, "The law after O.J.," *ABA Journal* 81 (1995): 72.
39. Ibid.
40. Gill Garcetti expressed in a post-Simpson trial news conference that the verdict was "based on emotion that overcame reason." See Henry J. Reske, "Observers say prosecution lost the case over a bloody glove, racist cop," *ABA Journal* 81 (1995): 48. University of Michigan Law School professor Yale Kamisar stated that Garcetti "is in real, real trouble. He ought to think about resigning" (p. 48).
41. Jo-Ellan Dimitrius participated in the selection of the Simpson jury as a private jury consultant to the "Dream Team." Thus, the information provided in this section mostly come from her involvement in the trial.
42. Dr. Vinson, former University of Southern California communication professor, was the founder of the most successful and profitable jury consultant firm, Litigation Science Inc. (LSI).
43. Donald Black, *Sociological Justice* (New York: Oxford University Press, 1989).
44. Fukurai et al., *Race and the Jury.*
45. *United States v. Wiley,* 492 F.2d 547, 555 (D.C. Cir. 1974).
46. *McCleskey v. Kemp,* 481 U.S. 279, 387, 1987.
47. Bill Boyarsky, "Garcetti faces political pitfalls at every turn," *LAT,* September 11, 1994; Jim Newton and Ralph Frammolino, "Prosecution won't seek death penalty," *LAT,* September 10, 1994.
48. David C. Baldus, George Woodworth, and Charles A. Pulaski, Jr., "Reflections on the 'inevitability' of racial discrimination in capital sentencing and the 'impossibility' of its prevention, detection, and correction," *Washington and Lee Law Review* 51 (1994): 359–428.

49. Of 7,563, black residents only constituted 63, i.e., 0.83% of the entire city community.
50. Fukurai et al., *Race and the Jury,* p. 63.
51. Thus, it is not surprising that in the first McMartin trial, only 43.4% of assigned jurors were white. Subsequently, half of the final jury included members of racial and ethnic minorities.
52. Fukurai and Butler, "Sources of racial disenfranchisement," pp. 238–275.
53. Ibid.
54. Fukurai et al., *Race and the Jury.*
55. For more discussions on cluster sampling with probability proportionate to size (PPS), see chapter 7 in Fukurai et al, *Race and the Jury,* pp. 165–192.
56. Eberle and Eberle, *Politics,* p. 89.

Subject Index

Name Index